£6.95

D1514683

*Patriot-Heroes
in England and
America*

Patriot-Heroes in England and America

Political Symbolism and Changing Values over Three Centuries

PETER KARSTEN

The University of Wisconsin Press

Published 1978
The University of Wisconsin Press
Box 1379, Madison, Wisconsin 53701

The University of Wisconsin Press, Ltd.
1 Gower St., London, WC1E, 6HA, England

First printing

Printed in the United States of America

For LC CIP information see the colophon

ISBN 0-299-07500-1

*Publication of this book was made
possible in part by a grant from the
Provost's Research and Development Fund
of the University of Pittsburgh*

To Merle Curti

Mentor and Friend

Lives of Great Men oft remind us / we should make our own sublime.

Henry Wadsworth Longfellow, "A Psalm of Life"

On his shoulders we hang our ideals of courage, manliness, and the power of truth and right and justice. That uplifted brow indicates our mental and spiritual aspirations. We may exalt a hero and in so doing we approach somewhat the height of his noblest aims.

Frances Davis Whittemore, *George Washington in Sculpture*

We are none of us without respect for the past—not even the most radical of us—especially when it can be pressed into the service of the present.

Ernest Barker, *Oliver Cromwell and the English People*

Heroes are created by popular demand, . . . and what does the historian know, more than you and I do, about popular demand?

Gerald W. Johnson, *American Heroes and Hero-Worship*

Contents

1 Introduction: A Primer on the Strength and Significance of Patriot-Hero Symbols in England and America

An awareness of the types of patriot-symbols that persons have admired, held in veneration, and attempted to emulate, together with an understanding of the nature of such public or private veneration, should be of value to the student of political culture. If patriot-heroes "are exemplars and champions of ideal values," if "the group sees its values realized" in patriot-heroes, if the patriot-hero is "the perfect expression of the ideal of a group in whom all human virtues unite,"[1] then the study of the veneration of patriots should reveal the contours of the political values existing within a culture that may otherwise be overlooked.

This examination of patriot-worship in England and the United States during the last three centuries has necessary limits. It would be quite beyond my capacity to deal with each and every case of patriot-worship over a period of more than three centuries. But ticking off such incidents of patriot-worship, without further organization, would be of little value to anyone. Analysis of the use of seven of the more important and frequently utilized symbols of patriotism in this period (1650–1975) has yielded some worthwhile returns.

In several years of examining English and American pamphlets, newspapers, novels, autobiographies, census records, poems, speeches,

1

paintings, and art objects, I found that a small handful of patriot-symbols was particularly important, recurrent, and interchangeable on both sides of the Atlantic. Of these John Hampden, Algernon Sydney, Oliver Cromwell, King Charles I, George Washington, Thomas Jefferson, and Abraham Lincoln received the greatest, most interesting, and most impassioned attention.[2] It would be entirely possible to consider the evidence of the rise and fall of the reputations of these men[3] on one side of the Atlantic alone, but this would not necessarily be the most logical way to proceed. The slightest examination of such evidence immediately suggests the transatlantic, "Anglo-American" nature of the subject.

In examining the ways in which these figures were perceived and made use of by eighteenth-, nineteenth- and twentieth-century Britons and Americans, we should learn something significant about changes taking place in both English and American political values, and we should be able to offer some informed guesses about the direction in which these societies may be moving.

Before proceeding with any discussion of the use of patriot-hero symbols by Britons and Americans, I ought to make clear that I have done what I could to determine the strength and meaning of the reputation of patriot-heroes among the great mass of Britons and Americans who neither led a movement, spoke to an audience, wrote a poem or history, edited a newspaper, nor left any other deliberate record of their views on patriot-heroes. Most of the readily available evidence of patriot-symbolism is the product of the articulate—men and women who left a record for posterity of their views of the subject, whether by forming a public patriotic or political organization, publishing a pamphlet, conducting lectures on "great patriot-heroes of the past as models for the present," or painting a historical canvas. They certainly spoke for themselves, and it may often be allowed that they spoke for groups that they claimed to represent. But I cannot assume that they spoke for others without providing substantial evidence to support such a thesis. After all, there were always competing symbols of patriotism. Englishmen of 1750 or 1900 could hear appeals from one camp to venerate Hampden and Sydney, or Cromwell, and to derogate the house of Stuart, and from another camp to venerate "the Royal Martyr," King Charles I, and vilify his family's enemies— Hampden, Sydney, and Cromwell.

Of course, they could ignore both camps, as many (particularly many lower-class persons) undoubtedly did.[4] Or they could cultivate heroes of their own—some might call them "antiheroes" today—symbols unfashionable with the articulate middle- and upper-class public. A lower-class debating society of the 1750's was called The Robin Hood, and in 1795

Joseph Ritson drew attention to the folklore celebrating Robin Hood, a symbol rarely extolled in the literature of the educated classes.[5] In 1907 Cecil Sharp noted that "the outlaw and freebooter appeal to [the English folk-singer's] imagination with greater force" than any "establishment" symbols. "Robin Hood, Dick Turpin or Henry Martin are his real heroes."[6] More recently Maurice Keen, Kent Steckmesser, A. L. Lloyd, Russel Ward, and Eric Hobsbawm separately concluded that "popular legend" revealed in ballads, nursery rhymes, and oral tradition "can tell [the historian] what his records so often conceal, what it is (common) men really believe in and what they really desired."'[7]

To these scholars the heroes of the lower classes have been the legendary figures of the local countryside who responded to the injustices of distant authorities, who charted their own futures—Robin Hood and Dick Turpin in England; Henry Martin and Rob Roy in Scotland; Ned Kelly, Jack Donahoe, Ned Hall, and the bushrangers in Australia; Billy the Kid, Kit Carson, Wild Bill Hickok, and the Molly Maguires in the United States. Where these scholars tend to disagree is in assessing the meaning of this rustic resistance to authority. Some, like Ward, conclude that the popular mind was fundamentally democratic and virtually anarchistic in its rejection of outside authorities. But while this may well describe the nineteenth-century Australian bushmen and diggers, it does not appear to other scholars to be a sufficient description of the political values of *their* common folk. It is quite possible that the same agricultural laborer in Yorkshire who admired Robin Hood also venerated Cromwell or the ruling monarch, that the same Pennsylvania miner who admired the Molly Maguires also named his son after George Washington or Thomas Jefferson. Resistance to regional injustices and veneration of national figureheads could be complementary phenomena.

In any event, the question before us in this essay is that of determining the strength and significance of the reputation of a handful of seventeenth-century Englishmen and eighteenth- and nineteenth-century Americans who were, to the articulate public, for nearly two centuries symbols of English and American patriotism. Who venerated them, why, and what does this tell us of Anglo-American culture in the eighteenth and nineteenth centuries?

Ideally, one might proceed by analyzing the results of professionally conducted samplings of Anglo-American opinion. No such data are available, of course, until the turn of the century. We do have a few relevant samplings of the views of British and American children, taken between 1899 and 1963, and several of my students and I conducted further samplings of public opinion in 1969 and 1974.[8] But while I shall have occasion to refer to these data later in discussing recent trends, it must be clear that few if any generalizations valid for the previous two centuries can be drawn from data collected in the twentieth century.

Lacking such "hard" sociological data, one must rely on "softer" evidence. Discussions with regional folklore specialists and folk singers, for example, can uncover verses celebrating the heroes (or the *lack* of heroes) of the common folk. Though the French and American governments made a serious effort in World War I to identify the "war to make the world safe for democracy" with one of America's first allies, the Marquis de Lafayette, they may have failed to impress many doughboys. With speeches, ceremonies and the popularization of the A.E.F. motto, "Lafayette, we are here!," the elite celebrated the American return of a favor. And at least one small group of Americans responded enthusiastically to the appeal to the name of Lafayette: the squadron of American volunteers who flew for France before America's entry into the war was named the Lafayette Escadrille. But the typical doughboy may not have been as enthusiastic if the verse many doughboys sang returning from the front line in 1918 is any indication: "We've paid our debt to Lafayette: Who the hell do we owe now?"[9]

Such evidence is "soft" because it is difficult to determine how genuinely "common" some of the songs and rhymes are, both in origin and frequency of use, and also because of their occasional ambiguity. Some may be clear enough.[10] But what (or how much) is one to make of these old English rhymes:

> Oliver Cromwell lies buried and dead;
> Heigho, "buried and dead"
> There grew a green apple tree over his head;
> Heigho, over his head (etc.),
> The apples were ripe and ready to drop
> There came an old lady to gather the crop,
> Oliver rose and gave her a crack,
> That knocked the old woman flat on her back.
> The apples are dried now, they lie on the shelf;
> If you want any, well you can get them yourself!

and

> As I was going by Charing Cross
> I saw a black rider on a black horse
> They told me it was King Charles the First
> Oh dear! my heart was ready to burst.[11]

(From remorse? Affection? Fear?)

Who sang such songs, and how seriously did they take whatever messages they may be said to have contained? M. R. Toynbee tells us that as recently as the early nineteenth century in the Shetlands, King Charles's gold coins were used as a cure for scrofula ("the King's evil"). But are we necessarily to assume that those who used such sacred relics were concurrently devotees of the "cult of the Royal Martyr" in *all* of its ramifications?[12] Similarly it has been reported by several writers that "the country mind" or the "rustic tradition" credited "Cromwell the Destroyer" with Satanic powers, and that as late as the 1880's in Oxfordshire "some of the older mothers, and grandmothers still threatened naughty children with the name of Cromwell. 'If you ain't a good gal, old Oliver Cromwell'll have 'ee!' they would say, or 'Here comes old Crumell!' "[13]

But it is also maintained that as late as the 1930's in at least one Cotswold village Oliver Cromwell's memory was "still very much respected among the labouring folk."[14] Thomas Carlyle discovered some evidence of this in the 1840's on the battlefield of Worcester where a laborer told him he "wished to God we had another Oliver, sir, times is dreadful bad."[15] Perhaps socioeconomic class is at work here. As significant might be the religious affiliation of Oxfordshire grandmothers, Cotswold villagers, and Worcester laborers. But one must always read with caution an educated man's description of the views of common folk. Carlyle's battlefield acquaintance may well have spoken in honesty, and we have no reason to doubt that Carlyle reported the conversation as it occurred. John Adams engaged in a similar exchange of views with "people in the neighborhood" of Worcester some fifty years earlier, which exchange became heated when Adams found them "ignorant and careless" of the "Holy Ground" that was their own. He lectured them on "Liberty" and found that "this animated them, and they seemed much pleased with it. Perhaps their awkwardness before might arise from their uncertainty of our Sentiments concerning the Civil Wars."[16] He was probably right; they may well have been the ideological ancestors of Carlyle's Cromwellian companion. But one can never be certain of this simply by reading Adams. After all, it may have been that Adams's vigorous defense of the Parliamentarians simply frightened them into agreeing with this crazy American tourist. If that were the case, it would not be the last time such a thing were to happen.

Another source of information about the people's choice of patriot-hero symbols may be their child-naming practices and patterns. According to Alice Rossi and Daniel Smith, most children (about 60 percent) are named after relatives. Some parents (about 25 percent) may give their children distinctive or attractive first and middle names with no particular nonrelative in mind. Few children (Rossi estimates 5 percent) are named for particular nonrelatives, and fewer still (less than 1 percent) for any patriotic figure.[17] Wilbur Zelinsky maintains that "newsworthy events produce only minor and temporary fads for naming of infants after national . . . heroes [such as Washington or Lincoln],"[18] but it is still possible to detect and measure some of these fads and to add this evidence of the use of patriot-symbols to other data to enhance our understanding of those data.[19] Occasionally specific parental intentions can be ascertained, even without such verifying evidence, but names like John Hampden Pleasants (son of a Virginia gentleman politician) or Oliver Cromwell Comstock (son of a Rhode Island Baptist merchant) are unmistakable.[20]

Children were not the only recipients of patriot-heroes' names. Taverns, social clubs, mountains, streams, towns, streets, colleges, ships, and the like also contain clues of popular patriot-hero veneration. This sort of naming is useful evidence, but here one faces again the problem of ascertaining how "common" in origin and "popular" in fact the choices really were. How many American city fathers in 1780 or 1820 actually polled their community's inhabitants before entering the name "Washington, Pa." or "Lafayette, Indiana" in their state's official register? In 1786 the town of Hamden, Connecticut, was named in honor of John Hampden (the English "p" is silent), but the choice of the patriot was not popularly determined; Amesah Bradley, head of the town's most prominent and powerful family, made the decision.[21] How popular was a "Cromwell Inn" likely to have been in a respectable Church of England community (unless it was the only inn within reach)? In the late 1960's I communicated with inhabitants and officials in a dozen American towns named after Sydney and not one of them had any idea for whom their towns had been named (for that matter, very few cared).

Sometimes, however, one can find good indications that the leaders of a community or organization are truly representative of their constituency. When Joseph Linnett, a young agricultural laborer who was chairman in 1875 of the Naseby branch of the British National Agricultural Labourer's Union, called for a ceremony to commemorate the bicentennial anniversary of Cromwell's victory over the royalists, he was joined in the call by the National's president, Joseph Arch, and on June 14 of that year some 2,000 agricultural labourers gathered around the Cromwell Obelisk at Naseby battlefield to hear Linnett and Arch invoke the spirit of the Lord Protector and demand better wages, the franchise for propertyless farm hands, and reform of the Game Laws.[22] While it might be unwarranted to assume that *all* working class people, or for that matter all agricultural laborers, were enthusiastic admirers of the kind of political values that these particular workers felt Cromwell epitomized, it would be difficult to claim that Linnett's commemorative movement was itself elite-inspired.

Many movements clearly *were* elite-inspired, however; some unabashedly so. Unfortunately one can only speculate on how "popular" were the 1895–99 protests against the proposed statue of Oliver Cromwell on Parliament's grounds at Westminster or Captain Henry Stuart Wheatley-Crowe's Royal Martyr Church Union, established in 1911.[23] We have some respectable evidence, however, that the gift of a statue of Cromwell to the city of Manchester in 1875 (pl. 33) was popular with a large element of that city's populace, for although one critic protested the unveiling of this statue of one whom he called a symbol of "bloodshed, rapine, pillage and tyranny," some 50,000 trade unionists "spoke" on behalf of the act by marching in a subsequent demonstration in support of its donor and her equally Cromwellian spouse.[24]

Evidence of popular interest in a patriot-symbol can occasionally be deduced from the efforts of elites to capitalize on what they perceived to be existing popular veneration of a particular patriot-symbol. I think this partially explains the enthusiastic use of Hampden and Sydney by John Wilkes and Samuel Adams in the decade preceding the American Revolution (see Chapter 2). It may also explain Major John Cartwright's decision to name the English Parliamentary reform movement that he was instrumental in organizing in the second decade of the nineteenth century the "Hampden Club," for, as he wrote in 1818, "The Hampden Club . . . has by its name, and the use that has been made of that name, been very instrumental in generating the petitions for reform of more than a million of men."[25] We need not necessarily accept Major Cartwright's claim that Hampden's name was as influential as he implies, but he thought it was, and, as he says, a great many Englishmen did identify with the political objectives of the Hampden Club, whether because of or despite the name (see also p. 118).

A good example of such a successful use of a patriot-hero symbol may be Lord Rosebery's speech in 1899 at the ceremonies commemorating the tercentenary of Cromwell's birth. Within a month of his unstinting praise of the Lord Protector, he received a note from a fellow Liberal Imperialist, Sir Robert Perks: "Your 'Cromwell' speech has produced a wonderful effect on many non-conformists. I have always said that any statesman who can completely command the confidence and gain the ear of *non-conformity* and *Labour* in this country would sweep the field." Six weeks later Rosebery received some evidence that at least one member of *"Labour"* had been suitably impressed. One W. Herbert Spencer, who identified himself as a journeyman tailor, told Rosebery:

> The poor, the homeless, the teeming millions verging between a mock respectability and starvation cries from every city, town, village and hamlet to their leader of the liberal Party for help and succour. . . . Will your Lordship . . . be the People's Protector: "We need another Cromwell" [here Spencer was quoting Rosebery].[26]

Another reasonable indication of popular reception of elite-projected patriot-symbols is the occasional record we are left of popular reaction to pamphlets, editorials, paintings, and speeches. Often speeches were published or reproduced by local newspapers with such internal indications of their enthusiastic reception as: "(Loud Cheers)" or "(Hear, Hear!)." But it is difficult to tell whether these entries represent the heavy hand of a sympathetic editor or the Voice of the People itself. And how much is one to make of the occasional heckler (or hecklers) or, similarly, the overenthusiastic member (or members) of the crowd who get a bit ahead of the speaker. One unidentified member of the audience did just that in 1850 when Chartist George Thompson addressed a meeting of the National Party and Financial Relief Association. While speaking of Parliament's rejection of the Chartist petition, Thompson was interrupted twice by a person invoking Cromwell's name; this caused Thompson to remark: "My friend says 'Oliver Cromwell!' Now I never want to see an Oliver Cromwell, but millions rolled into an Oliver Cromwell."[27]

Sometimes a lecturer will record that "the people approved" of some new twist; sometimes one can detect evidence of public interest in a particular patriot-hero in the form of recorded purchases of large numbers of books and pamphlets or in significant withdrawals of such publications from libraries. Occasionally, but only very occasionally, a Voice of the People writes a book and reveals the source of his or her veneration of a particular patriot-hero. Such was the case with Alexander Somerville (pl. 18), the son of a carter of coal and lime in the Firth of Forth region. In his maturity Somerville penned *The Autobiography of a Working Man*, in which he recalled his experiences as a laborer, a soldier, and eventually as a freelance writer. He told of working in a stonequarry in the winter of 1831, during the rise to power of Earl Grey, Lord Brougham, and the Whigs, and remembered that he and his fellow workers followed the Whig rise to power with interest and pleasure. One day "when we had been reading in the newspapers a great deal about the tyranny of the tories and the tyranny of the aristocracy in general," a stonemason struck a common laborer and Somerville recalled warning these stonemason representatives of labor's aristocracy:

We have been reading in the newspaper discussions about [suffrage and Parliamentary] reform, and have been told how much is to be gained by even one person sometimes making a resolute stand against oppressive power. We have only this day seen in the papers a warning to the aristocracy and the anti-reformers, that another John Hampden may arise. Come on, he who dares! I shall be John Hampden to the tyrannies of [stone] masons![28]

An exceptionally revealing illustration of the transmission of political symbols from an articulate elite to (at least one of) "the people." Or is it? There is no questioning Somerville's working-class origins, and it is perfectly possible that he recalled the incident substantially as it happened. But by the time Somerville wrote this autobiography, he had broken with the reform movement, which, by the late 1840's, was invoking Oliver Cromwell and Wat Tyler more often than John Hampden. It is possible that Somerville was "recalling" for the benefit of his new associates his early veneration of their favorite patriot-hero, and that neither he nor many members of his social class ever really invoked Hampden in the fashion that Somerville would have us believe that he had. If, for example, we were to discover other evidence, suggesting that common folk paid little or no attention to Hampden-worship among the educated, then Somerville's tale might be held in doubt.

Similarly suspect, but still worth consideration, are the efforts of the educated to represent the common man's heroes to us. The people venerate Hampden, they tell us, or Cromwell, or Charles the First. The less partisan the writer, the more likely he is to be reasonably accurate. But educated objectivity is no substitute for the professional sociologist's randomly selected survey. The most disinterested Etonian's description of the East End of London is still an Etonian's view of the East End. It is helpful to know what Ralph Waldo Emerson and Thomas Carlyle felt that the common man believed, but their views are no more useful to us than the common man's impression of Emerson and Carlyle. Both provide the insight afforded by a different perspective, but neither can be relied on to be precise, for each must reflect the personal values of the man who offers it.

Nonetheless, elite perspectives are sometimes all the evidence of popular values that are now available; when other evidence is available, it sometimes confirms these insights of the educated. Inasmuch as I have said something of the use of patriot-symbols in child-naming, I will offer two examples of how English and American writers (both novelists) imagined typical parents naming their children for national patriot-hero figures. The American novelist Sarah Josepha Hale described the naming of "Sidney Romilly," the hero of her novel, *Northwood* (published in 1852, but written in 1827), thus:

> Mr. Romilly was well read in English history, and from admiration of the splendid talents and devoted patriotism of the famous Algernon Sidney, selected the name for his own son. He would have given him both names, but Mrs. Romilly objected seriously to Algernon. It sounded, she said, too much like "Algerine" [a North African pirate label], and she detested it.

So the name was shortened to "Sidney" alone. Thereafter his father took such delight in identifying "the noble sentiments and exalted character" of the English patriot with his son that "at times, when pronouncing [the boy's name] he would almost feel an assurance of his own son's future usefulness and distinction."[29]

Similarly, the English novelist, C. S. Forester, described the decision of the mother of his hero in *Brown on Resolution* (1929): "She called him Albert. . . . About the name there clung a flavour of association with the Royal Family [the setting was 1893] which endeared it to her rather bourgeois little heart."[30]

These marvelously illuminating literary glimpses from the past need not be regarded as self-sufficient sociological "proof" of anything, but in these two instances other evidence suggests that the descriptions are valid.

For the most part, this essay necessarily examines the least effective evidence of the popular mind's veneration of patriot-heroes—namely, the voices of the articulate elites who wrote the pamphlets, editorials, speeches, and broadsides that they then aimed and fired at what they considered to be the people. As it is often impossible to measure their effectiveness or reception, I have often been reduced to recording the frequency with which and manner in which elites used a particular patriot-symbol and then extrapolating to estimate that symbol's overall popularity and significance. Obviously such extrapolations are of questionable value, but at least it is possible to say what a number of educated people of any given age felt, and I have done what I could to go beyond that.

Chapters 2–5 contain the evidence I have found for the generalizations I have offered throughout and which I have summarized below and in the final chapter. To that chapter are referred readers who are willing to take my first word of advice: that I have no axe to grind in this book, no particular, favorite, patriot-symbol of my own, and that I have consequently been able to let the evidence shape the thesis. But my second word of advice is not to accept my first, for one of my "conclusions" could be that no one is ever really "objective"—in the sense of being value-free. Even those who exhibited no intense passion for or against a particular figure nonetheless revealed something of themselves in the ways that they treated that figure. And this is also a caveat about the brief biographies of the patriot-heroes offered herein to help the reader place in perspective the various views of these figures discussed in the main body of this essay. I say again that I hold no brief for any particular one of these patriot-heroes, but readers will have their own opinions after reading the essay, and the truly conscientious may want to search out phrases, emphases, omissions, which, unbeknown to me, reveal my own values and attitudes.[31]

Of course, the biographies themselves are but "benchmarks." What is at issue herein is *not* the precise character and history of each figure, but the way in which each was perceived by future generations, for this is a study of the uses, over time, of patriot-symbols in England and America and of what these uses tell us of English and American culture.

What is the thesis of this study? Briefly, that for many centuries (and, in particular, for the past three centuries) the sense of what constitutes "patriotic" behavior and of who might be deemed to be a "patriot" has steadily undergone change and redefinition as developing societies (and, in particular, England and the United States) steadily shift their interests, affections, and esteem from local units, via confederations, to more centralized national units. The desire to remain independent, to be free from the interference or domination of strong central leadership, while still important today, was a more vital impulse in groups and individuals in the past. And the types of patriot-heroes venerated then and now reflect these changes.

In ancient Greece, in republican and imperial Rome, one's "patriotism" consisted of love of one's city. During the feudal age in the West, "country" meant county, one's loyalty rarely reaching beyond "one's native town or village." [32] To the twelfth- or thirteenth-century rustic "England" "was hardly larger than his native Hundred, and his politics reached no further than the local manor house . . . [for] the life of the manor-community was so intensely local."[33] Loyalty beyond the manor was largely either personal (to one's lord) or religious (to one's Lord and His Church). Nonetheless, by the fourteenth or fifteenth centuries a kind of national patriotism was clearly on the rise, as the monarch sought to strengthen his hand with the nobility and to link his authority to that of the Church. An able king reigning in the late middle ages might well be venerated by some as a national hero, a *corpus mysticum*. But such a monarch's task was considerable, for resistance to his authority was inherent in the "underdeveloped" medieval world. His taxes *pro defensione regni*, while enabling him to assume command of national armies, made him unpopular with those who had to pay. His knights followed where he might lead, but they did so for booty, personal glory, or a feudal sense of honor, not for any nationalistic sense of patriotism. His subjects might well fear the king's troops as much as or more than those of his enemies, for while they were free to resist the latter, they were compelled to endure the former.[34]

The monarch, then, was a national hero to some, a matter of indifference to others, and a veritable menace to still others. Were he to exceed his grasp, he might be confronted by angry nobles determined to bind him to a set of promises or to oust him altogether. His ministers might be set upon by knights, merchants, or peasants (such as the followers of Sir John Oldcastle, Wat Tyler, or Jack Cade) who were incensed by decrees affecting their religious tastes, by adverse local economic conditions, or by the fall from grace of some local political figure. In time legislative bodies, acting in defense of local, religious, civil, political, or property "rights" or traditions, grew more important and more powerful. "Patriots" rose to defend "the rights of Englishmen" against "a grasping court."

But the "grasping court" eventually yielded to democratic impulses. The central government became more representative in the same years that it was increasingly viewed as being necessary and legitimate. The disorder flowing from industrialization and modernization led some to seek "iron men," leaders capable of action, who could reorder their world. Some local interests and personal liberties might have to yield, and that was regrettable, but "the times" demanded it.

The difference between such antistatist patriot-symbols of the eighteenth and early nineteenth centuries as Hampden, Sydney, and Jefferson, and the more cosmopolitan, statist symbols admired in the late nineteenth and twentieth centuries, such as Cromwell and Lincoln, is a useful measure of the cultural distance between the two eras.

We begin our account in the seventeenth century when the first four of our patriot-heroes make their appearance.

2 Patriot-Symbols of the English Civil Wars: The Men and Their Reputations before 1755

Dramatis Personae Anglicae

Charles Stuart, King of England and Scotland

Born into a world where earls knelt to cut his meat, Charles Stuart was weaned on the divine right of kings. Neither Parliamentary prerogatives nor religious tolerance were part of his royal education: he quickly lost his patience with Parliament and the more Puritan of his subjects shortly after ascending the throne. Two disastrous naval and military expeditions against Spanish and French strongholds obliged him to convene Parliaments which did not hesitate to express their dissatisfaction with his most trusted ministers nor to bind their grants to his promise (part of the terms of the Petition of Right in 1628) never to levy taxes without their consent.

Angered by what he considered the bold and unsympathetic character of this Parliament, he eventually dissolved it and imprisoned its leader, Sir John Eliot. (Eliot died in the Tower in 1632; John Hampden served as guardian to his sons.) Throughout the 1630's he ruled without Parliament by means of his own courts, broke several promises he had made to Parliament, and offended many local interests when he sought to integrate local units of government into a centralized framework and to extend the financial base for the English Navy into the interior of the country.

13

He raised his family with much affection and care, and claimed to have as much interest and affection for all his subjects. But a significant number of his subjects found his interest and affection insufficient cause for rejoicing. His religious leaders seemed, to unsympathetic observers, to be bent on reinstituting and improving formal, almost Catholic rituals in the Church of England. Charles himself began to personify the Evil Monarch to Puritans whose frequent rereading of the Old Testament provided them with examples of God's vengeance on Old Testament kings who had fallen from grace.

To a growing number of powerful Englishmen, Charles's military counselors seemed dangerously close to imposing a standing army on the nation. Eventual difficulty in collecting taxes from a resistant public, coupled with an invasion by an army of equally disaffected Scottish Presbyterians, caused Charles to convene a new Parliament in 1640. But this body proved too critical and uncooperative, and he dissolved it, only to be compelled again, in 1641, to turn to a Parliament for funds.

The "Long Parliament" that then convened numbered John Hampden and Oliver Cromwell among its members, and would soon include Algernon Sydney as well. It moved decisively against Charles, showering him with demands for reform, imprisoning and ultimately executing his most important religious and military councillors (Archbishop William Laud and Thomas Wentworth, Earl of Strafford). Appealing directly to the English people for support, it sought to seize complete control of the armies of England. Charles met some of the demands, but ultimately attempted to arrest its leaders. Unsuccessful, he left London in disgust and anger and rallied nobles and gentry from the West and North to his standard at Nottingham.

In the civil war that ultimately resulted, Charles enjoyed some initial successes at Edgehill and Roundway Down. But Parliament's numbers, wealth, superior organization, and leadership eventually counted against him at Marston Moor and Naseby, and in 1646 he fled to the Scots, who surrendered him to Parliament.

In May of 1647 he was taken from the more friendly hands of Parliament by a radicalized army, but six months later he fled to moderate army forces on the Isle of Wight. This proved no security, however, as throughout his captivity Charles continued to pit one faction against another, communicating with his own royalists, with the Scottish Presbyterians, and with the Parliament, as well as with his army captors.

Eventually the army and the republican faction of Parliament, tiring of his conspiracies and his refusal to yield, placed him on trial for high treason and sentenced him to death. He was beheaded on January 30, 1649, maintaining a royal demeanor to the end.

John Hampden

John Hampden (1594–1643) was the eldest son of an extremely wealthy Buckinghamshire gentleman who died when his son was three. Throughout the 1620's and '30's he made himself known for his opposition to the various efforts of Charles I and his ministers to raise a revenue independent of Parliament. A champion of "ancient liberties," he was "in the forefront of the struggle to secure the revival of ancient boroughs; and when they were revived, he demanded the widest possible franchise for them."[1] He is said to have declined knighthood in the 1620's when James I offered the honor to a number of wealthy gentry upon the payment of considerable sums to their monarch. In 1629, and again in 1634, he associated with leading Puritans who were establishing colonies in Massachusetts and Connecticut.

In 1635 he resisted Charles's "ship-money" impost both as a property-owner bent on upholding local privileges and as a member of the Providence Island Company, a group of entrepreneurs seeking to seize an advance base in the Caribbean for raids on the Spanish galleon convoys. The company (which included in its ranks other leading Parliamentary figures such as John Pym) was willing enough to see the Royal Navy grow but was not at all satisfied that the king's foreign policy was sufficiently anti-Spanish; hence the testing in the courts of this tax, which the king sought to levy without Parliament's consent[2] in order to finance his foreign policies. A contemporary writer, Edward Hyde, later Lord Clarendon, recalled that with his opposition to the crown Hampden "grew the argument of all tongues, every man inquiring who and what he was, that durst, at his own charge, support the liberty and property of the kingdom, and rescue his country, as he thought, from being made a prey of the court." The judges ruled against him seven to five, but, according to Clarendon, "the judgment that was given against him infinitely more advanced him, than the service for which it was given." When the Short Parliament sat in 1640, Hampden was "the most popular man in the house," and later, in the Long Parliament, "the eyes of all men were fixed on him as their *Patriae pater*, and the pilot that must steer their vessel through the tempests and rocks that threatened it."[3] After Charles's unsuccessful attempt to arrest Hampden, John Pym, and three other eminent members of the Long Parliament, 4,000 Buckinghamshire men were said to have ridden into London in a demonstration of their support for Hampden with copies of Parliament's protest stuck in their hats.

When civil war ensued, Hampden led a regiment of these men into battle; a year later, charging at the head of a squadron at Chalgrove Field, he received his death wound. He was buried with considerable ceremony in his family church at Great Hampden.

Oliver Cromwell

The Cromwells had risen to power in the sixteenth century by acquiring church properties sold by Henry VIII. Born in Huntingdon in 1599, Oliver Cromwell belonged to a lesser, but still significant, branch of that family. He studied first under the Puritan Thomas Beard (later a political colleague) and then under further Puritan guidance at Sidney Sussex College, Cambridge.

He represented Huntingdon in the Parliament of 1628–29, but was maneuvered out of political power in that borough by royalists in 1630. He thereupon sold his properties and moved to St. Ives. Here, he experienced a period of depression and melancholy, but after he inherited substantial property and underwent religious conversion to Puritanism, he eventually recovered sufficient self-confidence and political support to gain election from Cambridge to the Short Parliament in 1640 and the Long Parliament, which convened in 1641.

As a member of the Long Parliament, Cromwell pressed for the reform of a Church he regarded as too Arminian, ritualistic, and hierarchical. He pressed for war against rebellious Irish Catholics, pledged £500 toward the campaign in Ireland, and was promised nearly 1,000 Irish acres in exchange. Active in committee work in 1642, he raised a regiment, the "Ironsides," which included fewer gentry or nobility than was traditionally the case. These tradesmen, shopkeepers, artisans, and yeomen, all "Godly men," became the core of the well-disciplined Eastern Association Army, of which Cromwell was second in command. Created lieutenant general, he played a decisive role in the battles of Marson Moor and Naseby. Two years later, he led an angry and radicalized army into London to compel the "Presbyterian" (conservative) majority in Parliament to obtain pay for the army and to institute a number of social and political reforms. Not as radical as many of those he commanded, Cromwell regarded as impractical the demands of army "Agitators" and "Levellers" for suffrage, ecclesiastical, legal, and agrarian reforms. He appears to have helped the king, a prisoner of the radical elements of the army, to escape to forces loyal to Cromwell on the Isle of Wight. He first moved to repress the army radicals, and then, alarmed by royalist risings in the South and West and an invasion of England by Scots in 1648, he made his peace with the radicals, crushed the royalists, and defeated the Scots at Preston. While in the field, he was advised of the decision of his fellow army commanders to purge the Parliament of undesirables and to bring the king to trial. At first uncertain, Cromwell eventually decided that Charles had behaved treasonably and dishonestly in simultaneously treating with the army, Parliament, the Scots, and his own English royalist allies, and he threw himself wholeheartedly behind that monarch's trial and execution.

He then suppressed a Leveller rising at Burford, brutally and decisively crushed the Irish rebellion at Drogheda, Wexford, and Kilkenny, and soundly defeated two new Scottish armies under Charles II at Dunbar and Worcester.

When in 1653 he became persuaded that the purged ("Rump") Parliament intended to dissolve itself and control new elections which might return a Parliament opposed to the army, he dissolved the Parliament himself and called a new Parliament of carefully elected "Godly men" who were in sympathy with Cromwell and the army's leadership.

This Parliament continued the Rump's efforts to reorganize and modernize the organs of government, but it proved to be as ideologically divided as its predecessors. Its more conservative and proarmy members consequently surrendered their powers to Cromwell in December, 1653; he then accepted the conservative, army-conceived Instrument of Government as the constitution of England and received the title of Lord Protector. The Instrument authorized the raising of 10,000 horse or 20,000 footsoldiers and a substantial naval force without recourse to any Parliament. To the degree to which the civil war had been fought to secure the prerogatives of Parliament's propertied electorate from royally imposed ship-money taxes and the like, the establishment of the Protectorate, a victory for executive over legislative prerogatives, thus constituted a rejection of Hampden's original protest by a faction led by his cousin and co-Parliamentarian, Cromwell.

In 1638, while out of favor with the powers-that-be, Cromwell had championed those Ely commoners who opposed the draining of the Fens, which would increase the amount of arable land for some farmers, but would sharply reduce grazing land for poorer residents. By the 1650's, however, Cromwell was facilitating the drainage of Fen lands, and realizing some financial benefits in the process.

Throughout the 1640's, Cromwell appeared to champion the cause of Independency, and was throughout his life a supporter of religious toleration for all but Papists, agnostics, and atheists. But his Protestant religious policies proved to be too conservative in the 1650's to please many Quakers, Levellers, and Independents.

His Protectorate's largely anti-Spanish foreign policy was coordinated and effective; his navies were successful against the Dutch; his commercial policy substantially aided England's foreign trade; his imperial vision was sophisticated for his day. His major generals ruled England without substantial opposition, and brought tranquility to the land. He acted only when convinced that he was following God's will, but his administration was never sufficiently popular to warrant either a radical reform of the suffrage or a return to regular Parliamentary rule by the conservative, propertied class. He was offered the crown in 1657, but his army colleagues opposed the notion, and he eventually declined. Seemingly omnipotent to his enemies, he knew some fear of assassination. Charged with boundless ambition, he often seemed reluctant to assume new powers. "I called not myself to this place," he remarked during the Protectorate. He died of pneumonia in 1658.

Algernon Sydney

Algernon Sydney (or Sidney), (1623 [?]-1683), the second son of the Earl of Leicester, considered himself of noble status. "Though I am not a peer," he once wrote, "yet I am of the wood of which they are made."[4] In a sense, his birth determined his fate. The rights to his father's estates and title belonged to his older brother Philip. Primogeniture condemned second sons to a lower rung on the socioeconomic ladder—unless they could arrest their fall by catching hold of the tail of fate. Algernon sensed this, and did his best. While still in his teens, he sought and received a commission in the army sent to Scotland to subdue the rebellion. When that service proved unsatisfactory, he wrote for permission to return to England, "not being able to subsist here but upon credit, the most sure way to ruine the fortune of one that hath noe stock to rely upon." He assured his mother that "nothing but extreame necessity" would have brought him to consider bearing arms in a homeland now torn by civil war, "and yet, it is the only way of living well for those that have not estates."[5]

After considerable hesitation, the Sydneys chose to fight for Parliament, and served first at Dublin Castle. Algernon had found a career—in the service of those who held England's pursestrings. He was wounded at Marston Moor, retired to civil life, and entered the political arena. He opposed the killing of the king, but returned to Westminster a week after the blow had been struck to resume his seat in the Commons, and two years later was named a member of the Council of State. But his ascendance was short-lived; it sank with the Rump on April 20, 1653, when General Cromwell dramatically dissolved that body. Sydney was the last to leave; a show of force had to be employed to eject him. In 1656 he took the lead part in a play critical of the Protector performed in the Sydney ancestral home.[6]

With Cromwell's death Sydney returned briefly to power, but when Charles II returned from exile Sydney took his place. He wandered about Europe for seventeen years. When he was finally permitted to return to England in 1677, he lost little time in reentering politics. With the aid of William Penn he twice stood for a seat in the Commons in 1679 and 1680, but both elections were contested, and on neither occasion were his claims upheld; his Commonwealth past and fiery temper rendered him too suspect to "moderate men."

By 1682 Sydney was deep in intrigue with various dissidents in England and Scotland, and was engaged in writing a reply to Sir Robert Filmer's *Patriarcha*, a royalist piece of political theory. When the "Rye-House Plot" was revealed in June, 1683, Sydney was arrested, along with several of his associates. As he was charged with high treason, he was denied counsel, habeas corpus, and knowledge of the specific charges against him. When finally brought before Lord Chief Justice Jeffreys in November, he was convicted on the testimony of a single witness and the introduction into evidence of his manuscript reply to Filmer, contrary to the letter of the centuries-old "two-witnesses" rule for high treason, but apparently in keeping with the new Statute of Treasons of 1661. He was beheaded on Tower Hill, December 7, 1683.

Fifteen years later, after the "Glorious Revolution" and the expiration of the Licencing Act, his manuscript was published under the title of *Discourses on Government*. Laboriously, Sydney documented his claim that "God left nations unto the liberty of setting up such governments as best pleased themselves." He made much of the "ancient liberties" of Englishmen, and of the prerogatives of Parliament. Like Hampden, Sydney rejected legislation by royal decree alone. "We owe noe but what we freely give," he wrote. "None is, or can be, imposed upon us, unless by ourselves."[7] Frequently, he linked liberty with property, spoke with abhorrence of slavery, and referred his case to a "higher law."[8] One section was entitled "Unjust Laws are not to be Obeyed."[9]

Sydney was no radical democrat. When he wanted to describe the need for self-protection, he used the analogy of a man protecting his deer park (the Sydneys had several). And when he wanted to demonstrate the ridiculousness of the prosecution's case at his trial, he compared it to "the sense of porters and grooms."[10] He argued that men elected to Parliament should not be bound to vote as their local constituency directed, but that they should feel free to vote as they deemed best for the nation as a whole. He favored a balance of power between king, nobles, and commons and felt that

> No better defence has been found against the encroachments of ill kings than by setting up an order of men who, by holding large territories and having great numbers of tenants and dependents, might be able to restrain the exhorbitancies that either the King or the Commons might run into.

His "good old cause" was that of the "ancient," feudal, "constitutional" order. But, of course, none of this should come as any surprise. Algernon, after all, was the descendent of Sydneys and Percys. In his position, it was quite radical enough to assail the divine right of kings, and to suggest that the gentry were quite as good, in many ways, as the nobility.[11]

"Royal Martyr" and "English Monster," "Patriot" and "Rebel Saint": Contemporary Reputations

It is difficult to say with certainty what the average seventeenth-century Englishman thought of the leading contenders in the English civil war, chiefly inasmuch as there were very few "average" Englishmen. Anglican royalists adored Charles I and loathed the man they considered his murderer, Oliver Cromwell; many Independents despised "the tyrant" Charles Stuart and were devoted to the Lord Protector. Jews were no less partial to Cromwell, for the favor he had displayed towards them, but many Presbyterians, staunch Parliamentarians, evangelical millenarians (like the Fifth Monarchy Men), and primitive social democrats (Diggers and Levellers), had cause to dislike Cromwell's treatment of their convictions. Hampden and Sydney were perhaps less contentious figures, and by the 1690's they were solidly entrenched as Whig symbols of Parliament's prerogatives and of due process.

In the main, the reputations of Hampden and Sydney, Cromwell and Charles I in the seventeenth century were shaped by the needs of the various factions—royalist and commonwealthman, "Tory" and "Whig"—engaged in the political tug-of-war over who should rule in England. Personal recollections of these four figures made myth-making and the kind of idolization that would characterize their reputation in later years more difficult in their own age, but even in their lifetimes they were panegyrized or criticized to suit political predilections.

Charles I and Cromwell

No sooner was Charles I in his grave than exiled royalists began a torrent of lamentations, apologia, and broadsides elevating "the Royal Martyr" to heaven and consigning Cromwell and his colleagues to hell. *The Eikon Basilike, or Pourtraicture of His Sacred Majestie in His Solitudes and Sufferings* (1649), alleged to have been the product of Charles's own hand (but possibly that of Reverend John Gauden), appeared in some forty-seven editions and served a burgeoning "cult of the Royal Martyr" (see pls. 38 and 39). Answered by *Iconoclastes* (1649) of John Milton, Cromwell's Latin Secretary, the *Eikon Basilike* drew the fire of other Commonwealth and Protectorate pamphleteers and caricaturists as well.[12]

In the last decade of his lifetime, and for about a year after his demise, there was never a shortage of poets, pamphleteers, and divines willing to sing Cromwell's praises. John Milton, Edmund Waller, and Andrew Marvell were joined by others, less famed today, who praised the Lord Protector's wisdom, equity, righteousness, and abilities in leading England from the confusion of civil war to a state of prosperity at home and prestige abroad. But two years after Oliver's death General George Monck and a coalition of Presbyterians and constitutional royalists brought the Royal Martyr's son, Charles II, over from continental exile. Thereupon Cromwell's remains were gibbeted and his name vilified with as great a passion as but a few years before it had been praised (occasionally by the same person). Prints depicting Cromwell as the Antichrist appeared as early as 1656, and were to be seen in 1659, 1660, and for many years thereafter until at least 1683. In 1660, the year of the Restoration, there appeared such pamphlets as John Gauden's *Cromwell's Bloody Slaughter-House* and Abraham Nelson's *A Perfect Description of Antichrist*, and the anonymous tragicomedy, *Cromwell's Conspiracy*. Over the next few years, while Charles II continued his purge of those responsible with Cromwell for the death of his father, were published more of the same, among them Abraham Cowley's *A Vision, concerning his late pretended highness Cromwell the Wicked* . . . (1661), James Heath's especially brutal *Flagellum; or the Life* . . . *of Oliver Cromwell, the Late Usurper* . . . (1665) (see pl. 22), William Winstanley's *The Royale Martyrology and Dregs of Treachery* (1665), and Slingsby Bethel's *The World's Mistake in Oliver Cromwell* . . . (1668). Bethel, with dubious justification, blamed the decline of England's foreign trade in the 1660's on Cromwell's foreign policies, while Winstanley's exultation of the Royal Martyr had its counterpart in his treatment of Cromwell: "an English monster, the centre of mischief, a shame to the British Chronicles, whose horrid treasons will scarce gain credit of posterity and whose bloody tyranny will quite drown the names of Nero, Domitian and Calligula."

Such harsh publications as these did not reflect the views of all Englishmen, of course. Charles II's domination of the courts made it difficult for those anxious to defend Cromwell to respond, but Christopher Hill has pointed out that some Englishmen during the reign of Charles II looked back on the Protectorate years with considerable nostalgia.[13] And to Hill's evidence I can add another item pointing in the same direction. When in the late 1670's and early 1680's Lord Shaftesbury and the "Whigs" (among them Algernon Sydney) sought to exclude Charles II's Catholic brother James from succession to the throne, "Oliver Cromwell's Ghost, Dropt from the Clouds," was called upon by one (understandably anonymous) Whig pamphleteer to remind Englishmen of the dangers of Popery and the proper way to deal with it. This Lord Protector's spirit (which apparently descended from heaven, unlike its royalist-inspired counterparts) expressed its anger at the vacillating policies of the Court towards France and the perennial Irish Catholic rebels. He had known how to handle Popery in his day: "Oh, that I could pick up the Crumbs of my mangled body again. . . . Oh, that I might be suffered now to do as much for King *Charles* the Second, as I did against King *Charles* the First."[14] It does not necessarily follow that shaking Cromwell's fist at the supporters of the Catholic James implied any deep and abiding affection for the Lord Protector on the part of the author. But he clearly found it *useful* to identify the anti-Catholic sentiment he sought to arouse with the hero of Drogheda, the champion of the Protestant cause.

Moreover, once another champion of the Protestant cause, William of Orange, had displaced the Catholic James on the English throne, the defenders of Cromwell regained the right to speak, if only in guarded tones. In 1692 there appeared Nathaniel Crouch's carefully laudatory *History of Oliver Cromwell*, to be followed by the bolder (and hence anonymous) *Parallel between Oliver Cromwell and the Prince of Orange* (1695) and *A Modest Vindication of Oliver Cromwell . . .* (1698). Public celebration of the Lord Protector was frowned upon by the moderate men guiding England's destinies, men for whom Cromwell's image still breathed dangerous fire. But private celebration of his virtues may well have continued among many Englishmen, such as those bold souls who met every January 30th (the day Charles I went to the block) from 1693 on, at the Calves Head Club, to dine on calves' heads and to toast the "patriots who killed the tyrant."[15]

If there is evidence that some late-seventeenth-century Englishmen venerated Cromwell, there is also evidence suggesting that many others did not. The republican Edmund Ludlow remembered Cromwell as a tyrant who had sacrificed "the public cause to the idol of his ambition." In 1662 Parliament made January 30 a day of fasting and lamentation, and for centuries many Englishmen gathered on that day to hear the clergy sing the praises of the Royal Martyr, victim of Cromwell's and his fellow regicides' evil deed.[16] In 1682 Thomas May's squib, *Arbitrary Government Displayed . . .* , was as critical of Cromwell as it was of the Whigs, and the Whig author of *The Secret History of the Reigns of King Charles II and King James II* (1690) could think no more damning the means of attacking James II than by comparing him to *"Oliver Cromwell* himself," who "with all the Irreligion laid to his Charge" was never quite so foul a liar as James II. [17] Note that Cromwell was not unequivocally accused of villainy here. The author hedged his phrase to allow some relief for those sympathetic to Cromwell. But his words suggest that Englishmen were at least familiar with the charges made against the Lord Protector, and his choice of Cromwell as a negative symbol suggests that many must have accepted those charges as valid.

My sense is that within a generation after his death Cromwell's image had generally become a bipolar "Machiavellian" one, with some attractive and some repulsive features.[18] The first balanced examination of the Lord Protector, Henry Fletcher's *The Perfect Politician; or a Full View of the Life and Actions (Military and Civil) of O. Cromwell* (1680), was characteristic, with praise of his courage and skill mixed with criticism of his ambition and deceptiveness. Its ambivalence tells us as much of its author and, I think, its era as it does of its subject, Cromwell.

Hampden and Sydney

Hampden fared well enough in his day. To be sure, there were royalists like Sir John Denham who directed squibs against him as early as 1641,[19] but laudatory accounts were more numerous, particularly after his death. The *Weekly Intelligencer*, a Parliamentary paper, claimed that "the losse of Colonell Hampden goeth neare the hearte of every man that loves the goode of his king and country," and added its opinion that "his reputation in the future will more and more be had in honour and esteeme." Similarly, the *Weekly Account*, referring to the death of "that nobel patriot of his country, whose losse is infinitely lamented in all places," reminded its readers "howe much he suffered for the goode of his countrey . . . imprisonment in the Gatehouse . . . and . . . a great summe of money out of his owne estate in defence of the kingdome's right in the great case of ship-money."[20] One elegy, bidding farewell to Hampden's "Renowed Dust," asked:

> Was he not pious, valiant, wise and just
> Loyall and temperate? Everything that must
> Make a perfect harmonie?

and answered:

> Yee Know
> His constant action have declared him so.

In 1647 a royalist balladeer named Hampden as a guest in "Pluto's Court," but a more friendly elegy, the work of a Roundhead, extolled "The Patriot" in these terms:

> His purer thought were free
> From all corruptions: he not valued friends,
> A fair estate, or self-propounded ends,
> Any preferment, or ought else above
> A quiet conscience, and his nation's Love.[21]

During Cromwell's Protectorate "Hampden's Case" was invoked by one George Cony, a London merchant who challenged Cromwell's Instrument of Government in November, 1654, by refusing to pay customs fees because they had not been imposed by a duly-elected Parliament. Cony had no more luck with the courts than had Hampden, but it had been worth a try, for Hampden's cousin, the Lord Protector himself, spoke of "the Patriot" as "a very noble person" whose "memory" is very grateful to all."[22] Thomas Hobbes scoffed at Hampden's reluctance to pay the ship-money levy ("Mark the oppression; a Parliament-man of £500 a year taxed at twenty shillings"), but Clarendon, a constitutional royalist, but through his very moderation a credible witness to Hampden's character, was more generous. Clarendon expressed some disapproval of Hampden's "cunning" and Parliamentary "dexterity," but praised his action in the ship-money case, his "courage," "modesty," and sense of "justice." Clarendon acknowledged that "his reputation for honesty was universal, and his affections seemed so publicly guided that no corrupt or private ends could bias them."[23]

For many years after the restoration of Charles II in 1660, royalists dominated the printed page and, despite Clarendon's example, Hampden's reputation was assailed. Bulstrode Whitlocke, a key official of the Commonwealth and Protectorate, later recalled Hampden as one with a keen "affection to public Liberty," who was "well beloved in his country" and much "Lamented," but Abraham Cowley's unfinished poem execrated Hampden as

> the man that taught confusion's art,
> His treason's restless with a noiseless heart . . .
> Was he that taught the zealous rout to rise,
> And be his slaves for some feigned liberties.

By 1680 the old differences between royalists and Parliamentarians had resurfaced, and Hampden's reputation became a bit of a political football. On Christmas eve of that year the Commons voted breach of privilege, arrested, and brought to the bar of the House a minister named Thompson for traducing Hampden's name.[24] These "Whig" defenders of "Hampden the Patriot" were shortly sent packing by their monarch, but within a decade they and their friends were back in power, having driven the brother of their late royal foe from the throne in a gloriously bloodless Revolution. With their return, Hampden's reputation was once again respectfully honored in public.

Algernon Sydney's reputation took shape, in a sense, before his birth. His uncle was Sir Philip Sydney, the chivalric hero of Zutphen. When John Milton singled out Algernon for praise in his *Second Defence of the*

English People, he seemed to have more to say about the name Sydney "(which is a name indissolubly attached to the interests of liberty . . . an illustrious name I rejoice to see in the list of those who always adhered to our cause)," than he did of Algernon himself.[25]

Algernon's fame never eclipsed that of Sir Philip altogether, of course, but it soon surpassed Sir Philip's. Bishop Gilbert Burnet remembered Algernon as a man of "rough and boisterous temper," but "of the most extraordinary courage, a steady man, even to obstinacy, sincere." The English ambassador in Paris, Lord Preston, reported to George Savile, Marquis of Halifax, when news of the Rye-House Plot broke, that "Mr. Algernon Sydney is very much admired and spoken of by the French" (albeit it may be that his French admirers were also his employers, or at least his political allies).[26]

But Sydney's fame during his lifetime was negligible compared to what it was to become after his trial and death. The postmortem glory was partly the result of the "greate Courage, greate sense, greate parts, which he'd showed both at his trial and death." But the greater part of his fame is attributed to the more impersonal issues of political symbolism, due process, and the laws of evidence Englishmen deemed at stake in "Al. Sydney's case." John Evelyn noted in his diary the day after Sydney's execution that "it was thought he had a very hard measure."[27] Richard Wynne, a solicitor, and a Mr. Forth, "the king's joyner," were fined and committed to Newgate for referring to the "loggerhead jury" that tried Sydney. A Mr. Bridges, "Gentleman of the Bedchamber," was "suspended his place [by the King] for speaking words tending that Colonel Sidney had not a fair trial," and Sir Samuel Barnardiston was fined by Jeffreys for "maliciously writing . . . letters of false news . . . that a party had prevailed to get Sidney executed."[28] Roger Morrice noted in his journal that no man's life or property could be safe after the use made of Sydney's manuscript at his trial. John, Earl of Ailesbury, remembered that "great clamours were made relating to the executing Colonel Algernon Sidney."[29] Whig wags might avoid censorship by satirizing the case, as did the author of "A New Song of the Times" (1683):

> Algernon Sidney,
> of Common-wealth Kidney,
> Compos'd a damn'd Libel (ay marry was it)
> Writ to occasion
> Ill Blood in the Nation
> and Therefore dispers'd it all over his Closet.
> It was not the writing
> Was prov'd, or indicting;
> Tho' he urg'd Statutes, what was it but fooling,

Since a new trust is
Plac'd in the Chief Justice [Sir George Jeffreys],
To damn Law and Reason too by over-ruling.

Similarly in "Oliver's Porter, Fiddler and Poet in Bedlam" (circa 1685) "Hodge the Constant" (Andrew Marvell?) and "Johnny the Sincere" (John Milton?) try to persuade "Oliver's Porter" of the guilt of Sydney and his colleague, Lord Russell. "Porter" replies: "Yet to the Plot I firm belief Afford/ Of th' Evidence I credit not one word." "Johnny" then asks: "Can you distrust what [Forde, Lord] Gray and [William, Lord Howard of] Escrick say?" and "Porter" sarcastically answers: "What two such excellent moral men as they?" and then remarks:

One witness, and a Circumstance for Facts,
Is not enough: We must prove Overt-acts.[30]

Sydney may have been guilty, and his trial may have been conducted in a manner consistent with the state of civil liberties in his day, but some Englishmen were nevertheless angered, and Sydney became a martyr to the cause of liberty among the "Whig" faction.

"Tories," of course, took quite another view of "the Rebel-Saint," as he was already being styled. One of Lord Preston's royalist correspondents reported "how imprudently Mr. Sydney carried himself at his trial." And while accounts, whether Whig or Tory, agreed that Sydney had "dyed a great Hero," "like a gentlemen," or "like a true rebel and republican," the bishop of Oxford felt that he had "died with the same surliness wherewith he lived."[31] But churchmen would be less impressed with his courage than with his disregard for religious ceremonies.

Tory pamphleteers had a field day with Sydney. The officially edited, 1683 account of his trial was prefaced by remarks arguing that Sydney had been "given . . . all the play imaginable" to make his defense. Pamphlets charged, similarly, that "he had all the favour in the World shown him."[32] Poetasters assailed the convicted traitor. There were many such squibs; I shall quote from but one. *An Elegy on the death of Algernon Sidney* (1684) railed against the "Ungrateful . . . old stanch't Rebel":

Early in treason he began to excel
Wou'd in his cradle scratch, bite, and rebel.
As strength encreas'd, so spite and malice reig'n.
And still prevailed o're his ill-temper'd mind.

His commonwealth principles, it was charged,

. . . made the Rebel-Saint with cursed sword,
In wrath, pursue th'Annointed of the Lord.

.   .   .   .

>   Then farewell Sidney! now expect no more
>   To sport and roil in Royal purple gore.

It is difficult to say whether or not this, or any of the other critical broadsides, enjoyed substantial popularity. Perhaps all that Tories hoped for was that Sydney's case should serve as "a memorable warning and fatal example to all the English nobility and gentry of this, and all future ages," to quote Bishop Thomas Sprat, the official recorder of the "infamous Rye-House Plot."[33] Such language may well have had the reverse effect; it may have been a red cape to many "nobility and gentry." "Sydney's Maxims," deduced from his *Last Paper* and the record of his trial, appear to have been widely discussed in London taverns, Sussex estates, and North Riding country homes. Evidence of this is difficult to find, of course, but some of it may be suggested in such items as the report of an unidentified correspondent or "secret agent" of Lord Sunderland in October of 1684, to the effect that "a mighty party" espoused the cause of the victims of the 1683 plot prosecutions.[34] In June of the next year the rebel aspirant to the throne, James, Duke of Monmouth, charged James II, among other things, "with the murder of Colonel Sidney."[35] Two years later the Whig poetasters were still reminding men of Sydney, "A rebel bold, for striving still/ to keep the law above the will."[36] And as warning clouds filled the summer air in 1688, "Sydney's case" was brought to mind again. At the trial of the seven bishops, their counsel Heneage Finch, who had assisted in the prosecution of Sydney, was embarrassed when he opposed the admission into evidence of the petition of the bishops. William Williams, who had aided Sydney at his trial, and who now served the king, remarked, "Mr. Finch I remember in Al. Sidney's case you were of another opinion, for though his hand were not proved but by belief yet you then pressed it so far that you had the blood of that gentleman."[37]

In December of 1688, William of Orange entered London triumphant, followed by a train of Sydney's old associates, coconspirators, relatives, and friends, and, more important, by a revolutionary "Whig" faction anxious to justify their act and to produce martyrs that James II's precipitous flight had denied them on the battlefield. Sydney had been a friend of John deWitt, the Dutch republican foe of William; he had been the implacable foe of Charles II; he had expressed consternation at the thought of William ascending the throne of England. It mattered not. A Lords' bill reversing Sydney's attainder was passed by both houses and signed by the new monarchs, legitimatizing the Rebel-Saint. As the bill was read in Commons, Sydney's prosecutor, Heneage Finch, rose to defend himself, remarking that "I see many gentlemen's eyes upon me." He was severely rebuffed by the speaker and several members. "This is not to be suffered," Sir Henry Goodricke exclaimed, and Finch reluctantly took his seat.[38] The reversal of Sydney's bill of attainder may not have constituted the decisive blow on behalf of English liberty that a later generation was to consider it (for the same day the Lords drafted it, they also approved an act suspending the same habeas corpus that Sydney had himself been denied), but it represented a step in the right direction to many Englishmen.[39]

The accession of William and Mary loosed the bonds of those anxious to respond to Bohun, L'Estrange, Settle, and the rest of Sydney's royalist detractors. Sydney's *Last Paper* was reprinted in 1689, and again in 1693. The Quaker pamphleteer, Humphrey Smith the younger, paraphrased Sydney in *Sydney Redivivus, or the opinions of the late Honourable Collonel Sydney as to Civil Government . . . By which the late proceedings of the nation against James the II are justified*. Smith praised "that Honourable Patriot . . . by which being Dead he yet speaketh and Patronizeth the *Good Old Cause*, for which he professedly Died a Martyr."[40] This was followed by Sir John Hawles's *Remarks on the Tryals of . . . College, Russel, Col. Sidney, . . .* , who charged that Judge Jeffreys and the king's ministers had "packed the Jury" and that Sydney had been "talked to death under the notion of a Commonwealth Man." Hawles pressed for reform of the Treason Act of 1661.[41] In Rotterdam, Benjamin Furley, Sydney's old friend, published a mysterious *Copy of a Prophecy sent by Colonel Algernon Sydney . . .* (see Appendix A). Late in 1689, when Lord Griffin was found to have treasonable papers in his quarters, the Earl of Rochester argued for bail for his compeer, citing the reversal of Sydney's attainder. "Sydney's case" was cited by one Anderton, a Jacobite printer in 1693, and by several other Tories on trial for treason in the mid-1690's, including Lord Preston, his old critic.[42]

In January of 1694, an anonymous pamphlet appeared, listing *Some Paradoxes . . . .* Among them was the suggestion that "To *Reverse* the *Attainders* of *Russel, Sidney*, etc. and yet *Browbeat* a Bill of Trials [Treason Act], that might prevent the like hardships again" was hypocritical.[43] In 1696 the Treason Act was passed, and shortly thereafter Sir John Fenwick was arraigned in Parliament on a bill of attainder for high treason. Several who rose to speak for or against the attainder bill cited Sydney's case, and no one suggested that Sydney might have been guilty. Thomas Pelham, son of Algernon's sister Lucy and heir of the Pelham dynasty, observed that Sydney had not only been innocent, but that he had been entirely selfless in his insistence that the law of 25 Edward III that required two witnesses to an act of treason be observed to the letter in his case; Pelham quoted Sydney himself on the matter.[44] When the words of Sydney, a man convicted of high treason in 1683, were quoted as law at the proceedings of others less than a score of years later, it may be said that the Rebel-Saint had come to symbolize due process.

Not until 1698 was Sydney's manuscript reply to Sir Robert Filmer printed, "under the avowed Patronage of the Chief Magistrates of the City of *London*." No sooner had it appeared, the royalist Charles Hornby recalled, than its title page, along with those of Ludlow's *Memoirs* and Milton's *Works*, were "affixed to the Gates of the Royal palaces, as if it were in open Defiance of Monarchy."[45] In 1700 Sydney's old friend, William Penn, sent a copy of the *Discourses on Government* to his agent in Philadelphia for sale, and the Rebel-Saint crossed the Atlantic, bound in folio.[46]

Patriot-Symbols in Britain, 1700–1755

Charles I and Cromwell

By the early eighteenth century it had become the practice every January 30 for government-favored clergymen to deliver sermons before one or the other Houses of Parliament. These were then published, occasionally inspiring the publication of other January 30 "counter-sermons," delivered elsewhere by ministers who reflected the views of the political opposition. Anglican divines like Luke Milbourne, White Kennett, Gilbert Burnet, Francis Hare, John Harris, John Chapman, William Dawes, and Humphrey Nickel lashed out at one another's interpretation of the causes of the civil war and the rights and obligations of the dutiful subject towards his monarch. Needless to say the Royal Martyr was featured prominently in the efforts of Tory divines like William Dawes, Bishop of Chester, who bristled with maledictions for those who were "this day *feasting*, to *hinder* the *good effects* of our fasting."[47]

By 1758 the critics of the first Charles had so upset John Boswell that he published a two-volume defense, *The Case of the Royal Martyr considered with Candor; or, an Answer to Some Libels Lately Published in Prejudice to the Memory of that Unfortunate Prince*. To Tories and Jacobites especially, "the idea of a patriot king" was appealing, and the essay by Henry St. John, Viscount Bolingbroke, with that title surely reflected those sentiments. A "patriotic" monarch was well placed to rise above "factions" and serve the needs of all his subjects. He had an obligation as well as a right to lead them. Lord Bute, tutor to the future George III, prescribed Bolingbroke's *Idea of a Patriot King* as the young prince's guide. Bolingbroke, for long leader of the Tory faction, venerated the Royal Martyr, as would Royal George.

Whigs, content with the rule of the first two Georges, were capable of entertaining such an ideal as Bolingbroke's while simultaneously venerating Hampden and Sydney, their own models of antistatist virtue. But for Tories and many Whigs as well, this respect did not extend to Cromwell. Thus, when in 1711, a Tory pamphleteer assailed the virtue of the Whig champion, John Churchill, Duke of Marlborough, he used

"Oliver's Pocket Looking-Glass" to detect the inequities and warned Marlborough to cease his imitation of Cromwell's usurpation; the ensuing Whig defense of Marlborough bristled at the comparison of their champion to the satanic Lord Protector.[48] In that same year a High Church critic of the proto-evangelical Reverend Benjamin Hoadly depicted Hoadly writing a revolutionary sermon (with a copy of Sydney's *Discourses* close by) while a spectral Oliver Cromwell hovered in the background, axe in hand. Somewhat later in the same decade there appeared *A True and Faithful Narrative of Oliver Cromwell's Compact with the Devil* (1720), which soberly explained how Cromwell had sold his soul for a promise of seven years of supremacy. The radical Whig "Cato" (Thomas Gordon) criticized Cromwell in 1721 in *Cato's Letters* for "enslav[ing] those whom he was employed to defend," and the Whig historian John Oldmixon wrote of his "treachery, tyranny, and other vices."[49] George Cadwallader, Tobias Smollett, and George Green (author of *Oliver Cromwell: an Historical Play*) all accepted Lord Clarendon's verdict on the Lord Protector and pronounced him deceitful, ambitious, guilt-ridden, and a tyrant. The anonymous author of *Liberty and Right: An Essay, Historical and Political, on the Constitution and Administration of Great Britain* (1747) had no use for the "artful" Cromwell at all. "Freedom and Liberty" had suffered from his "Tyranny." He had "no Public Spirit," no "Virtue," and worst of all, to "moderate" men, he was "enthusiastick."[50]

But there were a few articulate (and probably many inarticulate) enthusiasts for Cromwell in these lean years as well. In 1725 a Baptist minister, Isaac Kimber, updated "Robert Burton's" favorable biography of the Lord Protector (which had gone through six editions by 1728). Kimber's biography, which went through at least five editions of its own, conceded Cromwell's "ambitious" nature. But Kimber insisted that the Lord Protector had always acted "with a passionate Regard to the Public Good," and he praised his firm conduct of "a Protestant foreign policy" —both of which qualities continually aroused the nonconformist conscience from the 1650's to the twentieth century.[51] Kimber's sympathetic life of Cromwell was followed in 1739 by another, the work of one John Banks. Banks had been educated by an Anabaptist minister, and he too was filled with enthusiasm for Cromwell, one of the chief "heroes and patrons of mankind."[52] The Banks biography also went through at least five editions.

Nonconformists were not altogether alone in their respect for Cromwell. Lawrence Echard, Paul de Rapin-Thoyras, Jonathan Swift, and Henry Fielding had generous things to say of Cromwell's foreign policies, and in the centennial years of the Protectorate Cromwell's reputation may have experienced a modest revival among a segment of the community.

Oliver Cromwell's Ghost (1755) attacked the ministry for its incompetent handling of the war with France, and similar broadsides in 1756 and 1759 carried the Lord Protector's supposed criticism of a foreign policy that appeared weak-kneed when contrasted to Cromwell's own a century before.[53] But Francis Peck's brief *Memoirs of the Life and Actions of Oliver Cromwell* (1740), like the earlier Henry Fletcher's *Perfect Politician*, was circumspect, carefully hedging its bets. Peck found Cromwell "full of good and bad qualities," and assured his patron, "Mr. Auditor Benson," that "Whatever there is aught amiss . . . in . . . Cromwell's Politics, those are things which I neither pretend to vindicate, or request you to patronise."[54] Cromwell's memory was still quite dangerous, at least for those subject to the laws governing the press in England.

Hampden and Sydney

Neither Hampden nor Sydney can be said to have risen to the stature of a national hero by 1700, but they were on the way there. Tories continued to snipe at Sydney in particular as a "dangerous author," who had received his "due rewards" on the scaffold. When Bishop White Kennett praised Sydney in his *Complete History of England*, Roger North went to great lengths to refute the notion he saw growing over the years that Sydney was anything less than a traitor.[55] And when John Oldmixon expressed Whiggish views on a particular subject in 1727, he distinguished between his own "moderate" position and one less "responsible": "I doubt not some thoughtless malicious People will take me all alone for as errant a Republican as *Algernon Sydney*," he wrote, "but they judge in that as wildly as in their other Cavalier *Sentiments*."[56]

But most Whigs were less wary than was Oldmixon to identify with the Rebel-Saint; they quoted him frequently throughout the period and transformed him into a moderate man, and a "classical" one to boot. The author of *Free Thoughts in Defence of a Future State* (1700) was the first to refer to the *Discourses* as being of a caliber to supply the loss of six books of Cicero's *de Republica*, a phrase some later biographers were to repeat. The next year Lord Somers quoted "what I take to be very moderate and just, which Colonel Algernon Sidney says in that Discourse which cost him his life," to the effect that members of Parliament sit for England, and not for their hustings.[57] John Locke recommended the *Discourses* to gentlemen who hoped to be fully educated.[58] William Pulteney, Earl of Bath, and Nicholas Amhurst, who together wrote *Three Letters to The Members of the Present Parliament with a Discourse on Kings and Members of State* in 1747 under the pseudonym "Caleb D'Anvers," quoted the "wise and virtuous" Sydney variously on the duties of monarchs, legislators, and citizens alike. The nonconformist divine Phillip

Doddridge quoted from the *Discourses* no fewer than twelve times in his celebrated *Lectures*.[59] John Trenchard (a nephew of one of Sydney's co-conspirators) and Thomas Gordon quoted Sydney in their popular *Cato's Letters*, and may have paraphrased him as well; note the following similarity:[60]

Sydney's *Discourses* (1698), p. 76:	Cato's Letters, 2:85:
Man can [not] come to be master of many, equal to himself in Right, unless it is by Consent or Force.	Men are naturally equal, and none ever rose above the rest but by Force or Consent.

Sydney's *Discourses* may have been popular, but they did not constitute the only path by which Sydney's reputation rose. More important than his political precepts was the memory of the trial and death of this "martyr to English liberty." Daniel Defoe reminded Englishmen in 1706 that after Sydney's manuscript had been seized and examined, "it was thought fit, instead of answering him with the pen, to answer him with the axe. . . . *So* they cut off his head, merely because they could not answer his book." The author of *English Advice to the Freeholders of England* (1714) offered a similar reminder.[61] As in the 1690's, "Sydney's case" was cited in a 1722 defense of another Jacobite, Christopher Layer, a supporter of the Pretender. Similarly, in 1723 the Tory Duke of Wharton spoke in defense of Francis Atterbury, Bishop of Rochester, and embarrassed his Whig peers by comparing the injustice done to Sydney, "that unfortunate gentlemen," to that which he felt the Whigs were about to administer to Atterbury.[62] Four years later, the poet James Thomson canonized Sydney as "The British Brutus," "firm to the cause of Liberty, her rough determined friend," in his famous poem *The Seasons*, and later, in *Liberty* (1736), Thomson bemoaned "Sidney bleeding for the unpublish'd page."[63] The author of *An Address to the . . . Free-Holders . . . [on] the General Election* (1734) cited Sydney's trial at length to establish the superiority of Walpole's administration to those under the later Stuarts, and spoke kindly of Sydney, "that great and good man . . . . [that] illustrious person (for such I must call him for his virtuous Principles and great Mind)." This defender of the Whig status quo reminded Englishmen that Sydney had not been permitted to do "in his closet" what Trenchard and Gordon were now doing openly, and signed himself "A Revolutionist," referring, it seems safe to suppose, to the "Glorious Revolution" of 1688 rather than to any more radical or violent a one.[64] Thirteen years later, in another election year, another Whig supporter of Walpole praised Sydney and his fellow victim of Stuart justice, Lord William Russell, "murdered by Form of Law, for having been the Champions of Liberty, and of the Protestant Religion."[65]

Caroline Robbins has found that Sydney's popularity was greatest among radical Whigs, the "eighteenth-century commonwealthmen."[66] But his name was clearly a symbol to more moderate, "party" men as well. Thus the first Duke of St. Albans could deliberately choose to honor the Rebel-Saint in naming his fifth son Sydney in 1703. And William Murray, later Lord Chief Justice Mansfield, often used the pseudonym "Algernon Sidney" in essays appearing in *The Gazetteer* from 1738 to 1740.[67] Walpole, after all, sought to preserve the fruits of the "Glorious Revolution," and, though these may have meant to him and his followers the security of the house of Hanover and their own lucrative offices, to others they symbolized "the rights of Englishmen." "Sydney's case" was particularly illustrative of the tyranny that had preceded their day and could descend on them again at any time they failed to exercise virtuous vigilance, the vigilance, in James Thomson's words, of "the Patriot's noble Rage,/ Dashing Corruption down through every worthless age."[68]

Like Sydney, Hampden drew some fire from Tories in early eighteenth-century Britain. In 1712, while Tories enjoyed a brief season of prominence under Queen Anne, one Tory pamphleteer called upon "Grandsire Hamden's Ghost" to admonish his Whiggish grandson to "forsake" his colleagues and to *"meddle not with those who're giv'n to change."* This spirit of one of the Whigs' patron saints was filled with regret that his

> Crafty Speeches rais'd the Good Old Cause,
> And made the House run counter to the Laws,
> I sowed the fatal seeds of discontent
>
> .   .   .   .
>
> to my eternal Shame.

His "faction" had

> Disguis'd our ill Designs to gull the Crowd,
> With that prevailing Cant, *The Publick Good*,
> *The safety of Religion and the Laws.*[69]

But if one Tory regarded Hampden's reputation with cynicism, some Whigs treated it with considerable respect. Hampden's ship-money *Tryal* was republished in 1719; he was remembered in Thomas Gray's "Elegy in a Country Churchyard," where he represented latent rustic-yeoman patriotism in the oft-quoted phrase, "some village Hampden"; and he appeared in several poems in which James Thomson sought to remind Englishmen of their heritage and responsibilities:

> A Hampden . . . is thine, illustrious land!
> Wise, strenuous, firm, of unsubmitting soul
> Who stem'd the torrent of a downward age,

To slavery prone, and bade thee rise again
In all thy native pomp of freedom bold.[70]

The popular, Whiggish, French historian of England, Paul de Rapin-Thoyras, referred in the 1720's to the ship-money litigation as "the most important case that has ever been argued in any Court of Justice."[71] And Philadelphia-born James Ralph, a paid Whig pamphleteer, listed Hampden, who had never written any notable paper or delivered any particularly memorable speech, along with Sydney, Locke, and John Trenchard, early Whig theorists and essayists whose "glorious Labours" Ralph described as being "too widely circulated" and "too universally known to be withheld from the Knowledge and Admiration of remotest Ages. From them Liberty will be understood, and by them [that is, by their spirits] it will be defended till Time shall be no more."[72]

Patriot-Symbols in America, 1700-1755

Generally speaking, there appear to have been few occasions in early-eighteenth-century America which evoked the spirit of English patriots. Nevertheless, whenever "tyranny" did rear its head, there were colonists who remembered that, as Englishmen, they were the heirs of "that ardent Spirit of Liberty, and that undaunted Courage in the Defence of it, which has in every Age so gloriously distinguished BRITONS AND ENGLISHMEN from the Rest of Mankind."[73] And at such times, John Hampden or Algernon Sydney frequently came to mind.

Two phenomena appear to account for the transmission of Sydney to the New World: the purchase of the *Discourses* by colonists, and the migration to the colonies of Englishmen who held the Rebel-Saint in high esteem.

After Trenchard's and Gordon's contemporaneous *Cato's Letters* and Locke's *Two Treatises on Government*, Sydney's *Discourses* were the most popular of all works on political science in the colonies. The *Discourses* had at first been slow in finding their way to America. The volume Penn had sent to the Philadelphia bookstore stood on the shelf unsold for eight years.[74] And when in 1713 White Kennett compiled a library for America under the auspices of the Society for the Propagation of the Gospel in Foreign Parts, he received treatises on fortifications, geology, astronomy, scaling-ladders, sea fights, mathematics, and a host of other areligious but practical subjects; nary a volume of *Hampden's Tryal*, Sydney, Harrington, Milton, or Locke.[75] The Society's subscribers do not appear to have seen a need to convey ideas such as these to the queen's colonies.

Some colonists procured them just the same. Reverend Ebenezer Pemberton of Boston owned a copy of the *Discourses* when he died in

1717.[76] Jeremiah Gridley (1702–67), James Otis's opponent in the writs of assistance cases, owned a copy of the 1702 French-language edition.[77] Benjamin Franklin, James Logan, and Thomas Godfrey ordered a copy in 1732 for "the Junto's" Library company.[78] H. Trevor Colbourn has listed the holdings of twenty-six colonial American libraries, together with records of booksellers of sales and special purchases, and has remarked that "[t]here may be special meaning in the frequent priority accorded Sydney's *Discourses* over Locke's *Treatises on Civil Government.*"[79] Actually, Colbourn's own records indicate that Locke's *Treatises* were slightly more popular, if one includes the copies of Locke's *Works* in the total, but Colbourn was understandably puzzled, for he had uncovered evidence of a considerable respect for Sydney among colonial merchants and gentry.

Using Colbourn's data, I have compiled some comparative figures (see Table 2.1) which tend to upset some presuppositions some historians have held regarding the importance of one political theorist or another.[80] Harrington and Montesquieu may have been of lesser importance in America than the Tory Bolingbroke, and the Whigs Gordon and Trenchard, Sydney, and Locke.

Table 2.1. Political Texts in Prerevolutionary American Libraries

Political theorists	Private and public library holdings	Special purchases	Paper advertisements	Total
Trenchard & Gordon (*Cato's Letters* only. If *Independent Whig* included, figures even higher)	12	16	11	39
Locke (*Two Treatises* and *Works*)	21	9	6	36
Sydney (*Discourses*)	18	8	6	32
Bolingbroke (Shaftesbury) (all works)	15	0	6	21
Harrington (*Oceana*)	11	0	2	13
Montesquieu (all works)	6	0	0	6

Source: H. Trevor Colbourn, *The Lamp of Experience* (Chapel Hill, 1965), pp. 199–232.

If Kennett and the Society for the Propagation of the Gospel failed to despatch a copy of the *Discourses*, other Englishmen were less reluctant. Jeremiah Dummer sent a copy to Yale in 1710.[81] Thomas Hollis of Lincoln's Inn brought out his own edition, and sent copies to Harvard and to Jonathan Mayhew.[82] James Alexander (1691–1756) brought his copy with him, and in 1737 he drew a comparison between Sydney's case and that of the printer-publisher, John Peter Zenger. Alexander, who was one of Zenger's attorneys, wrote *A Brief Narrative of the Case and Trial . . .* for the Philadelphia *Gazette*; in it he identified Sydney as "the sworn foe of tyranny," "a gentleman of noble birth" who had been tried for "*a libel.*" "This case," he wrote of Sydney's trial,

> is a pregnant instance of the danger that attends a law for punishing words; and of the little security the most valuable men have for their lives in the society where a judge by remote inferences and distant innuendoes may construe the most innocent expressions into capital crimes. Sidney, the British Brutus, the warm, the steady friend of liberty [note the paraphrasing here of Thomson], was for those very discourses MURDERED by the hands of lawless power.[83]

It little matters that Alexander somewhat misrepresented the issues in Sydney's trial. What is significant is that he saw fit to compare Zenger's plight to that of the Rebel-Saint.

Alexander's admiration of Sydney was comparable to that of young Sam Adams in 1743, and to that of James Ralph, an expatriate Philadelphian who dedicated part of his Whiggish *Of the Use and Abuse of Parliaments* in 1744 "as an Act of Justice to the Memory of a Great Man . . . , Algernon Sydney."[84] Lemuel Briant, the Great Awakening preacher heard by John Adams in 1747, and Andrew Eliot, minister to Boston's North Church, were both "prejudiced in favour of [Sydney] that martyr to civil liberty" whose *Discourses*, Eliot claimed, had taught him "to form any just sentiments on government."[85] Arthur Dobbs (1689–1765) an Anglo-Irish, one-time governor of North Carolina, quoted Sydney to support his case for a union of Ireland and England.[86] Jonathan Mayhew remembered "having been initiated in my youth, in the doctrine of civil liberty," as taught by Sydney.[87] In 1748 the editor of Boston's *Independent Advertiser* commented on the pending "nomination of officers" for the Massachusetts Bay Colony. He hoped "the ill consequences which attend an abuse of Power" could be avoided, and he quoted from Sydney's *Discourses* on the obligations of "the good Magistrate." Sydney, the noble "Sacrifice to Tyranny," he observed, was a valuable guide because of his "approved character."[88] Another colonist, writing anonymously to the Philadelphia *Gazette* in 1755, asked the editor to publish an extract from the *Discourses* of "the great ALGERNON SIDNEY, whose Life and Death rendered him truly illustrious, for asserting the *Liberty of Mankind*, for defending the Rights of the *British* Nation, for *declaring* against Tyranny & Tyrants, against Oppresion and against the *Ruin and Desolation of his Country* (by any Enemy whatsoever)." The correspondent (perhaps Franklin) offered Sydney's advice "at this Melancoly Juncture" (several months after Braddock's defeat)—namely "That is the best Government, which best prepares for War."[89] To Pennsylvanians fearful of a Franco-Indian attack, Sydney may have served as a symbol of resolution, fore-shadowing what was to come when colonists experienced different anxieties ten years later.

3 "Liberty and Property": English Patriot-Symbols in the Age of the American Revolution

In 1749 Gilbert Tennant delivered a Thanksgiving Day sermon before Governor Jonathan Belcher of New Jersey. He gave thanks for the "Mildness and Equity" of George II's government, which he characterized in the following manner:

> He has expressed a just and tender Regard to the Rights and Liberties of his Subjects; nor has he stretched his Prerogative, to the prejudice of those wholesome Laws whereby it is reasonably limited, and his People's Properties secur'd. He has imprisoned none against Law, granted no Monopolies to the Injury of Trade, collected no ship-money, rob'd none of their Religious liberties, rais'd no subsidies without authority of parliament; all which . . . were flagrant in the *Tyrannical Reigns* of the Steward-family; whose violent attachment to *Popery* and *Arbitrary Power* (for the most part) made the oppressed nations groan.

This much of his sermon was reprinted in the Boston *Evening-Post* in early 1750, a month after the editors of the *Evening-Post* similarly defined a good king as one who "has imprison'd none against the law [and has] collected no ship money."[1] In short, a good king was one who displayed none of the faculties of the Stuarts, had generated no Hampdens, op-

38

pressed no Sydneys. As H. Trevor Colbourn has demonstrated, the more articulate colonists responded well to the admonition of James Burgh: "There is no kind of reading that tends more to settle the judgment than that of History and Biography."[2] And from the historians they had read— Rapin-Thoyras, Burnet, Kennett—many had, it is clear, acquired a healthy disrespect for Charles I, Cromwell, and Charles II, and a hearty affection for Hampden and Sydney. I shall not here consider the sad and bloody history of the Stuarts in the eighteenth century; it constitutes, in effect, the end of a chapter. But as the reign of George III advanced, Englishmen on both sides of the Atlantic were increasingly provoked to draw analogies between their own condition and that of their English ancestors of the previous century. The twin saints of liberty and property, Sydney and Hampden, accordingly drew ever greater public comment.

Sydney and the "Principles of Liberty"

Sydney's popularity, though still somewhat marred by his revolutionary character, continued throughout the 1750's,[3] although according to Thomas Hollis "the moderation of the late reign [of George II] has left [Sydney] in some degree of neglect."[4] For this seeming neglect James Otis, on the other side of the Atlantic, suggested a different reason when he confessed his reluctance to quote from Sydney to support his case against the writs of assistance. "Had any thing to justify them been quoted from *Col. Algernon Sydney*, or other British Martyrs, to the liberty of their country, an outcry of rebellion would not be surprising."[5] Otis found Locke's sentiments "less liable to insidious reflections and insinuations [of] Jacobites and other stupid Bigots" upon "moderate" men like himself.

Three events soon brought Sydney to the fore: the republication of his *Discourses*, the Stamp Act controversy, and the Wilkes Affair.

The first of these was probably the least important, for there had been two editions of the *Discourses*, published in 1750 and 1751,[6] but Thomas Hollis's 1763 edition is nevertheless remarkable because of its eccentric editor.[7] Hollis believed Sydney especially glorious for his "virtue" and "reasonable religion," free from "enthusiasm": "He had piety enough for a saint, courage enough for a general, or a martyr, sense enough for a king; in a word, if ever any, he was a perfect Englishman."[8] Hollis was Sydney's Parson Weems. His edition was the first to use the romantic Cipriani-Basire engraving of "the Rebel Saint" (pl. 3). He generated or transmitted a number of legends of his hero, crediting Francis Hutcheson, the philosopher, with one tale to the effect that Sydney had owned a fine white stallion in France, coveted by Louis XIV. On learning that the king intended to seize the horse, Sydney allegedly shot it, saying "this horse was born a free creature, has served a free man, and should not be mastered by a king of slaves."[9] Given Sydney's comfortable relationship with Louis XIV, the story seems apocryphal. But given the feelings of Englishmen in what one of them styled the "critical period"[10] of the 1760's, such an exercise in hero-worship and myth-making seems quite feasible.

In little more than a year after the appearance of Hollis's edition of the *Discourses*, the passage of the Stamp Act heralded a torrent of invocations of the Rebel-Saint. Letters protesting the act appeared in newspapers, bearing the signature "Algernon Sydney."[11] Pamphleteers referred their readers to "Sydney's case," and chanted the praises of his *Discourses*.[12] James Otis was no longer reluctant to cite Sydney as authority. When friends of the Court disputed the colonist's claims, Benjamin Franklin reminded them that if Americans were mistaken in their views of the British Constitution, it was because they had been "reasoned into this mistake" by such admirable authors as Locke and Sydney.[13] After all, Sydney had maintained that

> Property also is an appendage to Liberty; and 'tis as impossible for a man to have a right to lands or Goods, if he has no Liberty, and enjoys his Life only at the pleasure of another, as it is to enjoy either when he is depriv'd of them. . . . For Liberty solely consists in an independency upon the will of another; and by the name of slave we understand a man who can neither dispose of his person or goods, but a man who enjoys all at the will of his master.

Stephen Hopkins featured these passages in his protest to the Stamp Act, *The Rights of Colonies Examined* (1765), and it seems safe to say that for those propertied Americans fearful of Parliamentary taxation, Sydney had become a respected authority on matters of state.[14]

The case of John Wilkes is a particularly interesting example of the use made of the Rebel-Saint by Englishmen of the 1760's. Wilkes's newspaper, the *North Briton*, was highly critical of George III and his ministers, and when the forty-fifth issue insulted the monarch directly, Wilkes was seized and his papers and house searched on the strength of a general warrant. To his friends this smacked of "Sydney's case," and comparisons were drawn. Sydney's correspondence with his father was reprinted in later editions of the *North Briton*. Charles Churchill, Wilkes's associate, assured readers of his poem "The Duellist" that "An everlasting crown shall twine,/ To make a *Wilkes* and *Sidney* join."[15] When the government later revealed that Wilkes had apparently written an obscene but unpublished poem, the "Essay on Woman," and took steps to prosecute its author, an anonymous *Appendix to the 1st 46 issues of the North Briton* compared the circumstances to Sydney's case.[16]

Wilkes fled to the Continent, where he remained for several years, like Sydney, a self-exile. When he returned to England in 1768, he stood for Parliament, and was elected three times. Each time he was denied the seat, and throughout, he was consigned to the Old Bailey. Purdie and Dixon's Williamsburg *Gazette* described his incarceration to sympathetic colonists:

> the house in the Old Bailey, built for the great Algernon Sidney, is taken for the residence of Mr. Alderman Wilkes; and as soon as Mr. Wilkes resides there his friends propose to call the Old Bailey by the name of Sidney Street, an alteration which will be extremely pleasing to the inhabitants.[17]

Just so was it pleasing to certain of the colonists.

Wilkes made the most of the comparison, albeit quite sincerely. He explained to all that Sydney's case bore a resemblance to his own and that he "therefore admired Sydney almost to enthusiasm" (the word was still somewhat offensive to "moderate" men). Wilkes disapproved of his friend Churchill's poem, "Gotham," which had romanticized "the Royal Martyr," and quoted Sydney's remark that the killing of Charles I had been "no crime." He spoke of writing a life of Sydney, and praised the *Discourses* in the introduction to a proposed "History of England."[18] "Thank God our Ancestors were Heroes and Patriots, not *prudent* Men," he wrote to the Maryland *Gazette* in 1770. "Russell and Sydney were considered by the Townshends of their Age as *imprudent* Men. They risked all for liberty."[19] Eventually Wilkes was seated in the Commons and in June of 1774 a group of Newcastle Wilkesite reformers with "patriotic interest" organized "the Sydney Club" to elect other reformers to Parliament.[20] Clearly Wilkes, Sydney, and Liberty were synonymous to many Englishmen, both in Britain and in America.

During these years, Sydney unquestionably served many as a symbol of resistance to "tyranny." Horace Walpole wrote George Montagu, praising John Dunning's *Enquiry into the doctrine of . . . Libels, Warrants, and the Seizure of Papers* (1764), and assured Montagu that it would "warm your old Algernon blood."[21] When Benjamin Rush visited Edinburgh in 1766, he was taught the merits of Sydney by one John Bostock, a medical student, who, upon learning that their grandfathers had both served the Parliamentary cause in the Civil War,

> opened his mind fully to [Rush] and declared himself . . . [a] republican. . . . He spoke in raptures of the character of Sidney, and said that he once got out of his carriage in passing by Sidney's country house, and spent several hours in walking in the wood in which [Sydney] was accustomed to meditate when he composed his famous treatise upon government. Never before had I heard the authorities of Kings called in question.

I had been taught to consider them nearly as essential to political order as the Sun is to the order of our Solar System. . . . from that time to the present all my reading, . . . and reflections have tended more and more to show the absurdity of hereditary power.[22]

Bostock must have been of the same mettle as another Scot, Sylas Neville, who frequently compared George III's "arbitrary principles" to "those of the House of Stuart," praised Sydney to the skies, adopted a passage from his *Last Paper* as his motto, frequently met with other "adorer[s] of the character of Sydney," and often instructed his landlady in Sydney's "principles of Liberty."[23]

It is by no means clear that Neville's landlady was as impressed by such arguments as Rush had been. The "eighteenth-century commonwealth-men" who worshipped Sydney may well have been a rather exclusive crowd, at least in Britain. But Sydney-veneration was not restricted to republicans, and it seems safe to say that by 1770 Sydney was well regarded as a model of political virtue by Whiggish Englishmen of all social classes.[24]

Sydney's *Discourses* were now cited with greater regularity to support a host of "noble causes." A cartoon in the London *Political Register* in 1769, depicting an episcopal bishop being literally driven out of America by a band of angry colonists, showed one colonist brandishing a volume marked "Sydney on Government." A decade later, when the monarch gave his assent to the Catholic Relief Act of 1778, an anonymous print, *The Invisible Junto*, depicted a grotesque George III being weighed and found wanting in divinely held scales that tested him against a copy of Sydney's *Discourses* and a cap of liberty.[25] In 1770 John Adams quoted Sydney, "a great and worthy man, a patriot, and a hero, and enlightened friend of mankind, and a martyr to liberty," in his defense of the Boston Massacre soldiers. Adams sought thereby to establish the importance of passionless due process, "without any regards to persons." He cited Sydney again on the eve of independence in 1775 to strengthen his case that revolution was sometimes necessary when tyranny had grown intolerable.[26] In 1771 Edmund Randolph delivered an address before the faculty of the College of William and Mary on Locke and Sydney. This may have been the same time that Thomas Jefferson read Sydney, for he recommended it to a friend in August 1771.[27] When Josiah Quincy, Jr., bequeathed the *Discourses* to his son in 1774, he prayed that "the spirit of liberty" might thus "rest upon him" more easily.[28]

The Reverend William Stearns, preaching before the newly formed Continental Army at Cambridge, spoke of the American's "righteousness" and "ardent love of liberty" and quoted the words of "the famous ALGERNON SYDNEY: NO MAN CAN GIVE THAT WHICH IS ANOTHER'S."[29] Jehovah had said it too, but Reverend Stearns chose to cite the Rebel-Saint as his authority on that particular subject. Englishmen friendly to the colonist's cause, like Capel Lofft and James Burgh, often quoted from Sydney in pamphlets and tracts.[30] The Society for Constitutional Information, a British group of "Honest Whigs," planned a pamphlet composed of abstracts of Sydney, Coke, Selden, and Blackstone.[31]

Radicals found Sydney more conducive to their purposes than "conservatives," but the latter were beginning to use the Rebel-Saint as well. In 1767 "New Light" western Connecticut reformers campaigned against a local political system that gave them higher taxes and fewer offices than their eastern Connecticut neighbors, and in the process they drove a number of "Old Light conservatives" from office in the state. Thereupon a conservative writing under the pseudonym "Algernon Sidney" complained that good men were being voted out of office for insufficient reason and vigorously defended the "Old Light" cause. And in May of 1776, while plans for a Declaration of Independence were going forward on all fronts, "Cato" attacked the idea in the Pennsylvania *Gazette*, and assured his readers that "the immortal SIDNEY" would have opposed such a radical step. He quoted Sydney to the effect that it was wiser to "repair the breaches" in the constitution than to upend it altogether.[32] Apparently this use of Sydney did not disturb the radicals, for the first published copy of the Declaration of Independence carried as a frontispiece a quotation from the *Discourses*: "All human Constitutions are subject to Corruption, and must perish, unless they are 'timely renewed' by reducing them to their first principles."[33] Machiavelli had been the first modern political theorist to insist on this, but the colonists preferred to quote from the *Discourses*.

There were other ways of invoking "old Algernon" than by quoting his *Discourses*. In 1774 Rind's *Virginia Gazette* (Williamsburg) printed Sydney's letter to his father, written in 1660, in which he had refused to compromise with the tyranny of the Stuarts. Six months later the same journal published an "open letter to a brother who is a soldier coming to America." Its author referred to "a man, or an angel, called SIDNEY, whom one cannot see," who warned the author of the evils intended by the "tories" and their "Intolerable Acts."[34] The same year, there was circulated in London a pamphlet entitled *Sidney's Exhortation in a Candid Appeal to Every True Lover of God, His Country, and Himself*, which denounced the government for its repeated refusals to redress American grievances. Its author, "Sidney," announced that he was "personally resolved never to become a slave to such arbitrary measures and will not resign his liberty unless with his life." And in 1778 an anonymous poetic eulogy to the late William Pitt, Lord Chatham, had Sydney praise "the patriot minister" and then advise Englishmen that

A real Briton glories to be free,
He loves, reveres, he worships liberty;

. . . .

If in thy bosom genuine virtue glow,
That spirit which . . . scorns the man to mental greatness blind,

. . . .

Then . . . ardent zeal wake to just applause
Of Sydney's fire in freedom's glorious cause.[35]

As some Americans braced for open rebellion their thoughts were often on the Rebel-Saint. Thus in 1773 the Petersham Committee of Correspondence advised other Massachusetts Sons of Liberty that, given a sufficient display of public virtue, the Lord would deliver New England from the oppressive grasp of arbitrary power to the glorious sunshine of liberty: "in a similar belief, that Patriot of Patriots, the Great ALGERNON SIDNEY, lived and Died, and Dying, breathed a like Sentiment, and prophecy, touching his own and the then approaching times."[36] "Who would not rather be brave, even tho unfortunate, in the cause of Liberty?" John Adams wrote to his wife in 1777, and added, "Who would not rather be Sydney, than [General] Monk?"[37] Adams may have been instrumental when the time came in establishing as the motto of the new Commonwealth of Massachusetts the second line of what was regarded as Sydney's own motto:[38] "*Ense petit sub libertate quietam.*"

"Black Dalrymple" and the Barillon Notes

Some Tories continued to snipe at Sydney, of course, but generally without effect. The Jacobite pamphleteer and author of *Ossian*, James MacPherson, for example, considered Sydney "a dangerous citizen" who had been too "enthusiastic" at his execution, but historian William Harris's view of Sydney, the "patriot" with "uncorrupt hands," reknowned for "virtue, probity and integrity," beloved by "respectable" Englishmen, was more like it.[39]

Sydney's reputation was too firmly entrenched by 1770 to be damaged or dislodged, even after the introduction of particularly damning evidence. In 1771 Sir John Dalrymple uncovered and published a host of dispatches from the French ambassador at the court of Charles II, Paul de Barillon d'Amoncourt. In 1679 this gentleman had advised his master, Louis XIV, that he had paid some 500 guineas to a number of leaders of the opposition to Charles II, among them, Algernon Sydney. Dalrymple was a Scottish Tory, but even he felt it necessary to say of his discovery, "I felt very near the same shock as if I had seen a son turn his back in the day of battle."[40]

Tories were delighted. David Hume repeated Dalrymple's findings with pleasure. It was, he wrote, "amusing to observe the general, and I may say national, rage" evinced by the Dalrymple discoveries. Hume himself allowed that the bribe was of little importance, but he was glad to see the bubble burst. The "blind prejudice of party had exalted [Sydney] into a hero," and now, the Whigs would lose much face.[41] Similarly, when Boswell asked Dr. Johnson about the matter, that gentleman replied that it was "well that all mankind" now saw Sydney and his associates to be "rascals."[42]

The worshippers of the Rebel-Saint, as Hume had noted, were enraged. In 1773 Dr. Joseph Towers published an *Examination into the Nature & Evidence of the Charges brought against Lord Russel and Algernon Sydney by Sir John Dalrymple*, wherein he exonerated both from Dalrymple's implications and praised Sydney's "generous ardour in defence of . . . liberties . . . and . . . the common rights of mankind," and his "nobleness & dignity of soul."[43] In March of the same year Horace Walpole instructed William Mason to "revenge Sidney & Russel" for the attacks of Dalrymple, who, Walpole was certain, had accepted a bribe from George III's ministry to blacken the reputations and sully the "blood of patriot martyrs." "I will never believe [the charges]," Mason replied. And the next year he published a poem bemoaning the fact that "Sydney's, Russel's patriot fame should fall,/ Besmeared with mire, like black Dalrymple's gall."

Walpole continued firm. In 1777 he wrote to Reverend William Cole, renewing his faith in his "saint," Sydney. And in 1781, after Hume attacked Sydney's reputation in the *Critical Review*, Walpole damned his "saucy blockhead tone," and accused Hume and his Scottish countrymen of attempting to "annihilate our [Whig] patriots, martyrs, heroes & geniuses, Algernon Sidney, Lord Russel, King William, the Duke of Marlborough, Locke."[44] Concurrently, Francis Blackburne, the proto-Unitarian Yorkshire divine, a friend of Sylas Neville, and compiler of Thomas Hollis's *Memoirs*, struck out at the "nefarious" debunking of "our patriot" by "writers employed or favoured by the government," and denied all the "charges" brought forward by "a profligate and licentious court and ministry."[45] Dalrymple, Lord Bute, and George III were in cahoots as far as Blackburne was concerned.

Americans seem to have rejected Dalrymple's evidence as well. Colonists were warned by an anonymous correspondent of the *Virginia Gazette* in September, 1775, to beware of the pamphlets of Sir John Dalrymple, the man who had "calculated almost solely to extirpate the very idea of patriotism by endeavoring to condemn to infamy the memory of two of the most celebrated patriots mentioned in British history, the illustrious and celebrated RUSSELL and SIDNEY."[46] And Sam Adams wrote to James Warren, comparing the slanders directed against Dr. Arthur Lee to those of Dalrymple:

> It is the old Game of mischievous Men to strike at the Characters of the good & the great, in order to lessen the Weight of their example and influence. Such Patriots as Lord Russell and Algernon Sydney of the last Age, have of late been falsely and audaciously charged by a Scotch Tool of the most nefarious Court, with having received Bribes from the National Enemy; and it is not strange that . . . Lee is also charged with a Criminal Correspondence with the Enemy, without even the shadow of Reason.[47]

Franklin had written in 1745 that Americans were a "kind of Posterity" for writers like Sydney: "We know nothing of their personal Failings: the Blemishes in their Character never reach us . . . and therefore we praise and admire them without restraint."[48] The result of this uncritical adoration was that by 1775 many Americans were unwilling to accept the "blemishes" Dalrymple claimed to have found. Sydney was a Whig hero—designed, decorated, and displayed by the Whigs of two worlds—and a century after his death he had become part of themselves; they could not give him up.

Hampden and "the Protection of Property"

In the third quarter of the eighteenth century, while Sydney's fame rose, John Hampden's came increasingly to mind as well. In 1754, John Dickinson, while a student at the Inner Temple, remembered the days of yore, when "a Hampden and a Holt opposed encroaching Power, and supported declining Justice," and four years later, when Virginia's Governor Dinwiddie sought to raise revenue with a retroactive land grant fee ("pistole fee"), Richard Bland protested such a violation of "ancient rights" and reminded Virginians of "Hampden, that Great Man," who had defended his nation's liberties against just such an attack on the rights of property.[49]

When Horace Walpole suggested in 1761 that Hampden had displayed "a tincture of self-interestedness" in his relations with Charles I, his friends rebuked him.[50] The Tory, David Hume, had the same doubts about Hampden's disinterestedness, and he was critical of what he deemed to be Hampden's republican spirit, but he also allowed, ambivalently, that Hampden "merited great renown with posterity for the bold stand which he made in defense of the laws and liberties of his country." "Historians of the most opposite parties," he observed, were united in praise of Hampden, and in private correspondence with Catherine Macaulay, Hume linked the "cause of liberty" to Hampden.[51] Macaulay herself depicted Hampden as the defender of the nation's liberties in combating "this new state-monster, Ship-Money." The Reverend Mark Noble praised his "courage to stand forth the Champion of liberty" and remarked that he was "beatified" by his countrymen. Lord Cobham placed Hampden's likeness "among the British worthies" in his "Elysium" at Stow. Thomas Hollis, Sydney's admirer, sought (in vain) to acquire an original portrait of Hampden. John Wilkes claimed to be imbued with Hampden's "spirit." And in 1769 "Hampden" offered a *Vindication of the Petition of Livery of the City of London to His Majesty as to the Charge upon the Ministry of raising a revenue in our colonies by prerogative*. Something was moving Whigs firmly towards the hero of the ship-money affair.[52]

As the Sugar and Stamp Acts had caused some Englishmen to invoke the name of Sydney, so it stirred others to remember Hampden. Stephen Hopkins had quoted from the *Discourses* in his critique of the Sugar Act; he offered Thomson's praise of Hampden as the essay's frontispiece, a gesture that infuriated his compatriot, Martin Howard, a Tory from Newport. Hampden's "sedition" in 1641 "overturned the English constitution," Howard complained, and this conduct was "little applicable to the present times." "Only a few disappointed [Rhode Island rum and molasses] traders," alarmed about the apparent resumption of long-defunct imperial trade regulations, would identify with Hampden, or so Howard maintained. Hopkins immediately responded that his reference to Hampden was not meant to serve as a comparison between an England on the eve of civil war and the present; the comparison intended was between the England of 1636, the ship-money days, and the present days of the Stamp Act. Hampden's brave and selfless resistance to the ship-money tax was the object of Hopkins's attention:

> When Hampden made this noble appeal, taxes were laid on the people of *England* otherwise than by their own representatives. Then it was that the people began to whisper that such taxes were illegal, and to *murmur* at their imposition. In the year 1764 it was proposed to tax the *Americans* without the consent of their own representatives. This occasioned whispers and murmurs among them. Now whether there be any resemblance between these cases and times, let every man judge.[53]

Daniel Dulany objected to the sacrilegious use made of "the name of Hampden" by William Knox, a defender of the Stamp Act, who had cast "an oblique reflection upon the colonies." No Tory could be permitted to invoke "the Patriot" in order to mask barefaced tyranny. Dulany duly reminded his readers of the true lessons of Hampden's ship-money case for the colonists. The "arbitrary and oppressive" acts of Charles I, "destructive of the essential principle of English liberty," had been opposed by the bold and virtuous Hampden; American colonists were worthy heirs of his mantle. When "John Pym" defended the Stamp Tax in the Boston *Gazette and Country Journal*, "John Hampden" (pl. 14) answered. He objected to "British subjects" being "taxed without their consent, and tried without a jury," reminded "Pym" of the ship-money controversy, and directed him to "relearn the great doctrines of British liberty taught in 1640."[54] Simultaneously "John Hampden," writing on behalf of the New York Sons of Liberty, warned the publisher of the *New York Journal* to continue to print critiques of the Stamp Act or face the consequences.[55]

Benjamin Franklin and James Burgh continued the pattern in 1770. Their essays in *The* [Philadelphia] *Public Advertiser* compared the resistance of the colonists to taxation without representation to "the conduct of the brave Hampden," whose example they recommended to the ministry. "Do the Grenvilleans [supporters of the Prime Minister, Grenville] hold this glorious Patriot to be a seditious and rebellious Person?" Surely they could not; he was a hero to Britons. The comparison must have been most annoying to the "Grenvilleans."[56]

Others in America played variations of the same theme. In 1771 Samuel Adams, anxious to secure a united front among the colonies, reminded Americans that "When Mr. *Hampden's* ship-money case . . . was tried, all the people of England, with *anxious expectation, interested themselves* in the important decision."[57] And when in 1773 Governor Robert Eden of Maryland claimed the right to fix the fees of crown officials, Charles Carroll of Carrollton compared Eden's claim to that of Charles I in the ship-money case, a comparison that drew applause from "Independent Whigs."[58] Later in the same year news of the East-India Tea Act reached the colonies and letters "to my fellow countrymen on patriotism," bearing the pseudonym "Hampden" and written by Benjamin Rush, among others, sounded "The Alarm" in the newspapers of several of the colonies, imploring Americans to "Think of your Ancestors" and "rescue Patriotism from Obloquy." "The chief end of all free government is the protection of property," one such letter explained; Hampden must have been deemed an appropriate figure to deliver that message.[59] The next spring, Edmund Burke rose to propose a repeal of the tea tax act and told the Commons that

> The feelings of the colonies were formerly the feeling of Great Britain. Theirs were formerly the feelings of Mr. Hampden. . . . Would twenty shillings have ruined Mr. Hampden? No, but the payment of half that sum, on the principle it was demanded, would have made him a slave.[60]

Two years later, Perez Morton rose in Boston to praise the first American patriot-martyr, Joseph Warren, and to compare his life to that of John Hampden.[61] In 1776 *Hampden's Tryal* was reprinted in London, in the first volume of Francis Hargrave's *State Trials*, and in April of 1776 "Hampden" argued for independence from the crown in the pages of Dixon and Hunter's *Virginia Gazette*.[62]

Hampden and Sydney: "Freedom's Genuine Sons"

Given the growing identification of Englishmen on both sides of the Atlantic with Hampden and Sydney, it is not surprising that the two began to appear together, as joint symbols of the rights of Englishmen. Churchill's "The Duellist" is the first example of this linking that I can recall seeing. In 1763 Churchill juxtaposed Hampden, "The Prop of Freedom," with Sydney, "his brother patriot." The next year George Montagu told Horace Walpole of his "litany" of patriot-saints, "John Hampden and Algernon," before whose "pictures" (see pls. 5 and 10) he made "daily orisons" with the "hours of Magna Charta in my hand." William Temple was more serious. He wrote to Boswell in the same year, eulogizing his hero:

> O Sidney! thou friend to mankind, thou foe to oppression, thou scourge of tyrants and guardian of liberty, citizen, philosopher, hero, what can atone for thy sufferings, what expiate thy blood? . . . some future historian shall record your virtues.

After going on in this fashion for several paragraphs, Temple remarked: "I trust there will not be wanting other Hampdens and other Sidneys to pull the tyrant down and trample him [in] the dust."[63]

Temple may have been more aggressively republican than many of his contemporaries, but his juxtaposition of the two patriots was perfectly in keeping with the views of all who came to disapprove of George III and his ministers. An anonymous letter to the *Boston Gazette* in 1765 joined the two, and then compared their noble struggles to the "prospect now before us in America." "Somebody or other in Great Britain" had set "a direct and formal design on foot to enslave all America," and the patriots of the past would prove to be useful models.[64] In 1769 Edmund Jennings presented to "the Gentlemen of Westmoreland," Virginia, an ambitious painting, depicting William Pitt, Lord Chatham, champion of the colonial cause in the Stamp Act controversy, on an altar supported by busts of Hampden and Sydney.[65] After Benjamin Rush visited with John Wilkes in the Old Bailey, he wrote home, praising the author of the

45th *North Briton*, "I have heard a number of sentiments from him that would have done honor to a SIDNEY or a HAMPDEN."[66]

A year later, in 1770, Ebenezer Richardson, a customs official's man, killed an eleven-year-old boy during an attack upon his house by a Boston mob. He was not brought to trial for some time, as Governor Hutchison hoped the passage of several months would mollify the city, but John Adams complained of the "unjustifiable confinement." "What is law for a *Richardson* is law for a *Sidney*," he reminded Bostonians: "If oppression is warranted by law, the Patriot is much more likely to fall victim than the pimp and pander. Hampdens will stain the scaffold with blood."[67] Several years later, Adams's associate, Josiah Quincy, Jr., called upon his countrymen to unite in opposition to the Boston Port Bill. Quincy felt certain that Americans would rise to the occasion, that forthwith would emerge "Bruti and Casii—her Hampdens and Sydneys—patriots and heroes, who will form a band of brothers."[68] Arthur Lee assured Englishmen that the colonists were only protecting the constitution in the same way as had "Hampden, Pym, Sidney, and Russel, than whom Greece with all her patriots, and Rome with all her heroes, produced no men who trod this mortal stage with more dignity, or quitted it with greater lustre." And from London, Lord Rokeby's frequently reprinted *Considerations . . . with Respect to the British Colonies in North America* (1774) complained that Englishmen were straying from the liberal principles of Sydney, Russell, Locke, and Hampden.[69]

When actual fighting broke out, the twin patriots came to mind even more readily. Twice John Adams remarked to friends of the "ordeal" of politics, and reminded them that "Hampden died in the field, Sidney on the scaffold."[70] The death of Joseph Warren at Bunker Hill, as has been pointed out, suggested the comparison of Warren with Hampden, but more frequently both Hampden *and* Sydney were invoked in memory of the heroic doctor. The New York *Mercury* printed a "toast," in September, 1774, to "The immortal memory of Hampden, Sidney, Warren, and every patriot who bled in defense of liberty."[71] The following July, two pieces of patriotic poetry appeared, one in the *Pennsylvania Packet*, the other in Providence, Rhode Island, in the form of a broadside. The first, "An Elegy to the Memory of Doctor Warren," suggested that as Warren's bier was lifted heavenward, patriots of former days thronged round his soul. "Immortal Hampden leads the awful band,/ And near him Raleigh, Russell, Sidney, stand." The second, *Lines sacred to the Memory of Joseph Warren . . . ,* praised those who died "to save their Country's Laws, the CATOS, HAMPDENS, SYDNEYS"—"Ye for Justice who did plead,/ Ye for Freedom who did bleed," who helped "install a HERO NEW." This poet, one "B.B.", was sure that Hampden and Sydney could be heard to curse modern Britain and to "Swear the Glory is transferr'd,/ YOUNG AMERICA'S preferr'd." Still another example of this is Hugh Henry Brackenridge's poem, *The Battle of Bunker Hill* (1776), where Warren was made to say

> . . . I go to mingle with the dead—
> Great Brutus, Hampden, Sidney, and the rest,
> Of old or modern memory, who liv'd
> A mound to tyrants, and strong hedge to kings,
> Bounding the inundation of their rage
> Against the happiness and peace of man.[72]

Warren was not the only patriot to be compared to Hampden and Sydney. In 1778 Governor William Livingston of New Jersey (1723–90) eulogized "His Excellency General Washington" in the Trenton, N. J., *Gazette*, where he suggested that when the Father of his Country entered heaven he was certain to be met by God, who would introduce him to his "glad compeers,/ The HAMPDENS, SIDNEYS, *Freedom's* Genuine sons!/ . . . Patriot demi-gods."[73] And in 1780 a portrait of that esteemed patriot, John Hancock, was published and sold in Boston, complete with insets of John Hampden, Oliver Cromwell, and Algernon Sydney—four patriots for the price of one.[74] Ships were named for the patriots, as were towns, streets, and children. The regard for Hampden and Sydney was such in the period of the war for independence that Presbyterian Virginians named their first college, founded in 1775, Hampden-Sydney Academy.[75] Obviously, Americans found something attractive about "Freedom's genuine sons!" What was it?

To begin with, it seems clear that Hampden represented both the prerogative of the legislature and the right of Englishmen to their property, unencumbered by what they considered extraconstitutional authority. At the same time, Sydney represented personal, or "civil," liberty. Liberty and property were indivisible rights to the American revolutionaries ("we cannot be free without being secure in our property," John Dickinson had written), and Hampden and Sydney appear to have symbolized these rights.

The pair also represented "virtue" to an age which placed immense premiums on honorable and "virtuous" conduct.[76] They had given their all for "the good old cause" of English rights; others might learn to emulate their noble example. And they personified republicanism as well. Surely their reputation as republicans must have appealed to Americans about to embark on a republican ship of state, just as it appealed to British republicans like Sylas Neville and Thomas Hollis.

But at the same time it must be remembered that neither Hampden nor Sydney may be said to have represented, prior to 1789, any truly "democratic" sentiments. Rather they were symbols of established common law and the law of the Commons. After all, it had been Sydney's *lack* of "enthusiasm" on the scaffold, his reluctance to appeal to the "rabble," that Thomas Hollis and others had found attractive. A certain Dr. Butson, later Bishop of Clonfort, penned a poem "On the Love of Our Country" while at Oxford in 1771, wherein he praised Sydney, "the boldest son of public zeal," as one who had disdained demagoguery: "Yet no diffuse harangue declaim'd aloud,/ To gain the plaudits of a wayward crowd."[77] Even John Wilkes, whom some had accused of demagoguery, rallied the trained bands during the Gordon riots of 1780 to protect the property of Lord Mansfield (the judge who had sentenced him) and other targets of the mob. Similarly, Jonathan Mayhew's disdain for "forcible, riotous and illegal" proceedings, such as the Stamp Act riots in the colonies, was matched by Timothy Hollis's distrust of "the lower class of people."[78] Mayhew, Wilkes, and the Hollises, all of whom adored Hampden and Sydney, were Whiggish gentry, "Brahmins," who believed that "nations flourish more by wisdom, magnanimity, of individuals, the leaders of them, than by their members."[79] If Hampden and Sydney represented revolution to Englishmen, it was "legitimate" revolution. "We are not exciting rebellion," John Adams insisted in 1775, "Opposition, nay, open, avowed resistance by arms against usurpation and lawless violence, is not rebellion by the laws of God or the land. . . . Hampden, Russell, Sydney, Somers . . . were no tyrants nor rebels."[80] They were symbols of resistance, to be sure, but the resistance was constitutional, directed against illegitimate, oppressive power.

Finally, the two patriot-martyrs appear to have represented "freedom" to an Anglo-American culture that placed considerable value on individual liberties and antistatism. Only a powerful devotion to unrestrained private action as a sublime ideal could bring an English gentleman to exclaim, "Algernon Sydney! a man now in the over-measure of heavenly bliss, to die a second time . . . for us all, were there need, and the possibility to die!"[81] Only a social condition of extraordinary personal independence would have resulted in so thorough a canonization of these two enemies of "tyranny." A "New song," celebrating the Boston Tea Party, captures their essence. Over the heads of the Tea-Party Indians,

> . . . aloft in Mid-sky,
> Three bright Angel Forms were seen;
> This was Hampden, that was Sidney,
> With fair Liberty between.[82]

The fact that a number of the admirers of the twin patriots were Dissenters (Congregationalists, Baptists, eventually Unitarians) should come as no surprise; Dissenters like Jonathan Mayhew, Thomas Hollis, Philip Doddridge, Capel Lofft, Joseph Towers, Samuel Rogers, Lemuel Briant, Andrew Eliot, Benjamin Rush, and Stephen Hopkins had been raised on a steady ideological diet of antistatism, and many were often engaged in political efforts to secure full civil rights for Nonconformists. Engaged in such activities, however, they were often allied with Anglican liberals in "the struggle against tyranny."[83]

The use of the two patriots by Britons on both sides of the Atlantic, and the constant flow of sympathy each side afforded the other, illustrates in one more way the British character of the colonial American experience. This is not to say, of course, that there was nothing "American" about the colonies by the time of the American revolution. Richard Merritt has clearly established that, at least in the colonial American press, purely American symbols were beginning to crowd purely British ones from the scene by the early 1760's.[84] But until 1775 the Americans had no patriot-heroes to venerate, and the twin patriots were both appropriate and handy. Moreover, the colonial American veneration of Hampden and Sydney indicates that many colonists still thought of themselves and their problems in terms of a British past, complete with British patriot-symbols.

Why did these Britons and colonists identify with Hampden and Sydney in these particular years of the 1760's and '70's? For the very reason that they identified the alleged oppression of George III with that of the Stuarts. By 1760 many Britons were in agreement on one matter—the House of Stuart had been a blight on the nation's body politic. Men like Sylas Neville soon became convinced that George III was "of as arbitrary principles as those of the House of Stuart," that Charles I + Charles II = George III.[85] And under these conditions, Hampden and Sydney, archfoes of the Stuarts, were the obvious symbols of patriotic conduct.

"Villainous Cromwell"

Cromwell, as anti-Stuart a symbol as one might hope to find, was still in partial eclipse, still "too enthusiastick." Few leading American rebels were Levellers or Diggers, but neither were they sufficiently Cromwellian to invoke the Lord Protector. This was a republican revolution, but it was a moderate "constitutional" one, organized and managed largely by antistatists, a revolution of the Rump and Commonwealth, *not* the Protectorate.

Generous things might be said of Cromwell in these years by some (especially in New England), as they had been for a century since his death, but generally speaking, his name was only rarely invoked to lead others to emulate him or stir others to action. In England itself his name drew only tepid praise. William Harris, a tradesman's son who became a Nonconformist minister, wrote a mildly laudatory life of Oliver in 1762, but Harris, a friend of Thomas Hollis, clearly preferred Hampden to Cromwell. Reverend Adam Ferguson had praise in 1776 for the efforts he felt Cromwell had made to secure legislative and electoral reform; Lord Mansfield and William Petty, Earl of Shelburne, had kind words for Cromwell's Protectorate and aggressive foreign policy, but Petty's family had itself risen with that Protectorate, and Lord Mansfield's defense of it was chiefly that of a jurist who disdained "anarchy, confusion, disorder and ruin."[86]

In New England "Oliver" was a fairly popular given name, which may reflect the regard some New Englanders had for "the Great Nonconformist." In 1742 Jonathan Edwards, delighted with the Methodist preacher George Whitfield, compared him to the Lord Protector. In one comfortable section of Boston a popular inn was called Cromwell's Head. This institution, dating from the 1750's, was advertised by a large sign depicting the Lord Protector; the sign "hung so low that all who passed were compelled to make involuntary reverence." British officers ordered the sign to be removed during the wartime occupation of the city, but it was speedily replaced when they withdrew.[87] In 1769 an informer reported that Cromwell had been styled a "glorious fellow" at a meeting in Boston of the Sons of Liberty, and that it had been deemed "a pity" that another Cromwell was unavailable "to espouse their Cause at present."[88] (But the informer also reported a number of other sentiments, purportedly expressed at the meeting, which do not seem very plausible unless they had been uttered by one who did not speak for all, or unless they were cases of hyperbole—"[we] had rather be under the Government of France than England"—and it is possible that the expression of affection for Cromwell was either incorrectly reported, uncharacteristic of the Sons of Liberty as a whole, or exaggerated.) In 1772 "Oliver Cromwell" wrote in the *Boston Gazette*, complaining of the degree of independence from the Bay Colony's General Assembly that Governor Hutchinson allowed to judges. Another pseudonymous Cromwell called on Bostonians to protect their rights during the Tea Act Crisis of 1773; still another call came in April of 1777. "Cromwell" was invoked by the author of the *American Chronicle of the Times* (1774), and appeared therein as the "Lord Protector of the Commonwealth of Massachusetts."[89] In the third quarter of the eighteenth century several colonists were given Cromwell's name, as were towns, inns, and Revolutionary War privateers. Indeed, in Virginia Patrick Henry was said to have reminded George III that he might "profit" by the "example" of a predecessor's fate at the hands of the Man from Huntingdon.[90]

But Cromwell more commonly appeared, like Charles I and Judge Jeffreys, as a kind of foil to the twin patriots, Hampden and Sydney. While he had fond regard for Hampden, Thomas Gray was severe with Cromwell, and Charles Churchill reminded the friends of Sydney and Wilkes that Cromwell had meant "discord" and "horror" to the "friend of Liberty and Law."[91] Catherine Macaulay, a fond admirer of Hampden and Sydney, despised Jeffreys and the Stuarts and was convinced that "no rational and consistent friend to civil freedom" could ever "be an applauder" of Cromwell. The Tory David Hume and the Whigs John Millar and James Burgh alike found Cromwell "villainous."[92] The anonymous Whiggish author of *The Patriot's Guide* (ca. 1770) asked whether "When canting Cromwell play'd the patriot's part,/ Was he than Charles less tyrant in his heart?"[93] The British critic of Samuel Adams had no compliment in mind when he called that admirer of the twin patriots "the Cromwell of New England." Neither did the loyalist author of *The Yankee Doodle's Intrenchments near Boston* (1776) when he described the American revolutionaries as devotees of "Old Oliver's Cause." And the same may be said of the Reverend Dr. Burney, who styled the Gordon rioters "Oliverian" in 1780.[94]

In colonial America, critics of the "enthusiasm" of Reverend Whitfield's sermons styled them "Oliverian," thus using the same comparative model as was Jonathan Edwards, while giving it the opposite value. Jonathan Mayhew, who idolized Sydney, objected to Tory worship of the Royal Martyr and was simultaneously critical of Charles's fatal enemy, the Lord Protector.[95] A leading New York Whig devotee of Hampden and Sydney told of a horrible dream of his in which Cromwell, a century after the creation of his Protectorate, was resurrected and restored to power. The same pamphlet of Stephen Hopkins which displayed his affection for Hampden and Sydney juxtaposed the power-hungry Cromwell to them. Fear of "an Oliver Cromwell" was expressed in August of 1776, and, deep in the Revolution itself, Benjamin Rush, a firm convert to Hampden's and Sydney's political values, displayed great distrust of those of Cromwell.[96]

Cromwell, after all, symbolized the very danger of a standing army that so distressed urban Americans in the 1760's and '70's. He was recalled as one who had usurped the powers of the legislature, and as one whose enthusiasm for colonial empire had set in motion the Navigation Acts. Some would invoke him as an antityrannical symbol, to be sure, but to invoke is not necessarily the same as to admire. He may have ground the tyrant into the dust, but many were persuaded that he had then become one himself, and that his example was one to be avoided. A century later different Americans would find cause to invoke Cromwell's name and to hold him up as a model of virtue (a measure of the change a century would see), but there was little admiration displayed in 1775. And, in any event, Americans soon had a model of patriotic virtue themselves, one who had avoided all of the temptations to which they felt Cromwell had succumbed.

4

Fading Stars and New Lights: On the Changing Nature of Patriot-Worship In Nineteenth-Century America

Fading Stars: A Failure in the Transmission of a Political Culture

With independence secured, American veneration of the twin patriots waned, but it did not die out altogether for nearly a century. When, in 1787 and '88, the Confederation explored the virtues of a federal constitution, Hampden and Sydney were invoked by localistic anti-Federalists fearful of the powers the new union might wield. When in 1798 another "anti-Federalist" representative, Matthew Lyon, was imprisoned, he was styled by his Democrat-Republican friends "the Hampden of Congress," and in 1808 Jedidiah Morse and Elijah Parish published the oft repeated but apocryphal story that Hampden had been present in Plymouth in 1623, that he had carried gifts to Massasoit, and that he had received from that noble savage a warning of unfriendly Indians in the area, which information "the Patriot" had used to save the settlement.[1]

Sydney saw more service. After successfully concluding the Treaty of Paris in 1783, the chief American negotiator, Benjamin Franklin, symbolically purchased his third copy of the *Discourses* from Thomas Brand Hollis, son of the editor of the 1763 edition. When Henry Rutledge went abroad in 1796, his father, Federalist Edward Rutledge, advised him to imitate the Rebel-Saint.[2] In short, the veneration of "old Algernon"

57

was sufficiently widespread in 1804, at least among the elite, for "Parson" Mason Locke Weems to propose an American edition of the *Discourses*: "a work," he claimed, that had been "much extolled by [John] Taylor [of Caroline], [Benjamin] Rush, & [John] Dickinson." He asked President Jefferson for a "word of your approbation," and received a reply that praised those unedited manuscripts to the sky.[3] Weems had been preparing this edition for several years. As early as December of 1801 he lectured state legislatures on *The True Patriot: or An Oration on the Beauties & Beautitudes [sic] of a Republic; and the Abominations & Desolations of Despotism, With an Affectionate Persuasive to the American People, to . . . Honor their Rulers . . . and to Beware of Discord*.[4] This lecture "points to Sydney," he told his publisher. Weems was convinced that the list of subscribers would be numerous. "Reputation," he allowed, "is a great thing."

"The great Algernon Sidney for Politicians" had a respectable sale throughout the South in 1805 and 1806. James Pleasants, later a U.S. senator and the Jeffersonian governor of Virginia, father of John Hampden Pleasants (b. 1797), ordered 100 copies. "In 18 hours subscriptioneering," Weems wrote his home office in January, 1805, "I obtain'd from the [Virginia] Legislature 100 sub.s to Sydney." Americans did not cite from the *Discourses* after 1775 as often as before, but some Americans must have felt that a copy of Sydney's famed work was rather like a well-stocked wine cellar; no gentleman would be without one.[5]

Sydney once again symbolized "due process" to some Americans. In 1807 Aaron Burr's counsel drew a comparison between the case of Russell and Sydney and that of his own client—an analogy that drew fire from the prosecutor, William Wirt, who would not permit the souls of these patriot-martyrs to suffer comparison to that of Burr.[6] In July, 1808, Henry Clay argued for better legal representation for men who had suffered slanders. In this early expression of the right to counsel, Clay suggested as a model for such public defenders "the defender of a Sidney and Hampden."[7] In the following year Benjamin Rush discussed with John Adams the possibilities of civil war over the issue of slavery, and Rush reminded Adams that Sydney had preferred civil strife to bondage.[8] (Rush failed to note that Sydney had never expressed his opinion of African slavery, but his reference to the Rebel-Saint was probably intended solely to add dignity and propriety to Rush's antislavery conviction, not to serve as proof of Rush's argument.)

The expatriate English republican and journalist James Cheetham, addressing a throng of DeWitt Clinton's supporters in 1809, maintained that the colonial Englishmen who rebelled in 1775 had been the heirs of Sydney and other "sages and martyrs of freedom . . . from which our correct notions of civil liberty are drawn." And later, when John Adams penned an introduction to a new edition of the briefs he and James Otis had prepared in the "writs of assistance" cases some sixty years before, he prefaced his remarks with the passage from James Thomson's "Liberty":

> Mid the low murmers of submission, fear, and mingled Rage,
> My Hampden rais'd his voice,
> And to the laws appeal'd.[9]

Invocation of the twin patriots was less frequent after the War of 1812, but examples of it can be found. Edward Brooks (1784–1859) wrote a long and highly laudatory review of George Wilson Meadley's *Memoirs of Algernon Sydney* (1813) in 1822 for the *North American Review*, and told his countrymen that "[t]he integrity, the virtue, the constancy of Sydney should animate us to hope and struggle, even in the darkest times."[10] When Benjamin Watkins Leigh, in the 1829 Virginia Constitutional Convention debates, described "the French School" (one-man, one-vote democracy) as a threat to property and public order, John Cooke invoked the respectable British patriots, Sydney and Hampden, and (incorrectly) placed them in the ranks of past egalitarians who "had poured out their blood in vain" for the democratic ideal. Cooke was seconded by Chapman Johnson, who explained that the "solemn truths" of the democratic-sounding Declaration of Independence had sprung, via Jefferson, from Sydney's "crown of martyrdom."[11]

In mid-century the *U.S. Democratic Review* pronounced Sydney's name "immortal": "Wherever liberty is known, the name of Algernon Sydney is a household word."[12] In 1853 Samuel Janney was delighted to be able to establish a link between the "enlightened" Algernon Sydney and his own subject, William Penn, in spite of the fact that Janney's evidence clearly indicated that Sydney had deeply offended Penn by *criticizing* Penn's First Frame of Government for Pennsylvania![13] Others, like Herman Melville, Colonel Ethan Allen Hitchcock, Navy Secretary Hilary A. Herbert, and Admiral Alfred Thayer Mahan, had praise for the twin patriots in the mid- and late nineteenth century.[14] Furthermore, throughout the late eighteenth and much of the nineteenth centuries Hampden and Sydney often appeared as pseudonyms in the American press, as placenames on the American landscape, and as first names of the American child. We will briefly consider each of these types of uses.

"Hampden" and "Sydney" often addressed the readers of newspapers and pamphlets in the 1760's, the 1770's, and the Revolutionary War years, as we saw in the previous chapter. The practice lingered on for another seventy years, and, though antistatist Jeffersonians did predominate, no single faction utterly monopolized the pseudonyms. Anti-Federalist "Sidneys" warned of monarchical pretensions in the nation's capital, of Federalist secret diplomacy, and of the "unconstitutional" Sedition Act and federal excise tax, while a Federalist "Sidney" warned Kentuckians in 1798 that there should be "No Convention" in the state to protest the passage of the Alien and Sedition Acts. Five years later another "Sidney" in Connecticut *defended* the Jeffersonian critics of the Alien and Sedition Acts, while a Federalist "Hampden" from the same state complained of the persecution of Federalists before a Jeffersonian circuit court. Meanwhile, a Jeffersonian "Hampden" attacked the aristocratic "speculator" and the banking system in Baltimore and another, in Cincinnati, reviewed decisions of the Federalist-dominated Supreme Court.[15]

"The eminent Algernon Sidney," slain "for [my] attachment to the rights of man," argued in 1826 for the gradual emancipation and colonization of black slaves, while "Hampden," a friend of the State Rights Association, presented the merits of nullification in Charleston in 1831. Another "Hampden" supported the Wilmot Proviso in 1849 and urged that slavery be excluded from the territories, while still another "Hampden" praised the labors of Confederate President Jefferson Davis.[16]

Various "Sidneys" attacked Connecticut "office-seekers" (1817), General Andrew Jackson (1819), the Supreme Court (1821), critics of "the American System" (1831), Democrats (1835), and critics of those advocating annexation of Texas (1837). Various "Hampdens" defended states' rights (1819), General Jackson (1819), critics of Jackson (1827), critics of those advocating the annexation of Texas (1844), temperance lobbyists (1854), and foes of "Freedom and the Union" (1856).[17]

In short, a number of nineteenth-century Americans thought the twin patriots sufficiently inspiring to cause them thus to set their own names aside, and these Americans held quite diverse political views.

The pseudonymous use of Hampden and Sydney was only a temporary borrowing, however. More lasting were the instances in which one or the other patriot's name was bestowed for life on a devotee's innocent male offspring. Arthur Schlesinger, Sr., argued that Americans discontinued the use of English names "as the quarrel with the mother country developed and increasingly fired the popular emotions," that they attested their devotion "to the American cause at the baptismal font" by selecting the names of native-American heroes. There is much truth to this, of course; George Washington became "the Father of His Country" in more ways than the figurative one, as we will see. But Robert C. Winthrop, the Massachusetts legislator and a popular public orator in the mid-nineteenth century, was speaking with some authority when he referred to Algernon Sydney as "an American name—American in all its associations and American in its influences."[18]

About some of the namesakes of Sydney we have precise information: we know, for instance, that Joseph Willard, president of Harvard (1781–1804), and an enthusiastic advocate of independence, named a son born in 1780 after the Rebel-Saint, as did George Logan, the Philadelphia supporter of the Jeffersonian Democrat-Republicans, whose son Algernon Sydney Logan was born in 1791. Sidney Morse (b. 1794), son of a Federalist, the distinguished geographer-historian Jedidiah Morse, may have represented his father's Burkean reaction to French Jacobinism.[19] Algernon Sidney Crawford (b. ca. 1812), Algernon Sidney Butterfield (b. ca. 1813), and Algernon Sydney Newcomb (b. ca. 1815), all from Massachusetts, were the children of New England Federalist parents out of step with President Madison's war with Britain. Sydney Gay (b. 1814), the journalist and abolitionist, may have been at least a spiritual heir to the Rebel-Saint; his mother was a niece of James Otis. Among more obscure figures, Algernon Sidney Porter (b. ca. 1815) (the father of "O. Henry"), Algernon Sydney Sullivan (b. 1826) ("the American Chesterfield"), Algernon Sidney Paddock (b. 1830), Algernon Sidney King (b. 1835), Algernon Sidney Morgan (b. ca. 1840), Algernon Sidney Worth (b. 1842), Algernon Sidney Crapsey (b. 1847), Algernon Sidney Oddie (b. 1864), and Algernon Sydney Rush (b. ca. 1865) are unmistakable recipients of their parents' veneration. But if the parents of Sidney Rigdon (b. 1793), Sidney Breese (b. 1800), Sidney Lawrence (b. 1801), Sidney George Fisher (b. 1809), Sidney Law Johnson (b. ca. 1810), Sidney Williams (b. 1810), Sidney Dillon (b. 1812), Sidney Holmes (b. 1815), Sidney Thomas (b. ca. 1815), Sidney Dean (b. 1818), Sidney Edgerton (b. 1818), Sidney Shufeldt (b. 1824), Sidney Webster (b. 1828), Sidney Clarke (b. 1831), Sidney Andrews (b. 1835), Sidney Wilmot Winslow (b. 1854), Sidney G. Simms (b. 1851) and Sidney W. Simms (b. 1859), Sydney Mudd (b. 1858), Sydney Epes (b. 1865), and Sydney Bowie (b. 1865) did not use the Rebel-Saint's *first* name, there is sufficient evidence to establish that they had him in mind when they gave his *last* name to their son.[20]

Hampden, though apparently less popular a name, does offer some examples. Lachlan McIntosh, a colonel in the Georgia militia during the Revolutionary War, named a son after Hampden the Patriot, as did James Pleasants, a cousin to Thomas Jefferson, whose son John Hampden Pleasants (b. 1797) received his name while his father was voting for the Virginia Resolutions. And there was John Hampden Chamberlayne, a Confederate artillery officer, the son of a Virginia physician and a gentlewoman (b. 1838).[21] Other examples could be given, but the point has probably been made. The twin patriots lived on vicariously in a number of American families.[22]

They survive, mostly, it must be granted, in fossil form, in the names of counties, towns, streets, and buildings as well. There are over a dozen Hampdens (or "Hamdens"—the English "p" being a silent one) and Sydneys (or "Sidneys") throughout the nation (chiefly in New England and the Midwest), and a Hampden-Sydney in Virginia, where the college of that name is located. There are Hampden Avenues and Hampden Restaurants, Sidney Centers and Sidney Plains, and possibly a few creeks and peaks as well.[23]

Some Americans, then, of the revolutionary and early national eras left a number of different measures of their admiration for the "immortal Patriot" and/or the "Rebel-Saint." But the questions that have thus far been studiously avoided, and which must now be posed are: What did these displays of respect signify? *Which* Americans venerated the twin patriots? And why did the practice die out by the late nineteenth century?

The veneration of Hampden and Sydney, like that of other patriot-symbols, was more pronounced in periods of intense political and moral tension and debate. I have plotted chronologically the 202 instances I detected of the invocation or other respectful use of Hampden and/or Sydney in America from 1700 to 1901, and it appears (see Figure 4.1) that the pre-revolutionary and Revolutionary War era, the faction-torn 1790's, the years of the War of 1812, and the pre-Civil War and Civil War era were years in which the use of the twin patriots by elites was particularly pronounced. A few examples of these moments of anxiety may be appropriate here.

In the early 1840's Rhode Island experienced a virtual rebellion, when advocates of universal manhood suffrage, led by Thomas Dorr, sought to leapfrog a state legislature unwilling to reform the state's constitution. One of Dorr's supporters recalled that "our good friend and helper, Algernon Sydney," was constantly in the thoughts of Dorr and his fellow enemies of "the BANKRUPT ARISTOCRACY."[24] As we have noted before, Sydney was no democrat, but that did not trouble this Dorrite.

The patriot-martyrs appeared during another dialogue of political and moral tension: the antislavery movement. William Lloyd Garrison referred to the *Discourses* in his prospectus to the *Liberator* in 1830. He was furious, subsequently, when a defender of slavery used the pseudonym, "Algernon Sydney," in 1836. The illustrious "ALGERNON SYDNEY," Garrison responded, was "an enemy of slavery, . . . an Abolitionist of the modern school." Senator William C. Rives of Virginia told his colleagues

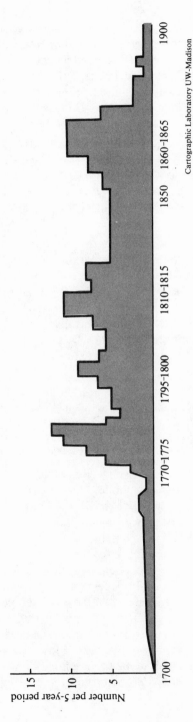

Figure 4.1. Rise and decline in the various uses of Hampden and Sydney in America, 1700–1900 (citations, invocations, pseudonyms, names). 202 cases in all were noted.

Cartographic Laboratory UW-Madison

in 1836 that slavery was "an evil, never a positive good," as Calhoun and "the new school" had suggested, and compared Calhoun's philosophy to that of Sir Robert Filmer, "exploded a century and a half ago by the immortal works of Sidney and Locke." (Calhoun felt compelled thereupon to rise and dissociate himself from Filmer's tenets.)[25] Fourteen years later, during debate on the Clay-Douglas Compromise Bill, Senator William Seward rose to quote Sydney's motto and tell the Senate

> Algernon Sydney expiated with his life the offence of writing as mere abstractions the fundamental principles of our own Constitution; and among them was the Wilmot Proviso [sic], thus expressed by that immortal patriot: "The liberty of one man cannot be limited or diminished by one or by any number of men, and none can give away the right of another."[26]

Abolitionists like John Greenleaf Whittier and Theodore Parker indicated their affection for "the great martyr of political freedom, Algernon Sydney,"[27] and in 1859, in the wake of John Brown's abortive rising, Wendell Phillips offered "the principles of the sublimest chapter in Algernon Sidney's immortal book," to establish that Governor Henry Wise of Virginia was misbehaving in his magisterial position.[28] The abolitionist Unitarian minister, Moncure D. Conway, another of Brown's admirers, asked his Cincinnati congregation:

> Do we admire Hampden, who, rather than pay an unjust tax of twenty shillings, risked his head that he might bring a throned tyrant to the block?—how much more should we admire the old Puritan [Brown], who for a protest against the great crime of our country . . . gave himself and his sons to a cruel death. The traitor of Charles I [Hampden] is our hero. The traitor of Governor Wise [Brown] will become our saint.[29]

Phillips returned again to Sydney in his 1881 Harvard Phi Beta Kappa address, "The Scholar in a Republic," in expressing his approval of Russian nihilism. He understood, he stated, the need for "dynamite and the dagger" in countries without "Faneuil Hall and the *Daily Advertiser*." Born in a commonwealth which had adopted Sydney's motto as its own, Phillips insisted that he could ask for "nothing less."[30] Phillips's revolutionary invocation of the Rebel-Saint was the exception to the rule, however.[31] In the nineteenth century the twin patriots generally symbolized the respectable, legitimate defense of personal and property rights ("liberty") against the encroachment of popular and "tyrannical" public rights ("equality"). "I am an aristocrat," remarked John Randolph of Roanoke, an ardent admirer of Sydney. "I love liberty; I hate equality." Edward Brooks suggested in 1822 that emulation of Sydney's character would improve respect for property and the existing order of things.[32]

When John Quincy Adams was invited to speak in strife-torn Providence in November of 1842, he avoided outright support of the Dorr faction, and told the assemblage that Sydney's motto in no way legitimatized "the anarchy of the Rump and the bayonets of Cromwell." Rhode Islanders were admonished to appeal to the courts. And after all, Adams concluded, neither the *Discourses* nor the American Constitution had said anything of democracy; they merely spoke of a "republican" form of government.[33] Similarly, the Baptist clergyman John Overton Choules, writing in 1846, distinguished the "glories" of the English Civil War and its heroes, based on "eternal verities," from the horrors of the French Revolution, "a living curse, a widespread damnation."[34]

In 1851 George Van Santvoord (1819–63), a New York State attorney, published the first, and only, full-length American biography of either patriot, *The Life of Algernon Sidney*. He found the "Rebel-Saint" to have been the "liberal and philosophical" champion of the ancient "Anglo-Saxon race." Unlike William E. Channing and the British romantic poets of the early nineteenth century, however, Van Santvoord considered his hero to have been of a "calm and placid disposition"; though exemplary, not "sublime."[35] Van Santvoord, who also published a work on *The Study of the Law as a Science* (1856), was representative of what Perry Miller called "the legal mentality"—unenthusiastic, logical, cool, unwilling to classify its heroes as "sublime." So was William C. Rives (1793–1868), a man devoted to the memory of Hampden and Sydney, with their "noble lessons and examples." Rives, a Virginia attorney, politician, and diplomat, was willing to style Hampden "sublime," but it was a sublimity of "moderation," "dignified by station." To Rives, the primary lesson the patriots taught was to regard "law as the rightful mistress of human conduct." It is noteworthy that many of those who gave the patriots' names to their sons, or borrowed them themselves, were by the mid-nineteenth century predominantly men of the law— Crapsey, Sullivan, Oddie, Paddock, Pleasants, Johnson, Gay, Henry Winter Davis, Charles Hammond, to name a few.[36] To a considerable extent, by 1850 Hampden and Sydney had been appropriated by the "legal fraternity" and had become symbols of "law and order," eminently conservative bulwarks of the existing social and constitutional order.

If Robert C. Winthrop (1809–94) is at all representative of those who in 1850 still worshipped the twin patriots (and I think he is), then this is precisely what happened. Winthrop was Whig to the core; Jackson was a "tyrant" in his eyes. He viewed with alarm in the 1860's and '70's the shift in the federalist balance from local power to "the government which is over us" in Washington. He opposed the democratic, one-man, one-vote scheme of reapportionment proposed at the 1853 Massachusetts

Constitutional Convention. He considered the national Whig party as the "party of LAW and ORDER—which seeks reforms by no riotous or revolutionary processes." He abhorred the likes of John Brown and "Nihilisms, Communisms, [and] Fenianism." He considered "the great right of revolution as having been, once for all, asserted, and the great work of revolution, once for all, accomplished, by those who have gone before us."[37] Henceforth, he felt, "occasional grievances" could be dealt with in a "peaceful and legitimate" manner, without "burn[ing] constitutions and batter[ing] down courthouses." After Garfield's assassination, while Phillips reminded Harvard men of the merits of violence in certain circumstances, Winthrop took a different tack. "It is not by murdering Emperors," he maintained, "that the welfare of mankind or the liberty of the people is to be promoted. Lawless violence and bloodshed cease to be regarded as a redress or remedy for anything."[38]

In the eighteenth century one who espoused Winthrop's conservative social or political views might have invoked the twin patriots, but with some misgivings, or self-restraint. To Winthrop, however, these two patriots were unquestionably of the highest order of sainthood. The name of Algernon Sydney was "an American name." Hampden's motto and spirit "were in the minds and hearts and wills of all our American patriots." His death was parallel only to that of Warren's at Bunker Hill. After the defeat of the Whigs in Massachusetts in 1850, Winthrop remarked, "I grieve for the good old cause," making use of an expression generally associated with Sydney. In December of 1853 Winthrop gave a lecture-address in Faneuil Hall on Sydney; in 1881 he spoke about Hampden. He quoted Sydney on the importance of union to preserve strength, and, in criticizing the Kansas Emigrant Aid Society, he suggested that "quieter action would have answered a better purpose, but *Quietus* [Sydney] is not the patron saint in these times, notwithstanding his bones have been [figuratively] brought over and enshrined on our soil." "I was born a Conservative," Winthrop proudly declared, "and . . . I have something of the Hampden . . . but not a particle of the Cromwell."[39] It would appear that by 1850 to be "something of the Hampden," to Winthrop and his ilk, was not to be unduly radical.

It is significant that Winthrop was not comfortable as a politician. He was named Speaker of the House in 1848, and was elevated to the Senate on the death of Webster, but in 1851 he was defeated by Charles Sumner, and eventually he withdrew from active politics. Fundamentally, Winthrop was a Brahmin, a friend of Holmes, the Adamses, George Ticknor, Emerson, George Peabody, and Edward Everett. The New York *Tribune* jeered at him:

a gentleman who lives in a very genteel square in a very genteel locality in the very genteel city of Boston. Quite *up*, you know; miles away from vulgar people; in a very good house; with a very good library.[40]

His championing of the twin patriots could not have advanced their reputation with many of his countrymen.

Perhaps Winthrop represents the phenomenon Francis Grund noted in 1839—the tendency of upper-class Americans to "vie with the splendour of the English nobility" and assimilate as much of British culture as feasible.[41] Winthrop viewed American patriotism as "the valor of Old England, inflamed . . . in the heart, mind, and muscle of New England." Such a definition had less and less meaning to his countrymen as the first century of full-blown American nationalism wore on. Winthrop acted perfectly in character when, in 1886, he penned an "Ode to Queen Victoria." As Charles Francis Adams said of him, he would have been more at home in Great Britain, where he could "have vindicated and justified an aristocracy, while in a democracy, even though born and brought up in it, he was never in all respects fully at home."[42] Nor would Winthrop's heroes, Hampden and Sydney, be "in all respects fully at home" in the hagiography of America.

Other examples of the absorption of the twin patriots into the American conservative camp can be offered. The parents of Sidney Willard, Sidney Morse, Sidney Breese, John Hampden Pleasants, Sydney Gay, were hardly of "the people." The names of Algernon Sydney Oddie's brother and sister, Albert and Victoria, suggest that their parents could have been quite at home with Robert C. Winthrop. A scanning of several hundred thousand names in various early nineteenth-century census returns, street directories, and other records suggests that a very small proportion (about one in every 5,000) of "working-class" American parents made use of either of the twin patriots in naming children. The further up on the social ladder the greater the frequency with which the names were used (about one in every 500 cases among the well-to-do). As late as 1899 Sydney George Fisher reported that there were "still Algernon Sydneys to be found among some of the prominent families in Philadelphia."[43]

Similarly, a great many of those who borrowed the names of the twin patriots for their pseudonymous broadsides were political conservatives. Benjamin Watkins Leigh, "Sidney" in 1819 and 1830, was one. Obsessed with "chivalry," his "style was classical." Indeed, he was, by his eulogist's own admission, "too senatorial" for the very proper Virginia Senate of the 1820's. His "high-toned" spirit was that of a "lofty citizen."

He was not of the unpropertied "people," whom he sought to continue to deny the vote in 1829. Neither was Noah Webster, "Sidney" in 1837 and 1838. Webster was disgusted with Jacksonian Democracy. The Founding Fathers would never have left England, he maintained, if they had known how "incapable of self-government" the "stupid" people were. His "Sidney" abused the voters for their rejection of the Whigs and recommended the creation of a hereditary executive, a monarchy!⁴⁴ With such models of Whig political views as Webster's "Sidney," it is not surprising that the Jacksonian, Robert Rantoul, could assail the Whig Party as a collection of English-American "antiquities and curiosities . . . contrasting . . . with rational American democrats." Rantoul thoroughly rejected "that British influence," as did the Whigs themselves in the 1840 "Log Cabin" election.⁴⁵

As the century progressed the identification of Sydney with the cause of conservatism became even more marked. A sketch of Sydney's life appeared in an 1872 volume, *Triumphs of Enterprise, Ingenuity, and Public Spirit*, by the journalist-historian James Parton. The Rebel-Saint at first seems ludicrously out of place amid the inventors and businessmen of Parton's volume but, on second glance, Parton's Sydney fitted the mold quite nicely. He was a "gentleman" of "high tone and noble breeding," whose most distinguished act was his (apocryphal) destruction of his property (his horse) rather than surrendering it to "the government" (Louis XIV). This act marked Sydney, in Parton's eyes, as "a man of the heroic type," above "ordinary" men.⁴⁶ In the same decade an admiring sketch of Sydney by the lawyer S. P. Scott contrasted his hero's conservative political model to that of the democratic model, "the most ruinous and implacable of all despotisms."⁴⁷ Perhaps the assimilation of the twin patriots into the liturgy of conservatism and the pantheon of the new American baronial elite was effected symbolically in 1899, when Horace Walpole's copy of the *Discourses* was purchased by John Pierpont Morgan.⁴⁸

To be sure, not all those who invoked the spirits of the twin patriots were aristocratic Whigs. But virtually all were antistatists, for whom the memory of the ship-money case and the foes of Stuart and Protectorate "tyrannies" were meaningful. And this antistatism is the most significant feature of American veneration of Hampden and Sydney. The Jeffersonian lawyer, Levi Lincoln (1749–1820), invoked the Rebel-Saint as the noble ancestor of the "republican principles" of the Democrat-Republicans who

> are not for enlarging [the constitution's] executive provisions, or abridging the people's rights. They are jealous of the discretion of an unchecked

power, of standing armies, of a host of dependents, or profuse expenditures, . . . unnecessary or unequal taxes, exclusive privileges, high salaries, and a monopoly of offices.⁴⁹

Similarly, an admirer of the twin patriots who was no Whig, the anti-Federalist John Randolph of Roanoke, argued for "retrenchment" in 1828 and attacked new "unconstitutional" taxes on gaming:

I have wondered that no rural, or rather rustic, Hampden has been found to withstand the petty tyranny which has as good a right to take away [by taxation] his wife's looking-glass or frying pan as his billiard table. By what authority is this thing done?⁵⁰

These were also the sentiments of other antistatist Virginian admirers of the twin patriots, Spencer Roane and Benjamin Watkins Leigh. (Roane's "Hampden" regarded the Marshall court's upending of Maryland's bank tax as a *coup de main* designed to prevent "some Hampden" from making "a stand against some ship-money measure of the government." Leigh's "Algernon Sidney" feared the "horrors" of military despotism in America and foresaw them coming "at no distant day.") They were the sentiments of the anonymous "Hampden" who attacked the powers of the "aristocratic" banking system in 1808. They were the sentiments of the Benthamite Asher Robbins, "Hampden" in 1808 and "Sydney" in 1823, who favored a condition "in which the *genuine* rights of man are amply secured, and where every man sits under his own vine and fig tree." They were the sentiments of Senator Theodore Frelinghuysen, who, objecting in 1830 to President Jackson's forcible removal of the Cherokee nation from its lands, compared their resistance to that of "the immortal Hampden" and spoke of liberty and "first principles." They were the sentiments of Nathan Loughborough, whose "Sydney" in 1831 complained of the "tyranny" and "slavery" inherent in the federal government's denial of political powers to residents of the District of Columbia. They were the sentiments of Francis Pickens, whose "Hampden" that same year compared the nullification controversy to the ship-money case, and urged his fellow South Carolinians to emulate Hampden's example and resist the "tyrant" in Washington. They were the sentiments of John P. Kennedy, the Maryland Whig Congressman, who in 1844 invoked "the great champions of Privilege against Prerogative, Russell and Sidney," in his defense of the Legislature against what he regarded as a Cromwellian executive.⁵¹ And they were the sentiments of the New York State Democrat, Adolphus Hart, whose two "Hampden" pamphlets in 1854 and 1855 argued against the spread of the "tyrannical" Maine antiliquor law to other parts of the States. Hart's "Hampden" identified the Maine law with general warrants, mob rule, antirepublicanism, and the tyranny of Charles I. He warned of infringements of basic human rights and threats to property. He referred frequently to the importance of "personal liberty," and explained that: "Morally and physically, man is a free agent, and any law which seeks to control his volition, is an insult offered to his person and dignity."[52]

Such antistatist concern for "personal liberty" became the trademark of the nineteenth-century Democratic Party,[53] but with a smaller percentage of British-Americans in their ranks than the Whigs or Republicans, the Democrats were only rarely inclined to adopt British, Whig patriot-heroes, despite the appropriateness of the political images and values they represented. The Republican Party, despite its name, would have none of these Whiggish-republican symbols either, as they were not only British in origin but also insufficiently statist for a party that spoke for those favoring the *active* intervention of the state in the affairs of men to curb evils (liquor, Sunday labor, adultery, slavery) and release energies (internal improvements, schools, incorporation).[54] (Thus the antistatist, Democratic elites who overthrew the activist—and hence "corrupt"—Tweed administration in New York in 1870 included at least one private admirer of the twin patriots.)[55]

Given their concern for "property rights" (slaves), their affection for the mores of the English gentry, their Whiggish aristocratic airs, and their views on the strict construction of the Constitution, articulate southerners were understandably the last firm devotees of Hampden and Sydney. D. K. Whitaker's "Sydney" in 1837 was adamant in his defense of slavery ("the sacred rights of property"). "The doctrine of the natural liberty and equality of the human race, having no foundation in truth and justice," "Sydney" wrote, "has ceased to be advocated by prudent men—and is to be found only in the creed of fanatics, agrarians, and abolitionists."[56] Abolitionists had invoked the Rebel-Saint, but when push came to shove, they deserted the Noble Failure for the more aggressive, and hence successful, Sword of Righteousness, the Lord Protector (see p. 75).[57] Southerners picked up the slack. By the mid-nineteenth century disproportionate numbers of parents who made use of the names of the two "foes of tyrants" in naming children were southern.[58] And when the Confederacy was created, in March of 1861, the Confederate Congress remembered that "our forefathers . . . were influenced by the spirit . . . of the great Hampden, *Vestiga nulla retorsum* [Hampden's motto]. . . . we think it good to imitate them."[59]

When the Confederacy collapsed, the southerner's affection for the twin patriots lingered on in some circles. William Gilmore Simms, the South Carolina author-poet, who named *two* sons after the Rebel-Saint, penned an ode "while strolling among [the] ruins" of his plantation and mansion in 1866, and signed it "Hampden Sydney." As late as 1910 the Georgia Jeffersonian Thomas Watson attacked Daniel DeLeon's statist brand of social democracy by contrasting it to his own "old Whig ideals," the ideals of "Charles [James] Fox, Henry Vane, Algernon Sidney, [John] Pym and Hampden." The ideals of these patriots, he explained, were *"the ideals of the Old South,"* and Watson warned his countrymen to beware of newfangled, "foreign-born," socialist ideals.[60]

Of course, not all nineteenth-century Americans who spoke of the twin patriots were uncritical. Horace Binney Wallace (1817–52), a young expatriate American essayist, took Lord Brougham to task in 1837 for his praise of "the hireling traitor Sydney and the selfish conspirator Hampden." Such " 'patriotic' lives" would never do, Wallace maintained, as models of public service for "a people rising to a sense of their responsibilities."[61] Wallace appeared to accept the most deliberate Tory debunking as fact, and this may have been characteristic of how some Americans looked upon their former heroes. But it is more likely that the Whig heroes simply didn't represent what most Americans came to treasure. E. L. Godkin (English-born-and-bred, to be sure) willingly associated Hampden and Lord Russell with an admirable aristocratic tradition of "courage and fortitude and generosity," but indicated that these were simply not enough. George Bancroft deserted Sydney because he was convinced that Sydney "stood for the liberties of his order, and not for new enfranchisements," that he "nourished the pride of patriotism rather than the sentiment of philanthropy." Sydney George Fisher (1856–1927), ironically bearing the same name as the man whom he claimed was unworthy of further attention and respect, felt that Sydney's trial and death had resulted in "an over-estimate of his importance."[62]

Perhaps by the 1850's Algernon Sydney had simply been shown to have been human (see p. 138)—a revelation that inevitably did violence to his mythical alter ego. The same cannot be said of Hampden. No historian unearthed embarrassing personal evidence of his humanity. (The British essayist Isaac D'Israeli tried, when he claimed that Hampden had refused to pay the ship-money tax "simply because he bore a grudge against the sheriff who levied it"; at least one proper Bostonian attorney, Samuel Quincy, was outraged by the charge.)[63] Yet Hampden's reputation declined in America just as surely as did Sydney's.

Robert C. Winthrop provides us with an illuminating account of this decline in his discussion of the portrait of John Hampden, donated to Congress in the 1850's, and placed in the White House. Winthrop first saw the painting in 1861, when, he later recalled, it drew respectful attention and admiration from all about him. Nine years later, while dining with President Grant, Winthrop noted that none of the company recognized the "glorious John Hampden," and he began to fear that the portrait might be removed. Consequently, he asked Grant to affix Hampden's name to the frame. Eight years later, however, while dining with President Hayes, Winthrop decided that the name alone would no longer suffice. So "a somewhat more detailed inscription was substituted." Nevertheless, three years later Winthrop was altogether uncertain that the portrait was properly "appreciated" by those who looked upon it.[64]

In spite of the effort of "Old Whigs" like Winthrop (and British immigrants like W. J. Linton) to keep alive the devotion of the Founding Fathers to their English patron saints, the transmission failed.[65] Winthrop hoped to dissociate the two from the concept of violent revolution—a self-defeating task, as it robbed the patriots of some of the very qualities that had attracted Jefferson and Adams. But even where the older image persisted, where Sydney continued to be portrayed as a revolutionary, his reputation declined.

The reasons for this decline are reasonably clear. As the young republic grew older, and its revolutionary days faded into history, Americans lost some of their respect for revolution. And with the advent of communism and socialism—*socioeconomic* revolution—the very notion of revolt became abhorrent.[66] Eventually, the Rebel-Saint and the Patriot drew fire *for* their "radicalism." It becomes evident that even conservatives were rejecting the twin patriots. Moses Granger, Chief Justice of the Ohio Supreme Court, complained in 1898 that *Hampden's Case* had "made bad law" in the sense that, like *Dred Scott*, it had been used by irresponsible politicians to exacerbate existing wounds to the body politic.[67]

There are other clear signs of the failure in transmission of the Hampden-Sydney image in America. When Winthrop referred to Sydney in an 1886 address, reporters quoted his praise of "Alderman Sydney." In 1883 Joseph Choate proudly referred to Sydney's and Massachusetts's motto, but in 1900 the editors of his address indexed the remark under "Sir Philip Sydney"; apparently they were not familiar with Algernon.[68]

Even the Brahmins, it would appear, eventually tired of the *Discourses*. And a generation gap was becoming apparent. In August of 1832 Charles Francis Adams, whose father and grandfather, both presidents, had been avid admirers of Sydney, planned first to read the *Discourses* of "one of the principal martyrs in the cause of liberty" and then to discuss with his father "the character and influence of public men." But the young man's classical plan went awry. Sydney, he noted in his diary a few days later, "is rather dry." The next day he found himself disagreeing with Sydney's judgment, and he put the *Discourses* aside, marvelling that there had been a day when they "should have been needed." Changing literary styles and values reinforced the sense of increasing irrelevance that Sydney's work evoked. Oliver Wendell Holmes confessed to Sir Fredrick Pollock his distaste for the "dull books of the past, such as Harrington's *Oceana* or Sydney."[69] As George Van Santvoord intimated in 1851, the *Discourses* had "fulfilled their mission" and had "become obsolete."[70]

So had "Freedom's genuine sons." When Parson Weems, editor of the 1805 American edition of the *Discourses*, produced a *Life of William Penn* in 1822, not a word was said in its 300-odd pages of Penn's advisor and onetime political ally, Sydney. General Richard Taylor, a former Confederate officer, and Admiral David Potter, a veteran of the Philippine insurrection, had no more than tongue-in-cheek words for the twin patriots.[71] Algernon Sydney Rush's son was named Alan Sydney Rush, a pattern repeated elsewhere. Neither Sydney nor Hampden were discussed in the section on "Philosophy and Patriotism" of Samuel Adams Drake's *Our Great Benefactors* (1884). No mention was made of them in Harpers' *Stories from English History for Young Americans* (1892); nor were they found in the 250 biographies of *Historic Characters and Famous Events* (1895).[72] By the mid-twentieth century the twin patriots were faded stars indeed. To two biographers of William Penn, Clifford Smith and Colwyn Vulliamy, Sydney was, respectively, the "radical republican who would abolish the rule of kings and queens," and "a crazy philosophic enthusiast," unrestrained by any sense of honor, "whose philosophy could see nothing wrong in a timely assassination." In 1959 the editors of the Henry Clay Papers confused John Hampden with his grandson, Hampden the Younger, while in the conservative Russell Kirk's life of John Randolph of Roanoke, Randolph's praise of the Rebel-Saint is indexed under the name of his nondescript elder brother Phillip, third Earl of Leicester.[73] None of the officials or local historians in towns named for one or the other of the twin patriots had ever heard of either patriot.[74] But these dignitaries were in good company; while 60 percent of a randomly selected sample of some 2,000 residents of Allegheny County, Pennsylvania, who were surveyed in a 1969 poll, were able to identify his compatriot, Oliver Cromwell, less than one percent could identify John Hampden.[75] Hampden was probably never known to *all* Americans, but it seems safe to say that the figure was considerably higher in, say, 1769, among a people constantly witnessing his public veneration. Which is only to say that America in 1969 was different from America in 1769, and that part of the difference is revealed in the failure of one antistatist generation of Americans to transmit the same patriot-symbols to later less antistatist generations.

New Lights from the Old World: Cromwell, Napoleon, and "Progressivism"

To say that Hampden and Sydney, two seventeenth-century English symbols of personal liberty, had faded from the American hagiography by the mid-nineteenth century is not to say that Americans rejected *all* of the "Old World's" stock of political heroes. As Hampden and Sydney waned, other more potent symbols of power and order waxed, and two of these were also of the "Old World"—Napoleon Buonaparte and Oliver Cromwell.

These two men of iron had not been admired by the generation that had loved Hampden and Sydney. After all, Washington had rejected Cromwell's mantle at Newburgh. Forty years after the incident John Lovett's poetic celebration of Washington's birthday has the Father of His Country tell his Newburgh troops ("Freedom's Sons"): "O, dam it not to raise a *Cromwell's* fame." Benjamin Rush had worried lest there be found "Cromwells in this country."[76] Others warned of Cromwell's "usurpation," and "guilty ambition," and feared the coming of a Cromwell "or some such ferocious animal" if a large standing army were to be created or if the Union were imperiled.[77] The first Whig president, William Henry Harrison, damned the "love of power" and the "dictator," Cromwell, in an antistatist inaugural address brimming with the language of libertarianism, in 1841.[78] When in 1840 Thomas Carlyle lectured on Napoleon and Cromwell ("The Hero as King"), Ralph Waldo Emerson was aghast. "Carlyle takes Cromwell sadly to heart," he told a friend: "When I told him that he must not expect that people as old as I could look at Cromwell as he did, he turned quite fiercely upon me."[79]

Emerson also pondered the increase in American popular interest in Napoleon, an interest that grew steadily throughout the century.[80] Hadn't Francis Lieber demonstrated the shortcomings of this autocratic Corsican? (Ah, but only the elite paid any attention to Francis Lieber.) But eventually even Emerson found some kind words for Cromwell, for he was finally swept up in the general revival of respect for the Lord Protector, a revival that did not wait for the appearance of Carlyle's 1845 edition of Cromwell's letters and speeches, but appears to have been well under way in the early forties.[81] In his popular *History of the United States* (1837) George Bancroft praised Cromwell, as did young Charles Francis Adams, rejecting the heroes of his grandfather, Hampden and Sydney.[82] In 1842 the transcendentalist Charles Lane spoke of the Lord Protector's "real, soul-inspiring manhood," his "true greatness." He might be a "patching tailor at constitution-mending," but he was a man of action, and action was "the assertion of greatness." America had need of a "new Cromwell," Lane maintained.[83] The American artist Emanuel Leutze, creator of "Washington Crossing the Delaware," executed two paintings of Cromwell in 1843 and 1844 (pl. 29).[84] Joel T. Headley, a conservative friend of "law and order," was a prolific, if superficial, biographer whose works on Napoleon and Washington were resounding popular successes. In 1846 he penned an ecstatic review of Carlyle's *Letters and Speeches of Oliver Cromwell* for the Whiggish *American Review*, and published the first American *Life of Oliver Cromwell* in 1848, citing Carlyle as his inspiration. Headley also compared Cromwell to George Washington, and, as he believed that he could see "the inherent right to command" in his hero, he styled Cromwell's dissolution of the Rump "sublime."[85]

The *U.S. Democratic Review* was incensed by Headley's blatantly "anti-republican" and "sycophantic" defense of the "despotic" Cromwell,[86] but others (particularly evangelical others) apparently agreed with Headley's verdict. By mid-century towns and counties in America were being named for the Lord Protector. Abolitionist ministers Theodore Parker, John Wingate Thornton, and John Lord praised him, and when the Civil War came, northerners anxious to use his "heavy hand and fearless grasp" on the erring South invoked his name; some later linked it to that of the Great Emancipator.[87] One Episcopal minister, Reverend J. G. Gilchrist, himself no admirer of the "king-killer," nonetheless imagined in 1886 that it was "quite within the experience of nearly everyone [in the U.S.] to hear the most extravagant praises of Cromwell and his followers crowded into popular addresses." By the turn of the century both Samuel Church and Theodore Roosevelt had produced lives of Cromwell. Others focused on Napoleon and several magazines were publishing serialized biographies of both leaders.[88]

What was it that these Victorian-age Americans saw in Cromwell and Napoleon? Briefly, leadership, power, and action. America was moving rapidly now along the paths of industrialization and economic and political centralization and systematization. Throughout the world Western "powers" were racing to stake out claims in underdeveloped, less powerful areas. T. H. Huxley and Herbert Spencer were glorifying "the struggle." To those who perceived their world as being in flux, in need of guidance and control, what value was there in classical, antistatist symbols of personal freedom like Hampden and Sydney? Theodore Greene has found that "progressive" magazines of the *fin de siècle* dismissed antistatist virtues as mere "Mugwumpery" and stressed "inflexible will" and achievement. They depicted their heroes as forceful, shrewd, foresighted men, truly charismatic, in Max Weber's original sense of that word. Their modern political model was generally Theodore Roosevelt, whom they compared to Napoleon, Cromwell, and Abraham Lincoln, figures of "tremendous human powers" (in *Century*'s words), men of "action," who, like Roosevelt, had "the power to thrill the nation's blood and make the pulse beat faster." Indeed, in 1904 a statue of Frederick the Great was proposed for the nation's capital![89]

A few examples may make my point clearer. E. D. Mansfield, a nineteenth-century student of the American military, looked upon Napoleon as "the Representative of modern SCIENCE IN ACTION . . . the impersonation of Modern Intellect!—Clear as the Sun;—strong as the blast of the Tempest."[90] And well he might describe him. Napoleon had given France power, glory, and order, however momentarily. His code, civil service, and concordat were contributions with some durability. In America he was looked upon by many as the "businesslike, energetic, accurate . . . Efficiency Manager," or so Albert Guerard said in 1924.[91] Lincoln, as well, was a man of action. He had moved to reinforce Fort Sumter; he had called out the militia; he had galvanized the Union into a war machine to force the rebellious South to terms; he had brought the northern state governments into harness; and he had liberated the slaves. John T. Morse compared Lincoln to Caesar and Napoleon in his ability to seize opportunities.[92] The Baptist educator H. L. Wayland and the Congregational minister Frank Gunsaulus both compared him to Cromwell, and the two did have much in common. Homely to a fault, willing to dispense with civil liberties at least temporarily in a moment of crisis, shrewd, down-to-earth, moody, middle-class, remembered as a moral force, successful leader of the anti-Cavalier forces in a civil war in the English-speaking world, Lincoln understandably reminded some northerners of "the warty one."[93]

One of the first Americans to "revive" Cromwell was James Russell Lowell, who began work on a "radical" dramatic poem that would celebrate the struggle of Cromwell and his colleagues, "Pym, Sidney, Hampden, Milton," on behalf of "the poor and the oppressed." The poem, "A Glance Behind the Curtain," appeared in an 1843 issue of the *Democratic Review*. It contrasted Cromwell, a man of "patient power" and "iron will," with his cousin, John Hampden. Hampden, in Lowell's verse, proposes that the two migrate to New England with their friends, in light of the stifling policies of Charles I. Cromwell rejects this course of action. He will stand and fight. He spells out his philosophy and perspective:

> New times demand new measures and new men;
> The world advances and outgrows
> The laws that in our father's day were best

. . . .
Reason and Government, like two broad seas,
Yearn for each other with outstretched arms

. . . .
My God is heedless if a few be crushed,
As some are ever, when the destiny
Of man takes one stride onward nearer home.

. . . .
Nor think I that God's world will fall apart
Because we tear a parchment more or less.

. . . .
The future works out great men's purposes.

Lowell closes the poem with praise of Cromwell, "A name earth wears forever next her heart;/ One of the few that have a right to rank/ With the true Makers: for his spirit wrought/ Order from Chaos."[94] It is easy to see why Lowell also admired President Lincoln.

A few final examples may help to convince those as yet unpersuaded that these modern heroes symbolized statism and power. In 1911 J. N. Larned offered a *Study of Greatness in Men*, which was a comparative analysis of Washington, Napoleon, Lincoln, and Cromwell, the last of whom was (among other things) "great in the perfect fitting and powerful use of practical means to practical ends." The clergyman Newell Dwight Hillis (whose most important work was *Rebuilding Europe in the Face of Worldwide Bolshevism*) had no use for the "partial" and "unbalanced" antistatist, Thomas Jefferson, or the genteel liberal "patrician," John Hampden, but glowed with admiration for his cousin, "a giant . . . with naked fists," whose dictatorial conduct grew "out of the necessities of the times." Cromwell's dissolution of the Rump Parliament had been a heroic act. He had been "the only man" to understand "the emergency, the true king who can do the thing that needs to be done!" Hillis may have seen his likeness in Mussolini, who came to power in the years these words were set to print.[95]

Hamilton Mabie's *Heroes Every Child Should Know* (1908) preferred more romantic figures—St. George, King Arthur, Sir Galahad, Siegfried, Roland, King Alfred, The Cid, Robin Hood, Richard the Lionhearted, William Tell, Robert Bruce, Robert E. Lee, Perseus, and Hercules. But note that all were men of force. "Courage and achievement," he told his young readers, "are the two signs of the hero." He said nothing of virtue or love of liberty.[96] Neither did H. H. Bancroft, the late-nineteenth-century chronicler of the growth of California. He exuded "a profound admiration for men of superior efforts and accomplishments, for men of strength and ability. . . . They who accomplish most are greatest. They who achieve most are best." There was nothing noble in "the great hordes of humanity." "Subjects" needed "rulers." Bancroft was no royalist reactionary but a lover of "progress" in a republic.[97] Like many Americans of his age, he simply admired "practical" men who displayed an ability to solve concrete problems and a drive to accomplish great things, the kinds of things that had been needed to transform California wilderness into orderly, industrious communities. These were precisely the qualities that many "progressive" *fin-de-siècle* Americans admired in Cromwell, Napoleon, and one of their own, Abraham Lincoln.[98]

5 America's Own Patriot-Heroes and What They Represented in the Nineteenth and Twentieth Centuries

Dramatis Personae Americanae

George Washington

The descendant of English planter gentry, Washington was born in the agricultural region of Virginia in 1732. His education was of a practical sort, with little or no attention to the classics, history, or philosophy, and considerable attention to geometry, surveying, and agriculture. He inherited the family estate at Mount Vernon as a young man of twenty.

The following year, in 1753, he accepted Governor Dinwiddie's appointment as emissary to deliver an ultimatum to French forces moving east along the Ohio Valley. Returning with militia troops in 1754, he threw up fortifications (Fort Necessity) in Great Meadows, Pennsylvania, but was forced to surrender after a brief French siege. He withdrew to eastern Virginia, but in 1755 he returned once more as aide to General Braddock. When Braddock fell in a French and Indian ambush of his forces on the Monongahela, Washington withdrew once more, and was eventually named to the overall command of Virginia's militia, this while still in his mid-twenties.

Washington was elected to the House of Burgesses in 1758 and as that colony's quarrels with king and Parliament grew, he developed into a full-fledged "radical." He attended colonial conventions attired in his militia uniform, and upon the outbreak of hostilities between colonials and British troops in Massachusetts, he was chosen commander-in-chief of the Continental forces.

General Washington was an ambivalent revolutionary—willing to apply radical principles of military tactics in the field but unwilling to apply such principles to the systems of military discipline, rank, and officer–enlisted-man relations in the camp. Keeping his army intact, a force-in-being, in the early stages of the war with Fabian tactics, he was eventually enabled to counterattack and (with French aid) to bring the British to terms. As the war came to a successful end, he firmly rejected the suggestion that he accept monarchic or dictatorial powers, and upon the signing of the peace, he parted with his colleagues and retired to his estate, a widely respected, genteel public figure.

Several years later, when nationalists (many of them Continental veterans) sought to strengthen the newly formed confederation of American states by altering its constitution, Washington joined them at Philadelphia and was chosen to preside over this constitutional convention. Upon the adoption of the new constitution by the states, he was elected the first president of the new United States and, four years later, was reelected without opposition.

President Washington constantly sought to effect compromises among the various congressional and Cabinet forces, opposed as he was to the creation of "factional" parties. But when Madison and Jefferson finally parted company with the more statist Federalists during Washington's second term, the president began to lean towards the Federalists.

After warning of the dangers to Americans of "entangling alliances" with European powers, and upon reiterating his disapproval of "factions," Washington retired from public life in 1797, unwilling to serve a third term. He died at Mount Vernon two years later.

Thomas Jefferson

Born in 1743 to a father of comfortable means (but not affluence) and a mother, Jane Randolph, whose family was among the more prominent in Virginia, Thomas Jefferson enjoyed a happy childhood, many friends, and a good legal education. As a young married gentleman, he began the construction of Monticello, a mansion after the Roman style, which he designed himself.

In 1769 he was elected to the Virginia House of Burgesses, where he became an active member of the "radical" faction. In 1774 he helped to create the Virginia Committees of Correspondence, and in 1775 was elected to the Continental Congress. He was the chief drafter of the Declaration of Independence in June of 1776. Shortly thereafter, he left the Congress and returned to the Virginia legislature, now styled the House of Delegates. Elected governor of Virginia in 1779, he wrote the Bill for Establishing Religious Freedom, championing the separation of church and state with the claim that "the opinions of men are not the concern of civil government." An unaggressive administrator, he preferred that the House of Delegates shape public policy, and he was consequently accused of a lack of due diligence in having failed to provide adequately for the proper defense of the state when British forces under Benedict Arnold and Lord Cornwallis invaded Virginia. He defended himself satisfactorily against charges of misconduct and negligence and was exonerated, but he retired briefly from politics.

His *Notes on the State of Virginia*, published in France in 1784, represent remarkable scientific work, but his scientific pursuits were deferred in 1783 when he was elected once again to the Continental Congress. He served ably once more, drafting the reports on the governing of the western territories. A slaveholder himself, he lacked respect for the institution, and occasionally spoke out against it. His democratic, antislavery plan of settlement for the western lands was accepted only after considerable revision by his colleagues in the Congress; the antislavery feature, in particular, was rejected.

He served as minister to France from 1785 to 1789, returning to the States upon the creation of the new government to serve it as secretary of state. He favored the amending of the new Constitution to incorporate a bill of rights, opposed the newly organized Bank of the United States as unconstitutional, and disagreed generally with his colleague, Secretary of the Treasury Alexander Hamilton, on matters of public policy. His firm opposition to Hamilton's mounting authority was a prime cause of his retirement to Monticello in 1793.

He was persuaded to return to the government in 1797, as the vice-president, and wrote the *Manual of Parliamentary Practice* while serving as president of the Senate. He continued to oppose the policies of the dominant Federalist faction, drafting for the Kentucky legislature the famous resolution that insisted that those powers assumed by the federal government which were not specifically delegated to it under the Constitution were null and void, and that, in particular, the Alien and Sedition Acts, being violations of individual freedoms guaranteed in the Bill of Rights, were not law; the resolution called on state legislatures to join in rejecting the legality of these acts.

At the head of a new political party of localistic "Democratic-Republicans," Jefferson defeated President John Adams in 1800. Stressing simplicity, he walked to the new Capitol to take the oath of office. He continued to favor legislative prerogatives, but, seizing an opportunity, he arranged for the purchase of the Louisiana Territory while Congress was adjourned. While he had objected to the treatment of Democratic-Republican editors at the hands of Federalist judges, he countenanced the arrest of Federalist editors during his own tenure, and he displayed considerable vigor in pressing the prosecution of Aaron Burr, whom he despised.

Harassed by British impressment on the high seas of American merchant sailors, angered by the all-inclusive nature of the British blockade of Europe and H.M.S. *Leopard*'s attack on U.S.S. *Chesapeake*, Jefferson secured an embargo of all American shipping in an effort to bring the British to terms. In the process, he made considerable use of federal military power to enforce the law. He retired from public office in 1809 and died on July 4, 1826, the fiftieth anniversary of the signing of his Declaration of Independence.

Abraham Lincoln

Born in 1809 to a Kentucky frontier family of modest means, Lincoln was of more humble origin than any of the other six of our patriot-heroes. Like Cromwell, he moved about a good deal before reaching his full political maturity. His family relocated first in Indiana and then in Illinois, where he worked in a store, on a riverboat, and in a law office.

He served briefly and without particular distinction as a militia captain during the Black Hawk War before being elected as a Henry Clay Whig to the Illinois state legislature in 1834; to this body he was returned until 1841. After several years of legal practice, he was elected to the U.S. House of Representatives in 1847 for a single term, during which he virtually accused President Polk of violating the Constitution in usurping congressional warmaking prerogatives.

He retired to his law practice until 1856, when, following the lead of friends like his young law partner William Herndon, he joined the newly organized Republican Party. He challenged the popular Illinois Democratic Senator Stephen Douglas to a series of debates in 1858, and the two toured the state, locking horns over the issue of slavery in the territories. He received more support statewide than Douglas, but the Illinois legislature, which chose U.S. senators, was so apportioned that Douglas was reelected. Lincoln spoke on behalf of the Republican cause in a number of eastern and western communities throughout 1859 and 1860, and won the Republican Party's nomination for president as a moderate compromise candidate in the latter year. This time the electoral process worked to *his* advantage, and he was chosen president with only a plurality of the popular vote but a majority of the votes in the electoral college.

He assumed the presidency several months after the secession of southern states angered by his election, and was for some time in a conciliatory mood, hoping to forestall the further flight of the "border" slave states. But he demonstrated his firm intention to defend what "federal property and places" remained in the seceded states by attempting to replenish the army garrison at Fort Sumter, and this move led the secessionists to fire on the federal fort.

Lincoln's response—the proclamation of a blockade, the expansion of the army beyond the congressionally authorized limits, the spending of as yet unappropriated funds, and the suspension of *habeas corpus*—led some to charge him with the same sort of unconstitutional behavior he had seen in President Polk, and led others to praise his leadership and courage "in defense of the Union." Throughout the ensuing civil war, he dealt effectively with his cabinet, with his congressional critics, with the governors of the remaining states, and with the army high command. He proclaimed the emancipation of all slaves held within rebellious territory on the first of January, 1863, upon the failure of the South to come to terms. At Gettysburg, speaking at a memorial ceremony for those who had fallen there, he stressed the democratic objective of the struggle to insure a united nation. Successfully fighting off efforts by "radicals" within his own party to dump him, and the efforts of "conservative" Democrats to replace him with General McClellan, he was reelected in 1864.

His second inaugural address was a plea for reconciliation, and he authorized the offer of generous terms to the virtually defeated South. On the eve of victory, Good Friday, 1865, he was assassinated. As he expired, his secretary of war, Edwin Stanton, was heard to remark: "Now he belongs to the ages."

"Columbia's Fav'rite Son": George Washington, A Nineteenth-Century Phenomenon

John Adams could see it coming. In 1816 he complained to Thomas Jefferson, another admirer of the Rebel-Saint, of the passing of the popularity of Sydney's *Discourses*, a passing he attributed to the venom of the pens of Dalrymple and Hume.[1] In light of the vigorous rebuttal that lovers of the Rebel-Saint had offered "black Dalrymple" and other Tory debunkers, Adams may have erred in attributing Sydney's decline to criticism of his character. It was not that Americans were beginning to think of Sydney as base; it was just that they were beginning to think of him as British—and of themselves as American. And this is certainly a central reason for the decline of both Sydney and Hampden in the United States.

Some lovers of the twin patriots sought to have, quite literally, the best of both worlds. Thomas Condie, one of George Washington's first biographers, drew a comparison in 1798 between Washington and Sydney. In 1828 William Ellery Channing preferred to compare Washington to the "godlike" Hampden. To William C. Rives, the "sublime" Hampden and Patrick Henry were "kindred spirits." Moncure Conway's Hampden was akin to John Brown. James Parton regarded Sydney as "the forerunner of our Jefferson and Madison." As late as 1867 Confederate General Richard Taylor felt that the "names and characters" of two Louisiana rebel leaders, Alexander Mouton and Leclerc Fusilier, "should be revered here as are those of Hampden and Sidney in England."[2] But Taylor's language betrayed the change that had taken place, for he no longer claimed that Hampden and Sydney were in any sense themselves American.

A few, like Jefferson, Adams, Sumner, and Channing sought to declare republican patriot-heroes of all lands as fair game for veneration by Americans. "The principles of their greatness are diffused through all your breasts," Channing wrote. And there were enough Lafayette McLains (b. 1821), Simon Bolivar Buckners (b. 1823), and Kossuth Nileses (b. 1848) to attest to the willingness of some Americans to venerate republicans other than their own.[3]

But for every Lafayette Smith, Simon Bolivar Jones, John Hampden Brown, or Algernon Sydney Johnson, there were four George Washington Martins, Jefferson Rileys, Henry Clay Taylors, and Andrew Jackson Whites. Of some 895 patriot-hero first names (found in such sources as nineteenth-century census returns, city directories, and biographical dictionaries) nearly 80 percent were of American origin and only slightly over 11 percent of British origin (the remaining 8 percent being European, Latin American, or classical). Algernon Sidney Worth's sixty-odd U.S. Naval Academy classmates in 1859 included two George Washingtons (Wood and Carter), two Henry Clays (Taylor and Holt), two Albert Gallatins (Caldwell and Hudgens), two Benjamin Franklins (Day and Haskins), a John Adams Hopkins, a Sam Houston Baker, a William Pinckney Mason, a Tecumseh Steece, and a Napoleon Jefferson Smith.[4]

Of these 895 patriot-hero first names, "the Father of His Country" accounted for more than one in every four[5] (see Table 5.1). No fewer than 198 places (towns, counties, rivers, colleges, mountains, etc.) including, of course, the nation's capital, had been named after the Father of His Country by 1859, about twelve times as many as had been named for either Hampden or Sydney.[6]

Washington's elevation to national sainthood was almost instantaneous. In his lifetime the *Nordamerikanische Staats-Kalendar* was calling him "the Father of his Country."[7] Poems and biographical sketches

Table 5.1. Sampling of Patriot-Hero First Names (n = 896) in America: Inclusive Years, 1760–1920 (median year, 1832)

George Washington (or "Washington")	237
Benjamin Franklin (or "Franklin")	102
Thomas Jefferson (or "Jefferson")	75
Andrew Jackson	61
Henry Clay	45
Algernon Sydney (or "Alg. Sidney")	34
James Madison	31
Albert Gallatin	24
Oliver Hazard Perry	21
Napoleon Buonaparte (or "Napoleon")	18
Lafayette	15
Horatio Nelson	14
John Milton	14
Isaac Newton	13
Daniel Webster	13
Christopher Columbus	12
William Pitt (the Elder)	11
Alexander Hamilton	10
John Adams	10
Julius (or Augustus) Caesar (or simply "Caesar")	10
James Monroe	9
John Hampden	9
Simon Bolivar	9
Ethan Allen	8
John Marshall	8
Dewitt Clinton	8
Stephen Decatur	8
Joseph Warren	7
Abraham Lincoln[a] (or "Lincoln")	6
John Jay	6
William Wirt	4
Paul Revere	4
Oliver Cromwell[a]	4
Cincinnatus	4
William Penn	4
John Hancock	3
Samuel Adams	3
Brutus	3
John C. Fremont	2
Robert E. Lee[a]	2
George Dewey,[a] John Quincy Adams, Daniel Boone, Elbridge Gerry, Leonard Wood,[a] Theodore Roosevelt,[a] Woodrow Wilson,[a] John Tyler, Charles James Fox, Lewis & Clark, Roger Sherman, Ambrose Burnside, John C. Calhoun, Ulysses S. Grant,[a] and Albert Sidney Johnston[a]	1

Sources: *Dictionary of American Biography*; *Biographical Directory of the American Congress*; various city directories, census returns, and other comparable sources.

[a]My patriotically named subjects were predominantly of the late eighteenth or of the nineteenth centuries; hence the small numbers of those named for more recent patriot-symbols, such as Lincoln.

spewed forth in his own lifetime and were buried in an avalanche of funeral eulogies with his death in 1799. His notebooks, his account books, his speeches, his farewell address, his last will and testament were reprinted time and time again over the years. Virtually every year a novel or play appeared that dealt delicately and reverently with "the man who made us."[8] Dozens of statues, paintings, and engravings celebrated "the Nation Builder," and a national monument was erected.[9] And virtually all these paeans were couched in superlatives. Ignatius Thompson, one of hundreds like him, would remember Washington as "this greatest instance of human perfectibility, this conspicuous phenomenon of human elevation and grandeur, . . . the ornament, the deliverer, the protector, the delight!" Readers of Parson Weems's popular *Life of Washington* were informed that he had been "the greatest man that ever lived." Francis Glass's 1835 Latin life of Washington offered an imaginary "prophecy from the pen of Cicero" about the hero of the Revolution. The preface to Horatio Weld's 1845 *Pictorial Life of George Washington* advised parents that "the first word of infancy should be mother, the second father, the third WASHINGTON." In the mid-nineteenth century young George Lippard (1822–54) founded the fraternal Brotherhood of the Union and assumed its leadership with the title "Supreme Washington."[10] Clearly the Americans had found a new patriot-hero. But why, and what did it all signify?

The struggle for independence caused many Americans to give up more that was British than East-India tea alone. But if British symbols of patriotism were to be left behind, American symbols had to be found to take their place. A young, new nation needed native models of virtuous public service. Noah Webster was a lifelong admirer of Sydney, but even his 1783 speller wrote off Britain as a loss, where "a few struggles of patriotism" were habitually overpowered by corrupt governments. Caleb Bingham's 1807 reader posed the utterly rhetorical question: "why may not Columbia's soil/ Rear men as great as Britain's isle . . . ?" Parson Weems, another early admirer of the Rebel-Saint, explained that since America had been created "in a style of the *sublime*," great men like Washington were clearly "designed for America" by Providence. As Ruth Miller Elson put it, in the eyes of Americans, "British virtues" had "migrated to America." And they all seemed to coalesce in the person of Gentleman-General George—"Columbia's fav'rite son," as Richard Snowden styled him in 1796.[11]

In America's late-eighteenth- and early-nineteenth-century schoolbooks, Washington was the essence of prudence, modesty, courtesy, charity, obedience, religiosity, courage, industry, honesty, chastity, benevolence, and, of course, patriotism—everything the Readers wanted their readers to be. The fifty-seven "Rules of Civility" that Washington's teacher had made him copy into his notebook at the age of thirteen ("In the presence of others sing not to yourself with a humming noise, nor drum with your fingers or feet; . . . jog not the table or desk on which another reads or writes; lean not on anyone") were reprinted frequently for the edification of worthy (and the annoyance of unworthy) American youth.[12] An 1821 reader observed that "nature was endeavoring to improve upon herself" when she created Gentleman-General George. "All the virtues of the ancient world" were but "so many studies preparatory to the patriot of the new." E. D. Mansfield explained in 1846 that the young require "some personified FIGURE OF GLORY" (see pl. 50). That image must be an American one, he explained, and Washington was "the MODEL HERO of all Modern Times."[13]

John Adams grew a bit alarmed by it all. As he wrote to Benjamin Rush, it seemed to be "expressly agreed to blow the trumpet of panegyric in concert" in order to make Washington seem "popular and fashionable with all parties and with all persons, as a center of union, as the central stone in the geometrical arch."[14] Adams feared that the veneration of Washington would foster a brand of hero-worship inimical to the republican ethic, that it might lead to the very monarchic or Cromwellian cult that Washington had himself rejected at Newburgh. But there was little that Adams could do about it, for the cult of "Columbia's fav'rite son" grew steadily throughout the new nation's first century.

It grew, of course, at the expense of veneration for the British Whig patriot-symbols, Hampden and Sydney. Some still invoked the twin patriots, but others were more "American" in their tastes. When John Randolph of Roanoke told the House of Representatives in 1811 of the Sydney who had served as his generation's model of virtue, a "British influence which he could never shake off," he was quickly called to task by Robert Wright of Maryland, who called for "the nobler distinction" of American symbols ("the beardless Powhatan, and the immortal Pocahantas"). Wright preferred Patrick Henry, Jefferson, and Washington "for my patriotism."[15] John Lovett had kind words for Hampden, Sydney, and other British worthies, but kinder words for the "greater sage," "Earth's great Hero man." Upon the death of Joseph Warren at Bunker Hill in 1775 several bards had depicted Warren's soul rising to heaven in the arms of *"Freedom's* genuine sons," the martyred Rebel-Saint and the Patriot. But the scene Parson Weems offered in 1807 of Washington's arrival at the Pearly Gates included no British spirits. None but "FRANKLIN, WARREN, MERCER" and other American "martyred saints" were on guard that night.[16] The kindest encomium William Rives could offer Hampden in 1845 was to say that had he lived "he would have been the *Washington* of his country." English writers might equate the two—

in 1831 Thomas Babington Macaulay described Hampden as one comparable in virtue only to Washington, and in 1876 Sir Leslie Stephen called Washington "the American reproduction of Hampden"—but by 1903 the American Henry Van Dyke would express outrage at the suggestion that Washington had been "a second edition" of some antique Englishman.[17]

For a year or two at the turn of the eighteenth century Washington was essentially the property of the Federalists, but neither Federalists nor Jeffersonians suffered that condition to last for long. In 1800 the British minister to the United States reported that leaders of the Federalist Party were making use of Washington's Birthday eulogies not only to advance their own party's interests but also to foster "the formation of a *national character*, which they consider as much wanting in this country" (see pl. 42).[18] The following year President Jefferson embraced the spirit of Washington in his inaugural address, and thereafter, throughout the nineteenth century, Washington served Americans in the same diverse ways as had Hampden and Sydney. He spoke as the pseudonym of a Jeffersonian seeking national unity in 1800, as a High Federalist upset by "the Cimmerian gloom of democracy" and critical of his party's candidate DeWitt Clinton (a man "without taste") in 1812, and as a Clinton *supporter* ten years later.[19] He was invoked by both sides while the debates over the Great Compromise of 1850 were raging. Henry Clay, introducing a motion to purchase the manuscript of the farewell address, reminded the Senate that he had opposed "sectional division" and "disunion." John C. Calhoun, in his last speech on the slavery controversy, remembered him as "that illustrious Southerner" who had rebelled against oppression.[20] In 1858, at the unveiling of Thomas Crawford's equestrian statue of Washington in Richmond—a very notable occasion—there was an effusion of eloquence. John R. Thompson, editor of the *Southern Literary Messenger*, read a poem which clearly echoed Clay's sentiments:

> . . . we here in gratitude renew;
> The patriot-vows to country ever due;
> And on this holy altar firmly swear
> The blessed compact never to impair.

Virginia's unionist Governor Henry Wise similarly linked Washington to *"National Union,"* but Alabama "fireater" William Lowndes Yancy responded with a vision of Washington similar to that of Calhoun, as did James Barron Hope, whose Washington was "the Messiah" of the South (see pl. 48). In 1860 George Fitzhugh, another "fireater," maintained that Washington's example and philosophy justified secession—a view that Abraham Lincoln firmly denied in his famous Cooper Institute speech of 1860, claiming for his own party the mantle of Washington.[21]

When civil war finally did come, a number of Confederate poets sought to associate the "Rebel cause" with "The Great Rebel." Thus George Miles:

> *Rebel's* the righteous name
> *Washington* bore;
> Why, then be ours the same.[22]

Simultaneously, in the North, Lincoln, Oliver Wendell Holmes, Walt Whitman, Herman Melville, and others were claiming "the Father of His Country" for their cause. Charles Alexander's *Washington's Vision* was subtitled "the first Union Story ever written." Bostonian Morison Heady began his 1863 life of Washington with the explanation that he had written of Washington for American youth "in the period of mighty struggles and issues" in order to provide them with "the noblest examples of patriotism and virtue." Heady's Washington was a critic of slavery and had been so ever since boyhood, when he had confessed to cutting down his father's cherry tree upon his father's threatening to punish young George's slave companion, Jerry, for the deed. Samuel Osgood's "Second Life of Washington" borrowed from Milton's *Paradise Lost* to depict the spirit of Washington leading victorious Union generals, avenging angels, against the fallen angels and their Satanic hosts.[23]

In the decades between the Civil War and World War II Washington was depicted as a friend of religion, education, technology, Boy Scouts, expansionism, Masons, Irish-Americans, Polish-Americans, Jews, blacks, and businessmen.[24] But by the turn of the century his followers were increasingly of a particular sort—the nativist elite. As had been the case with Hampden and Sydney, as time passed, the veneration of Washington was increasingly an elite phenomenon (and this was as true in Great Britain; before vanishing from the culture, Hampden and Sydney increasingly became "Establishment" symbols, as we shall see in the next chapter). J. H. Plumb's comment that "the personal ownership of the past has always been a vital strand in the ideology of all ruling classes" is a valuable insight. Perhaps this is why persons of lower socioeconomic backgrounds are simply less interested in political figures (and politics in general) than persons of upper socioeconomic backgrounds (as Fred Greenstein and others have demonstrated).[25]

In any event, *Washington's Vision* was reprinted in 1880 for the edification of native Americans. Reprinted again in 1938 by the "Christian Workers Union," this tale consisted of the reflections of one Anthony Sherman, a veteran of the Revolutionary War, who "recalled" Washington's visitation by an angel who told of racial or ethnic conflict in America's future. Hordes of foreigners would invade the United States and would be driven from the soil by "legions of white spirits" from Heaven, led, conceivably, by the general himself.[26]

The creator of this tale may or may not have approved (had he lived long enough to witness it) of the German-American Bund's use, during a 1939 rally in Madison Square Garden, of a thirty-foot likeness of Washington leaning on a column of bound fasces (a blown-up photograph of Jean Antoine Houdon's statue).[27] He might, however, have approved of the conduct of Charles Gallagher, Most Worshipful Grand Master of Massachusetts Masons, who, like himself, beatified the general. Gallagher presented his Masonic followers in 1901 with a lock of Brother Washington's hair ensconced in an "urn of solid gold": "it appears before you a priceless relic, worshipped by the [Masonic] followers as coming from that noble head which a more imaginative people would have beatified with the halo of a saint."[28]

Formal veneration of this kind (see pls. 51 and 52) was, from very early in the nineteenth century, set off by signs of public weariness with the Washington symbol. As early as 1800 the romantic novelist and journalist Charles Brockden Brown was ready to dismiss as valueless the outpouring of formal grief in the form of funeral orations. Two later literary figures, Nathaniel Hawthorne and Ralph Waldo Emerson, seconded John Adams's irreverent critique of Washington worship. Charles Farrar Browne's "Artemus Ward" offered in 1862 a caricature of a nineteenth-century Fourth of July speech:

> G. Washington was abowt the best man this world ever sot eyes on.... He never slopt over!... He was a human angil in a 3 kornerd hat and knee britches.[29]

Browne was drawing on a eugolistic tradition possessed of considerable strength, variation, and tenure; he would not have bothered with something that was no longer a familiar part of the cultural landscape. But the fact that he could write so entertainingly of this preeminent American patriot-symbol suggests that Washington had lost some of his magical powers. A satirist would never have dealt irreverently with Washington in the *early* nineteenth century—at least not in print.

The naming of children after the Father of His Country began to taper off by the mid-nineteenth century (see Figure 5.1). The median of the birthdates of 100 persons selected at random from the *Dictionary of American Biography* and the *Biographical Directory of the American Congress* was 1833. The median of the birthdates of the 102 "George Washingtons" from these sources was 1825. Fred Greenstein's compari-

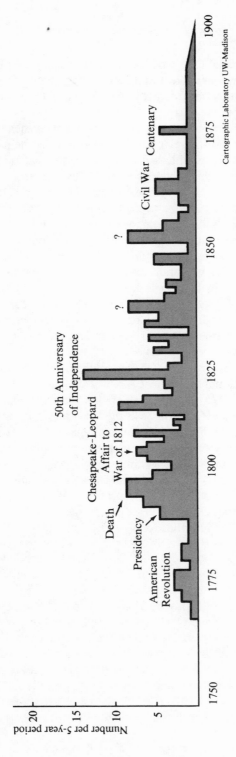

Figure 5.1. Relative popularity of the use of Washington's name as a first name in America. Sources: *Dictionary of American Biography; Biographical Directory of the American Congress;* various census returns for Massachusetts, Pennsylvania, and South Carolina; and other comparable sources. 237 cases in all were noted.

Cartographic Laboratory UW-Madison

son of student opinion surveys from 1902 to 1958 (see Table 5.2) indicates that Washington was of less and less significance to American school children with the passing of each decade. The public's devotion would appear to have begun to flag.

The efforts of those who sought to prolong the veneration crystallized in the obelisk in Baltimore and, more strikingly, in the nation's capital. In 1822 Sarah Hale was pleased that Americans had raised "no proud column" to "Columbia's fav'r'te son." "Thy monument's thy Name," she maintained.[30] But Hale was some seven years off. In 1815 some wealthy Baltimore residents, alarmed at the possibility that the removal of "the old Court House" building from their neighborhood might result in "the erection of unseemly structures on the site," had commissioned a "Monumental Shaft," capped by a statue of Washington in the act of resigning his commission as commander-in-chief to the Congress at Annapolis. The cornerstone was laid on Independence Day, amidst much fanfare and Masonic ritual, and the monument was finally completed and unveiled in 1829, at which time, according to one Washington marmorealizer, "a shooting star dashed across the sky and an eagle alighted on the head of Washington."[31]

Later, in 1833, a coalition of the socially prominent saw a need for a Washington National Monument Association which was designed to collect funds for another, even more impressive "proud column." Donations eventually tapered off, and in 1848 the Association persuaded Congress to incorporate them. That same year, members of the Masonic order laid the cornerstone for the Washington Monument in the nation's capitol and construction began, but within a decade work had ceased, as funds were only trickling in. The Association finally surrendered its dream of funding the project without public support and turned to Congress for funds. In 1876, the centennial year, Congress assumed the financial burden, and nine years later the monument was completed. It was dedicated by the same man who had delivered the address at the cornerstone ceremony in 1848, none other than the Honorable Robert C. Winthrop, who offered the antistatist's praise of Washington's "Anglo-Saxon trait of just resistance to the abuse of power."

The Washington National Monument Association's work was not done, however. The late nineteenth century's flood of "new immigrants" from southern and eastern Europe had to be made aware of the Father of Their Country, and the Monument Association reappeared as the George Washington Memorial Association, now an arm of the Sons and Daughters of the American Revolution. From 1898 until the 1930's this organization of worthies dispatched patriotic literature, sought to raise or acquire additional edifices in their hero's honor, purchased a graduate school

Table 5.2. Children's and Adolescents' Choice of Public Figures as Exemplars, 1902–58

Exemplars	Place, approximate date of field work, and investigator				
	1902 New Castle, Pa. (Chambers)	1910 Nashville, Tenn. (Hill)	1928 Birmingham, Montgomery, Mobile, Ala. (Hill)	1944 Springfield, Mass. (Stoughton, Ray)	1958 New Haven, Conn. (Greenstein)
Entertainment	4.7%	4.4%	15.5%	8.1%	37.9%
"Serious"	4.1	4.1	5.1	–	1.8
"Non-serious"	.6	.3	10.4	8.1	36.1
Business	1.6	1.0	1.0	–	.6
Contemporary political	12.5	2.3	2.4	3.1	6.3
Incumbent president	3.3	.9	.2	2.7	3.3
Other	9.2	1.4	2.2	.4	3.0
National hero	35.6	32.2	27.4	11.0	10.4
Washington	29.2	22.0	19.9	4.9	3.2
Lincoln	3.4	.6	2.4	1.5	3.6
Other	3.0	9.6	5.1	4.6	3.6
Miscellaneous figures from wider environment	17.2	20.6	15.6	33.4	14.8
Immediate environment figures	22.4	39.5	33.8	44.4	2.0
No response or invalid response	6.0	–	4.3	–	28.0
Total	100.0%	100.0%	100.0%	100.0%	100.0%
Ages included in present tabulation	7–16 yrs.	7–15 yrs.	6–20 yrs.	9 and 11 yrs.	9–15 yrs.
Number of cases	2333	1531	8813	259	659

Source: Fred Greenstein, *Children and Politics* (New Haven, 1966), pp. 388–89.

complex for Columbian University in exchange for that institution's promise to alter its name to George Washington University, and organized the elaborate Bicentennial Celebration of Washington's birth in 1932.[32]

This last affair was remarkable, involving essay contests, pageants, commemorative poems, songs, postage stamps, coins, historical accounts, and a three-volume compendium of the encomia. It serves both as a marvelous illustration of Washington worship by the long-established Anglo-Saxon elites and as a measure of that group's anxiety about the future. Instructions regarding the essay contest recommended 107 works on Washington, but included neither W. E. Woodward's *George Washington, The Image and the Man* (1926), Rupert Hughes's *Life of George Washington* (3 vols., 1926–30), nor any of the other debunking studies of the Father of His Country. One essayist, angered by these "deplorable" accounts "derogatory to the character of Washington," maintained that they "had little influence on the thinking public," and she may have been right.[33] But another, an Oregon schoolteacher, was fearful of what she regarded as the waning of Washington-worship among her young charges; she groped for an explanation:

> Today, when the laws of courtesy are forgotten, we may well remember Washington. . . . Modern Youth has declared a second War of Independence—a rebellion against restraint and formality. . . . Our daughters often forsake the ideal of feminine grace and charm, and our sons disdain the gallantry of other days. We . . . ignore culture.

Americans respectful of Victorian self-restraint and formality cherished the image of the venerable Virginia gentleman. ("He never slept over!") But many modern Americans, young and old, did not accept that model of virtue (captured in the widely circulated, dignified Gilbert Stuart portrait) as their own. This is not to say that Washington was passing from the scene in the fashion of Hampden or Sydney. One incident may serve to illustrate the difference between these patriot-symbols. The White House curators had consigned John Hampden to the cellar; the curators of the Metropolitan Museum of Modern Art similarly consigned Emanuel Leutze's "Washington Crossing the Delaware" to cold storage in 1930. Robert C. Winthrop had been virtually alone in his concern for the Patriot's portrait, but in 1932 the American Legion, the Sons and Daughters of the American Revolution, the Colonial Dames of America, the Grand Army of the Republic, the V.F.W., the Boy Scouts, the Girl Scouts, the Knights of Pythias, the Patriotic Order of the Sons of America, and the Democratic nominee for president of the United States united to demand the reappearance of the Leutze painting (which was duly resurrected and installed in an appropriately venerable setting in Washington's Crossing,

Pa.).[34] The Father of His Country was still a powerful symbol (as in Norman Rockwell's Bicentennial canvas). But his image *was* fading. At the turn of the century Professors Earl Barnes and Will Chambers analyzed the process by which American schoolchildren acquired models of patriotism. They noted a decline of interest in Washington among children as they matured (see Table 5.3) and attributed it to the "overworking" of Washington's character "for nursery purposes" by overzealous teachers who "lactated and peptonized" Washington "for infant food," giving him such "sentimental, distant, and vague" qualities as were expressed in "the hatchet story."[35] This appears to be the view taken by Grant Wood in his depiction of Parson Weems wryly unveiling "the hatchet story" scene of a young Washington with a bewigged, Gilbert Stuart head (pl. 55). N. C. Wyeth sought to alter this image. His Bicentennial Washington (pl. 54) is folksy, warm, down-to-earth—and consequently unfamiliar, absurd, unsuccessful. Many simply could no longer identify with "Columbia's Fav'rite Son." Marmorealized, he was too distant, cold, impersonal. Some (Table 5.2) preferred no hero at all; others a successful "self-made man" like Richard Armour or John Jacob Astor; still others an "antihero" like Jesse James or John Dillinger, and, increasingly, a "celebrity" hero (entertainer, astronaut, or ballplayer). The political hero that emerged to challenge Washington was the more down-to-earth "Abe" Lincoln, one of "the People," as Richard Henry Stoddard (1825–1903), in an ode to Lincoln, described him: "No Gentleman, like Washington."[36]

Table 5.3. Schoolchildren's Favorite Patriot-Hero, 1902, in New Castle, Pa., and Trenton, N.J.

	Age									
Hero	6	7	8	9	10	11	12	13	14	15	16
Washington	5%	9%	15%	31%	38%	43%	39%	33%	38%	17%	16%
Lincoln	0	0	4	4	2	3	5	5	11	12	15

Source: Will Chambers, "The Evolution of Ideals," *Pedagogical Seminary* 10 (1903):110. Cf. Estelle Darrah, "A Study of Children's Ideals," *Popular Science Monthly* 83 (1898): 88–98, for similar data from 1,440 schoolchildren in St. Paul, Minnesota, and San Mateo County, California.

"The Apostle of Liberty" and "The Savior of the Union": The Fitful Path of Jeffersonianism and the Rise of Lincoln

Perhaps we may gain a clearer insight into the relationship between cultural change and the veneration of patriot-heroes that I have thus far tried to describe if we consider the antithetical character of two of the more important American patriot-symbols: Thomas Jefferson, "The Apostle of Liberty," and Abraham Lincoln, "The Savior of the Union." As I hope to make clear in this chapter, to localistic, antistatist Americans of the nineteenth century Jefferson represented the virtues of freedom *from* government, and in that sense his image and fate were much the same as those of Hampden and Sydney. Lincoln, on the contrary, represented the virtues of orderly government and moral power, and in that sense his steady advance was akin to that of his ideological counterpart, Oliver Cromwell (a subject dealt with in the next chapter).

"The Apostle of Liberty"

Each of the patriot-symbols we have been considering to one degree or another served as an inspiration to many groups of differing political persuasions, and Jefferson was no exception. At one time or another he was invoked by abolitionists *and* nullifiers, by pro- *and* anti-Bank factions, by imperalists *and* antiimperialists, by New Dealers *and* their critics. He was something of a touchstone, as Merrill Peterson has demonstrated.[37] But, like Hampden and Sydney, he was primarily the symbol of localistic antistatism.

If Hampden and Sydney were too English to continue for long to serve Americans after independence, that did not mean that early-nineteenth-century Americans had dispensed with their antistatist values. Indeed, more so than Washington or any other American patriot-symbol, Jefferson inherited the antistatist mantle in America that Hampden and Sydney had shared. Had he not admired the Rebel-Saint and the Patriot? Throughout the days of the early Republic "Algernon Sydney" and "John Hampden" pseudonymously defended Jefferson and Jeffersonianism.[38] Jefferson, lover of "the twin patriots," champion of civil liberties and local prerogatives against Federalist "tyrannies," was a suitable antistatist figure for those nineteenth-century Americans who lived in fear of external, central authority and delighted in their personal liberties. Localistic Americans, whether early-nineteenth-century farmers, antebellum southern planters, late-nineteenth-century Populists and single-taxers, or Liberty Leaguers of the New Deal era, found inspiration in the sage of Monticello's philosophy and example. He had championed religious liberty in Virginia and political liberty in the Continental Congress; he had fought Federalist encroachments on civil liberties with the Virginia and Kentucky Resolutions; he had (at one time or another) been critical of cities, industrialism, and commercialism; his administration had abolished excise, land, and stamp taxes; he had opposed the "dangerous" growth of the regular army and navy; he had (at least initially) opposed a national bank. He became, in James Bryce's phrase:

> the representative not merely of democracy, but of local democracy, of the notion that government is hardly wanted at all, that the people are sure to go right if they are left alone, that he who resists authority is *prima facie* justified in doing so, because authority is *prima facie* tyrannical, that a country where each local body in its own local area looks after the objects of common concern, raising and administering any such funds as are needed, and is interfered with as little as possible by any external power, comes nearest to the ideal of a truly free people.[39]

But localism and antistatism were political principles more suited to the agrarian age to which Hampden, Sydney, and Jefferson belonged than to the commercial-industrial age of the late nineteenth and the twentieth centuries. Agrarian America, with its love of individualism and local control, was buffeted by the nationalizing impulses of democratic politics and the nationwide marketing system. Tocqueville felt this was inevitable: "individual independence and local liberties will ever be the product of artificial contrivance, centralization will be the natural form of government in a democracy."[40] Popular sovereignty was inherently centralizing and repressive of local differences. And Jefferson was no symbol of centralism.

Rather, he appeared a symbol of state rights, and later, to those living through a civil war, of secession.[41] (Was not the leader of the Rebellion his namesake?) Thus the nationalistic political theorists of the late nineteenth and early twentieth centuries rejected him.[42] Samuel Fowler found him too localistic in 1865 for a "progressive," commercial-industrial nation.

> The immense scale of modern enterprises, the stores of wealth which they create and demand, and the expenses attending them, have contributed to a degree hitherto unknown, to the force of [nationalism]. This is the day of great nations. The achievements in which the age delights, as well as that kind of progress with which its hopes are associated, are possible only among them.

Reason and science were revealing the unifying laws of the natural world. Nationalism was now the highest form of patriotism.[43] David A. Wasson agreed. Writing in the *North American Review* in 1874, Wasson doubted that the "weathercock rule" of Jefferson was a sufficient model for political leaders of the late nineteenth century. "New forces" active in the nineteenth century, "the new means of transportation, travel, and communication," had "effected a social transformation of vast importance." A revolution in high finance, "commercial centralization," the creation of modern corporations, modern mechanization, all affected labor and open competition. "One thing is wanting: a ruling order adequate to the new conditions," "a fine public regimen, a more effective public discipline."[44]

"The Savior of the Union"

To men like Fowler and Wasson, Jefferson was something of an anachronism. To Theodore Roosevelt and Henry Cabot Lodge he was downright "weak and vacillating." Lincoln, Cromwell, even Hamilton (Jefferson's nemesis), were more relevant figures. Frank Vrooman admired them all, and despised "Jeffersonian individualism." The future, for Vrooman, would reject Jefferson and all that he stood for and would espouse "a new *motif*," one of "rational association" and "nationally conceived and nationally coordinated law and order." Vrooman's government would be "of the people, by the people, for the people [sic]" and would be scientific in character. Hamilton, for Vrooman, "symbolized political 'mastery' against Jeffersonian 'drift,' the positive state against *laissez-faire*, . . . world power against isolation." In like fashion Herbert Croly's *Promise of American Life* (1909) called for "Hamiltonian" regulatory policies, centralization of power, and government by "experts."[45] But among symbols of statism it was Lincoln who loomed the largest.

The "Lincoln legend" grew steadily throughout the late nineteenth and early twentieth centuries, eventually surpassing that of both Jefferson and Washington. Republicans Robert Ingersoll in 1893 and Chauncey Depew in 1896 compared the tragic and human Lincoln favorably to the passive Washington, "now only a steel engraving." The Republican Party and the G.A.R. were certainly responsible for some of this Lincoln veneration, but most of it was quite spontaneous. If teachers were "overworking" the veneration of Washington, with the effects displayed in Table 5.3, another glance at that table will suggest that the maturing schoolchild's admiration of the Savior of the Union tended to wax as admiration of the Father of His Country waned. As had been the case with Hampden, Sydney, Cromwell, Washington, Jefferson, and Jackson, towns, parks, colleges, streets and children now bore Lincoln's name. He was the subject of poems, plays, novels, and biographies. "Savior of the Union," "Man of the People," "Great Emancipator," he was honored in marble and bronze in scores of American communities (north of the Mason-Dixon line), most impressively so in 1922 by Daniel Chester French in the Lincoln Memorial at Washington, D.C. Steadily increasing numbers visited his tomb in Springfield between 1874 and the present; millions have walked through his Memorial in the Capital.[46]

Films, and recently a television series, have paid tribute to his fame. Once again, why? What can we learn from the ever-growing image of Lincoln in the American mind?

To begin with, he *was* a "man of the people," self-made,[47] of frontier stock, "the mystic demi-god of common man,"[48] and this surely appealed to many Americans. Other statesmen were also of common stock, however, and others could similarly claim to have been "self-made." Lincoln's "plain" background and features certainly enhanced his appeal to egalitarian Americans, but these were not the qualities that caused his elevation to the first rank of the patriot-heroes, and, consequently, they are not the subject of our attention here.

Slain on Good Friday, after having led the Union through the Civil War, Lincoln was quickly and naturally apotheosized. Compared to Christ and Moses, he was venerated by the moralistic Americans, albeit located disproportionately in the Republican Party.[49] But others (Garfield and McKinley) had been the victims of assassins' bullets. Martyrdom alone did not elevate Lincoln to greatness.

The "Lincoln legend" was essentially a function of the twin roles Lincoln had played as "Savior of the Union" and as "Great Emancipator."[50] Both roles had required that he exercise righteous power and display "a will of iron"; it was these qualities (and especially the former one) that made him preeminent among modern patriot-symbols. Emerson grew to admire Lincoln's ability to act effectively under pressure and "to exert the enormous power of the continent." Francis Carpenter, whose historical canvas of "The First Reading of the Emancipation Proclamation" hangs in the Capitol, described Lincoln as one "grounded in righteousness, as immovable as one of the giant ranges of our own Rocky Mountains." Richard Henry Stoddard's Lincoln was "what the stern hour/Demanded that he was, . . . Power." He "preserved the State!"[51] William Herndon, Lincoln's old law partner, portrayed Lincoln as an earthly, but "Herculean" man.[52] Nathaniel Wright Stevenson's Lincoln was a consummate master of statecraft. Of "single will," "inflexible purpose, strong as steel, unwavering as fate," Stevenson's Lincoln had "refused to be the mere spokesman of the people," for he was "a statesman of nationalism, laboring for cohesion in a people" whose economy had "given a death-blow to geographical self-consciousness," but who still displayed such "deficiency in imagination that for them the world outside their [provincial] group" was "a world of shadows."[53] Lyman Allen's Emancipator was "Incarnate Conscience; Right's embodiment," wielding a "sovereign scepter" which "smote with such a stroke/The chains of centuries,/That earth was shaken to its farthest road." The Methodist minister G. E. Strobridge celebrated a Lincoln who "caught in giant hands" the "broken state," and "bound it fast in blood-cemented bands." To Francis Grierson Lincoln's "genius was superhuman." Edwin Markham's Lincoln "built the State,/Pouring his splendid strength through every blow." Fred Patee's Lincoln was "no Bismarck," void of conscience and of heart," but, nonetheless, of "granite will":

> Note the mighty power
> Coiled in his soul and waiting for its hour
> strong withal and mighty to control
> and bend the kinds of men to do his will.

> [He] drew our plan,
> The plan of empire that shall . . .
> make us strong forever, having him.

Ida Tarbell saw lessons for the modern world in Lincoln's "workmanlike, trustworthy" statesmanship; he was "steady in storms." Carl Sandburg's Lincoln knew how to get things done. He had said "Yes to the constitution when a help,/ no to the constitution when a hindrance."[54]

All these apotheoses had in common the praise of state power, always nobly used, to be sure, but still power, to achieve order, union, social change. They were also the measure of a transformation in American culture occurring between the opening of the nineteenth century, when *antistatist* symbols like Hampden, Sydney, and Jefferson were models of public virtue, and the closing of that century of civil war and socioeconomic change, by which time a symbol of order and power, a *statist* symbol, Lincoln, had taken their place.

Jefferson versus Lincoln

The replacement of the antistatist image of the "Apostle of Liberty" by the more statist, "Herculean" symbol of Lincoln did not come without a struggle. The "old" culture fought to preserve its ways, and its heroes. Mary P. Follett's *The New State* juxtaposed the old and the new concisely. She rejected Jefferson's philosophy of laissez faire, preferring "dynamic administration": "A constructive social policy is more democratic than the protection of men in their individual rights and property." John Dryden, head of Prudential Life, noted that "new conditions" had led to "new functions for the effective conduct of the nation's business and new laws to regulate the predestined expansion of American influence and diplomacy." He felt that "we are indebted to the spirit of Lincoln" for "much of this."[55] Over the years, the Republican Party's annual Lincoln Dinner Addresses reflect the tide of influential opinion. In 1900 Rabbi Emil Hirsch linked Lincoln to the nation's "industrial independence," "financial integrity," and municipal reform movement; he rejected the Democratic "party of everlasting negatives." John Baldwin, the Union Pacific's general attorney, was certain that if he were alive in 1901 Lincoln "would have brought to bear the same methods and principles" that he had used to save the Union on today's "great, portentous and momentous questions of finance, tariffs, capital, and labor." President Theodore Roosevelt spoke of Lincoln as the first "progressive," the founder of "a party of dynamics, not a party of statics." To Representative (later Senator) Albert Beveridge, Lincoln was "a logician of progress," a practical "great achiever," "the spirit of nationality incarnate." Representative Robert Bonynge went so far as to define "Lincolnism" (in 1918) in terms of war mobilization, unity, selective service, and "stamping out inefficiency wherever found in public service."[56] When in 1913 a group of cosmopolitan business and political leaders met to plan a lobby favoring a highway to span the nation, it was logical that they would name themselves the Lincoln Highway Association, that the nation's first transcontinental highway, completed by the 1930's, would be named for the "Great Martyred Patriot" who had signed the bill that had brought the Union Pacific Railroad into existence. The highway would "knit the many detached groups of the American people into a compact and homogeneous nation" and "make Americans cosmopolitans."[57] Its name was obviously appropriate.

Lincoln, then, was the hero of the "progressive" cosmopolitan; Jefferson, the villain. Walter Weyl's *The New Democracy* (1912) expressed the "progressive" rejection of Jefferson: "We are profoundly disenchanted," Weyl wrote, "with the fruits of a century of independence." The state had to take on responsibilities previously deemed beyond its reach, but "Our hand is stayed by ancient political ideas which still cumber our modern brains; by political heirlooms of revered—but dead—ancestors."[58]

Old-line Jeffersonians like Albert J. Nock, Claude Bowers, Oscar Underwood, Tom Watson, and Edgar Lee Masters were, of course, outraged. Masters, for example, though the son of a law partner of William Herndon, Lincoln's own partner, and a product of "Lincoln country" in central Illinois, was a Democrat, and four-year president of his local Jefferson Club. In defending his hero he attacked Lincoln, the archpatriotic symbol of what he called the "centralists" and "sordid imperialists" who had belittled Jefferson. Lincoln's "acts were against liberty," Masters intoned in his vitrolic *Lincoln the Man* (1931). His "centralist" administration had led to the "loss of liberty which at the present time is evidenced by daily decisions of the federal courts and by presidential usurpations." Masters suggested that Lincoln may have had the blood of the "arbitrary" Charles I in his veins, and compared the "pious reverence of Lincoln" in America to the remembrance of that tyrant by some misguided British royalists. Lincoln had committed numerous "unconstitutional" acts, such as the calling up of federal troops without congressional sanction, the imprisoning of some critics, the denial of the civil liberties of others, the suspension of *habeas corpus*, the creation of a national banking and currency system, and the imposition of a substantial tariff. He "played the part of the destroyer of the American system"—that is, the American system of Thomas Jefferson. Jeffersonians had defended the "altar fires of liberty" from the "violent winds of descending conspiracies":

> But all the while a patient, secret, self-conscious influence was gathering power, appropriating it from the people and from the states, and storing it in a central government for the purposes of business and money, and under the guise of law and order, of religion, and even of liberty. . . . Lincoln was . . . from the first . . . a centralist, a privilegist.

Power had been shifted into "the hands of central groups, courts and bureaus." The Republican "centralists" were "triumphant now" with their "armies and navies," their "amalgamation of wealth and government."

> The history of America since the days of Lincoln has been nothing but a filling in of the outlines of implied powers, which Lincoln did more than Hamilton or Webster to vitalize; it has been nothing but further marches into the paths which he surveyed toward empire and privilege.

Masters was outraged at the thoughtlessness of the "heedless throngs who have passed along the scene of life revering Hamilton, and making a demi-god of Lincoln," and he dedicated his study of Lincoln to Jefferson. But he was not overoptimistic about a possible revival of Jeffersonianism. After all, "every centralist historian and politician" since the Civil War had damned Jefferson and extolled Lincoln. And the public appeared to be following their lead. "Since America has largely discarded the principles of Jefferson, it is not remarkable that Lincoln overtops him."[59] And overtop him he did. But the election of a Democrat in 1932 gave the Jeffersonians one last hurrah.

The New Deal, deemed by many a sophisticated political effort to cope with the socioeconomic fruits of unregulated growth, was in many ways more Hamiltonian (or Lincolnian) than Jeffersonian. But since it was the work of a Democratic administration, since Jefferson was claimed both as a small and large "d" democrat, and since he *had* maintained that "the earth belongs to the living," he was offered as a symbol of the New Deal. Reviewing Claude Bowers's *Jefferson and Hamilton* for the *New York Evening World* in 1926, Franklin D. Roosevelt asked whether there was not another Jefferson "on the horizon." As president seven years later, he identified thoroughly with the Sage of Monticello, styling him among other things, the first "exponent of planning for the future." Jefferson's image appeared on the new nickel and the new 3-cent postage stamp. *And* he acquired a Roman temple.[60]

In 1936 the *New York Times*'s Elmer Davis permitted his newspaper column character, "Godfrey Gloom the well-known paw-paw planter and Jeffersonian Democrat from Amity, Indiana," to expire, struck down, appropriately, by an auto on a busy city street corner. Gloom's dying words, "the best place for a genuine Jeffersonian is in the tomb," were timely, for Jeffersonianism appeared to be out of step with the fast, statist pace of the new America.[61] Nevertheless, the Democrats, alarmed by the enthroning of Lincoln in a Grecian temple aligned with the Washington Monument and juxtaposed to the Capitol, were determined to honor one of their own patriot-heroes. The Jefferson Memorial, begun in 1937 and completed in 1943, just in time for the Thomas Jefferson Bicentennial ceremonies, captured his memory in a pantheon that was (appropriately) juxtaposed to the White House.[62]

But that was just it: The Jefferson Memorial *captured* Jefferson's memory; it did not rejuvenate it. Had it not captured his memory by 1943, it is entirely conceivable that no memorial would *ever* have captured it, for the "Jeffersonian image" was continuing to fade. The New Dealers had paid homage to Jefferson, but the people knew better. Critics of the New Deal styled it "Hamiltonian," and some reclaimed the more familiar, antistatist Jefferson. Southern Agrarians they were, and Liberty Leaguers, and Marxists. Edward Griggs, for example, was just as impressed with the "new and perplexing problems" posed by the "changing methods of industrial production" as were the more cosmopolitan "progressives," but he was clearly more troubled than they by "the vastly increased tendencies toward centralization and paternalism in government." Consequently, he felt that the values expressed by Jefferson "need reemphasis" at a time "when the popular mind is obsessed with the idea of multiplied legislation as the certain cure for all moral and social ills." Al Smith, a full-fledged opponent of the New Deal by 1936, proudly reclaimed the Jeffersonian mantle from FDR in an address to a Liberty League dinner. Russel Davenport, editor of *Fortune* and critic of many New Deal measures, fondly quoted Jefferson: "That government is best which governs least." His friend, Stephen Vincent Benét, an admirer of Jefferson and of the New Deal, was annoyed. He doubted that Jefferson could ever have said such a thing, but:

> Whether Jefferson said it or not, that [statement] seems to me completely outmoded thinking. If national government is merely "a necessary evil"

why the hell should anybody bother trying to set up any sort of *interna-tional* government or world order. . . . I think one of our great troubles has been this idea that "government" is something high sounding and far-off and scary that gets after you with a club. . . . That [statement] never was true of any complex civilization.[63]

But Jefferson *had* said such things. Any veneration Benét may have offered such an antistatist symbol seemed increasingly to have been misplaced. Indeed, the New Deal's own championing of the Democratic patron saint eventually ran out of steam. The Jefferson Bicentennial was managed by Edward R. Boykin, a retired advertising executive, who described it as "a piece of promotion business."[64] The choice of Boykin made some sense, for Jefferson's image, so strong a century before, did need promoting. The *New York Times* revealed in 1943 that, despite all of the public hullabaloo, only 16 percent of college freshmen could properly identify (let alone offer veneration to) Jefferson.[65] Later, in 1951, the Gallup Poll asked a sample of those whose names appeared in *Who's Who in America* to name "the President of the United States you regard as the greatest." The results (see Table 5.4) reflect the strength of Lincoln's reputation in the American mind, and the relative dispersion of the Jeffersonian image. In 1958 the general public was asked to name the "three famous persons in history—from the present or the past" that they would most like to "invite to your home" today. When ranked in order of frequency of mention (Table 5.5), once again, Abraham Lincoln was first, and Jefferson appeared in seventeenth place.

Table 5.4. Ranking of Presidents, June 1, 1951

A sample taken from the names in *Who's Who in America* was asked: "From your own personal point of view, which president of the United States would you regard as the greatest?"

President	Percentage
Lincoln	45
Washington	19
F. D. Roosevelt	7
Jefferson	6
Wilson	3
Theodore Roosevelt	2
Hoover	1
Cleveland	1
Others	1
Don't know	15

Source: *The Gallup Polls* (2 vols., New York, 1972), 2: 986.

Table 5.5. Gallup Poll, May, 1958

"If you could invite any three famous persons in history—from the present or past—to your home for dinner, which three would you most like to have?"

Choices 1–10[a]	Choices 11–21[a]
Abraham Lincoln	Jesus
Franklin Roosevelt	Herbert Hoover
Dwight Eisenhower	Richard Nixon
George Washington	Rev. Billy Graham
Harry Truman	Woodrow Wilson
Mrs. Franklin Roosevelt	Benjamin Franklin
Douglas MacArthur	Thomas Jefferson
Mrs. Dwight Eisenhower	Will Rogers
Winston Churchill	Adlai Stevenson
Theodore Roosevelt	Bishop Fulton J. Sheen
	Charles de Gaulle

Source: *The Gallup Polls*, 2:1560.
[a]Listed according to frequency of mention.

The New Dealers were not oblivious to the potency of the Lincoln symbol. And they eventually appropriated it. As early as 1929 Roosevelt had written to Claude Bowers of the need for "us Democrats to claim Lincoln as one of our own." Increasingly Roosevelt invoked Lincoln in speeches and fireside chats. Lincoln had maintained that government should "do for a community of people whatever they need to have done but cannot do . . . in their separate and individual capacities." Was this not the objective of New Dealers?[66]

Roosevelt was not alone in this effort to link Lincoln to the New Deal. Robert Sherwood's *Abe Lincoln in Illinois* (play 1938, film 1940), Carl Sandburg's monumental life of Lincoln, and Stephen Vincent Benét's several Lincoln-related poems all drew attention to the Savior of the Union in the years of crisis. And all three men explicitly associated FDR with Lincoln. Raymond Massey, who played Lincoln in the Sherwood play and film, told a *New York Times* reporter in 1938 that Lincoln "was definitely a New Dealer." And on the eve of the 1940 election Massey read a speech over the radio, written by Benét, which endorsed FDR and compared him to Lincoln. The *Times* reported that by the end of the speech Massey let his voice slip into "his Lincoln"![67]

Fascist aggression and the war in Europe added to the need for a symbol of order, strength, and union. An anonymous poet writing in the *New York Herald Tribune* called on the Savior of the Union: "Lincoln, the people invoke the spirit now—/ Preserve, protect, defend our sovereign state!'' Carl Sandburg stumped the country in 1940 with an address which asked ''What would Lincoln have done?'' Sandburg's answer: precisely what FDR was doing. FDR told the nation in the summer of 1941 that Lincoln had dealt with problems in his day ''not by words but by deeds,'' and that he would do the same. Later in the same summer he quoted Lincoln on the need for national unity and, to make more explicit his association with the Civil War president, he told reporters that their headlines ought to read: ''President Quotes Lincoln—and Draws Parallel.'' Clearly, if Jefferson was the first patriot-symbol of the New Deal, by 1939 he was overshadowed by Lincoln.[68]

The diverse pieces of evidence that I have amassed in this chapter may now be seen, I believe, as forming a pattern: first, we have reason to believe that popular attention to local, as opposed to national and international, affairs and issues has declined since the late nineteenth century, that America has become less localistic and more cosmopolitan (see, for example, Table 5.6). We know that Americans have increasingly expressed

Table 5.6. Geographical Scope of Muncie, Indiana, Newspaper Reading Matter, Sampled 1890 and 1923 by Robert and Helen Lynd, 1976 by the author

Scope of reading matter with an ascertainable scope	1890 (average of 2 evening papers)	1923 (average of morning and evening papers)	1976 (average of morning and evening papers)
Local	40.6%	24.6%	23.7%
County	6.1	8.5	8.2
State	11.7	12.7	11.0
National	33.1	40.9	43.0
International	8.5	13.1	13.9

Source: Robert and Helen Lynd, *Middletown* (New York, 1929), p. 533; content analysis of 1976 papers (May–June) by author (''sports'' divided according to character of activity).

a willingness to see decisionmaking shift from the local to the state and federal level (Table 5.7). I have detected a steady growth in attention to and affection for the cosmopolitan patriot-symbol of Lincoln at the expense of the more localistic figure of Thomas Jefferson, and I think one may also speak of a steady drift towards, and respect for, statism and order. Jefferson (like his antistatist predecessors, Hampden and Sydney) represented civil liberties and the prerogatives of legislative power; Lincoln (like Cromwell), those of order and the executive. It is quite clear that those today who fear ''big government'' also fear the loss of individual liberties to ''government interference'' (Table 5.8) and favor the

Table 5.7. Popular Attitudes Regarding National, State, and Local Decision-making Pre-rogatives in the United States, Reflected in Identical Questions Asked by Pollsters in 1937 and 1973

"Many people believe that there are certain policy decisions affecting our lives which should be decided on the federal level while other decisions should be made on the state level and still other decisions should be made at the local level—city, town, or county. Which kind of government—federal, state or local—do you feel should take care of relief?"

| Respondent's preference | Percentage (of those expressing a preference) | | "Which . . . should take care of health insurance" |
	1937	1973	1973
Local	30.5%	20%	11%
State	19.7	36	29
Federal	37.0	39	49
Don't know	10.3	5	11
None of them	2.5	—	—

Source: Roper-*Fortune* poll, October 1937, cited in Hadley Cantril, ed., *Public Opinion* (Princeton, 1951), p. 895; Harris Poll, May 28, 1973.

legislature over the executive (Table 5.9). Consequently, one would expect that "localism," a preference of "freedom" over "order," and a distrust of "big government" would all be positively correlated with a

Table 5.8. Individual Concerns by Operational Spectrum[a] (higher no. = higher concern)

Ideological concerns	Completely liberal	Predominantly liberal	Middle of road	Predominantly conservative	Completely conservative
Preserving our free enterprise system	201	212	228	237	257
Preserving our individual liberties against government interference	185	201	218	255	279
Preserving states' rights	169	186	204	232	260
The trend toward a more powerful federal government	161	177	185	230	263
Average score for all ideological items	179	194	209	238	265

Source: Lloyd Free and Hadley Cantril, *The Political Beliefs of Americans* (New Brunswick, N.J., 1967), p. 55.

[a]Defined by responses to questions regarding federal funding of a variety of programs ("liberals" favoring, "conservatives" opposing).

Table 5.9. Confidence in Branches of Government by Operational Spectrum (higher no. = higher confidence)

	Averages for executive	Averages for legislative
National averages	7.43	7.23
Operational spectrum		
Completely liberal	8.40	7.54
Completely conservative	4.07	6.01

Source: Free and Cantril, *Political Beliefs of Americans*, p. 118.

Table 5.10. Preference for Jefferson or Lincoln and Place in the Political Spectrum[a]

	Mean score on local-cosmopolitan scale (-4 to $+4$) (locals are lower)	Mean score on freedom-order scale (1–10) (preference for freedom is lower)	Mean score on statist-antistatist scale (-2 to $+2$) (statists are higher)
Prefer Jefferson to Lincoln (80)	$+1.392^c$	4.48^d	$-.157^e$
Prefer Lincoln to Jefferson[b] (119)	$+1.763^c$	5.09^d	$+.469^e$

[a] One hundred and ninety-nine respondents at the University of Pittsburgh were surveyed between September, 1974, and January, 1975. Responses were weighed in the following fashion: Those expressing a preference for one of these patriot-symbols over the other of only one point on the 1–10 scale (see Appendix B) were given a weight of 1. Those expressing a preference of this sort of 2 points were given a weight of 2. Those expressing a preference of more than 2 points were given a weight of 3.

[b] It is worth noting that the differences between those preferring FDR to Hoover (155) and those preferring Hoover to FDR (or seeing no difference between the two) (44) are similar to those depicted in Table 5.9 for the local-cosmopolitan and statist-antistatist scales. Apparently, FDR is attractive to cosmopolitans and statists, unattractive to locals and antistatists. But those preferring FDR scored *lower* (4.57) than those preferring Hoover (5.69) on the freedom-order scale. Thus FDR, the hero of statists and cosmopolitans, is also the hero of civil libertarians, in contrast to Lincoln, who correlated with the order end of the scale. Moreover, of the two, only FDR is nonpartisan; fully 35.5% of FDR admirers were Republicans (approximating the percentage of Republicans in the sample), whereas only 22% of Hoover admirers were Democrats.

[c] Differences in these means (calculated with the "t" test) are only statistically significant to the .33 level.

[d] Differences in these means are statistically significant to the .02 level.

[e] Differences in these means are statistically significant to the .01 level.

preference for Jefferson, while "cosmopolitanism," a preference for "order" over "freedom" and approval of "big government" would all be positively correlated with a preference for Lincoln. That is what the foregoing evidence, both "impressionistic" and quantitative, suggests, and that is precisely how some two hundred students unfamiliar with the author responded to a questionnaire in 1974 which asked them questions designed to test these hypotheses (see Appendix B). Those who regarded Lincoln as being "greater" than Jefferson (the majority of those expressing a preference) gave significantly more cosmopolitan responses to questions on a local-cosmopolitan scale than those preferring Jefferson; they placed themselves closer to "order" than to "freedom" on a freedom-order spectrum than did those who preferred Jefferson, and they were more negative towards the statement "that government is best which governs least" than were those preferring Jefferson (see Table 5.10). Moreover, this was not explicable in terms of political party loyalties; Democrats and Republicans divided almost evenly in their affections for the two patriots, with 62 percent of the group preferring Lincoln being composed of Democrats and 60 percent of those preferring Jefferson being Democratic. When asked to comment on their reasons for ranking one or the other patriot higher, the respondents gave revealing and, in light of what has been said in the previous pages, predictable responses. Lincoln was an "effective decisionmaker," a "strong leader," a "problem-solver" who "acted under pressure" and who "knew how to manipulate things." Lincoln "had guts," he "stuck to his point"; he "believed that freedom was important but order was of greater importance," and "after all, benevolent dictators are extremely rare." Jefferson was "insufficiently active"; he didn't "inspire me as a leader." He "had a tendency to sit and watch. . . . He never really participated, except verbally." "Anybody could have written the Declaration of Independence."[69]

The decline of Jefferson and of antistatism go hand in hand. America's own localistic "Apostle of Liberty" has receded into the background;[70] the more suitable statist figure of Lincoln has taken his place.[71] The changing tempers of American culture were reflected in the changing faces and character of American patriot-hero symbols. And what was true of America was true of Britain as well.

6 Romanticism and Imperialism, Democracy and Reaction: The Changing Character of Patriot-Symbols in Nineteenth- and Twentieth-Century England

Another Failure in Transmission: The Transfiguration and Death of the Twin Patriots

The year 1788–89 marked the centennial anniversary of the "Glorious Revolution," and throughout the realm Britons so inclined met to celebrate their freedom and (generally speaking) to venerate their patriot-heroes, Hampden and Sydney. Whig reformers in Parliament, men like the Earl of Shelburne, R. B. Sheridan, and Sir Francis Burdett and other members of the elite Society of the Friends of the People, joined their leader, Charles James Fox, in their veneration of the Patriot and the Rebel-Saint, for as Fox put it to them, "it will animate our zeal and invigorate our constancy, to pay grateful homage in our toasts to our glorious ancestors. . . . I trust we shall all be ready *to bleed like Hampden in the field, or like Sydney on the scaffold.*"[1] (Fox's last phrase was italicized, as it was one that had become commonly used as a toast by Whigs.) From that vantage point some suggested that Hampden and Sydney had "sowed a seed" in France, which was "now growing up to a glorious harvest." Three years later, in the spring of 1792, James Watt, son of the famous engineer-inventor, and young Thomas Cooper represented the Constitution Club of Manchester in a Jacobin rally; they carried a British flag and a bust of Sydney in a procession through the streets of Paris.[2]

When the French revolution grew more sanguinary, some Britons appeared less willing to lend their patriots to the French. The Scot Thomas Hardy (1748?-98) warned of the dangers of Jacobinism and "violent men" and suggested that such men tended to upset and disarm the honest work of more temperate reformers. Britons ought to "look back to the parallel case in the history of England, when the Hampdens, and Pyms, the great band of patriots and heroes who stood forth for the liberties of their country," were upset by "a new party" composed of "dark republican independents," who "scorned all moderate reform, drove the patriots off the stage, and overwhelmed them, the king, and the constitution, in one universal ruin, and set up Dictator Cromwell, to tread on the neck of England."³ Edmund Burke spoke of "canonized forefathers," and "illustrating ancestors," but only to warn that English liberty had a pedigree "which the French form," given to "misrule and excess," did not.⁴

But "moderate men" had no monopoly on the twin patriots. By 1793 the administration of Pitt the Younger was striking out at "radical elements" who admired some of the social and political changes the revolution had wrought in France and were hoping to introduce universal manhood suffrage and annual Parliamentary elections, and to abolish "rotten" and "pocket" boroughs from British political life. As Pitt moved against them, "radicals" and their sympathizers remembered Hampden's trial and "Sydney's case." Thomas Hardy (1752-1832), founder of the London Corresponding Society, and John Horne Tooke of the Society for Constitutional Information, compared themselves to Sydney during their trials for high treason. Thomas Spence, agrarian reformer and friend of the accused, read from the *Discourses* to London workingmen and deplored their economic plight. (Later, during his own trial for his "seditious attacks" on private property, Spence compared himself to none other than Hampden, the epitome of property rights!) Henry Redhead Yorke, another member of the London Corresponding Society, found it ironic that Burke and other "enemies of our cause" were "compelled" by convention "to render an involuntary praise" of the twin patriots. But ministerial lip-service to his heroes did not taint them in Yorke's eyes. His passion was still strong:

> Let us invoke the spirits of Hampden, Russell, Pym, Vane, and ALGERNON SYDNEY: And now that I mention Sydney, I feel my heart glow with a patriot's fervour, and I glory to hold up his life, writings, courage, and even his death to the imitation of Englishmen. He was ever plotting and scheming the subversion of a government which he considered as a cruel and iniquitous system of expression. . . . he boldly fought to establish an unintricate form of legislation, and became a martyr.

People had shed "tears of pity" for "the virtuous" Lord William Russell, Sydney's coconspirator, "but when ALGERNON SYDNEY, the GREAT CONSPIRATOR, mounted the scaffold no symptoms of effeminate grief were visible, but the spectators glowed with the fire of republican freedom."[5] The spectators were probably aglow from hot grog, for it had been extraordinarily cold that December morning in 1683; and most of the spectators had probably been either gleeful royalist enemies or bloodthirsty Tower Hill regulars, not hunted republicans. But Yorke's zeal understandably caused him to overlook such historical niceties.

By 1794 the twin patriots were on the minds of reformers of every stripe. Lord Charles Grey (later the second Earl Grey of reform bill fame, at this time an outspoken young Foxite), feared for his own safety as Pitt's arrests continued. "I am not, however, very ambitious of being classed even with Algernon Sydney," he wrote anxiously to a friend. A handbill appeared in London that same season, protesting against "crimping" houses (sites of deceptive military recruitment practices) and other such government activities. Such "atrocious" violations of the rights of Englishmen would not have been tolerated in the days of the Rebel-Saint and the Patriot: "Did Sydney and Russell bleed for this?" The Sheffield Constitutional Society held a public meeting and called for Parliamentary reform (a fairly courageous act in 1794). They concluded with a reminder to Englishmen of the importance of "Virtue," the "Holy flame of Patriotism," and "thy Hampden, thy Sydney, and thy Locke."[6]

In March, 1794, Joseph Gerrald's sedition trial began in Edinburgh. Gerrald, the author of *The Address of the British Convention to the People of Great Britain*, detested "the dead hand of the past," be it that of religion, political tradition, or the law of property. His hero was the iconoclastic Thomas Paine. But Paine had been tried *in absentia*, and was as dangerous a symbol in 1794 as Cromwell had been in 1660. Gerrald chose rather to identify his cause with those of Hampden and Sydney, alluding to these safer patriot-symbols no fewer than seven times in the course of the trial.[7]

In October of 1794 the Englishman Edmund Jennings and the American John Quincy Adams, meeting in London, agreed that the patriotism of Gerrald, John Horne Tooke, and a number of their associates was comparable to that of Hampden, Russell, or Sydney.[8] Early the next year Major John Cartwright petitioned Commons and reminded the members that a "*Sidney* and a *Russel* were accounted seditious, when a *Jeffries* was the pattern of Loyalty."[9] "Common Sense" offered "ten minutes advice to the People of England" in November of 1795; it consisted of a critique of the administration's proposed legislation to curb "dangerous speeches and assemblies." This fellow got the "old Whig toast" a bit mixed up—his Sydney bled "in the field"—but in any event the patriots were invoked. He asked Hampden, Sydney, and Russell whether it was possible that Englishmen might "so disgrace your names and render ourselves so undeserving of your spirited and pure exertions."[10]

John Baxter, a member of the London Corresponding Society, acquitted of charges of high treason in 1795, published *A New and Impartial History of England* the next year which was very partial to Hampden and Sydney (see pl. 7). An anonymous member of another unnamed organization that appears to have made the government's subversive activities list complained in 1798 of corruption in high places, the damage Pitt's policies were causing the economy, and the proposed income tax. In the past, the author recalled, "the decay of public virtue and the decline of national prosperity called forth the zeal and energy of the patriarchs of English liberty; of the Hampdens, the Sydneys and the Russels of former times."[11]

Concurrently, Charles James Fox compared Horne Tooke's case to that of Sydney in an address to Parliament, remarking that "the very sound of [Sydney's] name is still animating to every Englishman attached to the glorious cause [of Whiggish freedom]." Fox's remarks were public ones, and it is conceivable that the comparison was a ritualistic one, somehow bound by convention. But Sir Francis Burdett's letter to the banker Thomas Coutts was a simple, private note, and Burdett also compared Tooke to Sydney. And Fox himself remained consistent: in his *History of . . . James II* he expressed the belief that when Sydney's "memory shall cease to be an object of respect and veneration," it would require "no spirit of prophecy to foretell that English liberty [would] be fast approaching to its final consummation."[12]

Pseudonymous "Hampdens" in the 1790's demanded universal suffrage and the abolition of "rotten" Parliamentary boroughs, and scolded the Prince of Wales for his licentious behavior and false "puppet-show of patriotism." Pseudonymous "Sydneys" in the same years praised the conduct of French *philosophe* reformer-revolutionaries, criticized as devastating to "liberty" and the economy the "despotic" war policies of Pitt, condemned the sale of offices, and called for progressive tax policies to compensate for the "inequality of property."[13]

When the Tory Edmund Lodge attacked Sydney's right to "that niche in the Temple of Fame which those who celebrate him in mere shouts to the multitude" had awarded him, he was answered by Dr. Vicesimus Knox, who warned his countrymen to "be upon their guard" against those who would vilify Sydney's name.[14] It is clear that to many Englishmen Sydney's fame was linked to liberty so securely that the slightest anxiety over the security of one suggested an assault upon the other.

Radical Whigs like Francis Horner continued to visit Sydney's "shrine" at Penshurst. Horner "looked upon his image [portrait] with the raptures of a pilgrim" and confessed to John Murray his being "very Whiggish" for disbelieving Dalrymple's evidence. Sydney was "a *martyr*," he added, "and you know my superstition." Sydney's grave was opened in these years (Hampden's some thirty years later). "Curiosity was excited," Mark Noble recalled. "The body was very perfect."[15] When the Rebel-Saint was reinterred, the young Robert Southey penned an "Epitaph on Algernon Sidney" for *The Morning Post*. Southey was still a Radical, as was William Wordsworth, who also praised Sydney in his "Sonnet Dedicated to Liberty" (1802).[16] Radical politicians were seconded, then, by romantic poets.

An interesting example of the affection of the Radical and the romantic for Hampden and Sydney is the case of John Thelwall (see pl. 16). Thelwall was one of those arrested for treasonable activities in 1794. He discussed Sydney with Horne Tooke through the cell windows of the Tower, and both resolved to imitate his behavior. He prepared a speech for his own defense (which on advice of counsel he never delivered, because of its inflammatory nature) in which he intended to quote from the *Discourses* and to praise Hampden. Upon his release, he spoke on behalf of a Scottish radical, one Margot, who had been transported for his work as coordinator of the London and Edinburgh Corresponding Societies, referring to him as "*the Sidney of the British Convention*" and "a second Sidney."[17] His *Poems Written in Close Confinement in the Tower and Newgate* honor the virtuous, simple life of "rustic Liberty" and the "Patriot Heroes." He longed to

> swell to feelings
> but what the breast
> of Hampden or of Sidney might have swell'd.

He penned the London Corresponding Society's "Address to the People of Britain" in 1795, wherein he deplored the impact of the administration's war with France on "the national prosperity, diverted from the healthful channels of trade." This he linked to abuses of civil liberties—interference with Liberty and Property—and added: "Shall these things be done, and seven millions and a half of Britons breathe the same air that animated a Hampden, a Russell, and a Sydney?" His journal, the *Tribune*, was liberally sprinkled with references to the twin patriots. Its last issue in April of 1796 throbs with invocation:

> Spirit of our heroic ancestors, whither art thou flown? Venerable names of *Hampden*, *Pym*, and *Sidney*, have ye lost your charm? . . . No—no ye martyred patriots! . . . With what anguish must we regard a race of

Britons so sunk in vile and cowardly corruption. . . . Tis mercy to your names to hope for annihilation.[18]

In 1797 he rhymed the Radical goals for annual parliaments and universal suffrage and spoke of

> the voice of patriots and martyrs, oft array'd
> at dawn or even-tide, around my couch
> with presence all-inspiring . . .
> Twas for Mankind I suffer'd—for the cause
> For which a Hampden fought, a Sidney bled.

Thelwall named one of his sons Algernon Sydney Thelwall, another John Hampden Thelwall, and addressed lines "To the Infant Hampden":

> . . . Ah! sleep on—
> As yet unconscious of The Patriot's name,
> Or of a patriot's sorrows—of the cares
> For which thy name-sire bled.[19]

For better than two decades Britain fought France virtually without pause, and the twin patriots were sometimes called into service. Their association with the victims of Pitt's repression may have made them a bit dangerous to some, but they were national symbols now, hard to avoid. W. J. Denison's *Address to the People of Great Britain . . .* (1802) asked for unity in wartime "by Hampden's spotless shade . . . by Sydney's scaffold, and by Russell's wreath." *Britons, Strike Home!* (1803), an anonymous broadside, also called for unity and the defense of one's home and family:

> Repel the Foe that desperate dares invade
> The land protected by great SYDNEY'S shade;
> And in the cause for which your HAMPDEN bled,
> Should ev'ry Briton's blood be freely shed.

The Patriot, an anonymous poem published in Edinburgh in 1804 and dedicated to "the Volunteers in Scotland," may serve as another example. This was the work of one indifferent to factional strife. To its author, "INDEPENDENCE, for your country's RIGHT,/ Your homes, your altars, and your ALL you fight." No Jacobin, the author thought Great Britain quite acceptable in its present form: "Your King is just; your Nobles right decree,/ Your laws are equal, and yourselves are free." Stridently Francophobic, he recommended the example of "fearless NELSON" and his predecessors to the Volunteers:

> Your Sires, who erst priz'd Freedom more than life,
> Bend from their spheres, and view th' eventful strife.

> Lo! Wallace [a Scot patriot-symbol], Hambden [sic], Sidney, patriot band,
> Look from yon cloud and wave their shadowy hand,
> T'exalt your courage and inflame your zeal.[20]

Henry Redhead Yorke had remarked on the use of the twin patriots by conservative spokesmen; this may have been just such a case.

To the extent that the Rebel-Saint and the Patriot had been somewhat out of vogue during the war years, the Peninsular campaign brought a change. Samuel Taylor Coleridge maintained that with the appearance of "Spanish patriotism" in 1808 (when Spaniards united in opposition to Napoleon's occupation of their country) Englishmen were enabled "once more to utter the names of our Hampdens, Sidneys, and Russells without hazard of alarming the quiet subject or of offending the zealous loyalist."[21] The British had gone to the aid of the Spanish, provoking Radical Whigs to argue that the physician had best heal himself first. It was very commendable for Britons to aid others grappling with tyranny, "Sidney" maintained in his 1809 *Letters on the Affairs of Spain* . . . , but there were battles to be fought at home as well.[22]

One such occurred the next year, in 1810. John Gale Jones, head of the British Forum, a Radical debating society, had been imprisoned for a libel directed at the House of Commons. Sir Francis Burdett, a member of the Commons, spoke out in Jones's defense and was himself sent to the Tower. Charging the action to be unconstitutional, Burdett became a popular hero and was referred to as "the Hampden of his age." Other, similar instances brought similar comparisons. In 1817 William Cobbett, who sometimes invoked the twin patriots in the pages of his *Political Register*, withdrew to the United States in order to avoid prosecution by the government; he justified his flight by reminding his countrymen that Sydney had entered into self-exile as well to escape tyrannical persecution.

In the same year young Samuel Bamford, an active member of the Hampden Club, was imprisoned for his Radical activities. While in jail he penned impassioned lines to the causes of Reform, sanctified

> By the dear blood of Hampden, shed
> In freedom's noble strife!
> By gallant Sydney's gory head!
> By all that's dear to life![23]

We have already noted the interest shown by Southey, Wordsworth, Coleridge, and Thelwall in the twin patriots. Other literati loved them too. Lord Byron's notes to *Childe Harold* honored Sydney despite Byron's royalist ancestry, and Byron was a member of the Hampden Club. John Keats complained to his family of the lack of principle of reformers like Henry Hunt and Sir Francis Burdett; England, he lamented, was presently without an Algernon Sydney. In 1817 young Thomas Babington Macaulay called on Freedom to continue to

> pour the holy ray
> Which sooth'd the gloom of Sidney's parting day.
> O'er Hamden's life its beams of glory pour'd,
> And hallow'd Milton's life and Marlboro's sword.[24]

Percy Bysshe Shelley wrote in 1812 from Ireland (where he was distributing pamphlets demanding Irish home rule), of the *"good* there is in human nature." But this child of the Enlightenment found little good in either the continuation of what he considered an excessive royal prerogative or the particular monarch who ruled Britain. "[M]y blood boils," he told Elizabeth Hitchener, "to think that Sidney's and Hampden's blood was wasted thus." Several years later Shelley and Thomas Love Peacock considered refusing to pay taxes they considered "illegally imposed." His wife, Mary Wollstonecraft Shelley, conveyed this news to Leigh Hunt, and remarked, "As a prelude to this you must be reminded that Ham[p]den was of Bucks and our two worthies [Shelley and Peacock] want to be his successors."[25] Six months later, the Shelleys and William Godwin, Mary Wollstonecraft Shelley's father, journeyed to Hampden's Monument at Great Hampden to pay their respects. When the officers of the London Hampden Club asked for a copy of one of his pamphlets, Shelley proudly sent ten.[26] Concurrently, Shelley began (but never completed) a play, "Charles the First." Its hero, John Hampden, professed that

> The boundless universe
> Becomes a cell too narrow for the soul
> That owns no master

and gloried in

> the eagle spirits of the free
> . . . which range through heaven and earth
> Like eaglets floating in the heaven of time.[27]

Leigh Hunt, essayist and critic, is still another example of the affinity that liberal English literati felt for the two seventeenth-century patriot-symbols. Hunt learned of Sydney as a half-charity student at Christ's Hospital School in the 1790's. He frequently quoted from the *Discourses* in his periodical, *The Examiner*. Hampden was his hero from childhood as well, and in 1810, he ticked off a list of his "sages." Leading the list of English worthies were Hampden and Sydney. If Hunt's education was at all characteristic of that offered in other British schools in the late eighteenth and early nineteenth centuries (it was certainly characteristic of some), then the use of these patriots by Whigs and workingmen, intellectuals and Luddites, Jacobins and gentlemen becomes more explicable.[28]

Or does it? What did their use signify? And were there really any significant differences among those who venerated the Patriot and the Rebel-Saint? It seems that many of their admirers were either Radical-Whig friends of the working classes or working-class Radicals. The pseudonymous "Sydneys" of the 1790's directed their messages at "the lower class of people, as they are called," warned of the effects war would have on journeymen, members of the building trades, small manufacturers, and the poor, and called for soak-the-rich taxes.[29] Thomas Spence, the son of a netmaker, was certainly both working-class and very radical. And his admiration for the twin patriots was echoed by that of his working-class protegé, Thomas Evans, secretary of the London Corresponding Society and founder of the Society of Spencean Philanthropists. Evans's *Christian Policy, the Salvation of the Empire* (1816) honored Hampden and Sydney as patriots struggling for ancient Anglo-Saxon liberties lost during the Norman conquest; it called for the "restoration" of all land to "the whole people."[30] John Thelwall, whose speeches sometimes drew audiences of over 100,000, noted that his songs "sell like wildfire" among artisans and tradesmen, and these were songs saturated with Hampden-Sydney imagery.[31] There is evidence of significant lower-class affiliation with groups that held high the banner of the twin patriots—the London Corresponding Society, the Friends of Liberty, and the Society for Constitutional Information.[32] And there is evidence of Hampden-Sydney worship among some working-class movements themselves. In May of 1812, in the thick of the Luddite riots, an anonymous Jacobin from Lancaster, signing himself "Tom Paine," announced that "there is a regular, progressive organization of the people going forward. They may be called Hamdenites, Sidneyites, or Paineites," and, though they denied association with the "machine-breakers," they meant to "begin at the Source," and to "*demand* and *command* a redress of our grievances."[33] Later, when ministerial informers trapped a host of lower- and middle-class republicans in the web of the Cato Street Conspiracy, the doomed men called on Brutus, Cassius, Sydney, and "the brave Hamden."[34]

One organization that appears to have drawn members of all social classes together under the roof of one of the twin patriots was the Hampden Club. This locally organized "radical reform" lobby was founded by gentry like Major John Cartwright (see pl. 17) and Sir Francis Burdett, but it drew in many unfranchised tradesmen and artisans responsive to complaints of the "Norman Yoke" and the call for Parliamentary reform and the ballot. The Whiggish toast to "the Cause for which Hampden fell [or bled] in the field, and Sydney [and sometimes Russell] died

ALGERNON SIDNEY.
Execute le 7 Decembre 1683.

Algernon Sidney

In the century after Sydney's death representations of his likeness became increasingly fanciful, exaggerated, romantic. The earliest of these engravings (1) is based on an original portrait and is consequently close to reality, but a French engraving to be found in an eighteenth-century edition of Sydney's *Discourses* takes on a more stylized look (2). The frontispieces to the 1763 Hollis edition and the 1772 Robertson edition of the *Discourses* display similar qualities (3 and 4). The Cipriani-Basire engraving (3) clearly alters the appearance of the Rebel-Saint, bestowing classical Roman properties to the head.

5 The baroquely encompassed Sydney looking down on visitors to Anglesey Abbey was probably commissioned by a Whig grandee in about 1800.

7 The fact that Radicals could also worship Sydney is reflected in an illustration for *A New and Impartial History of England* (1796) by John Baxter, one of the London Corresponding Society members acquitted in 1794 of charges of high treason. Baxter's Sydney takes on the look of a Robin Hood.

6 This ambitious canvas, "The Trial of Algernon Sydney" (ca. 1825), commissioned by still another Whig grandee, was the work of Francis Philip Stephanoff (1788–1860).

8   A Whig grandee commissioned John Downman (c. 1810) to create a version of Sydney's
fellow patriot-martyr, Lord William Russell, bidding adieu to his wife and children. Now
in the possession of Lord and Lady Bedford, Woburn Abbey.

9   Downman's Lord Russell was more re-
alistic (given his subject's age at the time
of execution) than was George Noble's
more romantic engraving for the 1806
edition of Hume's *History of England.*

10

Representations of John Hampden underwent changes similar to those of his fellow Whig patriot-saint, Sydney, in the two centuries following his death. None of the stylized eighteenth- and nineteenth-century versions of "The Patriot" bore any resemblance to such portraits of him as survive. A 1740 print (10) associating Hampden, his motto, his death at Chalgrove Field, and the Magna Charta (the work of the Dutch engraver, J. Houbraken who modeled it after a 1725 engraving by Jean Audran) was widely circulated, and was recast as a plate for Tobias Smollett's *History of England* (1757). It later served as the basis for J. Posselwhite's engraving of Hampden for the Society for the Diffusion of Useful Knowledge in the early nineteenth century (11).

11

12 "Hampden's Burial" (ca. 1870) is the work of P. H. Calderon (1833–98), a member of the Royal Academy.

13 A dramatic statue of The Patriot was erected in the Buckinghamshire county seat of Aylesbury in 1911.

14 Paul Revere's engraving "A View of the Year 1765" depicts "Boston" and "loyal Hampden" (in robes with flint-lock) leading the colonies against the Stamp Act "Tyrant."

15 By the late eighteenth century "the twin patriots" served as patriot-symbols to Whigs *and* Radicals. An engraving of "English Patriots," from a book published in 1795, links Hampden and Sydney to William Pitt the Elder (Lord Chatham) and the Radical London alderman William Beckford, an associate of John Wilkes.

16   John Thelwall, a British admirer of the "twin patriots," in appropriately classical garb.

17   Major John Cartwright, founder of the Hampden Club.

18   Alexander Somerville, a working-class admirer of Hampden.

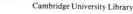

19   Cambridge University Library   20   Cambridge University Library

Depiction of Cromwell underwent a transformation similar to that of Hampden and Sydney over the centuries. Sir Peter Lely's portrait of the Lord Protector "warts and all" (19), was prettied up by the early-nineteenth-century engraver, H. Adlard (20).

British Museum

21   A late-nineteenth-century American engraving of Cromwell shows more signs of change (Justin Winsor, *The Memorial History of Boston* [4 vols., Boston, 1880], 1:348).

22   The Lord Protector's enemies were most irreverent, as this print from James Heath's *Flagellum* (1665) suggests. The artist had, of course, simply borrowed Cromwell's likeness from the Robert Walker portrait and had added a halter. Heath's Latin caption substitutes Cromwell for Sejanus in Juvenal's description of the death of that praetorian leader: "Cromwell is dragged out for all to see. 'What a puss!' 'Look at him!' 'Never think I was a friend of that man!' "

OLIVER CROMWELL.
From a Beautifull Medal by THO: SIMON.

Oliver Cromwell after the death of Charles I, set the Rump Parliament against the Army: for daring to prescribe laws to their Masters, then Enraged the Army against the Rump as betrayers of their trust. At length struck in with the Army, turned the Rump out of doors, and finally, leaving sworn against the government of a single person set up himself as Lord Protector.

British Museum

British Museum

23

24

Throughout the eighteenth and early nineteenth century Cromwell was generally depicted in this same unattractive mode, as tyrant and anti-Christ. James Sayers, a late-eighteenth-century Tory caricaturist, utilizes Cromwell's image in Charles James Fox's mirror (23) to convey his impression of Fox as demagogue in "The Mirror of Patriotism" (1784). Charles Townley's Cromwell (ca. 1801) is a hypocritical tyrant (24).

25   But Townley's engraving was modeled after this "Beautiful medal" by Thomas Simon (ca. 1785), a Staffordshire plaque in the Wheildon tradition. It seems to have been intended to *honor* the Lord Protector, whose reputation was beginning to revive, especially among dissenters (see page 149).

Print Room, Victoria and Albert Museum

26

Ford Madox Brown (1821–93) painted "Cromwell, Protector of the Vaudois" (26) in 1877, three years after completing this scene (27) of a brooding "Cromwell on his Farm." Impressed by Carlyle's *Letters and Speeches of Cromwell*, Brown toured the sites of Cromwell's youth and early manhood in Cambridgeshire and named his first son Oliver in 1855. Brown taught at the Working Men's College, Camden Town.

27

28 By the mid-nineteenth century, as Hampden's and Sydney's reputations waned, Cromwell's waxed. T. Maguire's "Cromwell Refusing the Crown of England" was exhibited throughout England in 1859 and 1860, and was widely and extravagantly praised, as much for its subject as for its artistic merits.

Leutze, *Cromwell and Milton*. In the collection of the Corcoran Gallery of Art

29 Simultaneously, the American artist, Emmanuel Leutze, depicted Cromwell with his family and friends listening to John Milton in the same thoughtful, domestic mood.

30 The religious quality of the renewed attention and respect for Cromwell in the mid-nineteenth century is reflected in Augustus L. Egg's "Night before Naseby" (1859) (see page 150).

31 Another paean to the hero of "the Nonconformist conscience" is "Cromwell at Dunbar" (1859) wherein Cromwell leads his Ironsides in the singing of "Old Hundred."

32

Numerous statues and monuments celebrating the Lord Protector rose throughout England in the late nineteenth century (see pages 156 and 158). The ones appearing here (32 and 33) may be found at Manchester and Westminster.

33

34

Eventually some authors of children's stories (especially Nonconformist authors, but others as well) projected warm images of Cromwell as a model of virtue, as in this illustration (34) in Laurence Peach's *Oliver Cromwell* (1963), and this one (35) in Estelle Ross's *Oliver Cromwell* (1915).

CROMWELL RIDES THROUGH LONDON

35

36 In 1962 the Speaker of the House of Commons opened the Cromwell Museum at Huntingdon to the public; over 150,000 persons had visited it by 1977.

37 This awesome symbol of force, cast against a blood-red battle-scene, was the strikingly appropriate image that served as advertisement for the Columbia film "Cromwell" in 1970.

38

39

William Marshall's allegorical plate for Reverend John Gauden's publication of King Charles I's *Eikon Basilike* (1649) may have been designed by Charles himself (38). It depicts the Royal Martyr, steadfast as the rock battered by the stormy sea, unbowed as the palm tree, setting aside the crown of gold to accept the crown of thorns, in anticipation of the crown of glory. Widely used throughout the seventeenth and eighteenth centuries (M. D. George, *English Political Caricatures* [2 vols., Oxford, 1959], 1: 34–36), it inspired other versions, like this one (39), Faber's "The Blessed King Charles the Martyr" (1717).

40 This mid-nineteenth-century romantic view of "King Charles I on his way to execution" is by Gustav Wappers.

41   This painted-glass version of Washington's ascension into heaven (ca. 1800) is one of
the more fanciful examples of Washington's glorification.

THE PRESENT State of our COUNTRY.

42   Soon after his death Washington was to be invoked by Americans for a host of purposes. Here he speaks from the clouds to feuding Federalists and Democratic-Republicans, a symbol of unity.

This Whig Party banner (43), dating from 1844, links the party and its principles to Washington, as does this 1916 Democratic Party campaign poster (44).

Grand in Peace, Brave in War,
Lovingly in the Hearts of His Countrymen.

First in Peace, First in War,
First in the Hearts of His Countrymen.

Copyright, 1908, by John M. Jones

Copyright, 1908, by John M. Jones

Stuart 1754-1828

45 Similarly, in 1908 William Jennings Bryan sought to identify both his principles and his physical features with those of Washington.

Smithsonian Institution

If the supporters of Abraham Lincoln and the supporters of his successor, Andrew Johnson, had somewhat different views of the federal balance (and I think that they did), then it may be said that Washington's symbolic value was rather ubiquitous by the 1860s. The banner reprinted above (46) was used in the 1860 Lincoln campaign. The banner reprinted below (47) was used by Johnson supporters during the congressional elections of 1866.

Smithsonian Institution

48 "Washington and Lafayette at Mount
Vernon" (1859) by Thomas Rossiter
and Louis Mignot captures the mid-
nineteenth century image of Washington as Virginia gentleman (see page 88).

49 In the early and mid-nineteenth century
a number of sculptors sought to capture
the immortal Washington. An example
of such marmorealizing is Horatio
Greenough's "Washington Renouncing
the Sword," commissioned by the
Congress for the Capitol (but now located in the Smithsonian Institution)
and completed in Italy in 1840, which
utilizes a Greco-Roman toga. Greenough regarded the work variously as
"natural and permanent," "decent,
dignified and simple." Greenough
(b. 1805), a Harvard graduate, Brahmin
Whig, and friend of Robert C. Winthrop, felt that "Washington's face and
form" were "identified with the salvation of our continent," that Washington was both "the old Hero" and "an
agent" (*Letters of Horatio Greenough*,
ed. Nathalia Wright [Madison, Wis.,
1971], pp. 173, 176–77, 194; F. Whittmore, *George Washington in Sculpture*
[Boston, 1933], pp. 47–50).

50 This engraving from John Frost's *Pic-
toral Life of Washington* (1853) is an
example of the nineteenth-century's use
of Washington as a model of virtue for
American youth (see p. 87).

CHARACTER TRAINING

Kenyon-Adams' The George Washington Readers*

Fourth Year *(Thoughtful-
 ness)*   .90
Fifth Year *(Adaptability)*   .90
Sixth Year *(Fidelity)*   .90
Seventh Year *(Self Reliance)* .90
Eighth Year *(Duty)*   .90

Contain well-graded stories selected from the World's Best Literature. These books are designed to inspire Courage, Loyalty, Self-Reliance, Correct Habits, High Ideals and to mould character.

The keynote of our modern education is to train students for life and its problems—Emphasis is placed on training in character. The *"George Washington Readers"* were made expressly for character training.

Character is made up of small duties faithfully performed, of self-denials, of self-sacrifice, of kindly acts of love and duty.   *—Matthews*

To form character is to form grooves in which are to flow the purposes of our lives.
                                —William J. Bryan

Faithfulness in little things fits one for heroism when the great trials come.   *—Louisa M. Alcott*

> Fame is what you have taken,
>   Character's what you give;
> When to this truth you awaken,
>   Then you begin to live.
>   *—Bayard Taylor*

> When wealth is lost, nothing is lost;
> When health is lost, something is lost;
> When character is lost, all is lost.
>   *—School Motto*

51

As the bicentennial of Washington's birth approached, the number of "readers" focusing on the Father of His Country grew. Among them were these "Character Training" readers (51), advertised in Alima Laird's *Complete George Washington Anniversary Programs for Every School Grade: New Ways to Honor The Father of Our Country* (New York, 1931), excerpts from which (52, 53) are offered on the following two pages.

WHAT DO WE SPELL

Characters: Sixteen boys or girls.
Costumes: None.
Staging: Each child holds a large pasteboard letter,
    corresponding with the line that he speaks.

G reat was the hero whose name we shall spell,
E ager to do his work nobly and well.
O rderly, too, in all of his ways.
R ighteous was he to the end of his days.
G ood, we are told, from his earliest youth.
E arnest his efforts for freedom and truth.

W ise with a wisdom sent from above.
A rdent his hope for the country we love.
S trong was his arm when in Liberty's fight.
H onest his purpose that right should be might.
I ndomitable was his courage, we know.
N oble in thought his worthy deeds show.
G rand in the record that's left us to read.
T rue to his God and his country in need.
O bedient ever to duty's command.
N one was so great in all the land.

In Unison And now you may see, when our spelling
            is done,
            We give you the name of good George
            Washington.

WASHINGTON PROGRAM
FOR
THE FOURTH GRADE

A WASHINGTON PLAYLET
One act play for four girls.

A ZEALOUS PATRIOT
Recitation for one boy.

WASHINGTON'S MUSIC
A recitation for three boys.

GEORGE WASHINGTON
Recitation for one girl.

THE MINUET
A dance.

A STORY ABOUT WASHINGTON
Anecdote for one pupil.

GEORGE WASHINGTON
One act play for five boys.

OUR GUIDE
Song for class.

TO LENGTHEN THE PROGRAM

OUR FLAG IS FLOATING TODAY
Recitation for one girl.

NEVER BREAK A PROMISE
Recitation for one boy.

WHAT DID WASHINGTON DO?
Dialogue for two boys and two girls.

53

54   N. C. Wyeth's "In a Dream I met General Washington" (1932) was one
      artist's effort to humanize the hero.

55   Grant Wood appears to be more epigrammatic in "Parson Weem's Fable" (1939).

56 Thomas Jefferson, "The Pride of America" in this early-nineteenth-century engraving by T. Gimbrede, was another important native-born American patriot-symbol.

The Je*ff*ersonian

Issued Monthly by the Democratic Union at 331 Madison Avenue, New York, N. Y.
Application for entry as second-class matter is pending, 20 cents a copy—$2.00 a year.

Volume 1	JULY, 1931	Number 1

57

For over a century Jefferson was widely used by the Democratic Party, as this party newspaper masthead (57) and this convention pass (58) indicate.

58

59 Frank Merrill's engraved version of the tale of Jefferson's tethering his horse to the White House fence, unaccompanied and without fanfare, before taking the oath of office appeared in Tom Watson's biography of Jefferson at the turn of the century. It captures the image of Jefferson popular among his admirers—that is, the image of a simple, rustic antistatist (see p. 97).

60 J.A. Arthur's 1865 engraving of America's "twin patriots" offers the Father of His Country greeting the Savior of the Union.

DRAWN BY ARTHUR I. KELLER.

ABRAHAM LINCOLN'S APPEAL FOR TOTAL ABSTINENCE
At South Fork Schoolhouse, Sangamon County, Illinois, in 1847.

61 Lincoln was an appealing symbol to temperance advocates, as this engraving of Lincoln as Temperance Man for the Reverend Louis Banks's tract, *The Lincoln Legend* (1903), suggests. It is comparable to the several prints of "the Lincoln-Lee Legion," produced by the Abstinence Department of the Anti-Saloon League (ca. 1905).

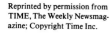

62

*"Just one thing more. If he invokes Lincoln before I invoke
Lincoln, who the hell do I invoke?"*

63

Efforts to identify one's policies with those of Lincoln are common, but potentially dangerous; cartoonists defend against untoward comparisons. William Spencer (62) is on the staff
of *Time*. Donald Reilly's material (63) appears in *The New Yorker*.

64   Daniel Chester French's statue for the Lincoln Memorial (1922) evinces strength and
stability.

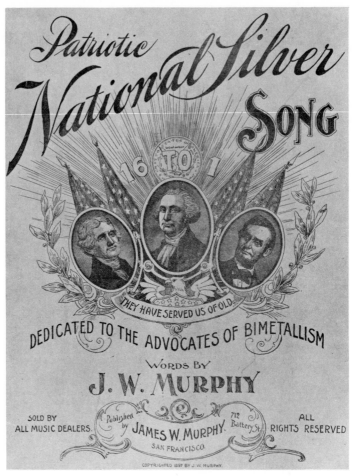

65

Jefferson, Washington, and Lincoln, the central patriot-symbols in America by 1900, were employed by the Populists in 1897 (65) and the Progressives in 1912 (66).

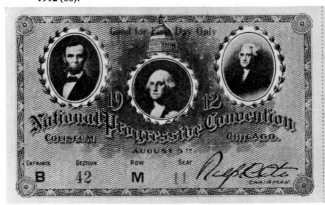

on the scaffold" decorated their publications and was repeated at their meetings. At the names of one or the other of the twin patriots "the youthful bosom" of the junior Hampden Clubber "beats high with the throb of patriotism, and expands with the glow of emulation. Their memory has long been consecrated by freedom and their country; they have been embalmed equally in the poet's lay and the patriot's harangue."[35]

Earlier I mentioned Major Cartwright's claim that the use of Hampden's name was "very instrumental" in gathering more than a million signatures. Cartwright may simply have mistaken support for "radical reform" with affection for his favorite patriot-hero, but if he did, there were others who made the same mistake. A "loyal" Tory address by a group of London merchants and bankers in 1816 complained of the use of Hampden's name by the reform club. "This idol of the people," the address raged, "was a traitor." In 1819 another Tory, the Anglican divine George Burges, damned "the young Hampdens of the country: (Whig reformers upon the radical, I had almost said the revolutionary scale)." These "aristocratical dictators of the Hampden school" were "very foolish and pernicious thinkers." And they had come to that sad state because "for many years past this nation . . . has been nurtured . . . in the very cradle of faction. . . . We have been seduced from our infancy to revere the principles of Milton, of Sydney, of Hampden, of Locke." Burges feared that "by and bye 'the glorious principles for which Hampden fought and Sydney suffered' " might "degenerate" (he was careful not to reject the twin patriots outright) into more "rebellious movements" such as those "for which Catiline was driven headlong from Rome and Caesar lost both his dictatorship and his life."[36]

Burges was clearly exaggerating the *revolutionary* character of "the Hampden school," but it is true that several veterans of the Luddite movement were "the principal leaders in the Hampden Clubs which are now formed in almost every village in the angle between Leicester, Derby and Newark [central England]" (according to one unsympathetic Derbyshire magistrate). "Hampdenism" (as Hampden Club activity was styled by Leicester elites) and "Hampdenites" were associated with "Luddism" and "Spence's Plan [radical land reform]" in 1817, and though the association was unwarranted, it is clear that Leicester and Manchester Hampden Clubbers were lower-middle-class craftsmen, artisans, and shopkeepers.[37]

Moreover, several devotees of the twin patriots in these years of war with France made clear that they were no mere ciphers of the Establishment Whig faction in Parliament. Thomas Lister, speaking through "Hampden," condemned the careless use by the Prince of Wales and the "opposition" party of the twin patriots and "the cause of liberty," a "puppet-shew of patriotism . . . serving but to give a zest to your wine, and evaporating in the quaintness of a toast."³⁸ Similarly, John Thelwall, perhaps the most devoted Hampden-Sydneyite ever to breathe their names, regarded "Whiggism" as a fraud, the high-flown addresses of Whigs and Tories little more than the rhetorical flourish of corrupt, office-hungry "OUTS and INS." Whig administrations of the past had saddled England with debts, a riot act, and a standing army; they had provided no schools, no parliamentary reform, no equitable tax system; they had sought to

> punish the poor journeymen who associate together for the increase of wages, while the rich manufacturers, the contractors, the monopolists of every description may associate as they please; and in their conventions, fix, at their arbitrary will, the prices of the commodities in which they deal.

In the wake of the "Peterloo" massacre in 1819, Thelwall scolded the Whig grandees: "Shall Plebian Reformers alone lift up the congregated voice of remonstrance on this occasion?" Indeed, the only credit Thelwall was willing to offer the Whigs was for their "having stamped with authority and approbation the political speculations of a *Sydney*" and for having "consecrated the memory of the holy martyrs of liberty [Hampden, Sydney, and Russell], engraving them as upon adamantine pillars in the temple of eternal fame and virtue; where to the end of time they will receive the veneration of mankind."³⁹

Many lovers of the twin patriots, then, clearly identified with "the People." But others either did not, or did so only with some trepidation and reserve, and very few were firebrand revolutionaries. Perhaps it was only discretion that caused the "Hampden" who criticized the Pitt administration in the *Morning Chronicle* in 1794 to deny that he was a republican, only discretion that caused John Millar, the "Sydney" of the following year, to deny that he was a leveller while he called for progressive taxation. But Millar quoted his friend, Adam Smith, no fast friend of Populism, as his authority. Millar was clearly an antistatist and a reformer, but he bore the unmistakable "air of the high-bred gentleman."⁴⁰ Samuel Ferrand Waddington, whose "Algernon Sidney" criticized Edmund Burke's conservative political philosophy, nonetheless restricted himself to orderly, "gradual reform." Francis Horner, Sydney Smith, Thomas Campbell, and Henry Brougham, the reform-minded founders of the Whiggish *Edinburgh Review* and admirers of the twin patriots, favored civil liberties, religious equality, and public education, but were never advocates of democracy. James Perry, the middle-class Whiggish editor of the *Morning Chronicle*, friend of Fox, Sheridan, Leigh Hunt, Thomas Campbell, and other avid Hampden-Sydneyites, and one of the founding members of the Hampden Club, made it clear that he was "no Jacobin," and pooh-poohed significant electoral reforms. The London Hampden Club reports themselves maintained that "the Hampden Association is composed of Noblemen and Gentlemen." ("The people" belonging to the Club, being unfranchised, were permitted to petition separately.) Major Cartwright, a "perfect gentleman of dignified and graceful deportment" (pl. 17), was convinced that British "Democracy" had none of the demagogic traits of its Continental fellows. He believed, with the American, Thomas Jefferson, in a "natural aristocracy," "disinterested," devoted to "the public good." And he explicitly rejected the Luddites and made clear that he was not directing his efforts at the working class alone. Sir Francis Burdett, "the Hampden of his age," angered the throngs that lined the streets of London upon his release from the Tower when he left quietly by the Tower's riverine rear door, thus avoiding the press of "the mob" in the streets. Burdett's case, moreover, was concerned with the privileges of Commons members; it did not involve questions of the suffrage or the "rotten boroughs." And if Burdett was initially close to the Radical reformers, he had done some backing and filling by the late 1830's, for he then became a Tory.[41]

Samuel Taylor Coleridge, another Hampden-Sydney devotee, had no patience with "the disgusting Trash of Westminster Meetings." His brand of reform was of the conservative, "respectable" sort, "as different from the vulgar seditions of Corresponding Societies and Manchester Clubs as A[lgernon] Sidney from Horne Took[e]." To Coleridge, Sydney stood for freedom, but "only freedom for gentlemen." Coleridge consistently invoked the twin patriots in his support of bills to abolish slavery, but he considered the thesis of the *Discourses* to have consisted of the maxim that "the men . . . are made for the state, not the state for the men."[42]

The Benthamite advocate of Parliamentary reform, George Meadley, planned a biography of Hampden, and actually completed one of Sydney in 1813. Meadley stressed Sydney's devotion to individual liberties and retold all of the myths the eighteenth century had supplied. Unlike the "moderates" of the preceding generation, he found Sydney's "enthusiasm" quite delightful. Reflecting the romanticism of his day, Headley imagined Sydney's heart to have been "vibrating with the most exquisite feelings."[43] At the same time, however, Meadley made it clear that Sydney's sensitivities were not "common." His "opinion of the dignity of human nature" was "too lofty a freedom for the passions and prejudices of the mass." Meadley's Sydney was antityrannical, but aristocratic. Note the drift of Meadley's invocation:

> If . . . the despotic prince and the profligate minister shall again prompt the patriot of noble birth to do or die for his country, then may the image of Algernon Sydney rise up to his admiring eye, and . . . fortify his spirit.[44]

Such language must have had its appeal to solid Whigs like Lord John Russell, who had words of praise for Sydney's "uncommon" spirit,[45] but it would not have inspired the Cato Street conspirators.

Even John Thelwall had his limits. Sharply critical of Marat and Robespierre in 1795, he rejected William Cobbett and Henry Hunt as "agitators" in 1819, on the eve of the "Peterloo" massacre. "To vulgarize," he opined, "is not to emancipate mankind." These "advocates of scurrility, malevolence, and tumultuary violence are not the Friends of Freedom." Describing himself now as a "Radical Reforming Whig," he praised the work of Sir Francis Burdett in the uncommon Commons and, calling the twin patriots to mind, allowed that "the people" were "worthy" of their "illustrious Whigs of old." And he was truly surprised when the Duke of Bedford, patriarch of Lord William Russell's descendants, declined to join him in a critique of the government's heavy hand at "Peterloo."[46]

Thelwall's language constituted no rejection of a proletarian tradition, for he was without one; he was the son of a "highly respectable" Anglican silk-mercer (pl. 16). Thelwall's sons, Algernon Sydney and John Hampden, both attended Trinity College, Cambridge (the well-endowed intellectual home of Radical Whigs), as did John Cam Hobhouse, John Hampden Gurney (b. 1803), and Russell Gurney (b. 1805), brothers of Sidney Gurney (b. 1800). Thomas Lister ("Hampden" in 1797) was an Oxford graduate and Staffordshire magistrate. Samuel Bamford's father was the manager of a cotton textile mill. Cartwright, Horner, Burdett, Fox, and Hunt were the sons of landed gentry or wealthy merchants, as was Thomas Campbell, whose *Pleasures of Hope* (1799) celebrated the patriotism of Hampden and Sydney. Samuel Rogers, whose hero in *Human Life* (1819) emulated Hampden, Sydney, and Russell, was the well-to-do son of a merchant. Even the unfortunate leader of the Cato Street Conspiracy, Arthur Thistlewood, was of well-to-do yeoman stock.[47]

A scanning of the 18,000 names of late eighteenth- and early nineteenth-century graduates in *Graduati Cantabrigienses*, of the London Post Office's *Law Directory* of 1851 for the 4,700 names of solicitors, barristers, and attorneys active in the mid-nineteenth century, of the manuscript census records for the 250,000 names of residents of Notting-ham and of the East (lower-class) and West (upper-middle-class) Ends of London, of *Who Was Who, 1897–1916*, of the *Dictionary of National Biography Supplement*, and of the Home Office's lists of 4,000 convicts transported to New South Wales in the late eighteenth and early nineteenth centuries indicates that the upper middle classes were five to ten times more likely to give their children patriotic names (be they John Hampden, Algernon Sydney, or Horatio Nelson) than were the lower or lower middle classes.[48] Radicals and Liberals might join Whigs in idolizing the memory of Algernon Sydney in this fashion; the common folk but rarely.[49] John Dobell, the author of *Man Unfit to Govern Men*, married the daughter of a leading London Radical; their first son, born in 1824, was named after the Rebel-Saint. John Hampden Snowden (b. 1828), the son of a well-to-do Taunton gentleman, was educated at Eton and University College, Oxford, and became Prebendary at St. Paul's Cathedral. Syd-ney Grundy (b. 1848) was the son of the mayor of Manchester. Algernon Sydney Aspland's father was a barrister; he became a barrister himself. The classicist John Hampden Haydon (b. 1840) was "of gentle birth," as were Algernon Sidney (b. 1803), a Parliamentary agent at Lincoln's Inn Fields, Sydney Evershed (b. 1825), Sir Sydney Hedley Waterlow (b. 1822), Sydney Owen (b. 1827), Sir Sydney Webb (b. 1816), Sidney Paget (b. 1860), and Sydney Oliver (b. 1859). Other examples might be given, but nearly all would be from the upper and middle classes. Either the lower classes felt that bestowing the name of a noble patriot on one of their off-spring would be regarded as overreaching and pretentious, or they were simply uninterested in such patriot-symbols as impressed the elite. The endless recurrence of such names as Sarah, Jane, Elizabeth, Mary, Robert, Henry, Thomas, John, and William suggest that local, family traditions were more powerful than the more cosmopolitan impulses that moved the elite to honor patriotic names. It is certainly conceivable that some of these lower-middle-class folk who named their children Elizabeth, Henry, or William were inspired by what C. S. Forester called the "flavour of association with the Royal Family."[50] But, for whatever reason, be it deference or lack of interest, lower- and lower-middle-class English fam-ilies appear to have behaved in the same fashion as their American coun-terparts (see page 67). Patriot-symbols appear to be the property of the elite, at least insofar as the naming of children is concerned.

In 1899 Earl Barnes surveyed the opinions of several thousand Lon-don School Board children (chiefly lower-middle-class) aged eight to thirteen and compared their responses to those of children from a school "located in a better part of London, having a superior staff of teachers." When asked to name a "famous person" they would "most want to be like" the children from the "better school" gave the names of historical or national patriot figures, rather than local or family ("acquaintance") figures, significantly more often than did their lower-class London contemporaries.[51] As Barnes put it, the more affluent children were "dropping their local ideals and taking on their larger ideals more rapidly, year by year, than the children in the average London school" (see Table 6.1). It appeared to Barnes that "the great men and women" who had "made England's name glorious" had "no very intimate place in the hearts of the Board School children of London."[52]

Table 6.1. Ideals of Children by Age and Socioeconomic Cast of School District, London, 1899

	Age					
Ideal	8	9	10	11	12	13
Acquaintance						
All-London	46%	45%	31%	19%	17%	14%
Special school	38	22	20	18	12	7
Historical or public character						
All-London	21	15	28	45	53	56
Special school	50	62	52	55	62	63

Source: Earl Barnes, "Children's Ideals," *Pedagogical Seminary* 7 (1900): 8–9.

Other evidence might be offered, but perhaps the point has been made—many of those who left records of their devotion to Hampden or Sydney were not truly "of the people." Many Luddites and laborers may well have admired the twin patriots too, but the more passionate admirers were generally gradualists, more "radical" in many cases than the eighteenth-century "moderate men" who had enshrined the twin patriots, but only rarely the revolutionary republicans that they may have seemed to distraught royalists.

Some of the reasons for the popularity of the twin patriots have been suggested—the advent of "Jacobinism" in England, with attendant anxieties about the fate of civil liberties; the impact of the Industrial Revolution on a hard-pressed artisan class eager for political rights; romanticism, with its affection for "Liberty" and patriot-heroes of the past; and, above all, the coming-to-age of a philosophy of individualism. Perhaps a marginal economy finds it more difficult to produce devotees of "the dignity of man" or "the love of liberty," for its members are simply too busy trying to survive. Flourishing economies would appear to be more likely to nourish the creed of "freedom from Government," and the members most likely to hold that creed are the economy's more prosperous ones. If revolutions occur in periods of rising expectations, so do symbols of freedom. Hampden and Sydney had themselves been economically independent; so were many of their admirers in the eighteenth and nineteenth centuries. "In some eyes the love of liberty is paramount to every other passion," a Hampden Club official wrote in his *Sketch of the Life of John Hampden*. But paramount chiefly to those unfettered by the passions of hunger or cold.[53] The anonymous bard who penned *The Patriot* in 1804 praised "Hampden, Sidney, patriot band," who "erst priz'd Freedom more than life"; he then exalted "Commerce," "blooming Labour," "the busy hum of Industry," and "thy merchants . . . enriching and enrich'd." The struggle raging with France on "old Ocean . . . Pregnant with weath," was for "the wealth of ages." But the pecuniary motive was entwined with a defense of "INDEPENDENCE" and "priz'd Freedom," and necessarily so, for the bard clearly regarded freedom and prosperity to be interdependent:

> Long may [Britain's] sons, with shining virtues crown'd,
> For courage, skill, and industry renown'd,
> To distant realms and future ages show
> What giant energies from Freedom flow.[54]

There does not appear to be any evidence of a conscious struggle in these years for possession of the patriot-martyrs. Nonconformist Radicals and conservative Anglican Whigs both managed to venerate the twin patriots without displaying any particular sense of discomfort with the other's use of these patriot-symbols. Indeed, Major Cartwright's use of "the Patriot's" name may have served to *unite* the gentleman Whig reformer, the Benthamite, the romantic, the Nonconformist, and the lower-middle-class democrat on one point—the antityrannical nature of British patriotism. High birth was not essential; "virtue" displayed in the defense of "liberty" was the key mark of distinction. On this most of Cartwright's Hampden Club colleagues were in agreement.[55] And Hampden and Sydney were considered the models of the virtuous patriot. They had defended British rights against tyrants. They had been totally "disinterested." If they had interpreted the law to encompass unwritten, higher human prerogatives than the king's courts would allow, that was to be expected, for they had something about them that was "sublime."[56] Like Shelley's Hampden, they were "the eagle spirits of the free," soaring above a libertarian, antistatist culture that gazed rapturously upon them from a land writhing in industrial and social change.

The "Peterloo" massacre of 1819 brought the reformers back to earth, but their affection for the twin patriots survived. Hampden and Sydney continued to be invoked throughout the early nineteenth century in election speeches, journals, novels, poems, and plays. The young Robert Browning, the young Alfred Tennyson, and a host of other novelists and poets celebrated their virtues.[57] Radicals such as William Hone and Richard Carlile, liberal Whigs like Thomas Babington Macaulay, John Cam Hobhouse, Lord Brougham, and Lord Nugent wielded the names of "our great watchwords of liberty" on behalf of Parliamentary reform, freedom of the press, temperance, abolition of slavery in the West Indies, and a host of other causes. The *Westminster Review* noted that, were the nation to adopt the philosophy and attendant public policies of Jeremy Bentham, "Hampden and Sydney will not have died in vain."[58] Pseudonymous "Hampdens" and "Sydneys" now spoke of the dangers of "Popery," the need for church democracy, the "deception" of "our present circulating money," the virtues of republics, the rights of artisans, the cause of "radical" Parliamentary reform, and the "tyrannical" exclusion of Lord Byron's monument from Westminster Abbey.[59]

By the 1830's, then, it appeared that "the twin patriots" were held in fond regard by Whigs and Radicals alike, their reputations secure. Just as Leigh Hunt, John Cam Hobhouse, and their generation had learned of Hampden and Sydney in late-eighteenth-century schools and publications, so future Chartists, trade unionists, and Anti-Corn Law Leaguers learned of them in their early-nineteenth-century cultural milieu, as orators, poets, essayists, and artists held these twin "watchwords of liberty" up for emulation. Alexander Somerville remembered learning to admire Hampden from the "reform" newspapers in 1831 while he was a young laborer. Chartist Robert Lowery read of them as a boy in William Godwin's *History of the Commonwealth of England*. "Our own Sidney, Hampden, and Russell were my heroes," he later recalled.[60]

This generation of Hampden-Sydneyites invoked the twin patriots no less often than had Hollis, Fox, or Thelwall. Somerville recalled casting himself as Hampden in his colleague's struggle with the "tyrannical" stonemasons. Lowery compared the Rebel-Saint to the Tolpuddle martyrs and the "Peterloo" heroes. His message: "Be true to the unions" and "all would be well." In 1834 Ebenezer Elliott, "the Anti-Corn-Law poet" praised the "race of Englishmen born in Hampden's dwelling place," and warned "despots" that "by the death which Hampden died," Englishmen would "tame your pride—stormily, or tranquilly." Five years later he rhymed for "labour in despair," and recalled the twin patriots: "Who would not die as Hampden died,/ That looks on Sidney's grave?"[61]

In the same year, 1839, the year that Chartism experienced its first real test, Bronterre O'Brien and William James Linton also invoked the twin patriots in editorials with a "physical force" ring to them. An 1841 editorial by Linton compared Hampden's resistance to Charles I with the resistance contemporary British workingmen were offering to "class legislation."[62] *The Penny Magazine* offered Posselwhite's engraving of Hampden. "A London Chartist" reminded his colleagues in 1841 of "lion-hearted Hampden." That same year "a Bristol Radical" offered the readers of *McDouall's Chartist Journal and Trade's Advocate* a play, "Electioneering," in which "Hampden" and "Sydney" stood as Radical candidates. This playwright's "Hampden" was no friend to the established order, for, as he put it, "we must have such a House of Commons as will make the Whigs look as pale as death upon the black horse." "Hampden" would "help the poor and those that are in trouble," the hero (a shoemaker) maintained.[63] When Chartist organizer Thomas Cooper was imprisoned in 1843, fellow Chartists in Leicester formed a "Hampden Section" to continue his political activities. Simultaneously, Chartist Henry Vincent, lecturing at Leeds, recalled "generous-hearted and cool-headed John Hampden," the "mention of whose name was enough to awaken the patriotic feelings of every English heart." George J. Holyoake, an Owenite rationalist, had kind words for the deistic Sydney in 1846. Charles Kingsley's "Alton Locke," a fictional Chartist "tailor and poet," dreamed of Magna Charta, Hampden, and the Charter while imprisoned in 1848.[64] Thomas Cooper and John Alfred Langford recalled the days of yore:

> freedom's holiest time
> when loving Hampden breathed his words of energy and fire
> when mighty Cromwell drew the sword, and Milton struck the lyre.

In the same year (1850) the *Working Man's Friend and Family Instructor* ran articles on Hampden, Sydney, and Russell, "noble-minded men," true "champions of liberty." *The Star of Freedom*, a republican journal, linked "the [blessed] names of HAMPDEN, PYM, and VANE" in 1852 to criticism of slavery and oppressive factory conditions. And two years later W. J. Linton's *The English Republic* attacked the "tyranny" of an unrepresentative Parliament and invoked the "Spirit of Wyckliffe, of Hampden, and of Milton," and the *People's Paper* serialized "The Trial of Sydney the Patriot."[65]

These were no Whig pamphleteers nor gentlemen reformers; they were generally middle- and lower-middle-class tradesmen and artisans. All were democrats; many were republicans. And their Hampden, Sydney, Pym, and Vane were no heroes of a Whiggish "Glorious Revolution," but "Heroes of the English Commonwealth."

The shoemaker-Chartist, Thomas Cooper, may serve as an example. His *Commonwealthsman, or Chartist Advocate* presented "the cause for which Hampden bled in the field, and Sydney died on the scaffold" as its motto and offered biographical sketches of Hampden, Pym, and Sir John Eliot in 1842. One of his poems, "A Chartist Song," called on "Labour's Children" to sing

> For the high foe of Wrong, great Hampden, a song
> The fearless and the sage!
> Who, at king-crafts' frown, the gauntlet threw down,
> And dared the tyrant's rage;
> Who away the scabbard threw, when the battle blade he drew,
> And with gallant heart led on!
> How he bravely fell, our children shall tell,
> When a thousand years are gone!

Cooper's Workingmen's Clubs held classes for young workers which he named for "the worthies of Old England" (who were all of the Commonwealth era): the "John Hampden Class," the "Algernon Sydney Class," the "Andrew Marvell Class," etc. When Cooper was imprisoned in 1843, he planned a dramatic trilogy, "The Commonwealth," which was to have centered upon Hampden, Cromwell, and Sydney, and he penned a popular "Ode to Liberty." Cooper warned therein against the use of physical force—"the pike, the brand, the blaze"—most unBritish means, he maintained, for effecting revolution—yet he called on "Liberty" to bring forth a new breed of Sydneys from the womb, "or wake our fathers from the tomb!" Elsewhere he invoked the "true-born Briton's darling champion," and appealed to the working classes to secure "the Toiler's Rights." He applauded the newly constructed monument to Hampden at Chalgrove Field and called for a similar memorial to Shell, the Chartist hero of the Newport Rising of 1839. He compared the twin patriots to Thomas Paine, William Cobbett, Feargus O'Connor, and other contemporary "friends of liberty." He recalled the "day in which Englishmen awoke and broke the power of a Crowned hypocrite," the "day when Hampden led the patriot hosts." And he was persuaded that "the blood of Hampden and Sydney" called Englishmen to do their part "to render the future England, and yourselves, worthy of such glorious memories."[66]

Whiggish gentry and aristocrats who venerated the twin patriots often had a quite different image. Attorney-biographer John Forster's Sydney was "gallant" and "chivalrous"; his Hampden, "the high-bred English gentleman, calm, courteous, reticent, self-possessed," was a "leader and governor of men." To Forster, a friend of Charles Dickens, Hampden's "love for all men and for all good and graceful things" were the qualities that "made Hampden a patriot." Little or nothing was made of the twin patriots' resistance to "unlawful oppression" or their "love of the People," qualities that Chartists saw in them.[67]

Edwin Paxton Hood, a middle-class, mid-century admirer of "England's great political martyr, Algernon Sydney," was troubled by the "noisy and illiterate demagogues" who stirred "the people" to action. He preferred the "illustrious names" that "adorn our library," Milton and Sydney, "apostles of liberty . . . deserving of the profoundest study."[68] Similarly, when Anti-Corn-Law Leaguers and some Chartists condemned the great landowners for high prices and unfair treatment of agricultural laborers and tenant farmers, Sir Edward Lytton Bulwer-Lytton defended his fellow landowners before a Hertfordshire Agricultural Society dinner, and identified their cause with Hampden and Pym, "names forever dear and sacred to every class and every party—the plain country gentlemen of England (loud cheers)."[69]

Sydney figures as the hero of Emma Robinson's well-bred novel, *Whitefriars* (1844), but he is not the Sydney of Chartist devotees. His "open and constitutional" motives are distinguished from Lord Shaftesbury's "dark and violent" ones. Sydney tells his friends, "I am no mutiny-stirrer." He is made to appear altogether innocent of the charges at his trial ("the brightest and saddest of the great martyrology of English liberty"). The foe both of Charles II's tyranny and Shaftesbury's plotting, Sydney emerges as the nineteenth-century laissez-faire liberal that Emma Robinson so admired.[70]

The same could be said of John Minter Morgan's *Hampden in the Nineteenth Century*. This dialogue between "John Hampden," an imaginary descendant of the Patriot, and his friends reveals the new "Hampden" and a friend, "Mr. Sidney," to be genteel Owenite reformers. "Hampden's" wife tells him that he has become a moderate man. An admirer of Lord Brougham's education reform proposals, Morgan's "Hampden" hopes they will "help prevent occasional ebullitions dangerous to the peace" and provide "order."[71] "Hampden's" views would hardly have endeared him to many Chartists.

George Grenville, Lord Nugent, is another example of the genteel Whig devotee of the twin patriots. Nugent (b. 1789) was the second son of the Marquis of Buckingham and a resident of Hampden's corner of England. At Oxford he associated with Brougham, Samuel Romilly, and other young Whig grandees. Fond of reciting "the old Whig toast" to the twin patriots, he clearly cherished the Patriot from Buckinghamshire. In 1828, in the company of a number of other prominent barristers and sergeants-at-law, he opened Hampden's tomb, examined the remains, cut off some locks of the Patriot's hair, and described the incident for *Gentleman's Magazine*. Four years later, while a Junior Lord of the

Treasury in Lord Grey's Whig government, he was interviewed by Benjamin Robert Haydon, who described him:

> He is of race, and looks like a noble. His manners are graceful and commanding. . . . He took down with the grace of high birth a print of Hampden, which hung in an old English frame, and presented it to me, writing his name on the back. He said some capital things.[72]

The occasion for Haydon's interview was the publication of Lord Nugent's two-volume life of the Patriot, the culmination of the work Nugent's Benthamite friend George Meadley had begun. Nugent's Hampden was a model Whig, "practically wise and industrious," opposed to any government infringements on personal liberty or "the rights of property," and bountifully endowed with "patient discretion." Nugent juxtaposed this image to those of Wat Tyler and the French revolutionaries; Hampden, less rude, democratic, and violent, was much to be preferred. Needless to say, Lord Nugent was present when John Henry Foley's statue of Hampden, the Patriot, was unveiled in St. Stephen's Hall, Westminster, in 1847.[73] Thus, Nugent was in every regard the counterpart of Robert C. Winthrop in his conservative zeal for the Patriot.

To Whigs, Anti-Corn-Law Leaguers, many Chartists and Dissenters, and to other Englishmen as well, Hampden and Sydney continued to be symbols of antistatism, freedom from tyrannical government interference. Ebenezer Eliott used them in a critique of the window tax. Charles Kingsley linked Hampden to "freedom, progressive, expanding, descending," the "glory and the strength of England." John Landseer's "Algernon Sydney" was the Ned Ludd of the London Art Union, condemning the electrotype process as a violation of copyright privileges. The anonymous "Hampden" who appealed to mid-century "Wesleyan reformers" objected to the Wesleyan Conference of 100 ministers that ruled "with a rod of iron. You are its slaves." He counseled lay Wesleyans to withhold financial support until given the right to participate in church decision-making: "Tyrants must be checked. . . . The age of priestcraft is gone—gone forever. The people will not consent to be slaves!"[74]

William Howitt's "John Hampden, Jr." was an Anti-Corn-Law advocate of laissez-faire who objected to taxes as "an incubus on our manufacturing exertions." "John Hampden the Younger," the anonymous author of *An Income Tax: A Remedy for all Political and Social Abuses* (1848), was an anti-Chartist, Peelite reformer. An admirer of Adam Smith and Jeremy Bentham, he was annoyed by special privilege, and regarded all sales and excise (indirect) taxes as inequitable, levied as they were on needs rather than abilities. John Minter Morgan's love of Hampden and Sydney was matched only by his regard for Jeremy Bentham. It was Daniel Eaton, a close confidant of Bentham, who had, earlier in the century, published the first inexpensive edition of Sydney's *Discourses* in weekly installments (sixpence a week) with the hope that by "dispassionately" reading Sydney, the middle and lower middle classes would see that "as self is the first principle of every individual," laissez-faire political systems were much to be preferred to all others.[75]

Whig grandees and Luddites, Hampden Clubmen and Cato Street Conspirators, had shared "our watchwords of liberty" in the early nineteenth century. Liberals, Utilitarians, Anti-Corn Law Leaguers, and Chartists shared them in the 1820's, '30's, and '40's. But within a generation Hampden's and Sydney's reputations were in sharp decline, and by 1900 they had nearly vanished from the culture. The forces that tore them loose from the hearts of reform-minded Englishmen were some of the same forces that simultaneously lifted Oliver Cromwell to the fore.

As time passed, and a pragmatic, "natural-leader" Whiggery drew many middle-class Radical Englishmen away from their Chartist, working-class, democratic allies, the more democratic devotees of the twin patriots became more and more uneasy about the common heritage. At first the democrats and republicans, as had Radicals like Thelwall and Lister before them, sought to oust the Whigs from any claim to the twin patriots. In 1818 Richard Carlile criticized Henry Brougham and other Establishment defenders of "natural leaders" (Brougham's phrase) and "blind Patriotism" (Carlile's term), while praising Cartwright and other "Reformados," the true heirs of the Patriot:

> Rise again, thou shade of HAMPDEN!
> Teach us once again the way
> To foil villains, to foil tyrants,
> And Establish Freedom's sway.

In 1820 *The Black Dwarf* insisted that "the spirit of Hampden is not extinct, though it may have left its immediate descendants." The republican Carlile was after Brougham and the "damned Whigs" again in 1833, and was critical of their misuse of his saints:

> Why think you [Brougham], have the present [Whig] ministers throughout their lives toasted the names of Hampden, Russell and Sydney? Why, but that Hampden took the field against Charles the First and was in that field wounded to death; and Russell and Sydney conspired against James the Second—either of them a much better man than is now on the throne of England.[76]

But the Whigs, it appears, had no intention of surrendering their patriot-martyrs. Eventually the democrats and republicans themselves began to fall away. Six months after he had flung the names of Hampden, Russell, and Sydney at his Whig foes Carlile was counseling his allies to forget them.

> There must be no constitution nonsense . . . nothing Whiggish . . . no demagogue trash—no toasting of "Hampden that died in the field, and Russell and Sydney on the scaffold." That was all very well in its day; but that day has gone by, not again to return.

Carlile preferred a figure more symbolic of "solid political principles"; one that allowed for no "distinction of classes by birth, or property, or title"; one who could be admired by trade unionists. Thomas Paine was his man.[77]

Democrats and republicans did not uniformly follow Carlile's lead in opting for Paine, but many did, and others were visibly troubled by a sense of the growing irrelevance of the twin patriots. Whereas Whigs tended to stress the ancient and hence, the irrevocable character of the Anglo-Saxon "constitution," Chartists tended to reject such ultimately antidemocratic appeals to the past and to derive their political theory from *a priori* reasoning. Thus though the chairman (a brushmaker) and the secretary (a silk weaver) of the Kettering Radical Association quoted from "the truly great Algernon Sidney" on the question of the aristocracy (the "Norman Yoke") in their 1839 presentation of "the Just Claims of the Working Classes," they must have sensed the tenuous relevance of Sydney to the matters at hand in 1839 for they declined to base their case on such evidence, "amidst the dust and cobwebs of antiquity." "Every generation" had both "the capacity and the right of acting for itself." When "any given mode of conduct" was propounded, the correct question to ask was "not how far does it accord with the customs of our ancestors, but how far is it in accordance with justice, and sound policy." John Collins, a Birmingham working-class Chartist, advocated cooperation in 1840 with enlightened members of the middle class but he had no use for their books. The "middle and higher classes" were "notoriously ignorant of the opinions and feelings and labels of the working classes." Collins probably did not spend much time quoting from Sydney's *Discourses on Government*.[78]

Lord William Russell, Sydney's colleague, came in for a few body blows as well. Chartist G. W. M. Reynolds's "People's Edition" of *The Ryehouse Plot* avoided any mention of the Rebel-Saint but was merciless with his fellow martyr, probably because Russell was the venerable ancestor of the hated Home Secretary in 1839, Lord John Russell. Reynolds's

Lord William Russell, had "no genius, and only mediocre talents." His "liberality" was "essentially aristocratic":

> He did not see that it was precisely the same to the people whether they were held subservient to the will of a monarch defying an aristocracy, or the will of an aristocracy, holding the monarchy in check. . . . If he had possessed the power of carrying out his aims, the Aristocracy would alone have benefited—the people would have been enslaved.

Reynolds explained that he had gone to some lengths in his critique of Lord Russell because "history has generally depicted him as an ardent liberal of even a democratic class; and popular error, down to the present day, has clung to the belief, fostering and perpetuating it."[79] This was pretty close to the mark, and if it is at all representative of what Chartists and other Britons were thinking, then the decline of Russell's more illustrious patriot colleagues is understandable.

The Poor Man's Advocate had praise for both Nelson and Napoleon, but no apparent interest in either Hampden or Sydney, probably because its editors were disgusted by what they called the Whiggish "burlesque upon liberty." ("Talk of British freedom!")[80] There was no mention of either Hampden or Sydney in Henry Hetherington and William Lovett's *Working Men's Association Gazette*, in *The English Chartist Circular*, or in *The Bread Eater's Advocate and National Daily Bread Society's Journal*. Ernest Jones had nothing to say of Hampden or Sydney in his *Notes to the People* (1851–52). His heroes were the less well-heeled Spartacus and Heraclides of Syracuse. And his advice may explain his lack of interest in the twin patriots: "Never trust a rich man as the poor man's advocate. Never trust another class, working man, to achieve the rights of your own."[81]

As late as 1850 William Howitt continued to claim the twin patriots among his list of fifteen patriots "of the people" (as opposed to the five patriots he allowed that the nobility had sired). But in the same month the Chartist journal that carried his article included a warning to "Distrust the 'liberals!' History hath proven them to be the deadly enemies of the people." A week later the anonymous Chartist poet who invoked "our martyrs" omitted Sydney and linked the name of Hampden to a Chartist hero, one Fitzgerald. Moreover, he chose a pseudonym increasingly popular among social democrats—"Spartacus."[82]

With the passing of Chartism, neither Hampden nor Sydney served again as champions of the people. They had seen their last masters of the radical left. Thomas Attwood, the banker and Radical M.P., resigned from the chairmanship of the Birmingham Political Union in the critical year of 1839, explaining that he was too much of a moderate to be comfortable at the head of a powerfully Chartist organization. He was satisfied that political reform could proceed quite well without all the talk of the use of physical force that he was hearing. He would remain true to the spirit of Hampden.[83]

Attwood's association of moderation with "the immortal Patriot" anticipated precisely Hampden's characterization by late-nineteenth-century Britons. Thus Oxford don Arthur Butler urged Englishmen in 1874 to embrace "with reverence" the "Hampdens," the "moderate party of all ages," representative as they were of the "purer virtues," and to "recoi[l] from the picturesque attractions of a strong Government, whether of Absolute Monarchy [Charles I] or Military Despotism [Cromwell]."[84] The Tory Anglican Reverend A. D. Crake warmed to "the gallant Hampden," a "moderate Churchman," and made him the hero of his novel *Fairleigh Hall* (1882). Another Anglican divine, Reverend William Selwyn, assumed the Patriot's name in his pseudonymous critique in 1869 of a bill to disestablish the Church of England in Ireland.[85]

Other late-nineteenth-century Hampden admirers were gentry who remained true to localistic, antistatist values. Thus the anonymous Anglican critic of the "despotic" London School Board in 1876 who signed himself "John Hampden, Ratepayer," regarded the publicly funded education of all children to be "oppressive Taxation," "Compulsion," and the School Board comparable to "the old Star Chamber." Such "Centralization and Uniformity" were contrary to the "voluntary principle," the "genius of this free people." The Hampden of the 1630's who had "defied the . . . shipmoney," were he "alive now," would have "denounced this unconstitutional demand for schoolmoney." The whole "fantastic and extravagant" theory was a product of "the land of the Barnums," and had been sponsored by so-called "advanced Liberals" oblivious to the "mischief" and "dangerous" consequences to "the natural leaders" of such education:

> It is usually wrong . . . to rob a clerk . . . of his hard earnings and to prevent him sending his children to a proper school, in order to give a first class education, full of "ologies" and "ometries" to the children of the chimney-sweep. . . . That is bad enough in all conscience! But what I want to know is—where are we to find the chimney-sweeps of the future? . . . Tell the young sweeps that much learning is their birthright . . . and soot will never suit them, and we shall come down to "every man his own chimney-sweep!" . . . But look, sir, we must have scavengers and scullery-maids. . . . Listen to a Seer.[86]

Ada Bayly's "Hampden" in *To Right the Wrong* (1894) sounded like a late-nineteenth-century Conservative. Eliza Pollard's "Hampden" in *A Soldier of Fortune* (1903) brimmed with Whiggish noblesse oblige.[87] Hugh Williamson's 1933 life of Hampden reduced him to a "law-abiding" squire to whom "rebellion was anathema." Cecil E. Lucas Phillips recalled the older antistatist imagery for a moment in 1938 when, annoyed with "creeping socialism," he invited Englishmen "to brood upon the example of a man who would put all to the test for the sake of twenty shillings." But even these were but peripheral remarks in a book that had reduced Hampden to one of "Cromwell's Captains."[88] Perhaps the crowning blow had already come in 1905, when Edward VII defused Hampden of any remaining vestiges of revolutionary spark by presenting the Patriot's portrait to President Roosevelt on the eve of Roosevelt's inauguration.[89]

In 1832, when veneration of the Patriot by Whig and Radical alike was common, Tory essayists Isaac D'Israeli and Robert Southey had attacked the Hampden cult. The Patriot had been little more than a self-seeking politician who "designed to Hampdenize all England." D'Israeli and Southey may have "convinced" those Tory readers who were already persuaded that any Whig or Radical hero was necessarily corrupt; they probably had little impact on the veneration of Hampden by others. (Indeed, Isaac D'Israeli's famous son Benjamin felt compelled to offer praise of Hampden, Pym, and other "heroes of our earlier movement" in condemning the Whig ministry of 1835. Hampden was, by comparison to Grey, Brougham, and Russell, a man "of a heroic mould of mind, . . . a marvellous sublimity.").[90] But by the twentieth century, bereft of his mystical powers, Hampden was fair game to critics and debunkers. To the royalist barrister Walter P. Dodge and the royalist Cambridge don Esmé Wingfield-Stratford in 1912, he was "the advertising Hampden, the Labour Member of the time," a "hard-bitten political intriguer" and "cunning extremist" whose character could "hardly be said to rise above the dignified mediocrity of the important landowner." The tercentenary of his death in 1943 became, in Wingfield-Stratford's King's College overkill, "the occasion for an orgy of hagiographical ballyhoo worthy of the purest Victorian tradition of the [Hampden] cult."[91]

In 1832 Hampden's biographer, Lord Nugent, found it no trouble at all to venerate both Hampden and the Royal Navy. But in 1898 Sir John Skelton was not so sure. After all, the navy was important to all. And Hampden's challenge of the ship-money tax had hindered Charles I's naval program. "One does not exactly see where the heroism comes in." More recently, G. M. Trevelyan was also unable to forgive Hampden for his obstructionism, for the navy was important to Trevelyan too.[92]

So Hampden faded from the scene, one of the "mere grand, silent shades, walking the Elysian fields of the past," as Elizabeth Charles put it in 1868, "far off, among the heroes, Leonidas, Brutus, or the Gracchi, but in no way disturbing the pursuits or influencing the thoughts of the present."[93] Lord Nugent would have been very disappointed. In 1843 he and others had raised a monument to the Patriot at Chalgrove Field, celebrating Hampden's "defense of the free Monarchy and ancient liberties of England." Gentry and country folk had come "from all round" and "many thousands" gathered on the fields to enjoy the festivities. "Two bands play'd all 'long t' road," one aged participant recalled in 1905. But the Reverend J. Howard Swinstead, vicar at Chalgrove Church, who interviewed others in his parish in search of popular memories or folklore, could say no more, for "to this brief reference to the monument commemorating our great Patriot, the simple folk add little by way of tradition."[94]

Sydney fared no better. By the late nineteenth century he too was a back number. Despite his mid-century rejection by "radicals," Sydney, like his fellow saint, Hampden, continued to be held in fond regard for years by "moderate," "Liberal," and eventually even some "Conservative" Englishmen. And "the old Whig toast" continued to see service. In 1853 Lord John Russell "trotted out Sydney from that eternal scaffold" in a Parliamentary speech *opposing* the introduction of the secret ballot.[95] Others stressed Sydney's noble birth, "moderation," and opposition to Cromwell's "extreme measures."[96] In 1873 Sydney's biographer, Alexander Charles Ewald, reported that the Rebel-Saint was

> no longer called a rebel, but a pioneer—a reformer, not a demagogue. . . . Extreme Radicals of the present day [had no claim on him, for he was] a republican—not a democrat. The League and the International would have certainly declined his services; he was a Reformer—not a Revolutionist.

Ewald assured his readers (probably correctly), that Sydney would have spurned "the miserable men who call themselves the Republicans of the nineteenth century." He urged the reader to emulate old Algernon, the "philosophical Liberal" (which was generous of him, since Ewald may very well have been a Conservative; his biography of D'Israeli celebrated that man's "preservation of the lower classes from the counsels of the agitator").[97]

Several *fin-de-siècle* novelists offered the same mellow image. Mary Rowsell's Sydney and Lord Russell were "lofty spirits," high above the "grovelling, revengeful self-seekers" of the Rye-House Plot. Ada Bayly's fictional Sydney was a critic of dueling and the death penalty. "Half

barbarians," he called his countrymen, "sadly wanting in common sense."
Miss Bayly wholeheartedly approved of Gladstone's "Principle of Liberalism"—"*trust in the people*, qualified by prudence." Her Sydney epitomized that prudence.[98] W. J. Escott's fictional Sydney was "a young
gentleman in the plain habit of a lawyer," whose features reminded Escott's hero "of the bust of the Emperor Aurelius in the Stadhaus at the
Hague." And Julia Cartwright Ady's fictional "Sydney" represented
the purest "noblesse oblige."[99] The monarchical editor of the 1885 edition
of the *Roxburghe Ballads* spoke of Sydney's "disdain" on the scaffold
for the rude multitude, and insisted that "the servile hirelings" of Charles's
court who attacked Sydney in verse after his death themselves displayed
"the vileness of the mob, as a result of indulgence in Revolutionary ran-
cour." Distinguishing Sydney from his "baser" contemporary, Cromwell, the *Roxburghe Ballads'* editor assured his readers that the noble
Sydney was simply "incapable" of joining in any king-killing: "We feel
this now two centuries later." In that same year Gertrude M. I. Blackburne's short "review" of Sydney's life compared him to "the king-errant
of romance, who had but one motive—his lady's safety and release from
captivity," and referred to him as "a moderate man," "first in order of
time among our modern politicians," a "man of the nineteenth century."[100]

But worship of the Rebel-Saint was tapering off, even among moderates and conservatives. Thomas Forster's discovery of Sydney's atten-
tiveness to "the affairs of his private fortune" and fondness for spiritous
liquor may have troubled some.[101] And Dalrymple's old "French money"
charges were beginning to trouble others in the heavily nationalistic climate of the nineteenth century.

John Landseer's "Algernon Sydney" remarked in 1843: "No man
questions my Patriotism";[102] he must have been unaware of the growing
chorus of questioners. William Cobbett dismissed the "romance" attached
to the Rebel-Saint and questioned Sydney's loyalty in 1824, as did the
more conservative Robert W. Blencowe. Blencowe, who had edited the
diary of Sydney's brother, Henry, described Algernon as the "visionary
and splenetic politician whom neither noble birth nor lofty theories of
political perfection saved from tarnishing his character by acceptance of
French money." Blencowe may have been echoing Tory Robert Plumer
Ward's critique of the Rebel-Saint. Ward had launched a squib in 1838,
directed against "one of the sacred articles of the creed of Whiggism"—
the prejudice "in favor of this canonized person [Sydney]" which had become "so widely spread . . . that most writers seem afraid even to inquire
into it." Ward was not afraid. He scolded Sydney for "amusing himself"
with "visions of commonwealth and liberty" during the Cromwellian
years, "while his country was bleeding." He repeated Dalrymple's charge

that Sydney was guilty of "betraying his country to France." He criticized the "dangers" inherent in the *Discourses*, and suggested that they had been responsible for "the reformatory revolt" of William Lyon MacKenzie in Canada.[103] Of course, Plumer Ward's critique serves to demonstrate the very real strength of Sydney's reputation in 1839. Indeed, the very severity of the criticism by Ward, Blencowe, and the twentieth-century royalist heirs to Dalrymple's charges (Esmé Wingfield-Stratford, Sir John Marriott, and H. M. Imbert-Terry) could be dismissed by Sydney aficionados as mere Tory partisanship.[104] But Thomas Babington Macaulay's attack on the Rebel-Saint was more serious.

Macaulay, a prominent Whig apologist, originally had nothing but praise for Sydney's "ardent public spirit." But he changed his mind at about the same time that Ward's critique appeared. In 1848 Macaulay confessed to the "pain" he felt in having found Sydney, "a man who is popularly considered as the personification of public spirit," to have been in collusion with the "enemy." Macaulay's volte-face may serve as a convenient datemark for the newer, more nationalistic definition of patriotism that was steadily displacing the older antistatist view of political virtue. Macaulay made clear that a public figure in the 1840's would be "thought lost to all sense of duty and of shame" if he were to enter the pay of a foreign (to say nothing of an "enemy") government.[105] He seems to have made no allowance for the patriot who might accept the aid of a foreign power to help rescue his compatriots from a tyrannical government at home—the interpretation given Sydney's conduct by Macaulay's late-eighteenth-century Whig counterparts (among them his namesake, Catharine Macaulay). Macaulay did not explain what it was that made Sydney's alleged acceptance of French monies in 1680 so much more intolerable to his value system than similar Whiggish appeals for Dutch aid in 1688. It may have had something to do with the success, and consequently legitimacy, of the "Glorious Revolution," or with the difference between France and Holland by the 1840's. But this latter difference could not have been what troubled the royalist Imbert-Terry in 1917, for he praised his hero, Charles II, for that "misjudged monarch's" friendly relations with Britain's World War I ally, France, at the same time that he gloatingly repeated Dalrymple's charge.[106]

In any event, Macaulay's dismissal of the Rebel-Saint may have made a difference; by 1850 most of Sydney's remaining admirers were articulate members of the Establishment, and many probably read or heard of Macaulay's criticism. A few Sydney defenders peppered *Notes and Queries* with attacks on Macaulay, and Ewald clearly rejected the Dalrymple claims, but many others accepted the views of either Dalrymple, Cobbett, Ward, or Macaulay, and defrocked the Rebel-Saint.[107]

The demythification of Sydney probably facilitated more objective analysis of his role in English political history. Sir Leslie Stephen noted that his *Discourses* were unpolished ramblings that should have been revised before publication (as they conceivably would have been had not Sydney been sent to the block). Armand Carrel noted that Sydney's virtues were not truly "of that class which interest the mass of the people." James MacKinnon properly described Sydney as "an aristocratic republican," and suggested that "a Whig party, supported by the middle classes, would practically have realized his ideal." In 1917 two gentlemen carried on a running debate in the *Times Literary Supplement* regarding the authenticity of a phrase attributed to Sydney. In the process, both projected their images of the Rebel-Saint into the world of Verdun and the Somme. One insisted that Sydney's motto was "anti-militarist" in tone; the other, that it was "as apt a statement of our present War-aims as could be desired." The two blasted away for some time until one got the upper hand, or the other decided the debate was no longer worthy of his dignity. It was the last instance I was able to find where Englishmen troubled themselves over old Algernon. Like Hampden, he no longer aroused any passions.[108]

Useful for over a century, the twin patriots had finally been cast down from the mystical heights. They had given way to patriot-symbols more relevant to the nineteenth-century world. The forces that tore them loose from the hearts of reform-minded Englishmen were some of the same forces that simultaneously lifted Oliver Cromwell to the fore.

The Resurrection of Oliver Cromwell and the Tenacity of the "Royal Martyr"

> Cromwell is the typical Englishman of the modern world. . . . To one of [his critics or admirers] he is the champion of liberty and peaceful progress, to another the forcible crusher of free institutions, to a third, the defender of oppressed peoples, to a fourth the asserter of his country's right to dominion. . . . he is a mirror to ourselves, wherein we may see alike our weakness and our strength.[109]
>
> S. R. Gardiner

Radicals and democrats angered by the shortcomings of the Reform Bill of 1832 and the refusal of Whigs to adopt "the People's Charter" turned on their former allies. In the process, they often deserted the Whiggish patriot-symbols, Hampden and Sydney, and invoked a new and more meaningful set of heroes—among them their own John Frost,

Feargus O'Connor, and the Tolpuddle martyrs; the venerable Spartacus, Wat Tyler, John Lilburne, Thomas Paine, Marat, Robespierre, and, frequently, the scourge of the Rump Parliament, stern Oliver Cromwell.[110]

This was something new. The Lord Protector had been in the darkness for well over a century before his nineteenth-century resurrection. And the century began with little changed. Edward Knatchbull-Hugessen recalled that, as a boy, in the 1820's, he had been "taught to believe that Oliver Cromwell was a person of low extraction and coarse manners . . . and a bad and ambitious man." Tories continued to blast away at his "deceiving, radically criminal" ways.[111] Irishmen continued to recall his cruelty and to associate him with evil ("the curse of Cromwell").[112] Many Whiggish gentry still complained of his "despotic" dissolution of the Rump.[113] And for years many commonwealthmen, republicans, Hampden Club democrats, Chartists, and socialists offered their own condemnation. The anonymous French or Belgian "Cromwell" who wrote "from Hell" in 1790 offered advice on how to "defoler l'ordre social" and praised the hypocrisy ("l'artifice") of "we who detest virtue."[114] In the same year two Tory High Church broadsides (designed by James Sayers and William Howard) attacked the Dissenter, Joseph Priestley; both associated him with Cromwell. And the next year, when a mob destroyed the home of Priestley and several other Birmingham Dissenters and Radicals, members of the mob were heard to call out: "Long live the King; No Oliver."[115] John Thelwall contrasted "the gallant patriot Colonel John Lilburne" to Cromwell, whom he condemned for his abuses of Parliament and trial by jury, and for his "warlike and ambitious spirit" which had "plunged the laborious orders of the community into miseries." Thelwall, Richard Carlile, and Henry Hunt compared the tyrannical behavior of Pitt the Younger and his successors to that of Cromwell ("the Oliverism of that cold-blooded monster," Carlile wrote of the Younger Pitt).[116]

Charles James Fox initially thought Cromwell "too odious ever to be the object of praise or imitation." Nonetheless, throughout his career Tories compared Fox's politics to those of the Lord Protector. A 1783 print by William Dent, *The Whig Club*, portrayed Fox presiding, beneath a bust of Cromwell. And in January of 1784, when Fox spoke out against two of the king's prerogatives (his rights to dissolve Parliament and to print and issue monies) Dent portrayed him as Cromwell again, presiding over the execution of the Royal Martyr. In like fashion, James Sayers's "Mirror of Patriotism" (see pl. 23) depicted him practicing a speech before a mirror which reflected back Oliver Cromwell. Other anti-Fox prints celebrated the Royal Martyr, implying that Fox possessed regicidal traits. Fox was most annoyed by these allusions, but later in his career he had cause to suggest that Cromwell may have had *some* admirable qualities, at which time "a member of no Party" took him to lengthy task for being so generous with this "abominable" tyrant. After Fox's death, in 1807, James Gillray linked him with Cromwell once again in his print, *Charon's Boat.*[117]

In 1819, W. T. Sherwin, a London printer, republished Edward Sexby's *Killing No Murder*, the tyrannicidal broadside Sexby had directed at the Lord Protector in the 1650's. It has been suggested (quite reasonably, I think) that Sherwin intended that the pamphlet serve as a critique of a ministry Sherwin felt was responsible for the "Peterloo" massacre, a ministry Sherwin was comparing to that of Cromwell, "the cunning and hypocritical despot" whose "tyrannical designs" Sexby, and Sherwin, despised.[118]

William Godwin's influential *History of the Commonwealth of England* was generally critical of Cromwell, and initially the Chartist movement and its allies had reservations as well. William Cobbett reminded Englishmen of "vile" Cromwell's "Legacy to Labourers"—the Protectorate's abolition of taxes on the estates of many wealthy landowners and the simultaneous imposition of the excise tax. In Cobbett's opinion the elimination of these taxes helped only the "aristocracy" and worked "against the people," who were compelled to make up Cromwell's lost land revenues with excise taxes "wrung out of the sweat of the [common man]."[119] Chartist Charles Westerton, commenting in Wandsworth in late 1838 on the division of "Charterists" into "the physical force men and the moral force men," offered a more delicate critique of the Lord Protector. He argued that the use of force was rarely "advantageous to the people," and that Cromwell had "been obliged to sacrifice his principles" in applying force in the past. Bronterre O'Brien, more sympathetic to the "physical force" school, also had some strong words for Cromwell and his "bloody Protectorate." A correspondent to the *Northern Star* complained in 1840 of the Home Secretary's use of the army and the police against Chartists, and wondered (perhaps with ambivalent feelings) whether "some Cromwell" would rise "like the days of old," and "establish a dictatorship" with that army. In 1842 Thomas Cooper contrasted "the great and virtuous Hampden" to Cromwell, whose "thirst for power" had led to his drift from "patriotism" into "a crafty Dictatorship." John Watkins, son-in-law of the Anti-Corn-Law poet Ebenezer Elliot and a one-time Chartist himself, wrote a play in 1848, *Oliver Cromwell, the Protector*, highly critical of Cromwell. As David Goodway has suggested, many Chartists preferred a patriot-symbol less tainted by apparent misuse of power than Cromwell's memory offered. "Power naturally tends to corrupt," a Hampden Club life of Hampden had explained, while execrating both Charles I and Cromwell.

Chartists were no less concerned than Hampden Clubbers about the abuse of power in a Parliament elected by only a fraction of the English public.[120]

The Lord Protector had become the butt of such a steady stream of abuse that Edmund Lodge could write in 1830: "Even the fierceness of democracy has not furnished a single champion to bedaub him with coarse and plain-spoken praise."[121] Lodge was, however, quite mistaken. A growing number of democrats and statists alike throughout the early nineteenth century were beginning to champion his name.

Independent descendants of the Ironsides, "merchant-born" venders "of hops and malt, of coals and corn," sturdy East Anglican Nonconformist yeomen, kept alive a faith in which "Cromwell was still their saint," his portrait the chief adornment on their walls (see pls. 25–30). He had opposed the Spanish and had defended Piedmontese Protestant victims of the Duke of Savoy's pogrom. He had brought prosperity and toleration for Independents. He breathed a Puritan air and spoke a Biblical tongue. He was their Englishman, "God's Englishman."[122] But he was now other people's Englishman as well. Nonconformists were his fondest and most enduring worshippers, but his resurrection could never have been accomplished by their will alone. It was not until his memory became relevant and useful to other vital segments of the society that he emerged as a truly national patriot-hero of Hampden's or Sydney's scale.

The socioeconomic unrest of the early nineteenth century gave new life to the Lord Protector, for men on both sides of the barricades found his example refreshing. Certain upper- and middle-class conservatives, anxious about the demands of the working classes for political equality and economic security, found the Lord Protector particularly worthy of their admiration. Had he not checked the Agitators, Levellers, and Diggers of his own day? The anonymous author of *Oliver Cromwell: A Poem* (1829) was sure that one could say that there was a more "kindly" public attitude toward Cromwell "of late years," but he was troubled by those who sometimes compared Cromwell and his kinsman Hampden to "the levellers of present times." They would have had nothing to do with such modern democrats or with "rebellious combinations of workmen." The Whig, Lord Brougham, agreed. Cromwell's Protectorate was admirable:

> The popular sense, or nonsense, had no voice in it. . . . Pertinacious opponents and disturbers of the government were, indeed, in some cases summarily enough disposed of, as was quite necessary; but nobody who chose to live quietly and in due obedience was molested.[123]

Edmund Clarke was of the same view. It was only Cromwell's "strong arm" that had preserved England from "anarchy." The "abstract principles of politics" had "not the slightest weight" with this level-headed Englishman. Clarke admired Cromwell's efforts to "preserve the rights of property undamaged, and to maintain the different classes of society in their proper and rightful position." He was delighted that Cromwell was not "afflicted with admiration of 'equality,' or yearn[ing] for the realization of the 'rights of man.' " And he was certain that his hero would have rejected the notion certain socialists and humanitarians were circulating, that "all poor people are suffering saints, and all rich people rapacious rogues."[124]

Clarke, Brougham, and their anonymous Scottish colleague had good cause to complain of popular misunderstanding of Cromwell's true nature, for the popular view of Cromwell does, indeed, appear to have been quite different from their own. In 1812 an anonymous worker angrily swore "vengeance" on the administration for ignoring "the *distresses* of the *People*," and promised that "a *second Oliver*" would "make his appeare to cleanse the Augean stable." Young Samuel Bamford's cardinal patriot-symbols were Hampden and Sydney, but when he visited the House of Commons in 1817 and thought of the unrepresented masses, his sentiments caused him to say (quietly, or to himself): "O! for the stamp of stern old Oliver on this floor."[125]

If Bamford's memory was good, it would not be surprising, for other Radical critics of Parliament were also recalling "the stamp of stern old Oliver." The *Poor Man's Guardian* called for a Cromwell to disperse Parliament in 1831, and in the same year the author of *The People's Book; Comprising their Chartered Rights . . .* suggested that a Cromwell had dissolved a corrupt Parliament once before, when the Rump's members had "quite forgot the original character of the *representative* constitution." J. Wade's *History of the Middle and Working Classes* (1833) spoke highly of Cromwell's policies towards "the labouring and productive classes" (thus coming to the opposite conclusion from William Cobbett). Young "Philip Stanton," the fictional hero of William Howitt's *Man of the People*, penned a "Bravo!" in the margin of an account of Cromwell's expulsion of the Rump Parliament. Feargus O'Connor alluded to Cromwell's act in an open letter to the Home Secretary, Lord John Russell, in July of 1839. Similarly, in 1848 a militaristic German radical, Friedrich Engels, longed for a German Cromwell to redeem the "honor of Germany" by dissolving a Frankfort Assembly which had allowed Denmark to hold Schleswig-Holstein.[126]

A growing number of democrats and Chartists appeared willing to recall the example of the Lord Protector as time passed. A letter to Carlile's *Gauntlet* in 1833 called for an "avenger of his country's wrongs," for a new Cromwell. Ebenezer Elliot, a staunch Hampdenite, warned in 1834 that "we *fight*, if fight we must," as had the "man of Huntingdon!"[127] Bronterre O'Brien recalled the Lord Protector in the tense days of early 1839. A laudatory account of Cromwell's life and achievements appeared in Manchester in 1840.[128] But the period when the Lord Protector's reputation blossomed was clearly the 1840's, the bicentennial years of the English Civil War.[129]

In those bicentennial years Cromwell was the object of considerable attention—in novels, poems, songs, essays, lectures, sermons, editorials, and surely in popular conversation as well. Matthew Arnold made him the subject of his prize poem at Balliol College, Oxford, in 1844. Emma Robinson, whose first love was Sydney, passed Hampden over with only a brief aside in her second novel, *Whitehall* (1845), and revealed her affection for Cromwell, the "master genius" of his age, who spoke from her pages of England's future: "Freedom, equality, glory, religion and happiness flourishing throughout her length and breadth, . . . Commerce free and unshackled." The hero of Henry Herbert's *Cromwell* (1848), one Edgar Ardenne, was no democrat ("corruption, anarchy, bloodshed, proscription, Caesar!"). He first found Hampden admirable and Cromwell a tyrannical democrat, but later decided that Cromwell's strong, honest government was worthy of his respect and support.[130] Throughout the 1840's and '50's Chartist and mechanics' institute lecturers like Henry Vincent, W. J. Linton, J. B. Langley, and George Dawson told avid audiences of the Great Commoner who had once "infused the loftiest energy into the common people, and showed them there was a soul in the plebeian, and a might in his arm."[131] George Robinson (Lord Ripon), the Christian Socialist M.P. from Hull and future governor-general of India, called his son Oliver in honor of the Lord Protector in 1852. The Cromwellian artist Ford Madox Brown (see pls. 26 and 27) did the same in 1855. Oliver Cromwell Ironside (b. ca. 1860), head of the Capitalist Commonwealth Association, and Oliver Cromwell Cox (born in Trinidad, 1901), author of *Caste, Class and Race*, must have had similarly inclined parents. When in 1845 the new Houses of Parliament installed effigies of the British sovereigns of the past, and Cromwell's was not among them, the nation's newspapers divided on the question of whether it was proper to omit the Lord Protector. Several offered the long-standing semiofficial view of Cromwell as a "vulgar" usurper who ruled with "brute force," and praised the decision. But others, among them the *Hampshire Telegraph*, the *Bradford Observer*, the *Liverpool Mercury*, and the *Bucks.*

Gazette were decidedly critical of the omission of one who had but "played the tyrant for the sake of liberty."[132] Chartist poets W. J. Linton, Gerald Massey, and Ernest Jones enthroned the Lord Protector as "*the* English hero!" If "red republicans" ever really *sang* Massey's "Song of the Red Republican," then such mid-nineteenth-century descendants of the Levellers whom Cromwell had crushed would have intoned that "a spirit of Cromwellian might is stirring at this hour." The anonymous poet "Spartacus," writing in G. Harney's *The Red Republican*, similarly called on fellow radicals to "swear by the strength of Cromwell's soul to win their freedom yet." Ernest Jones's celebration "of Cromwell's time" was reportedly sung (to the tune "God Save the Queen") by thousands in a Hyde Park meeting to welcome home the transported Chartist hero John Frost.

Of course, the fact that the gathering was reported to have sung Jones's words does not prove that the audience was as ready to embrace Cromwell as their patron saint as was the gentle-born socialist Jones. The fact that William Howitt's fictional working-class figures in *The Man of the People* (1860) asked a Hampden Club advocate of change: "But how did Cromwell do it?" does not prove that Cromwell *was* the people's benchmark.[133] But there are clear indications that some working-class Chartists and other working-class groups had much regard for the Protector. When George Dawson, a Birmingham Baptist minister, lectured on Cromwell at the Newcastle Mechanics Institute, Newcastle's libraries were reported to have experienced a run for some time thereafter on all books relating to Cromwell. *The Working Men's Friend and Family Instructor* ran a series of thirty weekly articles in 1850 on "Cromwell and his Times." The Chartist George Thompson was interrupted by enthusiastic cries of "Cromwell!" in 1850 while denouncing Parliament. And then there is the case of the Watlington Mutual Improvement Society, which debated Cromwell's character for seven nights in 1852 and then, by secret ballot, cast a strong vote approving of the Protector.[134] Working-class people themselves (artisans, mechanics, farm laborers, and tradesmen) may have been *more* enthusiastic admirers of the Proscribed one than were their "leaders."

Nevertheless, no account of the resurrection of Oliver Cromwell would be complete without some attention to those elite "leaders." There is available evidence suggesting that their handling of Cromwell had some impact on some Britons, though it may have been the other way around! Thomas Babington Macaulay first regarded Cromwell as a "buffoon." But in 1828 he noted that, "even to this day [Cromwell's] character, though constantly attacked and scarcely ever defended [by those who counted to Macaulay], is popular with the great body of our countrymen." Macaulay himself eventually came to champion Cromwell's "high, stout, honest English heart," representative of "the best qualities of the middling orders." So did a descendant of Huguenots, J. H. Merle D'Aubigne, whose *The Protector: A Vindication* (1847) throbbed with praise of Cromwell's foreign policy, which he regarded as having been favorable to commerce, but essentially religious. Cromwell had sought to evangelize "the entire world," and the "existing greatness of England" was "but the realization" of Cromwell's grand design. His accomplishments far outweighed his violations of Parliamentary rights, which had been necessary if England were to recover from her "confusion."[135]

Edmund Clarke paid homage to Merle D'Aubigne, and Howard Evans to Macaulay, for winning new admirers over to Cromwell. But both praised Thomas Carlyle.[136] They were not alone, for Carlyle's *Letters & Speeches of Oliver Cromwell* had impressed others. Adam Rushton, W. J. Linton, Joseph Barker, the editors of the *Christian Commonwealth*, and the *Liverpool Albion*, even the Whig John Forster had all been moved by Carlyle's "ennobling gospel." Linton praised Carlyle for "stirring young souls with higher aims than were deducible from socialistic materialisms, or from the Manchester morality of a generation of Whig utilitarians." Forster, whose 1839 life of Cromwell had been critical, was moved by Carlyle's view of the Lord Protector to revise the study; the 1860 edition is pure Carlyle. Joseph Barker remarked in his journal, *The People*, that he had

> just been reading the *Letters and Speeches of Cromwell* by Carlyle. I was not aware before, that Cromwell was so rational and superior a man. . . . I had always a favorable impression of Cromwell; but had no idea that his character was so superior, and that his talents were so transcendent.

Barker, a republican, was still somewhat offended by Cromwell's suppression of the Levellers, but he deferred to Carlyle's judgment here, and excused the act as one springing from a noble "sense of duty." He vowed to "enlighten the minds of the people" about Carlyle's "Greatheart."[137]

Carlyle's philosophy predisposed him to venerate Cromwell. Temperamentally distrustful of much of the economic and social change about him, Carlyle envisioned a neofeudal world in which things were simpler, more fundamental, and more orderly. He longed for "some Hero-worship," without which "this world does not promise to be very inhabitable long." "In these days," he wrote in 1831,

> man can do almost any thing only not obey. . . . whoso cannot obey cannot be free, still less bear rule; he that is the inferior of nothing, can

be the superior of nothing, the equal of nothing. Nevertheless, believe
not that man has lost his faculty of Reverence.

Initially he regarded Cromwell as a hero of the gentry. But, like Macaulay,
he found that "the people" quietly admired the Man from Huntingdon,
and in 1840 Carlyle began progressively to develop a profound admiration of the man. In July he wrote his brother that he longed to visit Cambridgeshire, "where Oliver Cromwell first came into being and action."
He visited Huntingdon, St. Ives, and Ely, where his eyes "filled with very
tears." He walked the battlefields, carrying off relics. By 1842 he had
come to regard Cromwell to be "almost a kind of god," whose reputation he found to be "steadily growing clearer and clearer in the popular
English mind." [138]

The Lord Protector was the epitome of "virtue" to Carlyle, but
unlike earlier admirers of the antistatist "virtue" of Hampden and Sydney, Carlyle's virtue translated as *"Vir-tus*, manhood, hero-hood." His
Past and Present (1843) was a paean to Cromwell's memory, "an everlasting encouragement, new memento, battleword, and pledge of victory
to the brave." Though he had little regard for the egalitarian and libertarian aspects of the movement, he saw Chartism as a force comparable
to Cromwell's Ironsides. Disturbed by the advent of industrialization
and social change, he was disgusted with the passive conservatism of the
landed gentry. The "just despotism of some armed Cromwell" was what
was needed in the "age of the cotton-mills." [139] "Mr. Thornton," the
capitalist hero of Carlyle's *North and South*, remarked, during a particularly tense scene of social conflict: "Cromwell would have made a capital mill-owner. . . . I wish we had him to put down this strike for us."
Carlyle hoped that "our first Chartist Parliament, or Oliver *Redivivus*,"
would impose taxes on the archaic landowners, if for no other reason
than to stir them to action. In 1846, after Sir Robert Peel had managed to
obtain the repeal of the Corn Laws, Carlyle sent him a copy of his edition
of *The Letters and Speeches of Oliver Cromwell* (1845) for Peel's "edification and strengthening." [140] As late as 1831 Sir Walter Scott had repeated
the remark that "a collection of the Protector's speeches would make . . .
the most nonsensical book in the world," [141] but many Britons found
Carlyle's edition of Cromwell's *Letters and Speeches* quite impressive; it
went through three editions in as many years. [142] Carlyle had touched a
resonant chord.

The bicentenary Cromwell revival provoked some to compare their
new saint to his cousin, the Whig hero, Hampden. Carlyle's Cromwell,
for example, utterly dwarfed Hampden, a "dreadfully dull" man of
"safe courses, . . . formidably thick-quilted." Carlyle "had *tried*" to

worship Hampden; he really had. But "with very indifferent success! At bottom I found that it would not do."[143] Goldwin Smith agreed. Hampden and Sydney were "obsolete," whereas Cromwell was "the greatest man, take him all in all, that ever trod the scene of history," for Cromwell had been able to "restore order." Edmund Clarke was more generous, but was basically of the same opinion. Hampden, "a man whose name expresses pure, noble, and lofty patriotism," was nonetheless too cautious. He might serve well in Parliamentary opposition; he might stand as a virtuous example; but in the crunch it was the leader, Cromwell, whose "zeal and resoluteness of purpose" really counted. When Colonels Hampden and Cromwell had discussed the Parliament's forces in 1642, Hampden had been dubious of Cromwell's proposal to recruit godly commoners for a New Model Army. And later Hampden had objected in Parliament to his cousin's get-tough policy with royalists. A fine enough fellow, Hampden, but not of Cromwell's metal; no model for leadership in the demanding years of the English Civil War, or of the nineteenth century.[144]

Lord Nugent, Hampden's champion, must have been distraught. In 1847 he published a spurious account he had"uncovered" of "a worthy discourse between Colonel John Hampden and Colonel Oliver Cromwell" (allegedly related by Hampden's chaplain, William Spurstowe). This "true and faithful relation" of the conversation of these two worthies was clearly intended to check the drift from Hampden to his cousin, for it placed Hampden in the more favorable light.[145] It could only have affected the handful of "articulate" elites who bothered with it, and in any event Nugent's fraud was eventually discovered. But it stands as a monument of one man's effort to check the cultural currents carrying one symbol into a backwater, the other into mainstream.

Nugent was not alone, of course. Other critics of the Man from Huntingdon responded to the Cromwell revival with elán as well. Irish writers continued to revile him, as did many Anglican divines. Reverend A. D. Crake, a Hampden devotee, repeated the old story of Cromwell's compact with the Devil. Reverend T. Lathbury's *Oliver Cromwell, or The Old and New Dissenters* (1862) denied Merle D'Aubigne's claim that Cromwell had not sought the destruction of "the Royal Martyr." Reverend Frederick Lee dismissed him as a "cruel, malicious, and blood-thirsty tyrant." J. B. Mozley, Regius Professor of Divinity at Christ Church, Oxford, reviewing Carlyle's *Letters and Speeches of Cromwell* for the *Christian Remembrancer*, vigorously dismissed Cromwell's "rolling, slippery colluvies of words," and continued to portray him as ambitious, coarse, vile, and a regicide.[146] Other royalists continued to point to his role in the killing of the king as well, and scornfully reminded "those modern English 'Democrats' '' who had made Cromwell their "pet" that "he would have been the first to despise" them.[147]

Constitutional scholars like Reginald Palgrave and Lord Acton had little use for the "Prince of wire-pullers," the "constant enemy of free institutions." Neither had socialists like John Morrison Davidson. Davidson's hero was the Digger, Gerald Winstanley, and in the 1890's socialists would sit in Tom Mann's Long Acre pub and hear Davidson damn "Cromwell the Liberticide," "the darling of the Army jingoes, of the trade capitalists, and of the 'elect,' or as we should now perhaps say, the 'Nonconformist Conscience.' ''[148] Davidson was referring to Cromwell's supporters of the 1650's, but he implied that little had changed, that Cromwell's late-nineteenth-century admirers belonged to the same groups. And this was clearly the case.

Cromwell's most devoted admirers continued to be the Dissenters.[149] Prior to the repeal of the Test and Corporation Acts in 1828 Nonconformists were extremely sensitive about the limitations of their political rights, and in these years Hampden and Sydney had been at least on a par with Cromwell to them. But as they lost some of their sense of persecution, they began to shift their attention to a more appropriate symbol. With the repeal of the hated acts Congregationalists, Baptists, and other Nonconformists slowly gained political power. Though representing at best a quarter of the English populace, they were well organized, self-conscious, and anxious to learn all about one of their own who had trod the same path before them.

In 1829 one of their number complained that "those devoted to the national church" seemed to consider it "as an axiom" to insure "that Cromwell shall be proscribed through all ages"; he and his fellow Dissenters were determined to put an end to that. As K. M. R. Short has argued, the development of Nonconformist self-confidence in the nineteenth century was in part a function of their frequent recollection of the Cromwellian era; his day was their golden past, his success their beacon.[150]

Cromwell's religiosity and zeal had been behind Edmund Clarke's praise in 1846. He was remembered (incorrectly, but that matters little) as a foe of tithing and church rates by the Baptist minister W. T. Henderson in 1857. Henderson likened Cromwell to Edward Yates, an Islington Libertarian Society figure and foe of establishmentarianism whom Henderson was supporting for a seat in Commons. Cromwell's opposition to "ritualism" recommended Cromwell to A. J. Bray in 1869, for the Oxford Tractarians were reopening that wound. In 1873 the editors of the *Congregationalist* expressed their delight that after "two centuries of humiliation and subordination" they could now "proudly claim for our own the Lord Protector and the godly host" [his "Ironsides" army].

Artists honored "the Great Nonconformist" (see pls. 31 and 32). Various Independent churches raised his standard in the late nineteenth century. Reverend Henry Bell regarded him in 1883 as "one of God's true prophets." Reverend Robert Horton told "the Young Free Churchmen of England" in 1897, "You need Cromwell. He is the man of the hour for you. Your work for England and the world, if it is to be done, must be done precisely as he did his."[151]

The "Nonconformist conscience" was somewhat divided over the question of imperialism, but both sides claimed Cromwell. F. W. Aveling, a Methodist educator who found parallels between the "ancient and modern" followers of "one of God's truest heroes," called for "modern Cromwells" to lay claim to "the world for Christ," but Aveling sought a nonviolent conquest; he was no supporter of the military, of imperial power, or of the Boer War. Similarly, John Matthews, a Congregationalist minister, maintained that Cromwell's "Imperialist legacy" was quite different from the "commercialism or Africanism" of the *fin de siècle*. Cromwell had rather envisioned a less militaristic, more voluntaristic "world wide federation for the service and progress of mankind."[152] But many of their fellow Dissenters did not agree. After all, Cromwell had subdued the Irish, one of England's first imperial subjects. Both Aveling and the Reverend Hugh Price Hughes, president of the Wesleyan Conference, reminded their colleagues of that in 1899.[153] And Dissenters had always remembered Cromwell's Continental policy with fondness, convinced that it was basically a Protestant one. Baptist William Jones's *Ecclesiastical History* (1831–38) gloried in Cromwell's protest to the Duke of Savoy over that potentate's treatment of the Piedmontese Protestants, and Jones delighted that Cromwell had made "the sound of his cannon" heard "in Rome itself."[154] Reverend Joseph Smith heard "enlightened men . . . anxiously exclaim—'*We want another Cromwell*'" in 1851. Smith agreed: "our colonies want him; the persecuted and downtrodden sons of Italy . . . want him. . . . *Oliver Cromwell is just the man which is required by the nineteenth century.*" The *Congregationalist* editor who had "proudly claim[ed] for our own the Lord Protector" reminded his Dissenting readers that "we, too, have imperial traditions."[155] More than one *Northern Echo* correspondent damned D'Israeli in 1876 for his failure to intervene on behalf of Bulgarian Christians suffering at the hand of their Turkish rulers, and reminded readers of Cromwell's policy towards the Vaudois. In 1879 Edwin Paxton Hood gloried in Cromwell's use of power on behalf of "freedom." "I love to behold him overawing bad nations so as I believe England has never overawed them since."[156] Later, in 1899, Dr. Rendel Harris, a Cambridge minister, told a Huntingdon Evangelical Free Church gathering that Cromwell

would never have stood by while Armenian Christians were being mas-
sacred by Turks.[157] Religion and foreign policy had blended comfortably
in the Lord Protector, and many late-nineteenth-century Nonconformists
found that example inspiring.

But there was more to it than that. Cromwell represented Protestant
diplomacy, but he also represented power and action, important qualities
to many nineteenth- and twentieth-century Britons, just as they were to
their American contemporaries. Many Dissenters admired these qualities
in Cromwell. He was the favorite of evangelical ministers "weary of
milk-and-water men," ministers like the Reverend J. Cranbrook, who
longed for an end to "the strife of parties" and sought a leader in Cromwell's image who might weld the nation into a single political force. His
military "genius," his "glorious victories," appealed to the anonymous
author of *Lays and Legends of Cromwell and the Nonconformist Heroes.*[158]
He was "the man . . . on horseback" to Congregationalist minister Joseph D. Smith, the "Hero" and "strong man" to his colleague J. Kirk
Maconachie. Reverend Adam Rushton admired his ability to stimulate
others to "deeds of heroism." Edwin Paxton Hood's Cromwell was
"most royal," "his power" stamped out "the imbecilities of anarchists,"
humbled "the proud empires of Europe at a glance":

> Hark! England feels his tramping,
>   our own Achilles comes;
> His watchword, "GOD IS WITH US,"
>   it thunders through our homes.[159]

Edward Knatchbull-Hugessen, a Baptist, Whig-Liberal member of Gladstone's cabinet, regarded "the great Nonconformist" as "the hero saint
of all true Baptists and Congregationalists." Cromwell's "strong hand"
had preserved English "liberty." But Knatchbull-Hugessen's "liberty"
was not quite the same as that of the admirers of Hampden and Sydney;
it was no antistatist code-word, except in the sense that it meant freedom
from government-controlled religion:

> I am not speaking now of liberty in the wild and exaggerated sense in
> which men often use the word nowadays. By "liberty" I do not mean . . .
> equality [or] fraternity. . . . The liberty I mean is the liberty of . . . security
> to life and property, and freedom to worship God without restraint.[160]

Many of Cromwell's Nonconformist devotees, then, saw him as an
active moral foe of disorder and evil, preeminently a man of force—
moral force, to be sure, but still force. But Dissenters were not the only
Britons to associate these qualities with the Lord Protector. Agnostics
and Anglicans also took note of his military prowess (*"he was never*

beaten"),[161] his successful foreign policy ("the Greatest Man in the World!"),[162] and his "practical" willingness to use power to bring "order" to a disorderly world.[163] Chartists like John Alfred Langford, W. J. Linton, and Henry Vincent invoked Cromwell's "might" and "wrath," the "bright flash of his sword" in freedom's cause. "Oh, for one hour of the stalwart Old Protector," Linton's *Republican* sighed in 1848. "Think you a Cromwell would have pleaded his amicable relations with despotism?"[164] J. B. Leno recalled that under the "spell" of Vincent's lectures "you could hear the sound of the great man's jack boots." Novelists like Charles Reade, Thomas Taylor, Elizabeth Charles, and Samuel Church celebrated "the memory of a man! . . . by soul an emperor," "a giant." Historian Samuel R. Gardiner styled Cromwell "the national hero of the nineteenth century" because he was the epitome of imperialism. Late-nineteenth-century Britain was following in Cromwell's footsteps in that she "has waged wars, annexed territories, extended trade and raised her head among the nations." The eclectic Goldwin Smith (who had been an anti-Chartist constable in 1848) noted in the late 1870's that "the opinion has been gaining ground" that Cromwell represented "the greatest human force ever directed to a moral purpose"[165] (a remark that suggests the distance between men like Smith and a past that would have reserved such a superlative for an apostle or saint). Military specialist William O'Connor Morris and Colonels Henry Clinton and T. S. Baldock recalled Cromwell's "manly and strong" conduct of the nation's naval, military, and foreign affairs. Leo Maxe, the hawkish editor of the *National Review*, was angered by parliamentary debates on the Boer War, and recalled with longing "the strong hand of Cromwell": "The axe, after all, is better than decay." Fredrick Payn's *Cromwell on Foreign Affairs* (1901) also damned the doves. Cromwell had known "nothing of such folly as 'rose-water wars.' " Arnold White, a staunch advocate of sterilization of paupers and criminals, and virulent critic of bureaucratic incompetence in his *Efficiency and Empire*, frequently invoked the Lord Protector. From his desk in the Admiralty, Winston Churchill sought George V's permission to name a battleship after the Man from Huntingdon.[166]

The tone of other late-nineteenth-century admirers of Cromwell was similar. He was the "divine hero" to John Tullock, a "Born King of Men" to Dr. M. Macaulay.[167] Frederic Harrison regarded his dissolution of the Rump to have been a "practical" move designed to "give the nation peace, good government." To Harrison, the positivist author of *Order and Progress* (1885), Cromwell was the "mighty statesman," whereas Sir Henry Vane, a leader of the Rump, was "only a noble character." Harrison was greatly annoyed by the Liberal John Morley's "excessive respect for Parliament and parliamentary methods" which had led Morley to compare John Pym favorably to Harrison's "favorite hero," Cromwell. After all, Cromwell had only been "a constable," who assumed "power to keep order, to stem the tide of anarchy." His legal reforms had many "modern" features, and he was the "founder of British Imperialism." Dr. Macaulay admired Cromwell for the same reason; it was "the ability to govern" that mattered, "not integrity and incorruptibility."[168]

J. Allanson Picton found Cromwell to be of "special interest" to "these times" in 1882. Had he not taught that "each unit in the multitude" should "willingly subordinate himself to the good of all"? Charles Bradlaugh's Cromwell used "a giant's might" to "govern well for the country which he held in the grip of his iron gauntlet." In 1886 the mature Chartist-republican George Julian Harney advised Friedrich Engels that he disapproved of the Irish republican advocates of "Secession and Dismemberment":

> What Ireland needs, and England too, is a Cromwell, who should begin
> by hanging Parnell and his gang, and [Liberals] Gladstone and [John]
> Morley along with them; and then . . . set about doing justice to . . .
> farmers, labourers, and others.[169]

Six years later Harney longed for "a Dictator" with the "hand and brain of Cromwell." "Is not Parliamentary Government an enormous humbug?" he asked Engels.[170]

Antistatist, libertarian admirers of Hampden and Sydney must have been shocked by the Cromwellian views of Harney, Dr. Macaulay, Harrison, Picton, Maxe, and others of their ilk. They were a new breed, but one attuned to the needs and wants of the day. "We English admire . . . a man of action," Frederick Payn wrote, praising Cromwell. Lord Rosebery, head of the Liberal Party and ex-prime minister, went further: "I wish sometimes for a dictator, a tyrant . . . a man of large mind, or iron will who will see what had to be done and do it." On the day after he made these remarks, Rosebery praised the "Imperialism" of Oliver Cromwell and remarked: "We could find employment for a few Cromwells now."[171]

Hampden and Sydney had been Whiggish symbols of the elite's resistance to "dictatorial power," of their love of freedom *from* government. The age of Darwin, industrialism, democracy, and empire worshipped different gods. Cromwell's very appeal lay in his *use* of power, his willingness to cut through formalities, to *act*. Cromwell's resurrection, and the demise of Hampden and Sydney, reflect a shift in Britain from a culture dominated by Whiggish prerogatives, the primacy of "natural" (that is, aristocratic) leaders, to one alert to the voice of Cromwell's "common folk" (especialy Dissenting "common folk") in the political order. This alteration in the relative strength of patriot-symbols also reflects a shift in the English-speaking world from a culture dominated by those who valued personal liberty over power or "order" to a culture dominated by those who preferred active, pragmatic leaders, "men of iron" who brought prosperity, morality, empire, and stability to scenes of decadence and disorder. Thus while the more moderate republicans and Chartists (men like Linton, Cooper, and perhaps O'Brien) remained true to Hampden and Sydney, the more extreme "physical force" Chartists and socialists (men like O'Connor, Jones and Harney) unfurled the colors of the Lord Protector. And while "natural leader" Whigs and members of the conservative, late-nineteenth-century Society for the Defense of Property venerated the twin patriots, moralistic social reformers in the Liberal Party enthroned "stern Oliver." Harrold Johnson, discussing evidence gathered in nineteen town and village schools throughout England at the turn of the century, associated the concept of patriotism with the empire.[172] Cromwell's image exuded imperial symbolism; Hampden's and Sydney's did not.

Cromwell was not the only "imperial" or "national" patriot-symbol, to be sure. Lord Nelson and Alfred the Great were also much venerated. Indeed, Lord Nelson has for a century or more been the most popular English historical hero among young schoolchildren,[173] as Earl Barnes in 1900 and Robert Stradling in 1969 have demonstrated (see Table 6.2). King Alfred had long been the subject of devoted attention from "divine-right" royalists and "Real Whigs" alike. It was from the masque *Alfred*, by James Thomson and David Mallet, that the patriotic song "Rule Britannia" emerged. Alfred was, to one playwright, *The Patriot King*; to another, the Victorian poet laureate Alfred Austin, he was "the one Englishman pre-eminently fitted to be a National Hero." His qualities were those "which founded, and which can alone maintain, the English empire." In 1901, in the year marking the thousandth anniversary of his death, there were numerous grand ceremonies at the several different sites he had made famous. Just as Nelson mounted a column in 1849 in Trafalgar Square, so a statue of King Alfred by Sir William Thornycroft rose in Winchester amid rituals in church, hall, and green, attended by "a vast assemblage of pilgrims." And shortly thereafter, in commemoration of his successful use of naval power against the Danes, he was honored as the founder of the Royal Navy by the commissioning of the battleship *King Alfred*.

Winston Churchill was to fail in his effort to persuade George V to allow a dreadnought to be named after the Lord Protector; Cromwell was still a regicide to the king. All the same, Cromwell was at least as

Table 6.2. Identification with Famous People among British Schoolchildren, 1900 and 1969[a]

1900 (2,100 London schoolchildren, ages 8–13)[b]		1969 (260 Essex schoolchildren, ages 8–12)[c]	
Public figures		Public figures	
Queen Victoria	13 %	Queen Elizabeth	12.5%
Contemporary political figure (Gladstone)	3.5	Contemporary political figures (Churchill, Wilson, Heath)	11.5
National heroes and historic models	20	National heroes and historic models	22
Lord Nelson	5	Lord Nelson	6
O. Cromwell, King Alfred, and others	15	Cromwell, King Alfred, and others	16
National heroes and historical models, among 13-year-old children only	56.5		
Total public figures	36.5	Total public figures	46
Family, neighborhood, sport, or entertainment figures	63.5	Family, neighborhood, sport, or entertainment figures	54

[a] Note the slight increase, by 1969, in the percentage of children identifying with national heroes or historic models, despite the fact that there were no 13-year-olds in the 1969 survey. (The older the child, the more likely he or she is to have shed local models and to have adopted a national or historic model.) This increase could be explained by one of my findings—namely, the steady rise of statist patriot-symbols in Britain over the past century or more. But compare this apparent rise of patriot symbols and national political figures in Britain with the apparent decline of such symbols in America (Table 5.2). In Table 5.2 it appears that incumbent presidents steadily become more important than other contemporary political figures—possible evidence of a rise in statism. But historical patriot-heroes appear to be declining. The apparent overall decline, however, is entirely a function of the decline in the importance of Washington.

[b] Barnes, "Children's Ideals," pp. 5–10.

[c] R. Stradling, in *British Journal of Political Science* 1 (1971): 121–28.

powerful a patriot-symbol as King Alfred. The use of Alfred as a patriot-symbol was ultimately shallow, as he was a distant, somewhat impersonal figure. Cromwell was more human, and more useful. James Willington wished that "our public conduct" might be "copied" after that of "the Protector," whom he compared to Julius Caesar, another admirable dictator.[174] Horace Groser urged English youth to choose "the heroic path" of "Enthusiasm," "Discipline," "Will and Action," and to imitate Cromwell, whose "name has become a watchword."[175] And in 1899 a statue of Cromwell, by Sir William Thornycroft, was unveiled near the entrance to the House of Commons on the tercentenary of "Greatheart's" birth.

In 1845, when such a statue had been proscribed (see page 145), the *Nonconformist* had not been offended. It was "sheer folly to contend for a marble Oliver," the editors observed in words similar to those Sarah Hale had used to protest any monument to her hero, Washington. Cromwell was above any of those mundane monarchs who owed their greatness only to their birth. But other Cromwell venerators disagreed, and a steady chorus mounted over the next half-century, demanding an "honorable niche" in Parliament to serve as a "perpetual remembrance" to their hero.[176]

Political leaders responded to a popular movement.[177] As early as the 1830's there were "friendly societies" named after Cromwell, and by the 1870's some seven or eight such societies were registered with the government. The Oliver Cromwell Lodge was founded in London in 1845, and in 1873 the International Workingman's Association met at "the Oliver Cromwell," which may have been an inn. Cromwell's statue was placed with those of other English rulers of the past in the new Town Hall at Bradford in 1874. In the next year "stern Oliver" rose in a Manchester square (see pl. 33), the gift of the mayor's wife to the city, and tens of thousands of trade unionists demonstrated their approval. In the same year some 2,000 members of the National Agricultural Labourers' Union celebrated Cromwell's victory over Charles before the Cromwell Obelisk on the fields of Naseby. "Arouse ye, Englishmen, there is yet another Cromwell," proclaimed the banners of the Tichborne Release Association and the Magna Charta Association in an 1878 Hyde Park demonstration. Carvings, tankards, busts, historical paintings, and the like were displayed at the Houghton Festival's "Cromwellian Celebration" in 1883.[178] Hence it was not entirely earthshaking for Parliament to reconsider its prohibition of Cromwell.

Nor, however, was it entirely inevitable. When R. L. Everett, a Liberal M.P., proposed a marble Oliver, Irish and Conservative M.P.'s joined ranks to vote down appropriations for it by a wide margin—an act that contributed to the collapse of the Liberal government the same week. The republican poet, Algernon Charles Swinburne, was furious. In 1880 Swinburne had complained of "the present fashion of blind and parrot-like Cromwell-worship," and of Cromwell's "selfish ambition and stupid shortsightedness." But he eventually succumbed to the worship himself, for three days after the defeat in Commons of the bill to authorize Cromwell's statue, Swinburne penned angry praise of the man who had given England

> The sundawn of her time—compelling power,
> The noontide of her most imperial day
>
> His hand won back the sea for England's dower;
> His footfall bade the Moor change heart and cower;
>
> .   .   .   .
>
> Him, who made England out of weakness strong,
>
> .   .   .   .
>
> Who bade fierce Europe fawn at England's heel,
> There needs no witness graven on stone or steel
> For one whose work bids fame bow down and kneel.[179]

Swinburne might take the high ground and scorn a mere graven image of his new hero, but others were less principled, or more stubborn. "Nonconformists," R. L. Everett told his allies, "would be most pleased" with a marble Oliver.[180] Workingmen and agricultural laborers might as well. And since the Liberals clearly sought the support of these groups,[181] Lord Rosebery, himself an outspoken admirer of the Man from Huntingdon, provided the funds himself, commissioned the statue, and presented it to Parliament in 1899.

Hundreds of petitions poured in protesting the statue. Lady Helen Clifford-Nellor, of 12 Hyde Park Place, published her own protest petition in an effort to rally the statue's opponents. She was astounded. England's proudest tradition had always been her "undying hatred of all oppression." Yet here were "opponents of despotism" and "lovers of freedom" willing "to applaud an insolent Caesarism" such as Cromwell represented. What could have possessed them? Had not their mentor, Gladstone, execrated Cromwell as "that great enemy of freedom?" (Arthur Balfour had made the same point in an 1895 debate when he had observed, with some justice, that Cromwell's "greatness was not of a kind which I should have thought would have appealed specially to the right honorable [Liberal] Gentlemen opposite.") Lady Clifford-Nellor was equally bewildered by those more conservative "upholders of Law and Order" who had managed to "revere one who scorned submission to any human authority other than his own." But while some Conservatives did support the elevation of Cromwell to the stature of national patriot-hero, most did not. The *Saturday Review of Politics, Literature, and Art*, as Conservative an organ as one might hope to find, was not one to join the Cromwell parade. It had been one thing for the *Review* to gather the noble Sydney to the fold (as it had in 1884); quite another to suffer Cromwell to enter. The *Review* angrily denied suggestions that Cromwell belonged among the enshrined. The statue was "the Cromwell Outrage." The House of Lords objected to the statue; Irish and Scottish M.P.'s re-stated their objections. But this time their protest was of no avail, and at 7:30 A.M. on September 3 an unidentified workman unceremoniously unveiled the statue and Cromwell began his guard over the institution he had dissolved two-and-a-half centuries before.[182]

The need for the Protector continued in the twentieth century. A few Royalists and radicals kept up the attack on "the imperfections" of the "idol" of "the Cromwell worshippers," but they were not nearly as vo-ciferous as their similarly disposed predecessors.[183] Lloyd George invoked him in attacking the House of Lords and ritualistic bishops. Henrietta Marshall recommended his "large soul" to youth seeking to understand "the beginnings of Greater Britain," and praised his treatment of the learned but "long-winded" members of the Rump Parliament who "did little or nothing." She allowed that he had been a tyrant, but a good one who "used his power . . . for the good of the people. He brought order out of hopeless confusion." Bonar Law contrasted Cromwell's popular handling of Irish rebellion with the Liberal Asquith government's pre-carious Home Rule policy for Ireland. By 1924 the playwright John Drinkwater could write of Cromwell: "I do not know that even the people who most dislike him any longer deny that he was an English patriot."[184]

In much of this Cromwell veneration there remained an authoritarian air. In the same year that Drinkwater's comment on Cromwell's patriotic standing was made, Andrew Dakers recalled with affection the "man of destiny whose name is cut deep and large into the tablet of Britain's Im-perial greatness." Dakers praised Cromwell's decision "not to turn swiftly from the temptation" of a crown. The Protector "preferred peace to riot" and was unmoved by "constitutional hair-splittings." An early pragmatist, Cromwell had experimented with military dictatorship and had found that "the experiment works." His modern counterpart, Dakers observed, was surely "Signor Mussolini," who was "saving his country from the onset of forces of destruction and disintegration, kindred to those which sought to undermine the greatness of England":

> Mussolini, battling with the insidious assaults of Communism and other systems of thought which ignore the realities of organized rational life,

presents a spectacle astonishingly like that of Cromwell grappling with the identical destroyers of his day.[185]

Several years later, in 1936, Ernest Barker entertained beer-drinking scholars in Germany with comparisons between Cromwell and Adolph Hitler. Barker expressed some reservations regarding his vision of Cromwell:

> We always tend to interpret the past in the light of the prepossessions which we cherish in the present, and when we idealize colonial expansion as a sign of national vigour, a symbol of national prestige, and an expression of national responsibility towards underdeveloped peoples and regions, we are apt to project our ideals into the past.

Professional caveats having been tendered, however, Barker ventured to reveal some of his "ideals" in his comparisons of the two strong men. Both leaders made admirable use of concentration camps to house the "unruly" ("a keeping of some in prison, as Cromwell called it"). Under Cromwell's masterful leadership the English people had been just as "transfigured" as the German people of the 1930's. Both were "religious" men. And both had brought order and prosperity to their chaotic times.[186] The German scholars, several of whom had suggested Cromwell as a model for fascism themselves, were an appreciative audience.[187]

Cromwell as fascist was a model offered by only a segment of the British Cromwellians, and was only fashionable until about 1938. Thereafter, as Britain and Germany moved towards war, Cromwell became less fascistic, and more English. Impatient with Neville Chamberlain's handling of foreign affairs, Leopold Amery repeated Cromwell's remarks on dissolving the Rump to Chamberlain ("You have sat too long here for any good you have been doing. Depart I say, and let us have done with you. In the name of God, go!") C. V. Wedgwood's 1939 biography of Cromwell found his "patriotism" relevant to British people in their hour of crisis, and insisted that Cromwell's Protectorate was quite different from Hitler's dictatorship. Isaac Foot, a Nonconformist M.P. who doffed his hat to Cromwell's statue daily on entering Commons, edited a Cromwell Association collection of the Protector's more stirring remarks in 1941 for the benefit of "our fighting forces," and suggested that they be read "alongside of the appeals of our leaders of today" in order to "strengthen our fortitude" in these days of crisis.[188]

Cromwell was compared to Winston Churchill, and Churchill himself discussed the Lord Protector's virtues with his fellow Conservative, Harold Macmillan, during the 1943 Cairo conference.[189] Moreover, whereas Churchill had failed to secure permission for an H.M.S. *Cromwell* in World War I, he saw to it that one of Britain's modern Ironsides, the

Cromwell tank, brought the Lord Protector into the fray. The Proscribed One had become a full-fledged national patriot-hero.[190]

In recent years the veneration of, or fascination with, Cromwell has survived despite the onset of a technologically inspired, present-minded climate of opinion, indifferent (or hostile) to patriot-heroes. Writers continue to hold Cromwell up to the young as "an inspiration" (see pls. 34 and 35). His handling of "anarchy" and the "foolish speeches" of the Rump is now regarded by many careful scholars to have been reasonable and temperate. Some "common folk" continue to utilize "stern Oliver" for their own purposes. When Greek nationalist terrorists on Cyprus began to assassinate British soldiers and officials in the 1950's, a group of British enlisted men began to launch reprisal raids of their own; their calling card read: "Cromwell!" The Cromwell Association commemorated the tercentenary of his death with elaborate ceremonies in 1958,[191] and in 1962 the Speaker of the House of Commons officiated at the opening of the Cromwell Museum at Huntingdon (see pl. 36), which now attracts over 10,000 visitors a year.[192] R.C.A.'s "Laureate Series" offered an Oliver Cromwell record, Cromwell became the subject of one of the "Jackdaw" historical series, and in 1970 Columbia Pictures, a seasoned judge of popular demand, released *Cromwell* to an enthusiastic public (see pl. 37).

But this film offered a sympathetic treatment of another patriot-hero figure as well; Columbia was sensitive to a second audience. Cromwell admirers might appreciate Richard Harris's steely version of the Man from Huntingdon, but others could delight in Sir Alec Guinness's portrayal of the noble Charles, the Patriot-Martyr.

Stuart Tenacity

Criticism of the Stuarts among devotees of Hampden, Sydney, and Cromwell continued in the nineteenth century. In 1859 the hierarchy of the Church of England ordered that the annual January 30 service honoring the "Royal Martyr" become optional, and in the 1870's Reinhold Pauli noted (in his laudatory biography of Cromwell) that "the old, enthusiastic, almost idolatrous ideas" about Charles I had "faded."[193] But Pauli, a staunch Dissenter, was hardly an objective observer: when the Anglican leadership made optional the observation of the "Royal Martyr's" day, they may have intended the move more as a recognition of Cromwell's new respectability than as a rejection of Charles. Indeed, there is reason to believe that the nineteenth century saw an *increase* in respect for the Stuarts.

Just as Hampden's and Sydney's physical remains became the object of attention to some of their early nineteenth-century admirers, so in 1813 the "cult of the Royal Martyr" was delighted by Henry Halford's account of the opening of the coffin of King Charles I. In the 1830's and '40's Isaac D'Israeli and his more famous son, Benjamin, presented Charles to their readers as a noble and patriotic soul, a staunch friend of the Church and "the poor."[194] Other evidence (psalms, poems, lays) of mid-century respect for the "Royal Martyr" is also available (among them curious old "Mr. Dick's" perpetual writing of a *memorial* to the "Royal Martyr" in Charles Dickens's *David Copperfield*), but the movement does not appear to have truly taken form and gained momentum until the end of the century. W. H. Davenport Adams's *The White King*, a eulogistic life of the "elegant and refined" Charles the First, appeared in 1889, and was followed in 1898 by Sir John Skelton's life of that monarch.[195] In 1904 Captain Henry Stuart Wheatley-Crowe's "defence . . . of one of the greatest . . . Princes that ever lived on God's earth" set the tone for Wheatley-Crowe's Royal Martyr Church Union and his Order of Merit, established in the Church of England in 1911 in honor of Charles. According to Walter Dodge, another sympathetic biographer, the Stuarts were "coming into their own again" by 1912. Anthony Ludovici's *Defense of Aristocracy* (1915) focused on Charles I, as did Mark Meredith's *Charles I, King and Martyr* (1922), and W. B. Redfern claimed that same year that there was a significant revival of January 30 observances in Charles's honor "in many [Anglican] churches."[196]

Much of this was clearly an aristocratic, or at least upper-middle-class movement;[197] I cannot say how well the "Royal Martyr" fared among common people in early-twentieth-century Britain. But if the first twentieth-century admirers were genteel, the movement seems to have spread to the middle and some of the lower middle classes by mid-century. Perhaps historical accounts of certain "social welfare" measures taken by Charles in the 1630's won him some new respect. In any event, he appears to have experienced something of a revival. A number of recent novelists have celebrated this monarch-martyr and his "sense of style."[198] While novelists themselves are imperfect guides to popular tastes, publishers are more sensitive weathervanes, and the publication of these historical tearjerkers, like Columbia's casting of Sir Alec Guinness as the noble Charles, constitutes some evidence of the proclivities of their potential audience.

No eighteenth- or nineteenth-century British monarch with any care for the likely reaction among Whigs or reformers would have given an heir to the throne the same name as that of the Royal Martyr or his rakish son. Only Stuart pretenders had dared to call their heirs Charles. Thus it is remarkable that the British enthusiastically approved of the naming of Elizabeth II's first son.[199] Charles III will become the king of a people who have lost their disdain and fear of "the cursed race of Stuarts."

What does this revival of interest in the "Royal Martyr" tell us of those who participate in it? Many have been attracted to Charles for the same conservative reasons that others were drawn to Cromwell—concern with the pace of socioeconomic change and affection for authority and order. Sir John Skelton feared that "the devotion to democratic rule" had "turned 'freedom' into a fetish." Confident that "the weight of too much liberty is apt to become oppressive," Skelton defended Charles's ship-money tax and other of his unpopular policies. To Anthony Ludovici Charles I represented "the cause of flourishing life" against "the powerful forces of modern capitalistic trade, of democracy, and of mere quantity as distinct from quality." His enemies had been "vulgar" people who raised "the specious cry of liberty and religious ardour to conceal their true and more material motives." His fight was a "last stand" made against the "spiritless" forces of "speed," "change," and "mere wealth." Charles Coit's *Royal Martyr* appeared in "times of confusion" (1924) "when society, religion, are rocking on their foundations." Coit found the example of Charles "refreshing and salutary." Joshua Brookes's *Vindication of Charles the First* (1934) was inspired by Brookes's conviction that monarchy had much to offer to "revolutionary" eras in need of order, as was Evan John's life of *King Charles I* (1933).[200]

Some of Charles's law-and-order admirers retained the traditional disdain for Cromwell, the regicide. But a good many others, W. H. Davenport Adams, J. S. Fletcher, Evelyn Everett-Green, Esmé Wingfield-Stratford, and Evelyn Anthony among them, displayed considerable respect or affection for the Royal Martyr's nemesis, Cromwell. Both, after all, were men of action, symbols of authority and order, the very qualities many of their admirers found so necessary in the modern world. It is not surprising, therefore, that Hugh Ross Williamson could write of *Charles and Cromwell* that they were "at last above the battle," "reconciled by 1940." They would have been "like Mussolini and King Victor Emmanuel in the modern age." Cromwellians could now join in the January 30 services honoring the Royal Martyr.[201]

Just as Jefferson, the antistatist, was yielding to the more potent Lincoln symbol in America, so Hampden and Sydney faded before the stronger image of Cromwell (and perhaps even that of Charles I as well). Whereas a preindustrial, preimperial age honored the protectors of local freedoms and antistatist prerogatives, the faster-moving, more complicated "age of anxiety" preferred "the Protector," the man of action, power, and purpose, the "doer." Antistatism survives, to be sure, but the trend is unmistakeable, and is unmistakeably reflected in both American and English patriot-symbols over the past two centuries.

7 Some Thoughts on Patriot-Heroes and the Recent Past, and a Summing Up

Patriot-heroes are the products of great crises and convolutions[1]—Hampden, Charles I, and Cromwell of the English Civil War, Sydney of the Glorious Revolution, Washington and Jefferson of the American Revolution, Lincoln of the American Civil War, Bolivar of the Latin American wars of independence, Juarez of *La Reforma*, and FDR of the depression and world war. Many heroes (like Jackson, Theodore Roosevelt, Wilson, Wellington, Lenin, De Gaulle, and for some time even Hampden, Sydney, Jefferson, and Cromwell) were largely partisan symbols. Only a few ever rise to the level of fully national veneration. But all represent something deemed of value to their societies.

Of late we have not seen produced in Britain or America any patriot-heroes of that order. Patriot-heroes "stood" for something in the past, when change was less rapid. It may be more difficult to "stand" for something in today's postindustrial world of flux and value modification. For many Britons and Americans social values are quite stable, to be sure, but the critic's pen and the investigative reporter's eye are more alive today than in the past; it may be difficult for elites to hold up models of political virtue for very long in the democratic tempest.[2] Neither Churchill nor FDR, perhaps the two modern political figures closest to patriot-hero

stature, appear as yet to be sufficiently free of partisan political association to be elevated by the public to the higher circles of patriot sainthood.
The only other political candidate for veneration, John F. Kennedy, did
not weather a crisis of significant intensity (the Cold War notwithstanding)
to galvanize a lasting image in the mind of America.

Antistatist, localistic figures (now styled "anti-Establishment,"
"populist," or simply "antiheroes") can still attract substantial numbers
of devotees. One need only think of the numbers who honor the memory
of John Birch or Senator Joseph McCarthy;[3] or of the recent property
tax "revolt" in California. But when one compares the strength of
these antistatist symbols today with the strength of Jefferson, Hampden,
and Sydney in a previous age, or when one considers that relatively few
today prefer antistatist figures to presidential figures, one has a sense of
the distance between Jefferson's world and our own. It is precisely because
we worry today of a "loss of leadership," because we now style our political heroes "leaders," and because they are nearly all presidents and
prime ministers,[4] that our political culture may be distinguished from
that of the eighteenth century.

In the 1930's the Democrats and Republicans in America reversed
their traditional roles. The story is familiar—the Democrats became the
party of strong central government and executive power, deserting Jefferson for Lincoln, while the once statist Republicans picked up the old
antistatist Democratic slogans of individualism, localism, and the tyranny
of strong central government (the most recent version of which has been
the Nixon administration's revenue-sharing plan). In the process, the
Democrats acquired a leader, FDR, who may, over time, develop into a
patriot-symbol with as much power as Lincoln or Washington.[5] Simultaneously, the Republicans, turning first to Herbert Hoover, and then to
Dwight Eisenhower, chose modern antistatist figures.[6]

In the future, one can imagine a war or serious depression which
might have the effect of producing a new-model hero, a new symbol of
patriotism (perhaps even one of *inter*national patriotism); but only if
such a person strongly reflected the dominant strands in British or American
culture. And this is precisely what the subjects of this book did.

The patriot-heroes that survive today are very different from those
of an earlier era. One student of American patriotism has defined patriotism as "love of country, pride in it, and readiness to make sacrifices
for what is considered its best interests." As such, it is "related" to "nationalism."[7] This definition accurately describes the *past* century, but it
does not suffice for an earlier era in the English-speaking world. As we
have indicated in the introduction, "patriotism" has its roots in a localistic, antistatist past. To the seventeenth-century Englishman a patriot was

one who supported "freedom" and the local "rights" of "the people" (however exclusive those "rights" and "people" might be) against a tyrannical court. Throughout the eighteenth and much of the nineteenth centuries a patriot was one "ever watchful for the public good" of excesses of government. Patriotism was "founded in great principles, and supported by great virtues."[8]

In that environment Hampden and Sydney were understandably attractive models.[9] They were localistic, appealing to libertarian Englishmen, Americans, French, and Germans. To the "Real Whig," the Benthamite and Radical, the Jeffersonian republican, they symbolized freedom *from* government, resistance to oppressive power; to the romantic they represented man's "sublime" soul, the glory of his "virtue"; to the legal community they represented due process, constitutionalism.

But by the mid-nineteenth century Hampden and Sydney, and their American counterpart, Jefferson, were being displaced by more potent, active, statist symbols. Industrialism and imperialism, nationalism and democracy, demanded more relevant patriot-heroes, and Hampden, Sydney, and Jefferson gave way to Washington, Lincoln, and Cromwell— gave way to men who would *act*—symbols of order, unity, righteousness, action, power, efficiency, organization, and the state. This alteration in the relative strength of patriot-symbols reflects the shift from a culture that valued personal liberty over "order" to one that preferred active, pragmatic leaders, "men of iron," who might bring prosperity, morality, unity, and order to scenes of decadence and disorder.

This essay also offers some substantiation of J. H. Plumb's claim that the elite tenaciously control the culture's vision of the past. Conservatives on both sides of the Atlantic successfully defended their claim to "the twin patriots." Radicals were forced to turn either to contemporary figures or to obscure symbols from the distant past. Their defeat is understandable; those in power have generally been able to decide on the shape of the nation's patriot-heroes, to determine the names of those to be numbered in its litany of patriot-saints. They choose carefully, and radicals are rarely able to make much use of patriots who had never been terribly radical themselves.

My expectations of what might be learned from this exploration of the nature of patriot-worship were, I think, modest ones. And necessarily so. The things that patriot-symbols tell us of cultural and political value change are not likely to be utterly unfamiliar to us, for, from other analyses, we already know something of the ideals and values of Britons and Americans. Nonetheless, I think this study has helped to clarify some of the central components of British and American political culture in these years, and I think it has helped to document important changes in that culture.

I speak of a single culture in referring to Britain and America. Obviously, there are many subtle differences between the two societies. But the mutual borrowing of patriot-symbols that both have engaged in for over two centuries reveals strikingly similar developments. Both societies have experienced a similar drift away from antistatism. And while no symbols have been quite as multinational as Hampden and Sydney were in the eighteenth century, it is clear that Cromwell had many American adherents; Washington, many British admirers. The same may be said of Lincoln, FDR, and even of Alfred the Great. Just as Britons were resurrecting King Alfred as a symbol of national unity and greatness, so Americans praised his "freedom from insular narrowness," his "cosmopolitan and international spirit," and his "genius for organization and administration."[10] Cosmopolitan and evangelical Americans intoned praise of Lincoln, and so did cosmopolitan and evangelical Britons. Viscount Haldane admired his "will" and compared it to that of Cromwell, as did John Drinkwater.[11] Godfrey Benson (Lord Charnwood), David Lloyd George, Frederic Harrison, and others proclaimed him a universal patriot-symbol of order and righteousness.[12] In 1920 a replica of the Saint-Gauden statue of Lincoln was placed near Westminster Abbey.[13] And these were clearly the same sort of persons as those who admired Lincoln in America. Drinkwater's patriotism was not "so narrowly local as to overlook the presiding interests of the state." Harrison's depended on one's willingness to reduce the powers of Parliament and to increase the powers of the prime minister in order to attain "more efficient government"; he had no use for Jefferson's "revolution once every ten years."[14] Conversely, American Jeffersonian critics of a powerful executive, of "Lord Abraham Lincoln," compared him in infamy to the Lord Protector.[15] Other examples might be given, but perhaps the point has been made: Britons and Americans often used patriot-symbols interchangeably and for the same reasons. The political cultures of Britain and America have had much in common over the past three centuries, particularly in the decline of antistatism, in the drift from localism to cosmopolitanism, and in the drift from a devotion to freedom to a devotion to order.

The decline of "the twin patriots," and the rise of their nemesis, Cromwell, reflects a growing tendency in the English-speaking world to reject antistatism, especially of the more revolutionary sort.[16] Thomas Jefferson, revolutionary and devout admirer of the twin patriots, had spoken of the possible need to "water the tree of liberty with the blood of patriots" every generation. Goldwin Smith's 1867 lectures on English political history began with the words: "Let us never glorify revolutions. . . . statesmanship is the art of preventing them."[17] We do not emulate the heroes of the English Civil War, the Commonwealth, or the American Revolution today. The Virginia and Kentucky Resolutions lie buried well beneath the Smith Act and its modern counterparts. While others in the world celebrate their zeal for change on the first of May, Americans observe "Law Day" or "Loyalty Day."

The decline of Hampden, Sydney, and Jefferson also reflects the shift in Britain and America from a culture dominated by Whiggish prerogatives to one alert to the voice of "the common people" in the political order: new symbols (Andrew Jackson, Abraham Lincoln, Oliver Cromwell) represented that "voice." But there is another important dimension to this veneration of Lincoln and Cromwell. Walter Prescott Webb has argued that with the industrial and population revolutions of the nineteenth century the Western world passed from a brief age of individualism, an antistatist age that gloried in the virtues of independence, acquisition, and constitutionalism, into a more "feudal," structured age of political, economic, social, and ideological rigidity. Samuel P. Hays emphasizes instead the drift from localistic, decentralized modes of thinking and acting toward cosmopolitan, systematized, centralized ways of organizing relationships.[18] As Tocqueville had observed, popular sovereignty and centralization do go hand in hand. The people get the vote, but they do not necessarily acquire the means to insure virtuous politics. The typical seventeenth- and eighteenth-century aristocrat or gentleman, facilitated by the socioeconomic power of his class and by his nearness to those in the legislature and at court, could wield much more influence, "clout," than any nineteenth- or twentieth-century voter. Hampden, Sydney, and Jefferson were of his class. Lincoln and Cromwell, Truman and Ike, were more democratic symbols. This democratic character of the patriot-symbols of the past century and half (beginning, perhaps, with Andrew Jackson) should not be lost sight of. But there is more to the veneration of Lincoln and Cromwell than that.

The veneration of Oliver Cromwell or Abraham Lincoln may not constitute a proto-fascist impulse,[19] but it does reflect a growing consciousness of the complexities of the modern polity. Lincoln and Cromwell were and are symbols of power, action, and order. And the rise of industry, cities, and macro-marketing systems yielded new sets of relationships so complex as to require potent political heroes. Roy Basler, a long-time student of "the Lincoln legend," recently expressed admiration himself for Lincoln's ability to solve problems within a rapidly changing socioeconomic context and "to use the executive power effectively."[20] These same qualities endeared Cromwell to many Britons.

This interest in the "iron" men does not necessarily mean that we are returning to an autocratic condition. The numbers who venerate Lincoln, Alfred, Charles, Napoleon, or "stern Oliver" today for the autocratic abilities they demonstrated at times are comparatively small. It is, I think, primarily their organizational skills that are respected. The heroes of America's schoolchildren and of the American Establishment's *Century* magazine at the turn of the century were individualistic figures from the past. But Theodore Greene has found that the typical patriot-hero to American magazines in the first few decades of the early twentieth century was increasingly modern and decreasingly individualistic. Organization men were what was needed; iconoclastic figures were less relevant.[21] Magazine editors are not "average" people, but Fred Greenstein's data suggest that "average" American people may feel the same way about patriot-heroes today.[22]

While this essay's findings regarding patriot-symbolism in Britain and America can hardly suffice as verification of either Webb's or Hays's hypotheses, it is worth noting that my conclusions appear to point in the same direction as both Webb and Hays. Rapid social change has led some of us to distrust the virtues of unabashed individualism or "town meeting democracy," and has provoked some to "escape from freedom"[23] and to experiment with more "efficient," hierarchical forms of government.[24] My own guess is that the movement in this direction will continue, for the socioeconomic changes that produced it continue to demand such political impulses as are epitomized by such men of power and order as Cromwell and Lincoln. To be sure, whether the process is inevitable, irreversible, or even undesirable, cannot be determined from our vantage point or by this analysis. Moreover, whether some final equilibrium will be reached between locals and cosmopolitans, between individual freedoms and collective rights, cannot be ascertained from any of the evidence I have offered here. All we can say with any certainty of the future is this: our analysis of the nature and meaning of British and American patriot-symbols constitutes evidence that these symbols do reflect changing values in the political culture. Hence, we can at least be sure that the patriot-heroes of the future will reflect the kind of settlement that will have been reached.

Reference Matter

Appendix A

One of the first examples of the use of the martyred Algernon Sydney by English Whigs is this *Copy of a Prophecy* . . . , published (and conceivably written) in the hour of victory by Sydney's friend, the Quaker merchant from Rotterdam, Benjamin Furley, an enthusiastic supporter of the "Glorious Revolution."

COPY

Of a Prophecy sent to B: F: in the Year 1666 from Montpelliers
by the late honourable Alguernon Sidney Esqr. & by him
Accidentally found among old Papers this $\frac{18}{28}$ February 1689

The Lilly shall remaine in the best part, & enter into the Land of the *Lion* wanting all help, because now the beasts of his owne Kingdome shall with their teeth teare his skin, and shall Stand among the Thornes of his Kingdome.

From Above *the Son of Man*, shall Come with a great army passing the waters. Carrying his armes beasts, whose Kingdome is in the Land of Wool, to be feared through the world.

The *Eagle* shall Come from the East parts, with his wings spread above the sun, with a great multitude of people to help the *Son of Man*.

That year Castles shall be left desolate, and great feare shall be in the World: and in Certaine parts of the *Lyon* there shall be Warr between many Kings, and there will be a deluge of blood.

The *Lilly* shall loose his Crown, with which the *Son of Man* shall be Crowned.

And for four yeares following there will be in the World many batailes among the followers of faith.

The greatest part of the World shall be destroyed: The head of the World shall fall to the ground.

The *Son of Man* and the *Eagle* shall prevaile, and then there shall be peace over all the World: and the Son of Man shall take the Wonderfull signe, and passe to the Land of Promise.

Appendix B

Questionnaire Administered to Students at the
University of Pittsburgh, 1974-75

A. Please respond to the following statements by indicating your measure of agreement or disagreement (circle the appropriate category):

1. That government is best which governs least.

   AGREE STRONGLY   AGREE   NEUTRAL   DISAGREE   DISAGREE STRONGLY

2. Complex modern societies require more effective central regulatory and planning agencies.

   AS   A   N   D   DS

3. The most rewarding organizations a person can belong to are local organizations serving local needs.

   AS   A   N   D   DS

4. I have greater respect for a man who is well-established in his local community than a man who is widely known in his field but who has no local roots.

   AS   A   N   D   DS

5. National and international events rarely seem as interesting and important as events that occur right in the local community in which one lives.

   AS   A   N   D   DS

B. Circle the number on this 1 to 10 spectrum which represents the point you place yourself in the tension between freedom and order:

   FREEDOM 1 2 3 4 5 6 7 8 9 10 ORDER

C. Circle the number representing your own "greatness score" that you feel appropriate for the following (1 is low, 10 is high):

George Washington	1 2 3 4 5 6 7 8 9 10
Thomas Jefferson	1 2 3 4 5 6 7 8 9 10
Abraham Lincoln	1 2 3 4 5 6 7 8 9 10
Theodore Roosevelt	1 2 3 4 5 6 7 8 9 10
Herbert Hoover	1 2 3 4 5 6 7 8 9 10
Franklin D. Roosevelt	1 2 3 4 5 6 7 8 9 10

D. 1. Why did you rank Jefferson in the way that you did?

   2. Why did you rank Lincoln the way you did?

175

E. 1. Please circle the political party you prefer:
        DEMOCRATIC   REPUBLICAN

    2. Your age is (circle correct category):
        UNDER 25   25–40   OVER 40

    3. Your parents' (or, if more appropriate, your own) occupation:

    4. No. of social science courses taken. _____

Notes

1: Introduction

1 Gottfried Salomon, "Hero Worship," *Encyclopedia of the Social Sciences* (15 vols., New York, 1932), 7:336–37. See also Paul Meadows, "Some Notes on the Social Psychology of the Hero," *Southwestern Social Science Quarterly* 26 (1945): 239–47.

2 Studies of the reputations of Lafayette, Jefferson, Washington, Cromwell, Lincoln, Charles I, Patrick Henry, John Milton, the Whig pamphleteers Trenchard and Gordon, the republican heroes of Greece and Rome, and "the Great Mr. Locke" have appeared, but as yet, little or no attention has been given to the strength and resilience of the reputations of Hampden and Sydney (which is why I give so much attention to their veneration in the text; I feel a "burden of proof"). The only treatment of the reputation of either man appears to be that of Caroline Robbins ("Algernon Sydney's *Discourses on Government:* Textbook of Revolution," *William and Mary Quarterly* 3rd ser., 4, no. 3 [July, 1947]: 267–96; and *The Eighteenth Century Commonwealthman* [Cambridge, Mass., 1959]), but while Robbins does provide a good account of the use made of Sydney's thought and writings, she does very little with what I consider the more important facet of his reputation— namely, the use of his name itself, quite apart from anything he may have written, as a symbol of martyrdom and patriotism. Moreover, J. H. Plumb recently remarked that a study is "badly needed" of the way in which the changing needs of nineteenth-century English society resulted in a reassessment of Cromwell (Plumb, *The Death of the Past* [Boston, 1970], p. 52n). See Merrill D. Peterson, *The Jefferson Image in the American Mind* (rev. ed., New York, 1962); Bernard Mayo, *Myths and Men* (Athens, Ga., 1959); Wilbur Cortez Abbott, "The Fame of Cromwell," in *Conflict With Oblivion* (London, 1924), pp. 163–95; Byron Stewart, "The Cult of the Royal Martyr," *Church History* 38 (1969):175–81; George F. Sensabaugh, *Milton in Early America* (Princeton, 1964); David L. Jacobson, ed., *The English Liberation Heritage* (Indianapolis, 1965); Richard M. Gummere, *The American Colonial Mind and the Classical Tradition* (Cambridge, Mass., 1963); Merle Curti, "The Great Mr. Locke; America's Philosopher, 1783–1861," *Huntington Library Bulletin* no. 11 (April, 1937): 107–52; P. M. Spurlin, *Montesquieu in America: 1760–1801* (Baton Rouge, 1940); H. F. Russell Smith, *Harrington and His Oceana: A Study of a 17th Century Utopia and its Influence in America* (Cambridge, 1914); Dixon Wecter, *The Hero in America* (New York, 1941); Marcus Cunliffe, *George Washington: Man and Monument* (New York, 1958); David Donald, "The Folklore Lincoln," in his *Lincoln Recon-*

sidered (New York, 1961); Wm. A. Bryan, *George Washington in American Literature, 1775-1865* (New York, 1952); Christopher Hill, "Cromwell and English History," in *God's Englishman* (London, 1970); Alan Smith, "The Image of Cromwell in Folklore and Tradition," *Folklore* 79 (1968): 17-38; and Maurice Ashley, *The Greatness of Oliver Cromwell* (London, 1957).

3 It should be obvious from the beginning, then, that women will play a slight role in this story. Elizabeth I occasionally figured as a patriot-hero to some seventeenth- and eighteenth-century Englishmen and women, but only occasionally. Female novelists and a handful of other articulate women offered opinions regarding one or another of these patriot-symbols, but the typical voice to be heard was that of a male (unless mothers play a significant role in naming their sons after patriot-heroes). Given the relatively small political role permitted women in Britain and America throughout most of the period under examination (see Fred Greenstein, *Children and Politics* [New Haven, 1965], pp. 107-27), my inability to detect much evidence of female attitudes towards patriot-heroes may be understandable, but I do not mean to imply that women were necessarily indifferent to political virtue and its symbols. I simply have not been able to discover sufficient evidence of their views to permit me to make any respectable generalizations about them.

4 C. P. Fitzgerald notes that the peasantry of ancient and feudal China took no part in the ancestor worship engaged in by the aristocracy and gentry, and J. H. Plumb argues that this was as true of medieval Germany and eighteenth-century Britain: "Myth, usually terrifying, provides for the worker; the official past is the property of the government! . . . The personal ownership of the past has always been a vital strand in the ideology of all ruling classes." Similarly, Fred Greenstein demonstrates that children from lower socioeconomic backgrounds in the U.S. are significantly less inclined to identify (either positively *or* negatively) with any famous public figure than are the children of upper socioeconomic backgrounds. Fitzgerald, *China* (New York, 1961), pp. 44-45; Plumb, *Death of the Past*, pp. 30-31; Greenstein, *Children and Politics*, pp. 100-101.

5 Joseph Ritson, *Robin Hood: A Collection of All the Ancient Poems, Songs, and Ballads Now Extant* (2 vols., London, 1795). The historical reality and the significance of Robin Hood were recently the subject of a debate in the pages of *Past and Present*. See R. H. Hilton, "The Origins of Robin Hood," *Past and Present* no. 14 (November, 1958):30-44; J. C. Holt, "The Origins and Audience of the Ballad of Robin Hood," ibid., no. 18 (November, 1960):89-110; Maurice H. Keen, "Robin Hood—Peasant or Gentleman?" ibid., no. 19 (April, 1961):7-15; and the communication by T. H. Aston, ibid., no. 20 (November, 1961):7-9.

6 Cecil Sharp, *English Folk Song* (London, 1902), p. 97.

7 J. H. Plumb, "Political Man," in J. L. Clifford, ed., *Man versus Society in Eighteenth Century Britain* (Cambridge, 1968), p. 17; Maurice H. Keen, *The Outlaw of Medieval Legend* (London, 1961); Kent Steckmesser, *The Western Hero in History and Legend* (Norman, Okla., 1965), pp. 244, 251, and

passim, and "Robin Hood and the American Outlaw," *Journal of American Folklore* 79 (1966):348–55; A. L. Lloyd, *Folk Song in England* (London, 1967); Russel Ward, *The Australian Legend* (Sydney, 1958), pp. 146–47; Eric Hobsbawm, *Bandits* (London, 1967), pp. 35–36, 48.

8 Greenstein, *Children and Politics*, pp. 100–101. I am indebted to Jema Cygnarovich and Fran Lezniak for their work on this project.

9 Anne Loveland, *Emblem of Liberty: The American Image of Lafayette* (Baton Rouge, 1971), pp. 154–58, quoting Laurence Stallings.

10 See, for example, Victor Daley, "A Ballad of Eureka," in Russel Ward, ed., *The Penguin Book of Australian Ballads* (London, 1964), pp. 215–17, celebrating Peter Lalor, a leader of the Digger rising of 1854.

11 Pansy Packenham, *King Charles I* (London, 1936), p. 142.

12 M. R. Toynbee, "Charles I and the King's Evil," *Folklore* 61 (1950): 14. Similarly, there are conflicting folk traditions in Scotland regarding "the Royal Martyr's" descendant, the Young Pretender Bonnie Prince Charlie. Some Highlanders (from the Isle of Skye) crooned of "the lad who's born to be King" and vowed that "Charlie will come again"; others (from the Isle of Barra) sang "O, young Charles Stuart, it was your cause that used me up."

13 "The Curse of Cromwell," *Saturday Review* 79 (1895): 819; J. A. Owen, *Drift from the Longshore* (London, 1898), pp. 116–17; M. W. Beresford, *The Lost Villages of England* (London, 1963), p. 98; Alan Smith, "The Image of Cromwell in Folklore and Tradition," *Folklore* 79 (1968): 25; Flora Thompson, *"Lark Rise" to Candleford* (London, 1965 ed.), p. 233. I am indebted to David Goodway of the University of Leeds and D. M. Palliser of the University of Keele, collaborators in a 1968–70 effort to gather information on the image of Cromwell in nineteenth-century England (a project hereafter referred to as "19C Cromwell") for the Owen and Thompson references.

    In the late nineteenth century the village boys of Harrow-on-the-Hill would shout "A stick and a stump/ For old Oliver's Rump," but it is not clear whether this was intended to commemorate Cromwell's dissolution of the Rump Parliament or simply to offer his posterior to posterity (Iona and Peter Opie, *The Lore and Language of Schoolchildren* [Oxford, 1959], p. 344).

14 J. Arthur Gibbs, *A Cotswold Village* (London, 1939), p. 81. I am indebted to Raphael Samuel of Ruskin College, Oxford, a 19C Cromwell participant, for this citation.

15 Hill, *God's Englishman*, p. 274.

16 John Adams, *Diary and Autobiography of John Adams*, ed. Lyman Butterfield et al. (4 vols., Cambridge, Mass., 1961), 3:185.

17 Alice Rossi, "Naming Children in the Middle-Class Families," *American Sociological Review* 30 (1965): 503; D. S. Smith, "Child-Naming Patterns and Family Structure: Bingham, Massachusetts, 1640–1880," paper delivered at the 1972 Clark University conference on The Family and Social Structure, pp. 16, 34, 35.

18 W. Zelinsky, "Cultural Variation in Personal Name Patterns in the Eastern

U.S.," *Annals of the Association of American Geographers* 60 (1970): 747. Cf. Harold Feldman, "The Problem of Personal Names as a Universal Element of Culture," *American Imago* 16 (1959): 237–50.

19 Sources ranged from nineteenth-century British and American census materials and street directories to dictionaries of American and British biography, biographic dictionaries of the American Congress, registers of graduates of universities and military academies, *Who Was Who, A National Register of the Society of the Sons of the American Revolution*, and a variety of other collections. The results are presented on pp. 63, 67, 91, 123, and 144.

20 Not as obvious are those named simply "Sidney," as this could be an innocuous family name, the pleasant-sounding but unintentional suggestion of an imaginative relation, or even a token of appreciation for an entirely different Sidney, the chivalric Elizabethan poet-knight Sir Philip, Algernon's granduncle. But sometimes it is possible to detect evidence that the "Rebel Saint" was indeed the reason that the parents chose "Sidney." Sidney Willard (b. 1780), for example, was certain that his first name was not given in celebration of Sir Philip and adds "it was the gift, I suppose of patriotism and the love of 'freedom.' " Willard, *Memories of Youth and Manhood* (2 vols., Cambridge, Mass., 1855), 1: 220.

More difficult to detect (but valuable because of what it reveals) are the instances of child-naming in which a patriot's name has been used but *altered* to fit the mood of the times. Thus Albert Sidney Johnston's parents first planned to name him "Algernon Sidney, out of esteem for the English Whig Martyr," but his older brother warned his parents that "so famous a name would be too much of a burden" to the boy. Charles Roland, *Albert Sidney Johnston: Soldier of Three Republics* (Austin, Texas, 1964), pp. 6–9. Cf. Sarah Hale in n. 29, below.

21 I am indebted to Alice Haugh of the Hamden Historical Society for this information.

22 I am indebted to Pamela R. L. Horn of 19C Cromwell for this information on the agricultural laborers.

23 Mark Meredith, *Charles I, King and Martyr* (Liverpool, 1922); Lady Helen Clifford Nellor, *Petition Against the Proposed Statue of Oliver Cromwell at the House of Parliament* (London, circa 1899), pp. 1–4; *The Times* (London), Nov. 1, 1899, p. 8; Nov. 10, 1899, p. 8; July 31, 1899, p. 13. See pp. 157 and 161 for further discussion of these movements.

24 *The Free Lance* (Dec. 10, 1875); James Middleton, *The Old Road* (London, 1920), p. 10. I am indebted to Raphael Samuel of 19C Cromwell for this information.

25 Frances Cartwright, ed., *The Life and Correspondence of Major Cartwright* (2 vols., London, 1826) 2: 143.

26 Perks to Rosebery, Dec. 2, 1899, Box 39, and Spencer to Rosebery, Jan. 27, 1900, Box 76, Rosebery papers, National Library of Scotland, Edinburgh. I am indebted to Keith Robbins of York and H. Matthew of 19C Cromwell for this information.

27 *Cheltenham Free Press*, March 2, 1850. I am indebted to Raphael Samuel for this reference.

28 Alexander Somerville, *The Autobiography of a Working Man*, ed. John Carswell (London, 1951), p. 87.

29 Sarah Hale, *Northwood, or Life North and South, Showing the True Character of Both* (New York, 1852), p. 10.

30 C. S. Forester, *Brown on Resolution* (London, 1929), p. 42. Compare Theodore S. Fay, *Sydney Clifton* (2 vols., New York, 1839), 1: 154; and see especially Anthony Trollope, *Doctor Thorne* (London, Pan ed., 1968 [orig. pub. 1858]), p. 139, for one explanation of the phenomenon Forester noted: "If one wishes to look out in the world for royal nomenclature, to find children who have been christened after kings and queens . . . the search should be made in the family of democrats. None have so servile a deference for the very nail-parings of royalty; none feel so wondering an awe at the exaltation of a crowned head; none are so anxious to secure to themselves some shred or fragment that has been consecrated by the royal touch. It is the distance which they feel to exist between themselves and the throne which makes them covet the crumbs of majesty."

31 Indeed, I sometimes catch myself wondering, like most twentieth-century English and Americans would, how it was that some of these figures stirred such emotions in eighteenth- and nineteenth-century breasts. Which is not to say that the values they stood for are meaningless for people today; on the contrary, many of the issues they fought for or represented are central to many of today's issues. It is simply that patriot-symbols representing a more relevant cluster of values have taken their place.

32 Ernst Kantrowicz, " 'Pro Patria Mori' in Medieval Political Thought," *American Historical Review* 66 (1951): 474–77.

33 V. H. Galbraith, "Nationality and Language in Medieval England," *Transactions of the Royal Historical Socety* 4th ser., 23 (1941): 120.

34 John Barnie, *War in Medieval English Society* (Ithaca, 1974), pp. 44, and 97–116 (Ch. 4, "Patriots and Patriotism"); Kantrowicz, " 'Pro Patria Mori,' " pp. 478–79; Johan Huizinga, *Men and Ideas* (London, 1940, trans. 1959), esp. p. 130.

2: Patriot-Symbols of the English Civil Wars

1 J. H. Plumb, *The Origins of Political Stability, England, 1675–1725* (Boston, 1967), p. 36.

2 J. W. Gough argues quite convincingly, however, that the five judges who concluded that Charles I had a *right* to levy such a tax to defend his realm were well within the law as it existed in the 1630's: *Fundamental Law in English Constitutional History* (Oxford, 1955), pp. 69–72.

3 Edward Hyde, Earl of Clarendon, *Selections from the History of the Rebellion . . .* , ed. G. Huehns (London, 1956), p. 168.

4 From his "Apology," in *Sydney's Discourses on Government* (3 vols., New York, 1805), 1:256; hereafter cited as *DOG*.

5 Sydney to his mother, June 18, 1643, in *History of the Irish Confederation and War in Ireland, 1641–1643*, ed. John T. Gilbert (7 vols., Dublin, 1882), 2: xiix.

6 "Journal of Robert, Earl of Leicester," *Sydney Papers*, ed. R. W. Blencowe (London, 1825), pp. 140–41; O. Cromwell, *The Writings and Speeches of Oliver Cromwell*, ed. Wilbur C. Abbott (3 vols., Cambridge, Mass., 1937–45), 2:631–55; Historical Manuscripts Commission, *Report on Mss. of Viscount de L'Isle* (London, 1966), 6:499, hereafter cited as HMC; J. R. Western, *Monarchy and Revolution* (Totowa, N.J., 1972), pp. 64–65.

7 *DOG*, 2: 477.

8 Ibid., 3: 73, 78, 97, 134–35, 146, 183, 347–48.

9 Ibid., ch. 3, sec. 20. Cf. J. W. Gough, *The Social Contract* (Oxford, 1957), pp. 128–29.

10 *DOG*, ch. 3, sec. 28; 1: 199; 3:431.

11 Ibid., 3: 223–24, 26.

12 See, for example, M. Dorothy George, *English Political Caricature* (2 vols., Oxford, 1959), 1: 37–48; anon., *Shuffling, cutting, and dealing, in a game at pickquet, being acted from 1653 to 1658 by Oliver, Protector, and others . . .* (London, 1659); *DNB*, John Gauden; Dr. Richard Hollingsworth, *Defense of Charles I* (London, 1692); Thomas Wagstaffe, *Vindication of Charles the Martyr* (London, 1687).

13 George, *English Political Caricature*, 1: 41, 42, 43 (for Winstanley), 60; Christopher Hill, *God's Englishman* (London, 1970), p. 254.

14 *Oliver Cromwell's Ghost, Dropt from the Clouds* (London, 1681), p. 2. See also Ferdinand Galardi, *La Tyrannie Heureuse* (Geneva, 1671). Robert Wild (an ejected minister), *Oliver Cromwell's Ghost, or Old Noll Revived* (London, 1679), offers a similar message.

15 Alan Smith, "The Image of Cromwell in Folklore and Tradition," *Folklore* 79 (1968): 19.

16 Wilbur C. Abbott, *Conflicts with Oblivion* (London, 1924), pp. 163–95; Byron Stewart, "The Cult of the Royal Martyr," *Church History* 38 (1969): 175–87. Stewart claims (p. 175) that the sentiments expressed in the 300-odd January 30 sermons of the late seventeenth and early eighteenth centuries that he consulted were "more indicative of the sentiments of the nation than any Whig doctrines." He may well be correct, but he offers no proof of this; I have seen many of these sermons myself and cannot see that they establish anything more than the fact that a great many Anglican divines whose January 30 sermons were published in these years were devotees of the cult of the Royal Martyr and defilers of the memory of Cromwell. Popular opinion simply cannot be deduced from collections of published sermons.

17 Anon., *The Secret History of the Reigns of King Charles II and King James II* (London, 1690), p. 201.

18 Cf. Felix Raab, *The English Face of Machiavelli* (London, 1965), pp. 130–54.

19 See "A Speech against Peace at the Close Committee," in *The Poetical Works of Sir John Denham*, ed. Theodore H. Banks, Jr. (New Haven, 1928), pp. 122-27, where Hampden is made to say that he divides his time between the king and Commons "To keep his Excellence in awe / and give the Parliament the Law."

20 The newspaper accounts and the first elegy are reprinted in full in John Forster, "John Hampden," in *The Statesmen of the Commonwealth of England* (New York, 1846), pp. 262-63.

21 Anon., *Elegies on the Death of Colonel Hampden* (London, 1643).

22 See Hill, *God's Englishman*, p. 169, on Cony; see anon., "The Member's Justification" (1647), in *Political Ballads of the 17th and 18th Centuries*, ed. W. Walker Wilkins (2 vols., London, 1860), 1:42; and *Oliver Cromwell's Letters and Speeches*, ed. Thomas Carlyle, in *The Works of Thomas Carlyle* (15 vols., London, 1907-20), 9, pt. 4, p. 60, on Cromwell's views.

23 Thomas Hobbes, *Behemoth* (London, 1682), p. 60; Clarendon, *Selections*, pp. 166-70.

24 R. Plumer Ward, *An Historical Essay on the Real Character and Amount of the Precedent of the Revolution of 1688* ... (2 vols., London, 1838) 1: 93.

25 John Milton, *Pro Populo Anglicano Defensio Secunda* ("A Second Defense of the English People"), vol. 8 in *The Works of John Milton* (New York, 1933), p. 235; see also Arthur Annesley, *England's Confusion* ... (London, 1659), p. 16.

26 Gilbert Burnet, *Burnet's History Of My Own Time*, ed. Osmund Airy (Oxford, 1900), 2: 352-53; HMC, *7th Report* (London, 1879), p. 343. For more on Sydney and the French see below, chapter 3.

27 *The Diary of John Evelyn*, December 8, 1683, ed. E. S. de Beer (London, 1959), p. 761.

28 Sir Richard Bulstrode, *Memoirs and Reflection upon the Reign and Government of King Charles the Ist and King Charles the IInd* (London, 1721), p. 357; Titus Oates, *A Display of Tyranny or Remarks upon the Illegal and Arbitrary Proceedings in the Courts of Westminster and Guildhall* ... (London, 1689), pt. 2, pp. 304-10.

29 Morrice is quoted in Doreen Milne, "The Results of the Rye-House Plot and their Influence upon the Revolution of 1688," *Transactions of the Royal Historical Society* 5th ser., 1 (1951): 97; *The Memoirs of John, Earl of Ailesbury* (Westminster, 1890), pp. 136-37.

30 *Poems on Affairs of State* (3 vols., London, 1697-1704), 1:218-19; 3:246.

31 H. Ball to Lord Preston, November 26, 1683, in HMC, *7th Report*, p. 375; John Stewkeley to Sir Richard Verney, 8th December 1683, in F. P. and M. M. Verney, eds., *Memoirs of Verney Family* ... , *1660-1696* (4 vols., London, 1892-99), 4: 272; ? to Richard Newdigate, December 20, 1683, in Lady Newdigate-Newdegate, ed., *Cavalier and Puritan* ... (London, 1901), p. 138; James, Duke of York, to William, Prince of Orange, December 7, 1683, in

Sir John Dalrymple, *Memoirs of Great Britain and Ireland* . . . (2 vols., London, 1771-73), 2: 54-55; Bishop of Oxford to Christopher, 1st Viscount Hatton, December 14, 1683, in Edward M. Thompson, ed., *Correspondence of the Family of Hatton*, Camden Society n. s., vols. 22 & 23 (Westminster, 1878), 23: 41.

Cf. ? to Increase Mather, December 10, 1683, *Collections of the Massachusetts Historical Society* 4th ser., 8 (1868): 636-37: "the relation that Coll: Sidney, when upon the Scaffold, tooke leave of a Minister as one of his friends, was a mistake, for upon further inquiry I find that if he bowed to any of that Function, it was gen^{ll}, as he stood amongst other company, the said Mr. Sidney altogether neglecting the assistance of any divine . . . he had no occasion for them."

32 An Exact Account of the Tryal of Algernon Sydney . . . (London, 1683), pp. 2-3; *Some Animadversions upon a paper delivered to the sheriffs* . . . (London, 1684), p. 3. Cf. Elkanah Settle, *Remarks on Algernon Sydney's Paper* (London, 1684), pp. 1-3; Edmund Bohun, *A Defence of Sir Robert Filmer against the misrepresentations of Algernon Sydney* . . . (London, 1684), passim; *The Animadversions and Remarks upon Collonel Sydney's Paper answered* (London, 1684).

33 Thomas Sprat, *A True Account of the Horrid Conspiracy against the late King* . . . (1685), in *Collectanea Adamantaea* (Edinburgh, 1886), 14, sec. 3: 36. Sprat also referred to another of the "conspirators," John Hampden the younger, grandson of the ship-money hero, and spoke of "the Hereditary Malignity of this House against the Royal Family; his Grandfather having been the most Active Instrument to widen the Breech between the late Blessed King, and the seduced part of his People" (sec. 1: 29).

34 ? to Sunderland, 29th October 1684, *Calendar, State Papers, Domestic, May 1684-Feb. 1685*, pp. 187-88.

35 *The Memoirs of Sir John Reresby*, ed. James J. Cartwright (London, 1875), entry for 14 June 1685, p. 332.

36 "The Metamorphosis" [circa 1687], *Poems on Affairs of State*, 2: 159; "An Epitaph in honour of Sidney" [circa 1687], in *The Memoirs of Thomas Hollis*, ed. Francis Blackburne (London and Edinburgh, 1780), pp. 780-81.

37 Edward Harley to Lady Harley, 30 June 1688, in HMC, *14th Report, Appendix, pt. 2, Portland, Mss.*, 3: 412. I have also examined the record of the trial, and find little difference in the accounts of the incident. Finch's reply, if any, is unrecorded.

38 William Cobbett, *The Parliamentary History of England* (12 vols., London, 1806-12), 5: 169-70.

39 HMC, *12th Report, Appendix, pt. 6, Manuscripts of the House of Lords, 1689-90* (London, 1889), p. 96.

40 Humphrey Smith, *Sydney Redivivus* . . . (London, 1689), pp. 2, 8. After summarizing the trial, the author noted: "the Blood of patriots is the Seed of Asserters of the People's Liberty." See also R. Burton, *The History of the Two Late Kings* . . . (London, 1693), passim.

41 Sir John Hawles, *Remarks* . . . , in *A Collection of State Tracts Published during the Reign of William III* (3 vols., London, 1705), 2:45–48.

42 Cobbett, *Parliamentary History*, 5:421; Thomas B. Howell, ed., *Cobbett's Complete Collection of State Trials and Proceedings for High Treason and Other Crimes* . . . (London, 1809–26), 12:645ff., 1245ff., 1291ff.; 9:846n.

43 *Poems on Affairs of State*, 3:327.

44 Cobbett, *Parliamentary History*, 5: 1039, 1077, 1137. Sir William Pulteney remarked, on the first reading of the Treason Bill (March 20, 1689), that "Colonel Sidney would not have lost his life if he had had counsel allowed him." Anchitell Grey, ed., *Debates of the House of Commons from the year 1667 to the year 1694* (10 vols., London, 1763), 9:174.

45 Charles Hornby, *A Caveat against the Whiggs* (2nd ed., 4 vols., London, 1711–12), 4:24.

46 Edwin Wolf, 2nd, "A Parcel of Books for the Province in 1700," *Pennsylvania Magazine of History and Biography* 89, no. 4 (October, 1965): 491.

47 William Dawes, *A Sermon preached before the Lords Spiritual and Temporal at Westminster-Abbey on January 30, 1710* (London, 1710), p. 20, and passim. See also Luke Milbourne, *The Traitor's Reward* (1702), *Impiety and Folly of Resisting Lawful Laws* (1710), *Animadversions on the 2 Last 30th of January Sermons of Bishop White Kennett* (1709), *A Guilty Conscience* (1710), and *Sedition and Rebellion* (1718); White Kennett, *A Sermon preached before Commons* (1706), and *A Compassionate Enquiry into the causes of the Civil war* (1708); Humphrey Nickel, *Duplex in Cardo-Cidas Querela* (1703); Gilbert Burnet, *The Royal Martyr and the Dutiful Subject* (1710); Benj. Hoadly, *A Layman's Lamentation* . . . (1710); George Fothergill, *The Danger of Excesses in the Pursuit of Liberty* (1737); and others in the collection of January 30 sermons in the Cambridge University library.

48 *Oliver's Pocket Looking-Glass; New Fram'd and Cleaned, To Give a Clear View of the Great Modern COLOSSUS* (London, 1711); *A Pair of Spectacles for Oliver's Looking-Glass Maker* (London, 1711), pp. 13–14. Cf. the anti-Cromwellian *Vindication of Oliver Cromwell and The Whiggs of forty-one to our modern low churchmen* . . . (London, 1712).

49 George, *English Political Caricature*, 1:68; *Cato's Letters*, no. 25, p. 71; John Oldmixon, *History of England* (London, 1730), 1:228.

50 George Cadwallader, *The Remembrance* (London, 1748), p. 88; *Tobias Smollett*, ed. G. S. Rousseau and P. G. Bouce (New York, 1971), pp. 38–39; anon., *Liberty & Right*, pp. 39–40. Voltaire accepted and repeated the criticism of Cromwell (*Oeuvres Completes* [52 vols., Paris, 1878], 13:62ff.). as did Frederick the Great (see his *Political Testament of 1752*, trans. in David Ralston, ed., *Soldiers and States* [Boston, 1966], p. 47).

51 Isaac Kimber, *The Life of Oliver Cromwell, Lord Protector of the Commonwealth* (London, 1725), pp. 393–99. See Chs. 4 and 5 for more on Cromwell and the Nonconformists.

52 John Banks, *A Short Critical Review of the Political Life of Oliver Cromwell, Lord Protector* (London, 1739), pp. 260–72.

53 See Hill, *God's Englishman*, pp. 264–67, on the general revival in the mid-eighteenth century; see George, *English Political Caricature*, 1:101, 103, 108, with regard to mid-eighteenth-century broadsides.

54 Francis Peck, *Memoirs . . . of Oliver Cromwell* (London, 1740), preface.

55 Jonathan Swift, in "Drapier Letter VI," *The Prose Works of Jonathan Swift*, ed. Temple Scott (12 vols., London, 1897–1908), 6: 167; Hornby, *Caveat*, 2: 2; White Kennett, *A Complete History of England* (3 vols., London, 1719 ed. [orig. published 1706]), 3: 403–5; Roger North, *Examen: or an Inquiry into . . . A Complete History . . .* (London, 1740), pp. 406–13.

56 John Oldmixon, *Clarendon & Whitlock Compared* (London, 1727), p. 207.

57 John, Lord Somers, *Jura Populi Anglicani . . .* (1701), in *A Collection of State Tracts*, 3: 281.

58 John Locke, "On Reading and Study," in *A Collection of Several Pieces of Mr. John Locke* (London, 1720), p. 244. Locke claimed never to have read Sydney's *Discourses*, but he did own a copy.

59 *Three Letters to the Members of the Present Parliament . . .* (London, 1747), pp. 29, 48; Anthony Lincoln, *Some Political and Social Ideas of English Dissent, 1763–1800* (Cambridge, 1938), p. 90.

60 See *Cato's Letters*, February 11, 1720, April 15, 1721, for Trenchard and Gordon's use of Sydney. In the first piece, Trenchard prefaced Sydney's famous motto *Manus haec inimica tyrannis . . .* with the observation that "every worthy Briton cries [it] out aloud." For evidence of Trenchard's family tie to Sydney the conspirator, see DNB, John Trenchard; and Forde, Lord Grey, 1st Earl of Tankerville, *The Secret History of the Rye-House Plot . . .* (written 1685; publ. London, 1754), p. 28. Cf. David L. Jacobson, ed., *The English Libertarian Heritage* (Indianapolis, 1965), p. xxxiii.

61 Daniel DeFoe, *Jure divino . . .* (a poem), in *The Works of Daniel DeFoe*, ed. William Hazlitt (3 vols., London, 1841), 3:28n; *English Advice to the Freeholders of England*, in *Somers Tracts* (13 vols., London, 1809–15) 13:555, 558.

62 *Rex* v. *Layer*, in *State Trials*, ed. Howell, 16: 94 (see also *Rex* v. *Hensey* [1758], ibid., 19:1341); Lewis Melville, *The Life and Writings of Philip, Duke of Wharton* (London, 1913), p. 284.

63 *The Complete Poetical Works of James Thomson*, ed. J. Logie Robertson (Oxford, 1951), pp. 109, 109n, 388. Thomson altered the verse in his 1744 edition of *The Seasons*, at which time Sydney became "the British Cassius . . . , of high determined spirit, roughly brave, / By ancient learning to the enlightened love/ Of ancient freedom warmed" (p. 109).

64 *An Address to the . . . Free-Holders . . . [on] the General Election* (London, 1734), pp. 17, 21–22, 30.

65 *A Proper Answer to a Late Scurrilous Libel Entitled, An Apology for the Conduct of a late Celebrated Second-rate Minister* (London, 1747), passim.

66 Caroline Robbins, *The Eighteenth Century Commonwealthman* (Cambridge, Mass., 1959), pp. 121, 137, 187, 260, 322, 358, 373.

67   J. H. Plumb, "Political Man," in J. L. Clifford, ed., *Man versus Society in Eighteenth-Century Britain* (London, 1968), p. 15; E. G. Withycombe, *The Oxford Dictionary of English Christian Names* (Oxford, 1945), p. 118; Robert Haig, *"The Gazetteer," 1735-1797: A Study in the Eighteenth-Century English Newspaper* (Carbondale, Ill., 1960), pp. 7, 282.
   I don't know what his politics were, but the gesture of one "Mr. Perry" was not noteworthy. In 1752, after acquiring some of the Sydney family's estates, Perry assumed the name "Algernon Sydney" (*The Letters of Edward Gibbon* [3 vols., New York, 1956], 1: 150).

68   See, for instance, *A Report of Some Proceedings on the Commission for the Trial of the Rebels in the Year 1746 in the County of Surrey . . . by Mr. Justice Foster* (3rd ed., London, 1792), pp. 198-99. See also James Thomson, *The Castle of Indolence* (London, 1748), Canto XXXII (Thomson was critical here of corruption in the Whig administration of Sir Robert Walpole, of course), and Bonamy Dobrée, "The Theme of Patriotism in the Poetry of the Early 18th Century," *Proceedings of the British Academy* 35 (1949): 7-13.

69   *Grandsire Hamden's Ghost, A Poem* (London, 1712).

70   *The Correspondence of Thomas Gray*, ed. Paget Toynbee and Leonard Whibley (3 vols., Oxford, 1935), 2: 749; Thomson's poem is cited in the frontispiece to the Hampden Club, *A Sketch of the Life of John Hampden* (Nottingham, 1817).

71   Paul de Rapin-Thoyras, *History of England*, trans. N. Tindal (London, 1730), 10:304.

72   James Ralph, *The Champion* no. 1 (1741): ix (a journal, edited by Ralph and Henry Fielding, that opposed Sir Robert Walpole's administration).

73   *Pennsylvania Gazette* (Philadelphia), October 9, 1729, p. 1.

74   Wolf, "A Parcel of Books," p. 432.

75   White Kennett, *Bibliothecae Americanae Primordia: An Attempt towards Laying the Foundation of an American Library . . . Humbly Given to the Society for Propagation of the Gospel in Foreign Parts* (London, 1713).

76   *A Catalogue of Curious and Valuable Books Belonging to the Late and Learned Reverend Mr. Ebenezer Pemberton* (Boston, 1717), p. 4.

77   Clifford K. Shipton, *Sibley's Harvard Graduates* (Boston, 1945), 8: 518-30.

78   Edwin Wolf, 2nd, "The First Books & Printed Catalogues of the Library Company," *Pennsylvania Magazine of History and Biography* 78 (1954): 57.

79   H. Trevor Colbourn, *The Lamp of Experience: Whig History and the Intellectual Origins of the American Revolution* (Chapel Hill, 1965), pp. 199-232. Harvard College possessed the only copy of *Hampden's Tryal* among the volumes listed by Colbourn.

80   T. Dwight, "Harrington and his Influence upon American Political Institutions and Political Thought," *Political Science Quarterly* 2 (1887): 1-44; H. F. Russell Smith, *Harrington and his Oceana: A Study of a Seventeenth Century Utopia and its Influence in America* (Cambridge, 1914); P. M. Spurlin, *Montesquieu in America, 1760-1801* (Baton Rouge, 1940); George

F. Sensabaugh, *Milton in Early America* (Princeton, 1964). The Sensabaugh study is particularly sensible.

81　A. S. Pratt, "The Books Sent from England by Jerimiah Dummer to Yale College," in *Papers in Honor of Andrew Keogh* (New Haven, 1938), pp. 15, 17.

82　Caroline Robbins, "Library of Liberty—Assembled for Harvard College by Thomas Hollis of Lincoln's Inn," *Harvard Library Bulletin* 5 (1951): 5–23, 181–96; Robbins, "The Strenuous Whig—Thomas Hollis of Lincoln's Inn," *William and Mary Quarterly* 3rd ser., 7 (1950): 432–44.

83　James Alexander, *A Brief Narrative of the Case and Trial of John Peter Zenger . . .* , ed. Stanley N. Katz (Cambridge, Mass., 1963), p. 230n23.

84　Moses Coit Tyler, *The Literary History of the American Revolution* (2 vols., New York, 1957), 2: 12; DAB, James Ralph; Ralph, *Of the Use and Abuse of Parliaments* (London, 1744), "advertisement" facing 1:1.

85　Catherine Drinker Bowen, *John Adams and the American Revolution* (New York, 1950), p. 32; C. N. Greenough, "Algernon Sidney and the Motto of Massachusetts," *Massachusetts Historical Society Proceedings* 51 (1917–18): 279; "Letters from Andrew Eliot to Thomas Hollis," *Collections of the Massachusetts Historical Society* 4th ser., 4 (1858): 403, Eliot to Hollis, May 13, 1767.

86　Robbins, *Eighteenth Century Commonwealthman*, p. 137.

87　Clinton Rossiter, "The Life and Mind of Jonathan Mayhew," *William and Mary Quarterly* 3rd ser., 7 (1950): 551–53, 545.

88　*Independent Advertiser*, May 16, 1748, p. 1. See also William Livingston's essays, "On Passive Obedience and Non-Resistance" and "Further Reflections . . . ," *Independent Reflector*, Aug. 16 and 23, 1753.

89　*Pennsylvania Gazette* (Philadelphia) November 20, 1755, p. 1. The passage from the *Discourses* is in 2: 212–13 (Chapter 2, Section 23) and on the next page (2: 214) Sydney wrote "God helps those who help themselves." Franklin must have read this and it is possible that "Poor Richard" borrowed it from the Rebel-Saint; but the phrase may have been "in the air" for a century or more.

3: "Liberty and Property"

1　*Boston Evening-Post*, April 9, 1750, p. 1; ibid., March 12, 1750, p. 1.

2　James Burgh, *Thoughts on Education* (Boston, 1749), p. 15, cited in H. Trevor Colbourn, *The Lamp of Experience* (Chapel Hill, 1965), p. 5.

3　Caroline Robbins, *The Eighteenth Century Commonwealthman* (Cambridge, Mass., 1959), pp. 274, 282. William Pitt and Arthur Onslow, Speaker of the House, read Sydney in these years. Franklin bought a second copy of the *Discourses* during his 1757–62 visit to London (John G. Shipley, "Franklin Attends a Book Auction," *Pennsylvania Magazine of History and Biography* 80 [1956]: 37–45).

4 Th. Hollis, *The Works of John Milton* (London, 1761), introduction.

5 James Otis, *A Vindication of the Conduct of the House of Representatives of the Province of Massachusetts-Bay, more particularly in the last session* (Boston, 1762), p. 20n.

6 There was also an edition in 1704, but none in 1740, as Sir Charles Firth had suggested in the *DNB* article on Sydney.

7 Robbins, "Library of Liberty—Assembled for Harvard College by Thomas Hollis of Lincoln's Inn," *Harvard Library Bulletin* 5 (1951): 183.

8 *The Memoirs of Thomas Hollis*, ed. Francis Blackburne (London, 1783), p. 187.

9 Thomas Hollis, "The Life and Memoirs of Algernon Sydney" (1763), reprinted in *DOG*, 1:79–80.

10 Francis Blackburne, in his edition of Hollis's *Memoirs*, pp. 186, 188.

11 See, for example, Rind's *Virginia Gazette* (Williamsburg), May 30, 1766, p. 2, where "Algernon Sydney," "showing my opinion," submits that "submission to the Stamp Law would have deprived us of our LIBERTY and PROPERTY." As the law was passed in violation of the rights of Englishmen in Virginia, Virginians "have a Right . . . to rise up and deny the binding efficacy of the Stamp-Act."

12 See, for example, anon., *Considerations on the Legality of General Warrants* (London, 1765), p. 14.

13 See Soame Jenyns, *The Objections to the Taxation of our American Colonies by the Legislature of Great Britain briefly Considered* (London, 1765), p. 79; and James Otis's reply, *Considerations on Behalf of the Colonists in a letter to a noble Lord* (Boston and London, 1765), p. 8. Cf. Benjamin Franklin's "Rejoinder to Tom Hint," London *Gazetteer*, December 27, 1765, in Benjamin Franklin's *Letters to the Press*, ed. Verner W. Crane (Chapel Hill, 1950), p. 41.

14 *DOG*, ch. 3, sec. 16; Stephen Hopkins, *The Rights of Colonies Examined* (Providence, 1765), p. 4.

15 *The Poetical Works of Charles Churchill*, ed. George Gilfillan (New York, 1855).

16 *The Correspondence of the Late John Wilkes*, ed. John Almon (5 vols., London, 1805), 5: 282; *An Appendix to the 1st 46 issues . . .* (London, 1769), pp. lxxxiii, xcii, civ.

17 Purdie and Dixon's *Virginia Gazette* (Williamsburg), March 30, 1769, pp. 1–2. See also Boston Sons of Liberty to Wilkes, June 6, 1768, *Proceedings of the Massachusetts Historical Society* 47 (1913–14): 191.

18 *Correspondence of Wilkes*, 4:219, 5:166; Caroline Robbins, "The Strenuous Whig: Thomas Hollis of Lincoln's Inn," *William and Mary Quarterly* 3rd ser., 7(1950):413.

19 *Maryland Gazette* (Annapolis), April 26, 1770, p. 1.

20 *Correspondence of Wilkes*, 5:166.

21 Walpole to Montagu, December 16, 1764, in *Horace Walpole's Correspondence*, ed. W. S. Lewis (Yale ed., 35 vols. to date, New Haven, 1941—), 10:139; Robbins, *Eighteenth Century Commonwealthman*, p. 358.

22 *The Autiobiography of Benjamin Rush*, ed. George Corner (Princeton, 1948), p. 46.

23 *The Diary of Sylas Neville, 1767–1788*, ed. B. Cozens-Hardy (London, 1950), pp. 23, 46, 48, 76, and 5 (on his instructing his landlady). Edward Gibbon (1737–94), the historian, copied Sydney's motto into his diary (London *Times Literary Supplement*, November 15, 1917).

24 Sydney Smith, of *Edinburgh Review* fame, b. 1771, appears to have been named for the Rebel-Saint.

25 The first of these caricatures is reprinted in the *William and Mary Quarterly* 3rd ser., 4 (1947):266, the second in M. Dorothy George, *English Political Caricature* (2 vols., Oxford, 1959), 1:160 and pl. 61.

26 *The Legal Papers of John Adams*, ed. L. Kinvin Wroth and Hiller B. Zobel (3 vols., Cambridge, Mass., 1965), 3:270. See also J. Adams and Jonathan Sewell, "*Novanglus and Massachusettensis*" (Boston, 1819), p. 62.

27 L. G. Tyler, "William and Mary College and Its Influences on the Founding of the Republic," *William and Mary Quarterly* 2nd ser., 15 (1935): 333; Millicent Sowerby, *A Catalogue of the Library of Thomas Jefferson* (Washington, D.C., 1952—), 3: 12–13. Douglass Adair, in "Rumbold's Dying Speech, 1685, and Jefferson's Last Words on Democracy, 1826," *William and Mary Quarterly* 3rd ser., 9 (1952): 521 ff., suggested that Jefferson lifted the expression regarding some men being born into the world booted and saddled to ride mankind from the last speech of Colonel Rumbold, a Rye-House plotter. It seems just as likely that he read the expression in the *Discourses* (*DOG*, 3: 264). In any event, the phrase was not exclusively Rumbold's.

28 Robbins, "Textbook on Revolution," p. 270.

29 William Stearns, *View of Controversy . . .* (Watertown, Mass., 1775), p. 18. See also Benjamin Franklin's quoting of "the great Sydney" in 1770: "We owe none but what we freely give; [none is] or can be imposed on us, unless by ourselves. . . . [we] think nothing too dear to be hazarded in Defense of [our Liberty]." *Papers of Benjamin Franklin*, ed. William Wilcox, vol. 17 (New Haven, 1973), pp. 47–48.

30 Robbins, *Eighteenth Century Commonwealthman*, p. 373; James Burgh, *Political Disquisitions* (3 vols., Philadelphia, 1775), l:vii, 191–92; 3:65.

31 Herbert Butterfield, *George III, Lord North, and the People* (London, 1949), pp. 345–47, 351.

32 Oscar Zeichner, *Connecticut's Years of Controversy, 1750–1776* (Chapel Hill, 1949), p. 146; Dixon and Hunter's *Virginia Gazette* (Williamsburg), May 25, 1776, p. 1.

33 Colbourn, *Lamp of Experience*, pp. 190–91; cf. Pauline Maier, *From Resistance to Revolution* (New York, 1972), pp. 31–42.

34 Rind's *Virginia Gazette* (Williamsburg), September 8, 1774, p. 2; ibid., now published by John Pinckney, May 18, 1775, p. 1. See also "Sidney," *The*

Scourge no. 2 (Boston, 1771) (copy in Massachusetts Historical Society Library).

35 HMC, *14th Report, Appendix, pt. 10, Earl of Dartmouth Mss.* (London, 1895), p. 376; *The Patriot Minister* (London, 1778), pp. 7, 15, 17.

36 Richard D. Brown, *Revolutionary Politics in Massachusetts* (Cambridge, Mass., 1970), p. 115.

37 J. Adams to Abigail Adams, April 13, 1777, in *The Adams Papers: Adams Family Correspondence*, ed. L. H. Butterfield (4 vols., New York, 1965), 2:208.

38 C. N. Greenough, "Sidney and the Motto of Massachusetts," *Massachusetts Historical Society Proceedings (1917–20)*, 51:259ff.

39 James MacPherson, *The History of Great Britain . . .* (2 vols., London, 1775), 1:402–5; Wm. *Harris, An Historical and Critical Account of the Lives and Writings of . . . Charles I and Oliver Cromwell . . .* (5 vols., London, 1814 [orig. pub. 1762]), 5: 336–37, 351. MacPherson was of the opinion that Sydney had delivered his *Last Paper* as a speech to the multitude before his execution, and thus accused Sydney of being too "enthusiastic." In fact, the speech was merely delivered to the sheriffs in writing.

40 Sir John Dalrymple, *Memoirs of Great Britain and Ireland . . .* (2 vols., Edinburgh, 1771–73), 1: 381–83; 2: vii, 287, 311–12.

41 Hume, *History of England* (London, 1803), pp. 44n, 89n.

42 *Boswell's Life of Johnson*, ed. G. B. Hill (New York, 1891), 2:241.

43 J. Towers, cited in *The British Plutarch* (London, 1791), 4:157–58.

44 *Walpole's Correspondence*, 28:67–68, 76. Walpole told Mason in January, 1774, that he had just read a book of poems, but was "disappointed in not finding a hecatomb offered to Algernon Sidney" (p. 127). The "Lord Russel" referred to here was, of course, William, Lord Russell, Sydney's co-conspirator in 1683, who also died on the scaffold (see pls. 8, 9). See also Walpole to Cole, October 13, 1777, ibid., 2:66; Walpole to Mason, February 5, 1781, ibid., 29:104–5.

In 1779 the Reverend J. Granger, who dedicated his *Biographical History of England* (4 vols., London, 1779) to Walpole, praised Sydney as a "martyr to patriotism" (4:96).

45 Blackburne, *Memoirs of Thomas Hollis*, pp. 188, 450, 452.

46 Purdie's *Virginia Gazette* (Williamsburg), September 22, 1775, p. 2. Dalrymple was believed to be the author of two antiindependence pamphlets: *The Address of the People of Great Britain to the Inhabitants of America* (London, 1775), and *The Rights of Great Britain Asserted Against the Claims of America* (London, 1775), but the latter may have been the work of the other critic of Sydney, James MacPherson (1736–96).

47 Samuel Adams to Warren, October 14, 1778, *The Writings of Samuel Adams*, ed. H. A. Cushing (4 vols., New York, 1904–8), 4:73.

48 Franklin to William Strahan, February 12, 1745, *The Papers of Benjamin Franklin*, ed. Leonard W. Labaree and Whitfield J. Bell (20 vols. to date, New Haven, 1960—), 3: 13.

49 John Dickinson to his father, March 8, 1754, "Dickinson's London Letters," ed. H. T. Colbourn, *Pennsylvania Magazine of History and Biography* 88 (1962): 257; Clinton Rossiter, "Richard Bland: The Whig in America," *William and Mary Quarterly* 3rd ser., 10 (1953): 43, 70.

50 *Walpole's Correspondence,* 34:103.

51 Hume, *History of England* 7: 213–19, 495–96; Thomas P. Peardon, *The Transition in English Historical Writing, 1760–1830* (New York, 1933), p. 70.

52 Catharine Macaulay, *The History of England . . .* (8 vols., London, 1765), 2: 220–24; Mark Noble, *Memoirs of the Protectoral House of Cromwell* (2 vols., 2nd ed., London, 1787), 2:70, 73–74; *Correspondence of Wilkes,* 3: 137; L. M. Donnelly, "The Celebrated Mrs. Macaulay." *William and Mary Quarterly* 3rd ser., 6 (1949): 203; Granger, *Biographical History,* 1:424.

53 Stephen Hopkins, *The Rights of Colonies Examined* (Providence, 1765), frontispiece; Martin Howard, Jr., *A Letter from a Gentlemen at Halifax to his FRIEND in Rhode-Island containing REMARKS upon a PAMPHLET entitled "The Rights of Colonies Examined"* (Newport, 1765), p. 4; "Some Account of a Pamphlet," *Providence Gazette,* Feb. 23, 1765, appearing in Bernard Bailyn, ed., *Pamphlets of the American Revolution* (2 vols., Cambridge, Mass., 1967), 1: 733.

54 Daniel Dulany, *Considerations on the Propriety of Imposing Taxes in the British Colonies* (Annapolis, 1765), p. 41. "John Hampden" debated "John Pym" in the *Boston Gazette,* December 9, 16, 23, 1765. (This "John Hampden" may have been John Adams—see *Diary and Autobiography of John Adams,* ed. L. H. Butterfield et al. [4 vols., New York, 1964], 1:282.)

"Hampden" appears to offer evidence in support of Edmund Morgan's side of the Morgan-Nettels debate regarding the colonists' alleged distinction between internal and external taxes. "Hampden" explained that the colonists were required to pay taxes, "call them direct or indirect, external, internal or eventual, as you please, it matters not. If the money is taken out of my pocket, it is of little importance what epithet is used, I shall not be a farthing the richer or poorer for words and names" (Dec. 23). "Hampden" also anticipates Oliver Dickerson's "era of customs racketeering," for he objects to "the great number of custom house and naval officers in the colonies" (Dec. 23).

55 George P. Anderson, "Pascal Paoli: An Inspiration to the Sons of Liberty," *Publications of the Colonial Society of Massachusetts 1924–28*(1926): 208.

56 *Papers of Franklin,* 17:17.

57 "Candidus," in the *Boston Gazette,* September 16, 1771, p. 1.

58 Colbourn, *Lamp of Experience,* pp. 138–39.

59 Bradford's *Pennsylvania Journal* (Philadelphia), October 18 and 25, 1773; Purdie and Dixon's *Virginia Gazette* (Williamsburg), November 11, 1773, p. 1, reprinted "from the Pennsylvania Papers"; Rind's *Virginia Gazette* (Williamsburg), November 11, 1773, p. 1, "from the *Pennsylvania Packet*" (Philadelphia); ibid., no. 4., November 25, 1773, dated "New York," October 27, 1773; later collected as "Hampden," *The Alarm* (nos. 1–5) (New

York, October, 1773); *Letters of Benjamin Rush*, ed. Lyman Butterfield (2 vols., Princeton, 1951), 1:82–84n.

60 April 19, 1774, in *Burke's Speeches*, ed. F. G. Selby (London, 1963), p. 12.

61 Perez Morton, in *Fifth of March Orations* (Boston, 1785).

62 Dixon and Hunter's *Virginia Gazette* (Williamsburg), April 20 & 27, 1776.

63 *Works*, pp. 105–6; Montagu to Walpole, May 13, 1764, and December 19, 1764, *Walpole's Correspondence*, 10: 124, 150; William Johnson Temple to Boswell, February 15, 1764, in *Boswell in Holland*, ed. Fredrick Pottle (New York, 1952), p. 150.

64 *Boston Gazette*, Nov. 4, 1765.

65 *Virginia Historical Register*, 1: 69–70; Rind's *Virginia Gazette* (Williamsburg), Apr. 20, 1769, p. 2.

66 Rush to his brother, Jacob, January 19, 1769, in *Letters of Benjamin Rush*, 1:72.

67 *Adams Legal Papers*, 2: 409.

68 Josiah Quincy, *Observations of . . . the Boston Port-Bill* (Boston & London, 1774), passim. Brutus and Cassius, of course, were also popular symbols of resistance to tyranny, similar rallying-flags of patriotism. Quincy asked his countrymen to dedicate themselves "Brutus-like" to the service of their country. A truly exhaustive analysis of patriot-worship would have to examine the Brutus image as well (see for instance, Sylas Neville's *Diary*, pp. 48, 62, 70, and Bishop Thomas Sprat, *Horrid Conspiracy . . .* [London, 1685], 1: 64, for mention of the popularity among English republicans of Brutus). But I think Quincy's juxtaposition of Brutus and Cassius, Hampden and Sydney, obviates the need for such analysis, since the two pairs of patriots appear to have been interchangeable symbols of antistatism. James Thomson, it will be remembered, compared Sydney first to Brutus and then to Cassius, and Montagu wrote to Walpole of "Brutus Hampden" (January 11, 1761, *Walpole's Correspondence*, 9: 333).

69 Arthur Lee, *An Appeal to the People of Great Britain . . .* (Boston, 1774), p. 28; Matthew Robinson-Morris, Lord Rokeby, *Considerations on the Measures Carrying on with Respect to the British Colonies in North America* (London, 1774), p. 10 (reprinted in Bailyn, *Pamphlets*, 1: 80).

70 *Memoirs of John Quincy Adams*, ed. Charles Francis Adams (Philadelphia, 1874), 1:148n; Bowen, *Adams*, p. 451.

71 R. J. Hooker, "The American Revolution Seen Through a Wine Glass," *William and Mary Quarterly* 3rd ser., 11(1954):67.

72 Richard Frothingham, *The Life and Times of Joseph Warren* (Boston, 1865), pp. 536–38; M. C. Tyler, *Literary History of the American Revolution* (New York, 1878), 2:216, for Brackenridge poem.

73 Francis B. Lee, ed., *Documents Relating to the Revolutionary History of . . . New Jersey* (Trenton, 1903), 2:137.

74 John W. Thornton, ed., *Pulpit of the American Revolution* (Boston, 1860), p. xxxiv.

75 Purdie and Dixon's *Virginia Gazette*, Nov. 2, 1769, p. 2; and June 5, 1779,

p. 2. Hampden-Sydney Academy, in Hampden-Sydney, Virginia, was founded in 1775, and incorporated in 1783 by the General Association of Virginia as Hampden-Sydney College (I am indebted to Mr. P. L. Grier, Librarian, Hampden-Sydney College, for this and other information about the school).

76 See, for instance, Sam Adams to Benjamin Kent, July 27, 1776, *The Writings of Samuel Adams*, ed. H. A. Cushing (4 vols., New York, 1904–8), 2: 305.

77 Quoted in *Burnet's History of Our Times*, ed. Osmond Airy (2 vols., Oxford, 1897–1900), 2: 405n.

78 Neville, *Diary*, p. 14; Jonathan Mayhew to Timothy Hollis, September, 1765, *Memoirs of the Life and Writings of the Reverend John Mayhew*, ed. Alden Bradford (Boston, 1838), p. 419.

79 Hollis, quoted in Robbins, "Library of Liberty," p. 188.

80 Thornton, *Pulpit of the American Revolution*, p. 75n.

81 Hollis to William Strahan, *Memoirs*, p. 449.

82 "A New SONG to the plaintive Tune of Hosier's Ghost," reprinted in A. M. Schlesinger, "A Note on Songs as Patriotic Propaganda," *William and Mary Quarterly* 3rd ser., 11 (1954): 78ff.

83 Lincoln, *Ideas of English Dissent*, pp. 8, 33, 35, 41, 90; Richard W. Davis, *Dissent in Politics, 1780–1830: The Political Life of William Smith, M.P.* (London, 1971); Alan Heimert, *Religion and the American Mind* (Cambridge, Mass., 1966), p. 255.

84 Richard Merritt, "The Colonists Discover America: Attention Patterns in the Colonial Press, 1735–1775," *William and Mary Quarterly* 3rd ser., 21 (1964): 270–87.

85 Neville, *Diary*, pp. 3, 23; Paula S. Preston, "The Severed Head of Charles I of England: Its Use as a Political Stimulus," *Winterthur Portfolio 6* (Charlottesville, 1970), pp. 1–13.

86 William Harris, *Historical and Critical Account*, 3: 490; Peter Brown, *The Chathamites* (New York and London, 1967), pp. 39, 153; J. R. Pole, *Political Representation in England and the Origins of the American Republic* (London, 1966), p. 438. Cf. Mark Noble, *Lives of the English Regicides . . .* (2 vols., London, 1798), 2: 261.

87 Bureau of the Census, *Population Schedule of the 2nd Census of the U.S., 1800* (Washington, D.C., 1960); George Reasons, "Oliver Cromwell," in *They Had a Dream* (Los Angeles, 1970); Oliver Cromwell Comstock (born 1780, son of Rhode Island Baptists) in *Biographical Dictionary of the American Congress, 1774–1971* (Washington, D.C., 1971); Christopher Hill, *God's Englishman* (London, 1970), p. 273; Samuel Adams Drake, *Old Landmarks and Historic Personages* (Boston, 1873), p. 61.

88 Alfred Young, "Pope's Day, Tar and Feathers and 'Cornet Joyce, jun.': From Ritual to Rebellion in Boston, 1745–1775," a paper presented at the Anglo-American Labor Historians' Conference, Rutgers University, April 26–38, 1973, 6: 2; Young, personal communication to the author, July 17, 1973.

89 R. D. Brown, *Revolutionary Politics in Massachusetts*, p. 53.
90 Purdie and Dixon's *Virginia Gazette* (Williamsburg) September 15, 1768, p. 2.
91 "Brutus," *Boston Gazette*, Feb. 1771; John Leacock, *The Fall of British Tyranny* (Philadelphia, 1776); Thomas Gray, "Elegy . . . "; Charles Churchill, "The Candidate" (1764) in *Works*, p. 365.
92 See T. Lathbury, *Oliver Cromwell, or the Old and New Dissenters* (Bristol, 1862), p. 9, on Catherine Macaulay, and C. Hill, *God's Englishman*, p. 266, on Hume. See also James Burgh, *Political Disquisitions* (London, 1774), pp. i, 9.
93 Anon., *The Patriot's Guide: A Poem* (London, ca. 1770), p. 31.
94 William Cushing, *Initials and Pseudonyms: A Dictionary of Literary Disguises* (2nd series, London, 1888), p. 71; George, *English Political Caricature*, 1: 152; Eugene C. Black, *The Association* (Cambridge, Mass., 1963), p. 165.
95 Heimert, *Religion and the American Mind*, pp. 58, 92, 148, 255, 275, 387, 457, 504; Jonathan Mayhew, *A Discourse Concerning Unlimited Submission and Nonresistance to the Higher Powers* (Boston, 1750), pp. 41, 47.
96 "Watch Tower," *New-York Mercury*, March 3, 1755; Stephen Hopkins, *Rights of Colonies*, p. 4; David F. Hawke, *Benjamin Rush: Revolutionary Gadfly* (Indianapolis, 1971), p. 74.

4: Fading Stars and New Lights

1 William Paca, in *Maryland Journal* (Baltimore), Feb. 13, 20, May 18, Aug. 3, 31, 1787; *New York Journal and Daily Patriotic Register* Jan. 28, 1788; J. F. McLaughlin, *Matthew Lyon* (New York, 1900), pp. 36–40; Jedidiah Morse and Elijah Parish, *A Compendious History of New England* (London and Boston, 1808), p. 87.

Americans were not alone in adopting Hampden the Patriot. A number of nineteenth-century Australians borrowed him too, and they were not even English to begin with, but Scots. They arrived in the 1820's and '30's and established sheep ranches on lands west of Melbourne in Victoria. By mid-century they were displaying one sure trait of colonial affluence: identification with English culture. Their homes came to resemble Sussex estates; their sons were sent to Oxford and Cambridge. They fought the mining community's efforts to democratize the Legislative Assembly. In 1848 they invoked Hampden's name in opposition to the Foreign Office's policy of transporting criminals to Australia. (Margaret Kiddle, *Men of Yesterday: A Social History of the Western District of Victoria, 1834–1890* [Melbourne, 1961], pp. 161, 457, 472, 475, 489–90; Geofrey Serle, *The Golden Age: A History of the Colony of Victoria, 1851–1861* [Melbourne, 1963], pp. 280–81; George Nadel, *Australia's Colonial Culture: Ideas, Men and Institutions in Mid-Nineteenth Century Eastern Australia* [Cambridge, Mass., 1957], p. 72).

If Andrew Carnegie's account of what students in India told him is accurate, Hampden, Sydney, Cromwell, and Washington were "revered" in India as well at the turn of the century. (But I do not claim to have an informed sense of the degree of Indian veneration of these English and American patriot-symbols.) See *Miscellaneous Writings of Andrew Carnegie*, ed. Burton Hendrick (2 vols., Garden City, 1933), 2:91.

2 *Writings of Benjamin Franklin*, ed. A. H. Smyth (10 vols., New York, 1905–7), 9:104; George C. Rogers, *Evolution of a Federalist: William L. Smith of Charleston* (Columbia, S.C., 1962), p. 291.

3 E. Millicent Sowerby, *Catalogue of the Library of Thomas Jefferson*, (4 vols., Washington, D.C., 1952–68), 3:12–13; *Mason Locke Weems: His Works and Ways*, ed. Emily E. F. Skeel (3 vols., New York, 1929), 2:307–9.

4 *Weems*, ed. Skeel, 2:204–7, 208, 322.

5 Charleston *Times*, July 1, 1806, p. 4; *Weems*, ed. Skeel, 2:318, 319–20, 346, 356, 310. (The Weems edition of Sydney's *Discourses on Government* (3 vols., Philadelphia, 1805], is, of course, the one I have quoted from in earlier chapters.)

   As early as 1776 John Adams was annoyed by the reluctance of educated people to *read* the works of Sydney, Locke, Harrington, and other political theorists. "No small fortitude is necessary to confess that one has read them," he observed (cited in Michael Kammen, *Deputyes and Libertyes* [New York, 1970], p. 199).

   Owning a copy of the *Discourses* did not mean that one was necessarily influenced by their contents. But the *Discourses were* expensive (in any but Daniel Eaton's 1794 sixpence-a-week instalment form in his "Political Classics" series for the English lower middle classes), and the sales clearly indicate a degree of respect for the Rebel-Saint.

6 *The Trial of Aaron Burr for Treason* (2 vols., New York, 1876), 1:131.

7 *Papers of Henry Clay*, ed. James F. Hopkins (6 vols. to date, Lexington, Ky., 1959—), 1:365.

8 Rush to Adams, March 13, 1809, in *The Letters of Benjamin Rush*, ed. Lyman Butterfield (2 vols., Princeton, 1951), 2:997–98.

9 James Cheetham, *The Life of Thomas Paine* (New York, 1809), p. 131n; Adams to William Tudor, Aug. 6, 1818, *Works of John Adams*, ed. C. F. Adams (10 vols., Boston, 1850–56), 10:338.

10 *North American Review* 14 (1822): 59–86.

11 *Proceedings and Debates of the Virginia State Convention of 1829–30* (Richmond, 1830), pp. 54, 260.

12 *U.S. Democratic Review* (Aug., 1851): 116, 129.

13 Samuel Janney, *Life of William Penn* (Philadelphia, 1853), pp. 192–93. For more on Penn and Sydney see my "Who was 'Colonel Sidney?' A note on the meaning of the Penn-Sidney letter of Oct. 13, 1681," *Pennsylvania Magazine of History and Biography* 91 (1967): 193–98.

14 Herman Melville, *White Jacket* (New York, 1850), p. 283; *U.S. Naval Institute Proceedings* 22 (1896): 561; A. T. Mahan, "The Practical Aspects of War," *National Review* 49 (June, 1907): 693.

15 "Sidney" [?], *Freeman's Journal* (Philadelphia), May 13, 1789, p. 2; "Sidney" [Abraham and Robert Yates], *Political Papers addressed to the Advo-*

cates for a Congressional Revenue (New York, ca. 1791); "Sidney" [?], *National Gazette* (Philadelphia), Apr. 23, 26, and 30, May 3, 10, 17, 21, and 24, 1792; "Sidney" [?], *No Convention* (Lexington, Ky., 1798); "Algernon Sydney" [Gideon Granger], *A Vindication of the Measures of the Present Administration* (Hartford, 1803); "Sidney" [Granger], *An Address to the People of New England* (Hartford, 1804); "Hampden" [?], *A Letter to the President . . . touching the Prosecutions under his Patronage Before the Circuit Court in the District of Connecticut* (New Haven, 1808); "Hampden" [?], *Letters Addressed to the People on the Undue Influence of Banks . . . whereby it will appear that the funds and capital of the different banks are devoted to the service of the speculator and shavfer [sic] instead of the industrious and deserving* (Baltimore, 1805); "Hampden" [Charles Hammond], *Reviews of the Opinions of the Supreme Court of the U.S.* (Steubenville, Ohio, 1821); Donald Stewart, *The Opposition Press of the Federalist Period* (Albany, 1969), pp. 84, 198, 228, 403, 505, 528, 553, 564. See also "Hampden" and "Sidney" [Ebenezer S. Thomas], in Charleston (S.C.) *City Gazette*, 1810-16.

16 "Sidney" [Rev. John Allen], *An Essay on the policy of appropriations by the U.S. for purchasing, liberating, and colonizing the slaves thereof* (Baltimore and Boston, 1826); "Hampden" [Francis Pickens], *The Genuine Book of Nullification* (Charleston, S.C., 1831); "Hampden" [Henry Winter Davis], *Alexandria Gazette* (Alexandria, Va.), April 25, May 3, 1849; *Jefferson Davis . . . His Letters . . .* , ed. Dunbar Rowland (10 vols., Jackson, Miss., 1923), 10:399.

17 "Sidney" [?], *Modern Toleration—Tyranny in Disguise* (Hartford, 1817); "Sidney" [Benjamin Watkins Leigh], *The Letters of Algernon Sidney in defense of civil liberty against the encroachments of military despotism . . .* (Richmond, 1830; first published in 1818-19); "Algernon Sydney" [Spencer Roane], *Enquirer* (Richmond, Va.) May 25, June 8, 1821; "Al. Sidney" [Asher Robbins], *Principles and Men* (Providence, 1823); "Sidney" [?], "Essays on the American System," *Boston Commercial Gazette* (Mass.), Oct., 1831; "Sidney" [Noah Webster], *Commercial Advertiser* (New York), Nov. 20, 1837, and *Appeal to Americans* (New York, 1838); "Sidney" [D. K. Whitaker], *Sidney's Letters to W. E. Channing, D. D. occasioned by his letter to Hon. Henry Clay in the Annexation of Texas to the United States* (Charleston, 1837); "Sydney" [Nathan Loughborough], *On Retrocession: To the Congress of the U.S.* (Washington, D.C., ca. 1831); "Alg. Sidney" [Salma Hale and J. Q. Adams], *The Administration and the Opposition* (New York, 1826).

"John Hampden" [Spencer Roane], *Enquirer* (Richmond, Va.), Dec. 27, 1817, June 11, 15, 18, 22, 1819; "Hampden" [?], *An Examination of the Charges preferred by General Jackson against Mr. Adams and Mr. Clay* (Washington, D.C., 1827); "Hampden" [Jabez Delano Hammond], *Letter to the Honorable John C. Calhoun on the Annexation of Texas* (Cooperstown, N.Y., 1844); "Hampden" [Adolphus M. Hart], *A Few Thoughts on the Liquor Question* (New York, 1854), and *The Impending Crisis* (New York, 1855); "Hampden" [John B. Jervis], *Letters Addressed to the Friends of Freedom and the Union* (New York, 1856). Cf. "Hampden" [Spencer Roane], *Enquirer* (Richmond, Va.), June 11, 15, 18, 22, 1819; and "Hampden Sydney" [William Gilmore Simms], *Charleston Mercury,* 1866.

18 A. M. Schlesinger, "Patriotism Names the Baby," *New England Quarterly* 14 (Dec., 1941): 613; Robert C. Winthrop, *Addresses and Speeches on Various Occasions* (4 vols., Boston, 1852–86), 2: 172; 4: 300, 263; and *Memoir*, p. 143.

19 Sidney Willard, *Memories of Youth and Manhood* (2 vols., Cambridge, Mass., 1855), 1: 220.

20 Secretary of the Commonwealth of Massachusetts, *List of Persons Whose Names have Been Changed in Massachusetts, 1780–1883* (Boston, 1885); Caspar Goodrich, *Rope Yarns from the Old Navy* (New York, 1931), p. 12; Frederick Tolles, *George Logan of Philadelphia* (New York, 1953), p. 130; D. Adair in note to C. Robbins, "Algernon Sidney's *Discourses* . . . : Textbook of Revolution," *William and Mary Quarterly* 3rd ser., 4 (1947): 4:271n; *Memorials of the Massachusetts Society of the Cincinnati*, ed. B. A. Whitmore (Boston, 1964); *Algernon Sydney Sullivan*, ed. Anne Holmes (New York, 1929); Louis Cornish, ed., *A National Register of the Society of the Sons of the American Revolution* (Washington, D.C., 1902), pp. 206, 345; U.S. Naval Academy Alumni Association, *Register of Graduates of the U.S.N.A.* (Baltimore, 1958); various registers of state militia and National Guard personnel; *The Letters of Wm. G. Simms*, eds. Mary Oliphant et al. (5 vols., Columbia, S.C., 1956), 5: 7; Elsdon C. Smith, *The Story of Our Names* (New York, 1950). In the *Oxford Dictionary of English Christian Names* (Oxford, 1945), the editor, E. G. Withycombe, comments (p. 118) that "the use of Sidney as a christian name was no doubt partly due to the Whig idolization of the memory of Algernon Sidney."

21 See, for example, Cornish, ed., *Sons of American Revolution*, p. 341; and *DAB*, John Hampden Pleasants; G. H. Chamberlayne, *Ham Chamberlayne, Virginian: Letters and Papers* . . . (Richmond, Va., 1932), p. 1. More modern family names may represent, at the least, fossilized tradition: the late John Hampden Lewis, Captain, U.S.N., born in Louisiana in 1901, may well have been named after a father or grandfather who had been blessed with the Patriot's mantle earlier in the nineteenth century.

22 Nathaniel Barber, who named his son after John Wilkes in 1770, expressed sentiments that must have been comparable to the views of those who named their sons after one or the other of the twin patriots. Barber told Wilkes that he had honored his son "by fixing an indelible mark . . . of the perfect Regard I have for you." He hoped to implant early in the boy "the true Sentiments of Liberty and Virtue" in order that he might never disgrace his namesake (*Massachusetts Historical Society Proceedings* 47 [1914]:215).

Sidney James, born within a day (Dec. 9, 1883) of the bicentenary of Sydney's execution, *may* have been named after the Rebel-Saint. See Clifford Drury, *The History of the Chaplain Corps, U.S.N.* (Washington, D.C., 1948), 1:163.

The Algernon Sidney who corresponded with Nicholas Biddle in 1812 may have been using the name simply as a pseudonym, but it hardly seems likely that he would disguise his identity while seeking subsidization of a publication entitled "Theory of our American Aborigines." It is more likely that his parents simply chose his first name with the same deliberation exhibited by others not already graced with the Rebel-Saint's last name as well. MSS. Division, Biddle Family Papers, III (Library of Congress, A. S. to N. Biddle).

23 See, for example, George Stewart, *American Place Names* (New York, 1970); and *Names on the Land* (New York, 1945); Irma Getchell, "History of Hampden [Maine]," *Sprague's Journal of Maine History* 13 (1925): 113–19; and my own curious correspondence with some fifteen bewildered mayors, town clerks, county recorders, etc. Australians named at least one shire after Hampden (in Victoria).

24 Mrs. Frances H. [Whipple] Greene McDougall, *Might and Right* (Providence, 1844), pp. 62, 132–34, 192–98. Cf. John Quincy Adams on the Dorr controversy, below, note 33.

25 Robbins, "Textbook on Revolution," p. 269; U.S., 24th Congress, 2nd Session, *Register of Debates* (Washington, D.C., 1838), pp. 719–23 (on Calhoun and Rives); *The Letters of William Lloyd Garrison*, ed. Louis Ruchames and W. M. Merrill (4 vols., Cambridge, Mass., 1971), 2:217.

26 Wm. Seward, "Freedom in the New Territories" (July 2, 1850), in *The Works of William H. Seward*, ed. George E. Baker (5 vols., Boston, 1884), 1: 102.

27 C. N. Greenough, "Sidney and the Motto of Massachusetts," *Massachusetts Historical Society Proceedings (1917–20),* 51:276; J. G. Whittier, quoted in *Byways in Quaker History*, ed. Howard H. Brinton (Wallingford, Pa., 1944), p. 52; Theodore Parker, *The Trial of Theodore Parker . . .* (Boston, 1855), pp. 50, 54; John Quincy Adams entered Sydney's motto in the autograph book of House Speaker Robert C. Winthrop during a struggle in the House of Representatives to repeal the Gag Rule (Winthrop, *Addresses and Speeches,* 2: 156).

28 Wendell Phillips, "John Brown and the Spirit of Fifty-Nine" (1859), in *Modern Eloquence* (15 vols., Philadelphia, 1900–1903), 14: 1598–99, 1602.

29 Louis Ruchames, ed., *A John Brown Reader* (London, 1959), p. 279. The degree to which figures like Brown eventually replaced the twin patriots will concern us in the final pages of this chapter. For now it is enough to note that comparisons were made in 1859.

30 *Speeches, Lectures and Letters of Wendell Phillips* (2nd ed., 2 vols. in 1, Boston, 1891), pp. 358–59.

31 More modern exceptions are those of the activist media firm *Pacifica* which recently produced a sixty-minute dramatization of the "conspiracy trial" of "a left-winger named Algernon Sidney," reenacted "from court records recently unearthed," and of the activist-historian Staughton Lynd, who reminds us of the truly radical and revolutionary character of many eighteenth-century American revolutionaries by noting how often they used "Hampden," "Sydney," and "Brutus" as pseudonyms: "They . . . knew what it cost to be a Sydney" (*William and Mary Quarterly* 3rd ser., 23 [1966]: 324–26).

32 Wm. Bruce, *John Randolph of Roanoke, 1773–1833* (2 vols., New York,

1922), 1: 238; E. Brooks, in *North American Review* 14 (1822): 86.

33 *Memoirs of John Quincy Adams*, ed. C. F. Adams (12 vols., Philadelphia, 1874–77), 9: 227–28; John Quincy Adams, *The Social Compact, exemplified in the Constitution of the Commonwealth of Massachusetts* (Providence, 1842), pp. 27–28, 29–31.

34 John Forster, *The Statesmen of the Commonwealth of England*, ed. J. O. Choules (New York, 1846), pp. v–vi.

35 George Van Santvoord, *Life of Algernon Sidney* (2nd ed., New York, 1854), pp. 22, 264, 329, 333; See *Appleton's Cyclopedia of American Biography*, George Van Santvoord. See the next chapter for more on Sydney and the romantics.

36 Perry Miller, *The Life of the Mind in America* (New York, 1965), esp. pp. vii–xi, 105, 121. William C. Rives, *Discourse on the Character and Services of John Hampden* . . . (Hampden-Sydney College Trustees, Richmond, Va., 1845), pp. 3–4, 26, 50, 62–65.

37 Massachusetts Historical Society, ed., *Memoir of Robert C. Winthrop* (Boston, 1897), pp. 15, 225, 164, 173–74, 213, 308. Winthrop was not alone in his distrust of the Democracy. See also R. McKinley Ormsby, *A History of the Whig Party* (Boston, 1860), for more pronounced statements of the Whig disdain for demagogy, "contrived for the captivation of the masses, by pandering to their passions and prejudices." Ormsby was critical of "the ignorant multitude," ill-equipped for government; he called for the return of government to the aristocrats, as a "reward for moral and intellectual excellence" (pp. 360, 361, 374).

38 Winthrop, *Memoir*, pp. 173–74, 307.

39 Winthrop, *Addresses and Speeches*, 2:171, 172; 4:263, 300; Winthrop, *Memoir*, pp. 143, 183–84, 205.

40 Winthrop, *Memoir*, p. 205.

41 Francis Grund, *Aristocracy in America* (2 vols., London, 1839), 1:119, 222.

42 Winthrop, *Addresses and Speeches*, 4:261; Winthrop, *Memoir*, pp. 323–24; *Tributes of the Massachusetts Historical Society to Robert C. Winthrop* (Boston, 1895), pp. 36–37.

43 S. G. Fisher, *The True William Penn* (Philadelphia, 1899), p. 218. It appears that by 1900 the name "Sidney" was favored somewhat disproportionately by minority groups—blacks and Jewish immigrants—but there is little evidence that the selection was consciously motivated by esteem for the Rebel-Saint. If it had become a more popular name with minorities, the popularity may be attributable to the very fact that the name had been selected in nineteenth-century America by the elites and arbiters of society (Matthew Josephson, *Sidney Hillman: Statesman of American Labor* [New York, 1952], p. 24; Smith, *The Story of our Names*, p. 26). Nonetheless, it is worth noting that one *fin-de-siècle* black separatist signed his "back-to-Africa" essays "Sidney," and that CORE had two "Sydneys" and one "Algernon" on its twelve-man Advisory Committee in 1969 (P. S. Stuckey, "The Spell of Africa," Ph.D. dissertation, Northwestern University, 1973).

44 William MacFarland, *An Address of the Life, Character and Public Services of the Late Benjamin Watkins Leigh* (Richmond, 1851), pp. 5–10; "Sidney" [Webster], *Appeal to Americans* (New York, 1837 and 1838), pp. 5–8; H. R. Warfel, *Noah Webster: Schoolmaster to America* (New York, 1936), pp. 424–29. Cf. "Sidney" [Robbins], *Principles and Men*, pp. 6–19. Not surprisingly, the General Committee of the Whig Young Men of New York dissociated itself from such "anti-republican doctrines as those of 'Sidney,' " while the Democrats "trotted out" the "Sidney" essay for years "as the bugaboo with which to frighten the populace into supporting the Jacksonians" (Warfel, *Webster*, pp. 428–29).

45 Rbt. Rantoul's 1836 July 4 address, as cited by Marvin Meyers, *The Jacksonian Persuasion* (Stanford, 1957), p. 224.

46 James Parton, *Triumphs of Enterprise, Ingenuity, and Public Spirit* (New York, 1872), pp. 602–4, 613.

47 W. A. Dunning, *History of Political Theories* (3 vols., New York, 1902), 2: 342–43; S. P. Scott, "Sidney," *Potter's American Magazine* (Philadelphia) 6 (1876): 335.

48 I am indebted to Mr. W. S. Lewis, editor of Horace Walpole's *Correspondence*, for this information.

49 Levi Lincoln, *Letters to the People* (Salem, Mass., 1802).

50 Russell Kirk, *John Randolph of Roanoke* (Chicago, 1964), p. 396n.

51 "Hampden" [Roane], *Enquirer* (Richmond, Va.), June 11, 15, 18, and 22, 1819; "Sidney" [B. W. Leigh], *Letters*, p. 42; "Hampden" [?], *Letters addressed to the people on the undue Influence of Banks . . .* (Baltimore, 1808); "Sidney" [Robbins], *Principles and Men*, p. 11; Theo. Frelinghuysen, "Speech on the Cherokee Lands," U.S. Congress, *Register of Debates*, 6, pt. 1 (Apr. 9, 1830), p. 313; "Sidney" [Loughborough], *On Retrocession*, pp. 3, 4, 11, 14; "Hampden" [Francis Pickens], *Genuine Book of Nullification*, pp. 52, 58–60, 154; J. P. Kennedy, *Defense of the Whigs . . .* (New York, 1844), p. 15.

52 "Hampden" [Hart], *A Few Thoughts on the Liquor Question*, and *The Impending Crisis*, esp. pp. 21, 26. Cf. "Hampden" [Asher Robbins], *A Letter to the President . . .* (New Haven, 1808), pp. 27–28.

53 See Paul Kleppner, *The Cross of Culture* (New York, 1970).

54 See the arguments in James Willard Hurst, *Law and the Conditions of Freedom in Nineteenth Century America* (Madison, Wis., 1956), esp. p. 9; Kleppner, *Cross of Culture*; and Ronald Formisano, *Birth of Mass Political Parties: Michigan, 1827–1861* (Princeton, 1971).

55 See, for example, Seymour Mandelbaum, *Boss Tweed's New York* (New York, 1965); *The Diary of George Templeton Strong*, ed. Allan Nevins (4 vols., New York, 1952), 4: 26; and *U.S. Democratic Review* (June, 1851): 494, (August, 1851): 116–25.

56 "Sidney" [Whitaker], *Letters to Channing*, p. 51.

57 This may explain why Charles Cowley compared the "noble" Confederate General Thomas Drayton to Hampden, and the victorious Union General

W. T. Sherman to Cromwell (Cowley, *Leaves from a Lawyer's Life Afloat and Ashore* [Lowell, Mass., 1879], pp. 44, 148).

The twin patriots *had* been symbols of "Union" to some before the war, however. John Jervis's "Hampden," for example, addressed *Letters . . . to the Friends of Freedom and the Union* in 1856, and John Wingate Thornton reminded Americans in 1860 of Hampden, Sydney, and their English heritage, and then quoted from the *Discourses* on the necessity for union: "There is no safety where there is no strength, no strength without union, no union without justice" (Thornton, ed., *The Pulpit of the American Revolution* [Boston, 1860], pp. 164, 333, 379n). And Charles Sumner quoted from the *Discourses* in an 1866 speech on the Senate floor in support of radical reconstruction legislation (see "Equal Rights of all," in *Works of . . . Sumner* [15 vols., Boston, 1870–83], 10: 155–56), but Cromwell proved a more potent symbol for those seeking to suppress rebellion. See p. 75 for discussion of abolitionist invocations of Cromwell.

58   For example, the parents of John Hampden Pleasants, Albert Sidney Johnston, Algernon Sydney Adair, Algernon Sydney Sullivan, Sydney Epes, Sydney Bowie, and the Sidney Simms brothers were all southern.

59   George H. Preble, *Our Flag* (Albany, 1872), p. 394.

60   *Letters of Simms*, ed. Oliphant, 5: 7n (Simms also used the pseudonyms "Old South" and "Old Southern Democrat"); Tom Watson's articles, "Socialists and Socialism," and "Populism and Socialism," written for *Watson's Jeffersonian Magazine* 4 (June & July, 1910) are quoted in C. Vann Woodward, *Tom Watson: Agrarian Rebel* (paperback ed., New York, 1963), p. 408.

61   H. B. Wallace, *Literary Criticisms and Other Papers* (Philadelphia, 1856), pp. 320–21.

62   E. L. Godkin, in Robert Stauffer, ed., *The American Spirit in Americans of Foreign Birth* (Boston, 1922), p. 49; George Bancroft, *History of the United States* (10 vols., Boston, 1840–74), 2: 379–80; Fisher, *The True William Penn*, p. 219.

63   Samuel Quincy, ed., *Reports of Cases . . . in the Superior Court . . . of Massachusetts Bay 1761–1772* (Boston, 1865), p. 237.

64   R. C. Winthrop, "The Portrait of John Hampden," a communication to the Massachusetts Historical Society, June 9, 1881, in *Addresses and Speeches*, 4: 243–44. Winthrop's anxiety was fully warranted, for soon after he expressed this concern for the future of the Hampden portrait it was consigned to cold storage by the White House (Carol J. Heinsius, Assistant to the White House Curator, to the author, May 4, 1973).

65   F. B. Smith, *Radical Artisan: William James Linton* (Manchester, 1973), p. 190.

66   See, for instance, "Editor's Easy Chair," *Harper's New Monthly Magazine* 25 (1862): 271–72.

67   Moses Granger, *Washington v. Jefferson* (New York, 1898), p. 81.

68   Winthrop, *Memoir*, p. 321; for Choate, see *Modern Eloquence* (15 vols., New York, 1900–1903), 1: 178; 10, index.

69 *Diary of C. F. Adams*, ed. Marc Friedlander and L. H. Butterfield (6 vols., Cambridge, 1968), 4: 328, 331, 338, 340; *Holmes-Pollock Letters*, ed. Mark De Wolfe Howe (2 vols., Cambridge, 1942), 2: 22.

70 Van Santvoord, *Life of... Sidney*, p. 15. Cf. Sir James F. Stephen, *A History of the Criminal Law of England* (3 vols., London, 1883), 1: 411.

71 Richard Taylor, an "unreconstructed" Confederate officer, offered sarcastic sympathy for a Radical Republican who had fallen from grace; Admiral Potter compared Hampden to a Filipino who had aided the American counterinsurgents! R. Taylor, *Destruction and Reconstruction* (New York, 1879), p. 259; D. Potter, *Sailing the Sulu Sea* (New York, 1940), p. 264.

72 S. A. Drake, *Our Great Benefactors: Short Biographies of the Men and Women Most Eminent in Literature, Science* ... (Boston, 1884); [?], *Stories from English History* ... (New York, 1892): A. R. Spofford, Frank Weitenkampf, and Prof. J. P. Lamberton, eds., *The Library of Historic Characters and Famous Events of all Ages and Nations* (10 vols., Philadelphia, 1895).

73 Clifford Smith, *William Penn* (New York, 1931), p. 88; C. E. Vulliamy, *William Penn* (New York, 1934), p. 147; *Papers of Henry Clay*, ed. Hopkins, 1: 367n; Russell Kirk, *John Randolph of Roanoke* (New York, 1964), pp. 307, 484. For further examples of the misuse of Sydney's name by authors and editors see Eugene C. Black, ed., *British Politics in the Nineteenth Century* (New York and London, 1969), p. 84; and John Osborne, *William Cobbett* (New Brunswick, 1966), p. 271.

74 I refer to the generous correspondence of such folks as G. K. Weeden of Sidney, Delaware, Ralph Greenwood of the Fremont County (Iowa) Historical Society, Clara Heckman, town clerk of Sidney, Indiana, and Geneva Combes of Sidney, Montana, with the author.

75 I am grateful to Ms. Fran Lesniak and Ms. Jena Cygnasovich for including my curious question in their survey.

76 John Lovett, *Washington's Birth Day—An Historical Poem* (Albany, 1812), pp. 30, 33, 41; *Letters of Rush*, p. 235.

77 "Washington," *To the People of the U.S. on the Choice of a President* (Boston, 1812); W. C. Rives, *Discourse on ... Hampden*, p. 62; "Democritus," *National Gazette* (Philadelphia), May 10, 1792, p. 224; Stewart, *Opposition Press of Federalist Period*, p. 518; "Hampden" [Hart], *A Few Thoughts on the Liquor Question*, p. 9; J. Q. Adams, cited in Richard Van Alstyne, *The Genius of American Nationalism* (Waltham, Mass., 1970), p. 155; *Diary of G. T. Strong*, ed. Nevins, 4: 92, 150.

78 *Messages and Papers of the Presidents*, ed. James Richardson (Washington, D.C., 1900), 4: 15-16. Cf. Merrill Peterson, *The Jeffersonian Image in the American Mind* (New York, 1960), p. 91.

79 *Correspondence of Emerson and Carlyle*, ed. Joseph Slater (New York, 1964), pp. 35, 274, 280. For an American Catholic's view of the late-nineteenth-century's love affair with Cromwell see the angry remarks of Reverend George McDermot, C.S.P., "Cromwell and Liberty," *Catholic World* 71 (1900): 487-99.

80 R. W. Emerson, cited in Theodore Greene, *America's Heroes* (New York,

1970), p. 110. See also Joel Headley, *Napoleon and his Marshals* (New York, 1846); Marcus Cunliffe, *Soldiers and Civilians* (Boston, 1968), pp. 399–402; Stephen Ambrose, *Duty, Honor, Country* (Baltimore, 1966), p. 138; Ruth M. Elson, *Guardians of Tradition: American Schoolbooks of the Nineteenth Century* (Lincoln, Neb., 1964), p. 141; Theodore Greene, *America's Heroes,* "The Hero as Napoleon"; James Malin, *Confounded Rot about Napoleon* (Lawrence, Kansas, 1961), pp. 185–204; Albert Guerard, *Reflections on the Napoleonic Legend* (New York, 1924); Francis Lieber, *Washington and Napoleon* (New York, 1864). Cf. A. L. Lloyd, *Folk Song in England* (London, 1967), p. 44, who noted that many early-nineteenth-century British folk songs dealt with the arch-enemy, Napoleon.

81 *Letters of Emerson,* ed. Ralph Lush (New York, 1939), 4: 534.

82 George Bancroft, *History of the United States* (rev. ed., New York, 1866); C. F. Adams, *Diary,* ed. Friedlander and Butterfield, 4:360 ff.; also quoted in *North American Review* 37(1833):164–89. Cf. R. Kirk, *John Randolph,* p. 412.

83 Charles Lane, "Cromwell," *Dial* 3 (Oct., 1842):258, 260, 264.

84 Anne Hutton, *Portrait of Patriotism* (Philadelphia, 1859), pp. 36, 123.

85 Joel T. Headley, "Cromwell," *American Review* 3 (1846):396–414, and *Life of Oliver Cromwell* (New York, 1848).

86 *U.S. Democratic Review* 26 (January, 1850): 28–30.

87 Theodore Parker, *Speeches, Addresses and Occasional Sermons* (3 vols., Boston, 1861), 3: 261–62; Thornton, *Pulpit in the American Revolution,* p. iii; *Diary of G. T. Strong,* ed. Nevins, 2:448–49 (on Lord). See also Charles Davis, Jr., *C. H. Davis, Rear Admiral, U.S.N.* (New York, 1899), p. 295; James MacPherson, "The Anti-Slavery Legacy," in *Toward a New Past,* ed. Barton Bernstein (New York, 1968), p. 129; Daniel Aaron, *The Unwritten War* (New York, 1973), p. 346; David Donald, ed., *Inside Lincoln's Cabinet: Civil War Diaries of Salmon P. Chase* (New York, 1954), p. 95; *National Quarterly Review* 14 (1867): 244–88; John W. Dean, *The . . . Embarkation of Cromwell and his Friends for New England* (Boston, 1866) (note that the hero of this flight-from-Stuart-tyranny story was now Cromwell rather than Hampden). Proslavery writers also displayed admiration of "stern Oliver." See J. R. Jones, *The Quaker Soldier* (Philadelphia, 1858), 326 ff.; and T. W. Hoit, *The Model Man: An Oration on Washington* (St. Louis, 1866), pp. 12, 28.

88 J. G. Gilchrist, "Charles I: A Martyr," [American] *Church Review* 47 (1886): 1; Samuel Church, *Oliver Cromwell* (New York, 1894); Clifton Smith, "Oliver Cromwell," *Munsey's Magazine* 11 (1894): 136–40; A. J. Gade, "Oliver Cromwell," *Cosmopolitan* 26 (1899): 564–70; 30 (1903): 339–42; Theo. Roosevelt, *Oliver Cromwell* (Boston, 1900); Greene, *America's Heroes,* pp. 120–26. Cf. Wilson Vance, *Big John Baldwin* (New York, 1901), an American version of an English historical novel which celebrates Cromwell.

"Cavalier" southerners generally seem to have despised the "Roundhead" Cromwell (Aaron, *The Unwritten War,* p. 344), but at least one rebel clergyman claimed Cromwell was on the side of the Confederacy. See Reverend Thomas V. Moore, *God Our Refuge and Strength in this War* . . . (Richmond, 1861), p. 14. In September, 1973, a letter to the editor of the *New York Post* called on Senator Sam Ervin to "be our Oliver Cromwell" in the struggle against "an absolute monarch" in the White House (Terry Ward to the editor, Sept. 10, 1973).

89   Greene, *America's Heroes*, pp. 81, 112n, 120–29, 137, 159; Hoit, *The Model Man*, p. 28; Peterson, *The Jeffersonian Image*, p. 421.

Roosevelt, in turn, admired Lincoln and Andrew Jackson. Jackson had, in his own day, been much admired for his "ceaseless activity" and "iron energy." Henry A. Wise (the Virginia governor who hanged John Brown) styled him "a Hercules of action" who took life "by main force." Joseph Baldwin, a southern lawyer and essayist, felt that Jackson was "built of Cromwell's stuff," and several compared him to Napoleon (see John William Ward, *Andrew Jackson: Symbol for an Age* [New York, 1955], esp. pp. 157, 212).

It would appear that Cromwell devotees tended to be Republicans and Progressives in the period from 1850 to 1915, and that their praise of Cromwell upset Catholics and ritualistic Protestants, who tended to be Democrats. This would be consistent with Paul Kleppner's findings, which show late-nineteenth-century Republicans to be pietists and moralists, willing to use state powers to ensure right behavior, and late-nineteenth-century Democrats to be ritualistic, anxious to maintain a separation of church and state and to protect "personal liberty" (Kleppner, *Cross of Culture*).

90   Cunliffe, *Soldiers and Civilians*, p. 399.

91   Guerard, *Napoleonic Legend*, pp. 105–11.

92   J. T. Morse, *Abraham Lincoln* (1893), cited in Basler, *Lincoln Legend*, p. 16.

93   National Republican Club, *Proceedings at the Annual Lincoln Dinner Addresses* (5 vols., New York, 1887–1919), 1: 52–57; 2: 47, 50, 55.

94   *The Complete Poetical Works of James Russell Lowell* (Boston, 1896), pp. 49–53.

95   As John P. Diggins has shown, Mussolini clearly was a hero to many Americans in the 1920's and was compared by some to George Washington (Diggins, *Mussolini and Fascism: The View From America* [Princeton, 1972], 183, 223, and esp. the chapter entitled "Mussolini as American Hero"). The account Diggins offers appears to indicate what one would expect: that cosmopolitan progressives were at least initially impressed with Mussolini, and that Jeffersonian, antistatist lovers of "personal liberty" (such as Albert Nock) were offended by him. See Dixon Wecter, *The Hero in America* (New York, 1941), p. 304; J. Larned, *Study of Greatness in Men* (Boston, 1911), pp. 166–67, 214, 300; N. D. Hillis, *Great Men as Prophets of a New Era* (New York, 1922), pp. 86, 89, 90, 103, 110, 113; N. D. Hillis, "Religion or Dogma?," *Forum* 70 (1923): 1681.

96   H. Mabie, *Heroes Every Child Should Know* (New York, 1908), p. xvi.

97 But if Bancroft was no reactionary, other lovers of the "strong man" were. Indeed, some might be more accurately have been styled fascists. Thus one New York chaplain to the Sons of the American Revolution in 1899: "If . . . a great number of soured and discontented men, their brains clouded by envy and passion, should, by the use of . . . universal suffrage, attempt to . . . derange the order of society, some strong man will come on the stage able to throttle the public enemy and drive him back" (quoted in Davies, *Patriotism on Parade*, pp. 290–91).

98 H. Bancroft, *Chronicles of the Builders of the Commonwealth* (6 vols., San Francisco, 1891–92), esp. 1: xi–xiii, 2. Cf. I. E. Levine, *Oliver Cromwell* (New York, 1966), a "personal liberty" view of Cromwell.

Kent Steckmesser has found that Western heroes like Kit Carson, Wild Bill Hickok, and Colonel George Custer were often likened to Cromwell, Napoleon, and other such self-reliant men of force. See Steckmesser, *The Western Hero in History and Legend* (Norman, Okla., 1965), pp. 244, 251.

Even Washington was now seen by some in these terms. To Stewart Woodford, Past Master of the New York Masonic Lodge, for example, he was a "robust, muscular man of magnificent physique" and inflexible will (Freemasons of the Pa. Grand Lodge, *Proceedings . . .* [1902], pp. 178, 255, 259). Cf. Edward House, *Philip Dru, Administrator* (New York, 1912).

5: America's Own Patriot-Heroes

1 Adams to Jefferson, Dec. 16, 1816, *Adams-Jefferson Letters*, ed. Lester Cappon (2 vols., Chapel Hill, 1959), 2:502.

2 Thomas Condie, *Memoirs of George Washington*, as reported in William A. Bryan, *George Washington in American Literature, 1775–1865* (New York, 1952), p. 57; W. E. Channing, "Likeness to God" (1828), in American Unitarian Society, ed., *The Works of W. E. Channing* (Boston, 1887), p. 298; W. C. Rives, *Discourse on the Character . . . of John Hampden* (Richmond, 1845), p. 8; Moncure Conway, quoted in Louis Ruchames, ed., *A John Brown Reader* (London, 1959), p. 279; James Parton, *Triumph of Enterprise . . .* , p. 602; Richard Taylor, *Destruction and Reconstruction* (New York, 1879), p. 104.

3 W. E. Channing, *Works*, p. 298. Names are from *Dictionary of American Biography* and other registers. On another European symbol, see George Anderson, "Pascal Paoli, an Inspiration to the Sons of Liberty," *Colonial Society of Massachusetts Publications* 26 (1926): 180–210; Anne Loveland's account of the American image of Lafayette, *Emblem of Liberty* (Baton Rouge, 1971), pp. 56–153, is also very revealing.

4 Napoleon Jefferson Smith's parents were being quite cosmopolitan, but they had nothing on the parents of Napoleon Jackson Tecumseh Dana (b. 1822), Hannibal Lafayette Washington Godwin (b. 1873), George Washington Bonaparte Caesar Towns (b. 1801), or Washington Lafayette Bolivar Elliot (b. 1825). After Albert Sidney Johnston's heroic death during the Civil War, some southerners used that alteration on the Rebel-Saint's name in naming

their own children. Thus did Sydney's name (once removed) survive his reputation.

5 Determining whether a name was "patriotic-heroic" or not was, of course,
crucial to the analysis. Some names, like those of Washington, Hampden,
Joseph Warren, Sydney, Napoleon, were clear enough. The father of Andrew
Jackson Smith (b. 1815) explained that he "had no other means in his power"
of showing his regard for "the Hero who achieved the Victory" at New
Orleans than by calling his son for him (*DAB*, Andrew Jackson Smith).
Others, like those of Columbus and Newton, were included to provide the
perspective of those who preferred scientific or explorer symbols. Political
figures (Jefferson, Jackson, Clay, Gallatin, etc.) were included, as their use
clearly indicates that some loyal Democrats, Federalists, Whigs, etc., were
making an effort to honor a "patriot" they admired.

But what is one to do with Benjamin Franklin? Was his name being
honored as a "patriot" or as the discoverer of electricity? And what of "Nelson" and "Milton"? Are these simply family names? Or do they honor
British "patriots?" And if they honor John Milton, colleague of Cromwell,
Hampden, and Sydney, do they honor him as a "patriot," a writer, or a
religious figure?

Religious symbols are more difficult to isolate, as names drawn deliberately from the Old and New Testament are hard to distinguish from innoc-
uously chosen, family or "common," areligious names. Daniel Smith has
found that Biblical naming steadily declined in its hotbed, the Massachusetts
town, from a high of 95 percent usage in 1695 to 70 percent in 1770, 55 percent in 1810, and 25 percent in 1850. Religious motives clearly *were* more
powerful than "patriotic-heroic" ones in child-naming, but they steadily
became less powerful over time as the world became less mysterious and
more secular, and as colonial America became the United States. (Smith,
"Child-Naming Patterns and Family Structure," paper delivered at Clark
University Conference on Family and Social Structure, 1972, p. 34.)

Of the nonreligious, identifiable, "heroic" names, 54 percent were of a
political nature, 33 percent military, 10 percent scientific-explorer, and 3 percent legal. The preponderance of political, "patriotic" names reinforces the
claim of "impressionistic" historians that early Americans were extremely
political, with a healthy fear of standing armies and military dictatorships.
But the high percentage (33 percent) of purely *military* heroes (higher among
nonelite elements of the society) reveals a clear affinity for the martial virtues
among a sizable number of early-nineteenth-century Americans. See Marcus
Cunliffe, *Soldiers and Civilians: The Martial Spirit in America, 1775–1865*
(Boston, 1970) for more on this subject.

No particular region or state appeared to generate disproportionate
numbers of patriotic-heroic names, though the names differed somewhat
from region to region. Not surprisingly, there were no John Jays from the
South, and precious few Thomas Jeffersons (four of seventy-five) from New
England.

In about 350 cases the political party of either the parents or the patriotically styled child could be determined, and it is clear that members of all parties used patriot-hero names. But certain names were clearly identifiable with particular parties. Jay, Hamilton, Webster, and Clay were favored by Whigs and Republicans; Jefferson, Jackson, Gallatin, and Madison by Democrats. (Indeed, James Fenimore Cooper told of a Federalist minister who refused at the font to christen an infant with such a "Satanic" name as "Thomas Jefferson," and substituted "Alexander Hamilton," which may not have delighted the parents.) Washington, Franklin, Sydney, Lafayette, and Oliver Hazard Perry appear to have been sufficiently ubiquitous, or above party identification, to be used by members of all parties.

Politicians, lawyers, and military officers were disproportionate bearers of patriot-hero names. Electors may have favored patriotic-sounding candidates, but there is a more likely explanation. Their parents had been sufficiently concerned to give them a patriotic label, and it is thus quite likely that many were strongly encouraged to pursue public service careers. (Not surprisingly, the military officers had disproportionately martial names—Decatur, Napoleon, Washington, etc.)

6 James Parton, cited in Marvin Meyers, *Jacksonian Persuasion* (Stanford, 1957), p. 3. Parton found that Washington led with 198, followed by Jackson (191), Franklin (136), Jefferson (110), and Clay (42). As placenaming is generally a pastime of elites, the large number of places named after Andrew Jackson may *not* represent what Parton and Meyers seem to imply, a popular affection for the "Symbol of an Age," because my own child-naming data, with a more popular source base than Parton's placenames, does not show such a high percentage of Jackson devotees. Perhaps the places were named by local Jacksonian politicos, anxious to honor their party's symbol and to *create* more veneration for it than existed.

7 J. J. Timaeus, ed., *Nordamerikanischer Staats-Kalendar* (Hamburg, 1798).

8 Eleven editions of the last will and testament to date; over 140 of the farewell address. See, for example, William Spohn Baker, *Bibliotheca Washingtoniana* (Philadelphia, 1889); William A. Bryan, *George Washington in American Literature, 1775–1865* (New York, 1952), p. 53; Samuel Shirk, *The Characterization of George Washington in American Plays Since 1875* (Easton, Pa., 1949); Percy MacKaye, *Washington, the Man Who Made Us: A Ballad Play* (New York, 1919); Edwin Markham, *Washington: The Nation Builder* (Washington, 1932).

9 See Frances Whittmore, *George Washington in Sculpture* (Boston, 1933); Joel T. Headley, *Illustrated Life of Washington* (New York, 1859); W. S. Baker, *The Engraved Portraits of Washington* (Philadelphia, 1880), and *Medallic Portraits of Washington* (Philadelphia, 1885). On the monument, see F. L. Harvey, *History of the Washington Monument and the National Monument Society* (Washington, D.C., 1903).

10 See Baker, *Bibliotheca Washingtoniana*, pp. 6n, 75–77, and passim; Ignatius Thompson, *The Patriots' Monitor*, cited in Ruth Miller Elson, "American

Schoolbooks and 'Culture' in the Nineteenth Century," *Mississippi Valley Historical Review* 46 (1959): 119; Mason Locke Weems, *The Life of Washington*, ed. Marcus Cunliffe (9th ed., Philadelphia, 1890; reprinted Cambridge, Mass., 1962), p. 8; Horatio Weld and George Lippard, cited in Bryan, *Washington in American Literature*, pp. 101, 214.

11 Noah Webster, *A Grammatical Institute of the English Language* (Hartford, 1783), cited in Ruth M. Elson, *Guardians of Tradition: American Schoolbooks of the Nineteenth Century* (Lincoln, Neb., 1964), pp. 110, 106, 118, 282–83; Caleb Bingham, *The Columbian Orator* (Boston, 1807), p. 58; Weems, *Life of Washington*, p. 6; Richard Snowden, *The Columbiad* (Baltimore, ca. 1796). Cf. Merle Curti, *The Roots of American Loyalty* (New York, 1946), pp. 56–60, 128.

12 *George Washington's Rules of Civility*, ed. Moncure Conway (New York, 1890), rules 2 and 4 (cf. William P. Stoddard, *George Washington's 57 Rules of Behavior* [Denver, 1886] and several other similar editions). See also Elson, *Guardians of Tradition*, pp. 198, 202, 228; Weems, *Life of Washington*.

13 Elson, *Guardians of Tradition*, 198; E. D. Mansfield, cited in Cunliffe, *Soldiers and Civilians*, p. 393.

14 Douglas Adair and John Schultz, eds., *The Spur of Fame* (San Marino, 1966), pp. 93, 206–15, 229.

15 U.S. Congress, *Annals of the Congress of the U.S.*, 12th Cong., 1st Sess., (Washington, D.C., 1853), pp. 452, 472–73 (I am indebted to Stuart Brandes for this reference).

16 John Lovett, *Washington's Birth Day—An Historical Poem* (Albany, 1812), pp. 49, 52; Weems, *Life of Washington*, p. 168.

17 Rives, *Discourse . . . on Hampden*, p. 62; *Historical Essays of Macaulay*, ed. George Watrous (New York, 1901), p. 108; Sir Leslie Stephen, *History of English Thought in the 18th Century* (2 vols., London, 1876), 2: 201; Henry Van Dyke, *The Americanism of Washington* (New York, 1906), p. 13.

Washington's fame not only eclipsed that of the twin patriots; it spread abroad as well. Irish, English, Australians, French, Venezuelans, Italians, and Romanians sang his praises. See George Kittridge, "An 18th Century Irish Song relating to Washington by Thomas O'Mechan," *Publications of the Colonial Society of Massachusetts* 13 (1911): 254–59; M. Cunliffe, *George Washington: Man and Monument* (Boston, 1958), p. 19; R. C. Winthrop, *Oration on the Completion of the Washington Monument* (Boston, 1885), p. 69; Amanda Ellis, *Rebels and Conservatives* (Bloomington, 1967), p. 94; "Crespy-Noher" [Alexis Manieres], *Oeuvre de propagande républicaine— Washington et Napoleon* (Bordeaux, 1871); "Columbian," *Bolivar i Washington* (Caracas, 1865); T. C. Giannini, *Giorgio Washington Visto da un Italiano* (Rome, 1933); C. Formichi, *Giorgio Washington* (Milan, 1933); Society of the Friends of the U.S., Bucharest, *Homage to George Washington* (Bucharest, 1932).

18 Bernard Mayo, *Myths and Men* (Athens, Ga., 1859), p. 49.

19 Ibid., p. 48; "Washington," *A Touchstone For the Leading Partymen in the*

U.S. (n.p., 1800); "Washington," *To the People of the U.S. on the Choice of a President* (Boston, 1812); "Washington," *The Constitution of the U.S. Defended and the Rights of the People Advocated* (Schenectady, ca. 1822).

20 Bryan, *Washington in American Literature*, p. 75.

21 Ibid., pp. 78–81, 164; George Fitzhugh, "Bonaparte, Cromwell, and Washington," *DeBow's Review* 28 (Feb. 1860): 139–54.

22 Bryan, *Washington in American Literature*, p. 81. Cf. Robert C. Winthrop's Unionist invocation of Washington in 1848, *Oration on the 4th of July, 1848, on the occasion of laying the cornerstone of the National Monument to the Memory of Washington* (Washington, D.C., 1848), pp. 34–35.

23 Bryan, *Washington in American Literature*, p. 165; Charles Alexander, *Washington's Vision* (Philadelphia, 1864); Morison Heady, *The Farmer Boy and How he Became Commander-in-Chief* (Boston, 1863), esp. 4, 44–45; Samuel Osgood, "The Second Life of Washington," *Harper's Magazine* 32 (March, 1866): 466–67.

24 W. H. Burk, *Washington's Prayers* (Norristown, Pa., 1907); *Religious References in the Writings . . . of Washington* (Washington, D.C., 1932); Leo Helderman, *George Washington, Patron of Learning* (New York, 1932); J. M. Toner, *George Washington as an Inventor and Promoter of the Useful Arts* (Washington, 1892); John A. Stevens, *Address to the New York Sons of the American Revolution* (New York, Feb. 22, 1900); Dudley Knox, *The Naval Genius of George Washington* (Boston, 1932); Augusta Stevenson, *George Washington, Boy Leader* (New York, 1942); Michael J. O'Brien, *George Washington's Association with the Irish* (New York, 1937); W. M. Kozlowski, *Washington and Kosciuszko* (New York, 1942); Walter H. Mazych, *George Washington and the Negro* (New York, 1932); Halsted L. Ritter, *Washington as a Business Man* (New York, 1931) (Ritter, a Florida Circuit Court judge, was impeached five years later); Edith Calisch, *The Jews Who Stood by Washington* (Cincinnati, 1932); Sidney Hayden, *Washington and his Masonic Compeers* (New York, 1866); Freemasons of the Pennsylvania Grand Lodge, *Proceedings at . . . the Sesquicentennial Anniversary of the Initiation of Brother George Washington* (Philadelphia, 1902); Henry Hill, *George Washington and Active, Aggressive and Progressive Masonry* (New York, 1919); John J. Lanier, *Washington, the Great American Mason* (New York, 1922).

25 J. H. Plumb, *The Death of the Past* (Boston, 1970), p. 31n; Fred Greenstein, *Children and Politics* (New Haven, 1966), pp. 100–101.

26 "General Washington's Vision," *National Tribune* 4 (Dec., 1880).

27 Dixon Wecter, *The Hero in America* (New York, 1941), p. 9.

28 Freemasons of Pennsylvania Grand Lodge, *Proceedings*, pp. 104–5. Cf. *A Memorial to Washington the Mason* (Alexandria, Va., 1910).

29 Bryan, *Washington in American Literature*, pp. 56–57, 71–72, 82–83, 84.

30 Sarah Hale, *The Genius of Oblivion and Other Original Poems* (Concord, N.H., 1823), p. 87.

31 Whittemore, *Washington in Sculpture*, pp. 81, 83.

32 U.S. Congress, *The Dedication of the Washington National Monument* . . . (Washington, D.C., 1885), p. 103, and passim; Harvey, *Washington Monument*; E. L. Kayser, *Bricks without Straw* (New York, 1970), pp. 189-90.

33 But see J. H. Plumb's argument in *The Death of the Past*, p. 53. Plumb maintains that the modern world is too sophisticated, too critical, to "marmorealize" anyone; historical analysis debunks the patriot-figures of the past and "undermines" their usefulness. A recent example of such demythologizing of Washington might be Marvin Kitman's recent edition of Washington's Revolutionary War expense account, a document reproduced several times in the mid-nineteenth century and praised then as a model of "economy" and "disinterestedness in the public service." By 1970 Kitman could offer a devastating critique of this "swindle sheet" of "the man second to none" in the preparation of padded expense accounts. Kitman's reward, appropriately, was some greenbacked Washingtons. (*George Washington's Expense Account*, by General George Washington and Marvin Kitman, Pfc. [Ret.] [New York, 1970], esp. p. 19.) It remains uncertain how much Kitman's irreverence is symptomatic of attitudes towards Washington, and to what extent debunking of this sort has an impact on popular attitudes.

34 Anne H. Hutton, *Portrait of Patriotism* (Philadelphia, 1959), pp. 153-55, 169.

35 Earl Barnes, "Children's Ideals," *Pedagogical Seminary* 7 (1900):239; Will Chambers, "The Evolution of Ideals," ibid., 10 (1903): 110-11.

36 U.S. George Washington Bicentennial Commission, *History of the George Washington Bicentennial Celebration* (3 vols., Washington, D.C., 1932), 1: esp. 394, 399; Bryan, *Washington in American Literature*, p. 166; Kent Steckmesser, *The Western Hero in History and Legend* (Norman, Okla., 1965), pp. 244, 251; see also Theodore Greene, *America's Heroes: The Changing Models of Success in American Magazines* (New York, 1970).

"We [already] have lives of . . . Heroes, Philosophers, and Statesmen," Freeman Hunt explained in the preface to his *Lives of American Merchants* (2 vols., Cincinnati, 1858). The new heroes of commerce, "pre-eminently the characteristic" of America, were what was needed.

37 Here, as elsewhere in this discussion of Jefferson as symbol, I am indebted to Merrill D. Peterson for his impressive study, *The Jeffersonian Image in the American Mind* (New York, 1960). I come to somewhat different conclusions from Peterson about the strength, meaning, and significance of "the Jeffersonian image in the American mind," however, and while I utilize much of the same evidence that he considered, I recommend that those especially interested in Jefferson's image consult his more complete study as well.

38 Thus while William Seward invoked *Sydney* in his defence of the Wilmot Proviso, Thomas Hart Benton and others styled it "the Jefferson Proviso," so certain were they that this check to slavery in the territories reflected *Jef-*

ferson's principles (Peterson, *Jeffersonian Image*, pp. 190, 198). Tom Watson also joined Jefferson to Hampden and Sydney in *Life and Times of Jefferson* (New York, 1903), p. 515.

39 James Bryce, *The American Commonwealth* (2 vols., New York, 1891), 2: 9.

40 Cited in Peterson, *Jeffersonian Image*, p. 211.

41 See, for example, J. Sheldon, "Thomas Jefferson, as seen by the Light of 1863," *Continental Monthly* 5 (February, 1864); and Moses M. Granger, *Washington vs. Jefferson: The Case Tried by Battle in 1861-65* (Boston, 1898), for Unionist critiques of Jefferson and "the doctrines of '98."

42 Peterson, *Jeffersonian Image*, pp. 212–20. In 1865 the Democratic historian George Bancroft found it necessary to depict Jefferson as one who had done much "towards consolidating the Union" while he had been president, thus giving Jefferson an image somewhat unfamiliar to Americans. Bancroft, "The Place of Abraham Lincoln in History," *Atlantic Monthly* 15 (June, 1865): 759.

43 Samuel Fowler, "The Political Opinions of Jefferson," *North American Review* 101 (October, 1865): 330–35; first noted in Peterson, *Jeffersonian Image*, p. 218.

44 David A. Wasson, "The Modern Type of Oppression," *North American Review* 119 (October, 1874): 257, 261–84. Cf. Wallace Farnham, " 'The Weakened Spring of Government': A Study in 19th Century American History," *American Historical Review* 69 (April, 1963): 662–80.

45 Henry Cabot Lodge, *The Democracy of the Constitution* (New York, 1915), pp. 122, 126; Peterson, *Jeffersonian Image*, pp. 333–40; Frank Vrooman, *The New Politics* (New York, 1911), pp. 12, 17, 21, 23, 96–97, 265, 273, 274. Brooks Adams regarded Washington, rather than Hamilton or Lincoln, as the "personification of the principle of consolidation" (though he admired the latter two as well). Washington, whom Adams compared to Cromwell in "organizing and administrative intellect," had the proper "contempt of the practical man" for such "abstractions" as Jefferson or men of his ilk might spin. Under his firm guidance the United States had become "a social mass capable of sustained and energetic action." Adams, "War as the Ultimate Form of Economic Competition," *U.S. Naval Institute Proceedings* 24 (1904): 838–41.

46 *Addresses delivered at the Lincoln Dinners of the Republican Club of the City of New York* (5 vols., New York, 1897–), 1: 71. For evidence of the veneration of Lincoln among diverse groups in society see Roy Basler, *Myths about Lincoln* (Boston, 1935); Montgomery Lewis, *Legends That Libel Lincoln* (New York, 1946); Michael Davis, *The Image of Lincoln in the South* (Knoxville, Tenn., 1971); *Lincoln Lore*, a weekly "bulletin of the Lincoln National Foundation," edited from the 1930's to the 1950's by Louis Warren of the Lincoln National Life Insurance Co., Fort Wayne, Indiana; Lloyd Lewis, *Myths After Lincoln* (New York, 1929), p. 261; W. Lloyd Warner, *The Living and the Dead* (New Haven, 1959), pp. 270–73; and F. L. Bullard, *Lincoln in Marble and Bronze* (New Brunswick, 1952). Cf. Victor Searcher's bibliography, *Lincoln Today* (New York, 1969).

47 For two clear statements of this "self-made" theme see the "dime novel" biography by J. O. Victor, *The Private and Public Life of Abraham Lincoln*, in Beadle's Lives of Great Americans Series (New York, 1864), and William M. Thayer, *The Character and Public Services of Abraham Lincoln* (Boston, 1864).

48 Percy MacKaye, *Ode on the Centenary of Abraham Lincoln* (New York, 1909).

49 See Paul Kleppner, *The Cross of Culture* (New York, 1971); Louis Banks, *The Lincoln Legend* [a temperance group] (New York, 1903); and Eugene Chafin, *Lincoln: The Man of Sorrow* (Chicago, 1908).

50 Of 126 "Political Tributes to the Memory of Abraham Lincoln," gathered in 1865, 60 celebrated Lincoln as "Savior of the Union," 60 offered praise to "the Great Emancipator," and 6 remembered him for both qualities (noted by Roy Basler in his original and valuable *The Lincoln Legend: A Study in Changing Conceptions* [New York, 1935], p. 202).

51 For Emerson see Basler, *Lincoln Legend*, pp. 5, 16, 30–32, 87, 142–46, 219–21, 227; for Stoddard see William Betts, ed., *Lincoln and the Poets* (Pittsburgh, 1965), pp. 11, 68.

52 William Herndon, *Herndon's Lincoln* (Chicago, 1889), pp. 111, 611.

53 Nathaniel W. Stevenson, "Lincoln and the Progress of Nationality in the North," *Annual Report of the A.H.A., 1919* (2 vols., Washington, D.C., 1923), 1: 361–63.

54 Betts, *Lincoln and the Poets*, pp. 8, 11, 68, and 96 (on Stoddard, Ailen, Grierson, and Sandburg); *Lincoln Dinner Addresses*, 1: 68 (on Strobridge); Benjamin Thomas, *Portrait for Posterity* (New Brunswick, N.J., 1947), p. 200 (on Tarbell). Cf. Thomas Dixon, *A Man of the People* (New York, 1920), a "Savior of the Union" play in which Lincoln defends ably his suspension of habeas corpus; and William B. Hesseltine, *Lincoln and the War Governors* (New York, 1948).

55 Mary P. Follett, *The New State* (New York and London, 1926), p. 182 ff; *John Dryden, Addresses and Papers . . .* (Newark, 1909), pp. 278, 280.

56 *Lincoln Dinner Addresses,* 1: 114–15, 186–87, 138–45, 251.

57 Lincoln Highway Association, *The Lincoln Highway* (New York, 1935), pp. vii, 23, 55, 62, 263, 268. Cf. Chesla Sherlock, *Tall Timbers* (Boston, 1926), pp. 329–30.

58 Peterson, *Jeffersonian Image*, p. 331.

59 Edgar Lee Masters, *Lincoln the Man* (New York, 1931), pp. 3, 4, 5, 98, 340, 400–401, 427, 446–47, 450, 497–98. Cf. Thomas E. Watson, *The Life and Times of Thomas Jefferson* (New York, 1903), pp. 15, 282, 470, 499.

60 See Alfred H. Jones, *Roosevelt's Image Brokers: Poets, Playwrights, and the Lincoln Symbol* (Port Washington, N.Y., 1974), p. 27, on Roosevelt's review of Bowers's book. See also Dumas Malone, "Jefferson and the New Deal," *Scribner's Magazine* 93 (June, 1933): 356–59; Richard Carlyle, *The Earth Belongs to the Living* (Los Angeles, 1936); T. T. McAvoy, "Roosevelt: A Modern Jeffersonian," *Review of Politics* 7 (July, 1945): 270–75; and John Dewey, *The Living Thought of Thomas Jefferson* (Philadelphia, 1940).

61 Quoted in Peterson, *Jeffersonian Image*, p. 375.

62 Ibid., pp. 356-65, 425-36.

63 Edward Griggs, *American Statesmen* (Croton-on-Hudson, 1927), pp. 5, 174; A. H. Jones, *Roosevelt's Image Brokers*, p. 28; Benét to Davenport, January, 1942, in *Selected Letters of Stephen Vincent Benét*, ed. Charles A. Fenton (New Haven, 1960), pp. 391-92.

64 Peterson, *Jeffersonian Image*, pp. 364-75, 432-35.

65 Ibid., p. 433. In the early summer of 1946 George Gallup had found that Lincoln ran just behind FDR (39% to 37%) and well ahead of Washington (15%) and Woodrow Wilson (5%) in a four-president race (Hadley Cantril, ed., *Public Opinion* [Princeton, 1951], p. 590). Wecter, *Hero in America*, p. 391, mentions similar results in a 1921 poll of college students who ranked Lincoln and Theodore Roosevelt well ahead of Jefferson.

66 Jones, *Roosevelt's Image Brokers*, pp. 26-27, 65-66. I rely on Jones for much of the evidence used in this and the following two paragraphs, but while I found Jones perceptive and useful, I was troubled by his stress on the egalitarian nature of the Lincoln symbol. This aspect is certainly there, but Lincoln the symbol of strength, order, unity is also vital, and I think Jones gives it inadequate attention.

67 Ibid., pp. 43, 80.

68 Ralph Gabriel, *The Course of American Democratic Thought* (2nd ed., New York, 1956), pp. 445-50; Jones, *Image Brokers*, pp. 28, 72, 77, 83, 108-10, 116. Throughout the war Robert Sherwood served as a ghostwriter for FDR, while Benét wrote several Lincolnesque radio scripts.

The use of the Lincoln symbols is a persistent phenomenon, of course. Most recently Lyndon Johnson, caught in the throes of his Vietnam policies, and Richard Nixon, trapped by his Watergate machinations, sought to associate themselves with Lincoln (see pl. 62).

69 Conversely, those who preferred Jefferson to Lincoln had positive things to say about the Declaration of Independence and negative things to say about Lincoln's alleged abuses of civil liberties: "I have the greatest respect for civil libertarians." Likewise, "I scored Lincoln lower for his transgressions against liberty." "[Jefferson] was a president, *not* a king."

70 Civil libertarians, to be sure, would invoke him in the McCarthy era; Jefferson's remark that "error of opinion may be tolerated where reason is left free to combat it" seemed appropriate. But this sort of invocation did little to improve his standing with many "everyday" Americans, and in any event one solid study casts serious doubts on Jefferson's own libertarian standards (see Leonard Levy, *Jefferson and Civil Liberties: The Darker Side* [Cambridge, Mass., 1963]).

71 Many Americans, of course, do not think of Jefferson and Lincoln in these terms at all. Some admire Jefferson for his intellect, Lincoln for his humanity, and give little other conscious thought to either men. But intellect and humanitarianism are apolitical traits, and we are primarily concerned here with the use of patriot-heroes as political symbols. Most Americans do distinguish

between order and freedom, statism and antistatism—most do take a position on one side or the other on such issues. And, whether consciously or unconsciously, Lincoln is the patriot-hero of order-conscious, cosmopolitan statists; Jefferson of freedom-conscious, localistic antistatists.

6: Romanticism and Imperialism, Democracy and Reaction

1 C. J. Fox, *The Speech of C. J. Fox . . . at the Whig Club of England . . .* (London, 1792), p. 7. For instances of such veneration see Dr. Joseph Towers, *An Oration on Occasion of the Commemoration of the Revolution* (London, 1788); Richard Price (1723–91), "Address to the Society for Commemorating the Revolution of 1688," November 4, 1789, in Basil Duke Henning, Archibald Foord, et al., eds., *Crises in English History: 1066–1945* (New York, 1949), p. 403; "John Hampden, Esq." *A General History of England* (London, 1784); *The Patriot: A Poem* (London, 1793), pp. 7, 17; Chris. Wyvill, *Political Papers* (6 vols., York, 1794–1802), 4: 219n; D. Eaton, "Address to the Public," advertisement for the "Political Classics" series in the frontispiece of his *Pigott's Political Dictionary* (London, 1794); Mary Moorman, *William Wordsworth* (London, 1957), p. 205.

2 I have not attempted anything like a thorough search of European sources to evaluate the reputation of the two patriots on the Continent, but there are some signs that their reputation was not insignificant. Sydney's *Discourses* were published in France in 1702, 1755, and 1789, in Holland in 1755, and in German editions in 1705 and 1793. Montesquieu owned a copy by 1734 (Shackleton, *Montesquieu* [Oxford, 1961], p. 417), as did Rousseau (L'infortuné Sidney pensait comme moi, mais il agissait; c'est pour son fait, & non pour son livre, qu'il eut l'honneur de verser son sang") (*Political Writings . . .* ed. C. E. Vaughan [2 vols., Oxford, 1962], 1: 240; 2: 205–6). Condorcet loved "the generous Sydney" for his faith in man's ability to understand and secure his natural rights (Bertrand Russell, *History of Western Philosophy* [New York, 1945], p. 722). Thomas Hollis sent copies of his edition to revolutionaries in Sweden (C. Robbins, "Library of Liberty," *Harvard Library Bulletin* 5 [1951]: 183). "Sidney" urged Frenchmen in 1789 to support an active, anticlerical, antiaristocratic National Assembly ("Milord Sidney," *Lettre de félicitation . . . aux Parisiens et à la Nation Française, on Resurrection de Milord Sidney . . .* [Paris, 1789]), and in December, 1792, the president of the French National Convention wrote to the British Society for Constitutional Information: "The shades of Pym, or Hampden, and of Sydney are hovering over your heads. [An English Republic is not far away.] The sons of liberty throughout the world will never forget their obligations to the English nation" (Thomas B. Howell, ed., *Cobbett's Complete Collection of State Trials and Proceedings for High Treason and other Crimes . . .* [33 vols., London, 1809–26], 25: 1211). In 1792 a member of the National Club of Bordeaux exclaimed: "O ye . . . guides in the career through which we pass—ye who have acquired a claim to the eternal gratitude of mankind, SIDNEY, [Richard] PRICE, HAMPDEN . . . arise from your tomb, partake with

us" (translated in the *Columbian Centinel*, March 31, 1792, p. 2). (Sydney had criticized French absolutism: *Discourses on Government* [3 vols., Philadelphia, 1805], 2: 193, 454). A year later several imprisoned Girondists compared their fate to that of Sydney (Moorman, *Wordsworth*, p. 208). Cf. H. T. Parker, *The Cult of Antiquity and the French Revolution* (Chicago, 1937).

The German historian, Barthold Niebuhr (1776–1831), noted in his diary in 1794 the 111th anniversary of Sydney's death, "in my eyes a consecrated day, especially as I have just been studying his noble life again." Niebuhr praised the "virtue and holiness" of the Englishman (Robert C. Winthrop, *Addresses and Speeches on Various Occasions* [4 vols., Boston, 1852–86], 2: 172). Frederick von Gentz was shocked by Karl Wilhelm von Humboldt's ignorance of the Rebel-Saint—"just imagine! He does not even know Algernon Sidney's name!" (quoted in Caroline Robbins, "Algernon Sidney's *Discourses on Government:* Textbook of Revolutions," *William and Mary Quarterly* 4, no. 3 [July, 1947]: 272). See also Jacob Venedey, *John Hampden und die Lehre vom gesetzlichen Widerstande* (Belle-Vue, by Constance, 1844).

3 Thomas Hardy, *The Patriot* . . . (Edinburgh, 1793), pp. 29, 57. This was a different Thomas Hardy from the English radical (1752–1832).

4 Edmund Burke, *Reflections on the French Revolution* (London, 1910), p. 32.

5 *Rex* v. *Hardy, Rex* v. *Tooke*, in Howell, *State Trials*, 24:199, 25:1; C. Robbins, *The Eighteenth Century Commonwealthman* (Cambridge, Mass., 1959), p. 322; Olive Rudkin, *Thomas Spence and his Connections* (London, 1927), p. 115; Henry R. Yorke, *These are the Times that Try Men's Souls! A Letter addressed to John Frost, A Prisoner at Newgate* (London, 1793), p. 30.

6 Grey is quoted in Edward Lascelles, *The Life of C. J. Fox* (London, 1936), p. 265; for the complaint against crimping houses, see George Rudé, *The Crowd in History* (New York, 1964), p. 230; and Rudé to the author, August 2, 1973; Sheffield Constitutional Society, *Proceedings of the Public Meeting . . . on . . . Parliamentary Reform* (London, 1794), p. 44.

7 *Trial of Joseph Gerrald* . . . (2nd ed., Edinburgh, 1794), pp. 93, 116, 203, 212, 215, 233. (I am grateful to E. P. Thompson for the Gerrald citation.) In like fashion, John Warden, on trial for organizing a Chartist "National Holiday" in Bolton, told a jury forty-six years later that his principles were "identical" to those of Hampden and Sydney, and that these principles "tend not . . . to anarchy . . . but to . . . the protection of property, to the preservation of social harmony, and to the defense of all that is time-hallowed and true in our institutions." Quoted in Patricia Hollis, ed., *Class & Conflict in 19th Century England, 1815–1850* (London, 1973), p. 237.

8 *Memoirs of John Quincy Adams*, ed. Charles Francis Adams (12 vols., Philadelphia, 1874), 1: 54.

9 John Cartwright, *A LETTER to the High Sheriff of the County of Lincoln . . . respecting the Bills . . . for altering the CRIMINAL LAWS OF ENGLAND respecting TREASON and SEDITION, including a copy of the Author's*

Petition to the Honourable House of Commons, presented by Mr. Fox . . . 25 November 1795 (London, 1795), p. 19; John Cartwright, *The Constitution in Danger* (London, 1795), p. 13. In 1803, Cartwright wrote to Charles James Fox, confiding his hope that the government should "get into the hands" of men like Sydney (*Life of . . . Cartwright* [2 vols., London, 1826], 1: 316).

10 "Common Sense," *Ten Minutes Advice . . .* (London, 1795), esp. pp. 4, 6.

11 John Baxter, *A New and Impartial History of England* (London, 1796), pp. 413, 532; *The Case of the People of England . . . By one of "the 80,000 Incorrigible Jacobins"* (London, 1798), p. 83.

12 Charles James Fox, *History of . . . James II* (London, 1808), pp. 47-50. M. W. Patterson, *Sir Francis Burdett and His Times* (2 vols., London, 1931), 1: 127. Cf. *Collected Works of S. T. Coleridge: The Watchman*, ed. Lewis Patton (Princeton, 1970), p. 371. Burdett also compared Tooke to Brutus and to Russell.

13 "Hampden," *To the Inhabitants of Nottingham . . .* (Nottingham, 1793); "Hampden," *Letters to the Duke of Portland on his Dereliction of the Cause of the People* (London, 1795), pp. 1-5; "Hampden" [Thomas Lister], *A Mirror for Princes* (London, 1797), pp. 17-18, 20; "Sydney," *On M. Petion's "General Rules of my Conduct"* (Manchester, 1792); "Sidney," *War!* (Nottingham, 1792); *Letters of "Sydney" [John Millar] to the "Scots Chronicle" on Inequality of Property* (Edinburgh, 1796), p. 17; "Sidney," *A Monody occasioned by the loss of the Viceroy Packet* (London, 1798).

14 *DNB*, Edmund Lodge; Lodge, *Portraits of Illustrious Personages . . .* (12 vols., London, 1823-34), 4: 79; Vicesimus Knox, *The Spirit of Despotism* (London, 1795, and Morristown, N.J., 1799), p. 218.

15 Mark Noble, *The Lives of the English Regicides* (2 vols., London, 1798), 2: 260.

16 S. Maccoby, *English Radicalism, 1786-1832* (London, 1955), pp. 260-63; *Memoirs and Correspondence of Francis Horner*, ed. Leonard Horner (2 vols., London, 1843), 1: 434; *Poems of Robert Southey*, ed. Maurice H. Fitzgerald (London, 1909), p. 429; Wm. Wordsworth, *Sonnets Dedicated to Liberty*, Sonnet 15 (London, 1802).

17 *DNB*, John Thelwall; John Thelwall, *Political Lectures . . .* (London, 1795), pp. 24-25, and *The Natural and Constitutional Right of Britons to Amend Parliaments, Universal Suffrage, and the Freedom of Popular Association . . .* (London, 1795), p. 54. William Godwin advised Thelwall to avoid quoting "from Sidney and others," but to "[a]ppeal to that eternal law which the heart of every man of common sense recognizes immediately" (Charles Cestre, *John Thelwall* [London, 1906], p. 202 [appendix]).

Alexander B. Grosart maintains that, over a century before Margot, one Robert Baillie of Jerviswood, a Scottish accomplice of Sydney's in 1682-83, became known as "the Scottish Algernon Sydney" (*DNB*, Robert Baillie).

18 John Thelwall, *Poems written . . . in the Tower* (London, 1795), pp. 5, 12, 20, 28; *Tribune*, June 3, 1795, p. 298; Oct. 23, 1795, p. 95; May 2, 1795, p. 176; Sept. 25, 1795, p. 344; April 8, 1796, p. 288; April 15, 1796, p. 333. Cf.

Stella Thelwall, *The Life of John Thelwall* (London, 1837), pp. 193 (on the "Address" in 1795), 207, 266, 400, 432, 471–72.

19 Cestre, *Thelwall*, p. 97; Thelwall, *Poems chiefly written in retirement* (London, 1801), "To the Infant Hampden," [October 1797], pp. 140–41.

20 M. D. George, *English Caricatures*, 2: 67 (for Denison's *Address* . . .); Frank J. Klingberg and Sigurd Hustruedt, eds., *The Warning Drum: The British Home Front Faces Napoleon* (Berkeley, 1944) (for *Britons, Strike Home!* broadside); *The Patriot* (Edinburgh, 1804), pp. 7, 9, 12. Cf. *The Life and Letters of Wm. Cobbett* . . . (2 vols., London, 1913), 1:259; *Correspondence of Wilkes*, ed. Almon, 1:iv; *The Complete Works of Wm. Hazlitt*, ed. P. P. Howe (21 vols., London, 1930–34), 1:241; 11:66; 12:320; 19:197, 268.

Samuel Taylor Coleridge noted that in 1809 Sydney was being cited by all parties, and Francis Wrangham claimed in 1816 that Hampden's "memory is revered to this hour by every lover of his country and every friend to the rights of mankind" (*British Plutarch* [8 vols., Perth, 1795–1815], 3:63).

21 *The Political Thought of Samuel Taylor Coleridge*, ed. R. J. White (London, 1938), p. 75.

22 "Sidney," *Letters on the Affairs of Spain* . . . (London, 1809).

23 S. Maccoby, *English Radicalism, 1786–1832* (London, 1955), pp. 260–63; John Osborne, *William Cobbett* (New Brunswick, 1966), pp. 74, 82; *Autobiography of Samuel Bamford*, ed. W. H. Chaloner (New York, 1967), pp. 166, 361. Bamford became disillusioned with some of "the 'gentlemen patriots' of the present day" (Henry Hunt in particular) who had not lived up to the example of "the gallant Sydney" (p. 245).

24 *Works of Lord Byron*, ed. E. H. Coleridge (13 vols., London, 1898–1905), 2: 504; Phil. A. Brown, *The French Revolution in English History* (London, 1965), p. 186; Keats to George and Georgina Keats, October 14, 1818, *The Letters of John Keats*, ed. Hyder E. Rollins (2 vols., Cambridge, Mass., 1958), 1: 396; John Clive, *The Shaping of the Historian: Macaulay* (New York, 1973), p. 81.

25 Shelley to Elizabeth Hitchener, February 27, 1812, *The Letters of Percy Bysshe Shelley*, ed. Frederick L. Jones (2 vols., Oxford, 1964), 1: 173; Mary Shelley to Leigh Hunt, March 2, 1817, *The Letters of Mary Wollstonecraft Shelley*, ed. Frederick L. Jones (2 vols., Norman, Okla., 1944), 1: 9, 24.

26 Ken Cameron, *The Young Shelley* (London, 1951), p. 317; *Mary Shelley's Journal*, ed. Frederick L. Jones (Norman, Okla., 1947), p. 85.

27 *The Complete Poetical Works of . . . Shelley*, ed. Thomas Hutchinson (London, 1961), pp. 505–6. Cf. Shelley, "A Philosophical View of Reform" (1819–20), in *Political Tracts of Shelley* . . . , ed. R. J. White (Cambridge, 1953), p. 216.

28 Carl R. Woodring, "Leigh Hunt as Political Essayist," in *Leigh Hunt's Political and Occasional Essays*, ed. Lawrence H. and Carolyn W. Houtchens (New York, 1962), pp. 7, 9, 107; Robert Zegger, *John Cam Hobhouse* (Columbia, Mo., 1973), p. 43.

29 "Sidney," *On M. Petion's "General Rules . . . "*; "Sidney," *War!*; *Letters of "Sydney" . . . on Inequality of Property*, p. 17.

30 Olive D. Rudkin, *Thomas Spence and His Connections* (New York, 1927), pp. 15, 151.

31 *Howell State Trials*, 25: 221.

32 Robert Birley, *The English Jacobins* (London, 1924), p. 9.

33 Edward P. Thompson, *The Making of the English Working Class* (London, 1963), pp. 550–65, 597, 602, 607; C. B. Roylance Kent, *The English Radicals: An Historical Sketch* (London, 1899), pp. 272–73. Cf. E. J. Hobsbawm and George Rudé, *Captain Swing* (London, 1969), p. 249.

34 Thompson, *English Working Class*, pp. 705, 716. Counsel for one of the conspirators cited "Sydney's case" in his client's defense. *Rex* v. *Thistlewood*, *Howell State Trials*, 33: 681.

35 Hampden Club, *A Full Report of the Proceedings of the Meeting Convened by the Hampden Club . . .* (London, 1816), pp. 4, 9; Hampden Club, *A Sketch of the Life of John Hampden* (Nottingham, 1817), pp. 2, 6, 7; *Sketch of the Life and Character of John Hampden, A True and Faithful Representative of the People in Parliament, A Staunch and Able Opposer of Tyranny, and a Reformer both in Theory and Practice . . .* (London, 1819), esp. frontispiece; *Life . . . of Cartwright*, 2: 127, 143.

36 George Burges, *Reflections on the Nature and Tendency of the Present Spirit of our Times* (Norwich, 1819), pp. 20–21 (on the "loyal" Tory address), 76, 147, 194, 216.

37 Thompson, *English Working Class*, pp. 550–65, 597, 602, 607; Roylance Kent, *English Radicals*, pp. 272–73; anon., *The White Hat* (Newcastle, 1819); A. Temple Patterson, *Radical Leicester* (Leicester, 1954), pp. 107, 110; Alfred Plummer, *Bronterre: A Political Biography of Bronterre O'Brien, 1804–1864* (London, 1971), p. 124.

38 "Hampden," *A Mirror for Princes*, p. 20.

39 John Thelwall, *The Tribune*, May 2, 1795, pp. 176, 180, 197–202; Oct. 23, 1795, p. 97; Thelwall, *The Champion and Sunday Review*, Sept. 12, 1819, p. 574.

40 "Hampden," *Letters to the Duke of Portland*, p. 7; *Letters of Sidney . . . on Inequality . . .* , p. 17, and passim; W. C. Lehmann, *John Millar of Glasgow* (Cambridge, 1960), esp. pp. 16–18, 64–67.

41 Samuel F. Waddington, *A. Sidney's Address to the People of the United Kingdom* (London, 1812), p. 12; Chester New, *Life of Henry Brougham to 1830* (London, 1961), esp. pp. 10, 19; *Full Report of Hampden Club*, pp. v, vii; John Cartwright, *The English Constitution Produced and Illustrated* (London, 1823), p. 227; *Life . . . of Cartwright*, 2: 96, 285; Zegger, *Hobhouse*, p. 285.

Cf. [anon.], *A Letter to the Right Honorable George Canning, M.P.* (London, 1818), p. 32, which allows that Hampden was a tyrannicide, but no "assassin."

42 S. T. Coleridge, *Philosophical Lectures*, ed. Kathleen Coburn (New York, 1949), p. 120. Coleridge to T. G. Street, December 7, 1808, *Collected Letters of Samuel Taylor Coleridge*, ed. Earl Leslie Griggs (Oxford, 1959), 3: 137; Coleridge, "The Statesman's Manual" (1816), in *Political Tracts of Words-*

worth, Coleridge, and Shelley, ed. R. J. White (Cambridge, 1953), pp. 47, 84, *Collected Works . . . The Watchman*, ed. Patton, p. 176, and *Collected Works . . . : The Friend*, ed. Barbara Rooke (Princeton, 1969), 1: 68, 180, 266.

43 *DNB*, George W. Meadley; Meadley, *Sydney*, pp. 286, 288, 302–3.

44 Meadley, *Sydney*, p. 303.

45 Lord John Russell (1792–1878), *The Life of William, Lord Russell* (2 vols., London, 1819–20), 1: 197–98; 2: 139.

46 John Thelwall, *The Tribune*, May 23, 1795, p. 246; Thelwall, *The Champion*, July 4, 1819, passim; July 19, 1819, p. 448; July 25, 1819, passim; Sept. 12, 1819, p. 573.

47 Stella Thelwall, *Life of Thelwall*, p. 4; Wm. Cushing, *Initials and Pseudonyms* (New York, 1885); Thomas Campbell, *The Pleasures of Hope* (London, 1799); Samuel Rogers, *Human Life* (London, 1819), p. 48; Rudkin, *Spence*, p. 129.

48 *Graduati Cantabrigienses, 1659–1823* (London, 1823); Henry Luard, *Grad. Cant., 1800–1884* (London, 1884); P.O., London, *Law Directory* (1851); "Census of Nottingham, 1841," and "Census of London, 1851," Public Records Office; *DNB Supplement; Who Was Who, 1897–1916* (London, 1919).

49 Withycombe, ed., *Oxford Dictionary of English Christian Names* (Oxford, 1945), p. 118.

50 Stanley Kunitz and Howard Haycraft, *British Authors of the Nineteenth Century* (New York, 1936), p. 190; C. S. Forester, *Brown on Resolution* (London, 1929), p. 42. Similarly, Jeffrey Kaplow argues that the Parisian laboring poor were more devoted to their monarchs than to any aristocratic or bourgeois liberal figures (*The Names of Kings* [New York, 1972], pp. 153–54, 157).

51 Gustav Jahoda's 1961 survey of the opinions of six- to eleven-year-old children of working-class, white-collar, and professional parents in Glasgow points in the same direction. The children of working-class parents were less able than the children of white-collar and professional parents to recognize the British national anthem (33% to 19%) or the Union Jack (45% to 22%), but equally able to recognize the Scottish poet Robert Burns. The children were equally Scottish (evidence of local or regional loyalties) but the lower-class children were less British (evidence of a more cosmopolitan patriotism) than were their more affluent peers (G. Jahoda, "Development of Children's Ideas of Country & Nationality," *British Journal of Educational Psychology* 33 [1963]: 143–53).

52 Barnes, "Children's Ideals," *Pedagogical Seminary* 9 (1900): 6–9.

53 Hampden Club, *A Sketch . . .* , p. 2; for similar arguments, with supporting evidence, see Seymour Martin Lipset, *Political Man* (New York, 1972), pp. 51–52, 157; and Fred Greenstein, *Children and Politics* (New Haven, 1965), p. 93.

54 Anon., *The Patriot*, pp. 12, 16, 21. Cf. Denison, *Address*.

Sydney's *Discourses* were still occasionally referred to. Rev. Francis Wrangham included a number of lengthy passages from both the *Discourses* and Sydney's letters home to his father in his laudatory account of the Rebel-Saint in *The British Plutarch* (8 vols., London and Perth, 1815), vol. 4, but the *Discourses* had clearly become less popular than they had been to eighteenth-century Sydney devotees. When William Scott, Baron Stowell, published *The Essence of Algernon Sydney's Work on Government* in 1795, he prefaced his remarks with the explanation that though he found none "among the learned" who would "be thought ignorant of the works of Sydney," few had actually read the *Discourses*. With the passage of time this would increasingly be the case (A Student at the Inner Temple [William Scott, Baron Stowell], *The Essence of Algernon Sydney's Work on Government* [London, 1795], p. vii. Lord Stowell's work was dedicated to "Stanhope & the Friends of Justice, Peace, & Liberty," and went through a second edition in 1797).

55 Thelwall, *Political Lectures*, p. 8; Meadley, *Memoirs*, p. 302. Shelley, in assailing the "HATED . . . Tyrant," Napoleon, complained of Napoleon's lack of virtue (*Works*, pp. 526–27).

56 Thelwall, *Political Lectures*, p. 8; Meadley, *Memoirs*, p. 302.

57 Esmé Wingfield-Stratford, *The History of English Patriotism* (2 vols., London, 1913), 2: 213, 289, 372; "S.E.A.," *Father John* (London, 1842), p. 69; Charles Phillips, *The Genuine and Correct Address of C. Phillips, Esq. to the Electors of the County of Sligo* (London, 1818), p. 6; George Smeeton, *The Unique* (London, 1824), p. III.

58 Richard Carlile, *Gorgon*, June 13, 1818; Carlile, *The Republican* 5 (Jan. 4, 1822): 23; (May 10, 1822): 604; *Black Dwarf* 4 (Jan. 19, 1820): 100; (Mar. 1, 1829): 286; Macaulay, "John Hampden," *Edinburgh Review* 54 (Dec. 1831): 93; William Hone, *The Right Divine of Kings* (London, 1821), p. 36; George Grenville, Lord Nugent, *Some Memorials of John Hampden* (London, 1860 ed.), intro.; *Speeches of Lord Brougham* (4 vols., Edinburgh, 1838), 2: 119–28; *Westminster Review* 18 (April, 1833): 143; "Hampdens and Hobarts File," Buckinghamshire County Record Office. (I am indebted to Mr. E. J. Davis of Bucks Co. Record Office for a look at these scrapbooks on Hampden, which included such notes as this clipping, from around 1820: "To all who deem themselves patriots, and to many who are really so, the name of Hampden is dear.") See also Hunt's *Essays*, pp. 318, 367, where Hunt called, in 1833, for monuments to Hampden and Sydney and the celebration of Sydney's birthday; and Richard Chase Sidney, esq. [a descendant], *A Brief Memoir of the Life of the Honourable Colonel Algernon Sidney . . . To Which is Added a Description of Mr. F. P. Stephanoff's Painting* [see pl. 6] (London, 1835), p. 54.

59 "Sidney, Junior," *The Republican* 5 (May 10, 1822): 604; *Letters by Sidney, Shewing by a Comparison of Its Present with Its Former Character that*

Popery is "semper eadem" (Cork, 1822); [Samuel F. Waddington], *"Sydney's Letter to the King . . . Connected with the Reported Exclusion of Lord Byron's Monument from Westminster Abbey* (London, 1828), pp. 54–55; [George Spencer-Churchill, Duke of Marlborough], *Letters of Sidney to the "Evening Star," 1829-1832* (London, 1834), pp. 18, 37; [John Landseer], *Algernon Sidney's Letter to Thomas Wyse, M.P. Concerning Art Unions, Electrotype, Prince Albert's Patronage, The Rights and Wrongs of Artists, etc.* (London, 1843), pp. 2, 8; "Hampden," *Slavery or Freedom? An Appeal to Wesleyan Reformers* (London, 1850); "John Hampden, Jun.," *The Theory of Money . . .* (Manchester, 1817); Zegger, *Hobhouse*, p. 28.

60 Alex. Somerville, *Autobiography of a Working Man*, p. 87; Rbt. Lowery, in *Weekly Record of the Temperance Movement*, May 24, 1856, p. 69, and *Newcastle Chronicle*, April 19, 1834. (I am indebted to Brian Harrison of 19C Cromwell for the information about Lowery.)

61 Ebenezer Elliott, *Poetical Works of Ebenezer Elliott . . .* (2 vols., London, 1876), 1: 114 ff.; Elliott, in Bronterre O'Brien's *The Operative*, Feb. 10, 1839. (I am grateful to David Goodway of 19C Cromwell for the latter reference.) By 1849 Elliott had added Vane and Washington to his litany of republican saints, supplementing Hampden and Sydney (Elliott, in G. J. Harney, *The Red Republican*, Nov. 9, 1850, p. 168).

62 Br. O'Brien, *The Operative*, Feb. 24, 1839 ("Britons, we have freed the African—shall we not emancipate ourselves? Have Hampden, Russell, Sidney, lived, bled, died in vain?"); W. J. Linton, in *The National* (London, 1839), pp. 114–15n, calls for a "new Constitution" for which "the countrymen of Hampden" may need to spend blood as well as treasure. Elsewhere Linton quoted Sydney on slavery and invoked "the unburied Hampden lying on the heart." F. B. Smith, *Radical Artisan: Wm. J. Linton, 1812-1897* (Manchester, 1973), p. 40; Linton, *National*, p. 214. Cf. *"The English Republic" by William James Linton*, ed. Kinton Parkes (London, 1891), pp. 82, 92.

63 "A London Chartist," in North London Charter Association, *The English Chartist Circular*, no. 10, Mar. 11, 1841; *McDouall's Chartist Journal and Trade's Advocate*, July 17, 1841, p. 124.

64 A. T. Patterson, *Radical Leicester*, p. 354; *Leeds Times*, Mar. 30, 1844; George J. Holyoake, *The Reasoner* 1 (1846): 159; Charles Kingsley, *Alton Locke* (London, 1850), p. 299.

65 *Thomas Cooper's Journal*, March 2, 1850; *Star of Freedom*, July 24, 1852; Smith, *Radical Artisan*, p. 229; *People's Paper*, July 22, 1854. (I am indebted to David Goodway, E. Royle, Brian Harrison, R.D. Storch, J. F. C. Harrison, Raphael Samuel, and Mrs. O. Anderson, all 19C Cromwell collaborators, for some of the preceding references.)

66 Thomas Cooper, *The Commonwealthman*, no. 9, April 12, 1842 (I am indebted to Raphael Samuel for this reference); *The Poetical Works of Thomas Cooper* (2nd ed., London, 1886), pp. 249, 285; *Purgatory of Suicides* (London, 1845), p. 180; Robert J. Conklin, *Thomas Cooper, the Chartist (1805-*

1892) (Manila, 1935), pp. 58, 96, 153, 211, 222; George Holyoake, *The Reasoner* 5 (1848): 227, 235; Cooper, *Eight Letters to Young Men of the Working Classes* (London, 1819), pp. 3–4; Patterson, *Radical Leicester*, p. 319.

67 John Forster, *Oliver Cromwell* (2 vols., London, 1838–39), 2:52, 64, 102; Forster, *John Hampden* (London, 1837), p. 315; Forster, *Arrest of the Five Members by Charles the First* (London, 1860), pp. 169–70.

68 E. P. Hood, *The Age and its Architects* (London, 1850), pp. 284–86 (I am indebted to J. F. C. Harrison for this reference).

69 Sir Edward Lytton Bulwer-Lytton, cited in *Buckinghamshire Gazette*, Oct. 4, 1845 (I am indebted to Tim Mason of St. Peters College, Oxford, for this reference).

70 Emma Robinson, *Whitefriars* (London, 1844), pp. 132–34, 160, 163, 183, 188, 190–91, 195, 197, 214–15, 230, 267.

71 J. M. Morgan, *Hampden in the Nineteenth Century* (2 vols., London, 1834), esp. 1: 25–42, 243; 2: 53–54, 90–120; Morgan, *Colloquies on Religion and Religious Education: Supplement to "Hampden in the Nineteenth Century"* (London, 1837), pp. 61, 121, 127, 141. Morgan's "Hampden" regards "our servants" as an entirely separate class of people, sentiments that would hardly have won him Chartist approval.

72 B. R. Haydon, *Autobiography and Memoirs of B. R. Haydon*, ed. Tom Taylor (London, 1926), 2: 310, 320.

73 Nugent, *Some Memorials of John Hampden* (2 vols., London, 1832), 1: xii, xxiii, 220; Nugent, *A Letter to John Murray* (London, 1832); Nugent, *The Ballot Discussed in a Letter to the Earl of Durham* (2nd ed., London, 1837); Reverend Frederick Lee, *The History . . . of the . . . Church . . . of Thame* (London, 1883), pp. 541–42.

74 Eb. Eliott, "England," in *The Operative*, Feb. 10, 1839; Kingsley, *Alton Locke*, p. 299; *Sidney's Letter to Thomas Wyse*, pp. 8 ff.; "Hampden," *Slavery or Freedom*.

75 "John Hampden, Jr." [Wm. Howitt], *The Aristocracy of England*, p. vi; *DNB*, John Minter Morgan; Morgan, *The Reproof of Brutus* (London, 1830), pp. xix, 12, 53; *DNB*, David Eaton, and Eaton, "Address to the Public," an advertisement for his "Political Classics" series in the frontispiece of his *Pigott's Political Dictionary* (London, 1794).

76 Zegger, *Hobhouse*, p. 61; Asa Briggs, "Middle Class Consciousness in English Politics, 1780–1846," *Past and Present* 9 (1956): 55–74; "A Call to the Electors," *Black Dwarf* 4 (Mar. 1, 1820): 286 (I am indebted to Sheila Rowbotham of 19C Cromwell for this reference); Rich. Carlile, *Gorgon*, June 13, 1818, esp. p. 191; Carlile, *The Gauntlet*, March 10, 1833, p. 67.

77 R. Carlile, *The Gauntlet*, Nov. 10, 1833, p. 625; John Nott, "The Artisan as Agitator: Richard Carlile, 1816–1843," Ph.D. dissertation, University of Wisconsin, 1970, argues that Carlile's colleagues were of the working class. See R. Carlile, *The Republican* 5 (1822): 368–69, for one "republican's" praise of Thomas Paine.

78 J. H. Plumb, "Political Man," in James Clifford, ed., *Man versus Society in 18th Century Britain* (Cambridge, 1968), p. 17 (on Paine's popularity); J. G. A. Pocock, *The Ancient Constitution and the Feudal Law* (Cambridge, 1957), p. 232 (on Whig veneration of the past); Kettering Radical Association (signed by G. T. Green and J. A. Leatherland), *The Just Claims of the Working Classes* (Henry Hetherington, London, 1839), reprinted (with Collins) in Dorothy Thompson, ed., *The Early Chartists* (Columbia, S.C., 1971), pp. 97, 137, 169.

79 G. W. M. Reynolds, *The Rye House Plot* (2 vols., London, 1884), 2: 88, and passim.

80 *Poor Man's Advocate*, March 10, 1832, p. 62; April 14, 1832, p. 101; June 2, 1832, pp. 159–60.

81 Ernest Jones, *Notes to the People* 1 (1851): 499.

82 *The Friend of the People*, ed. G. J. Harney, with Gerald Massey, George Holyoake, and Ernest Jones, 1 (Dec. 14, 1850): 8; (Dec. 28, 1850): 20; (Jan. 4, 1851): 32; Smith, *Radical Artisan*, p. 24. See the next section of this chapter for more on alternative Chartist heroes.

83 Francis Place Papers, XXXI, British Museum Add. MSS. 27, 819, folio 242.

84 Arthur Butler, *Charles I* (London, 1874), p. xix.

85 A. D. Crake, *Fairleigh Hall* (Oxford, 1882), pp. iv, 24, 99; *"John Hampden" [William Selwyn] to his Countrymen* (Cambridge, 1869); see also Reverend John Swinstead, *Chalgrove Field and John Hampden* (London, 1906).

86 *"John Hampden, Ratepayer," The Star Chamber on the Victoria Embankment: A True Bill Against the School Board for London* (London, 1876).

87 "Edna Lyall" [Ada Bayly], *To Right the Wrong* (New York and London, 1894), esp. pp. 46, 56, 510; Alfred T. Sheppard, *The Art and Practice of Historical Fiction* (London, 1930), pp. 156–57 (on Ada Bayly); Eliza Pollard, *A Soldier of Fortune* (London, 1903). Cf. Estelle Ross, *Oliver Cromwell* (London, 1915), p. 79; John Drinkwater, *John Hampden's England* (London, 1932), p. 285.

88 Hugh Ross Williamson, *John Hampden—A Life* (London, 1933), pp. 15, 16, 170; Freda Long, *The People's Martyr* (London, 1968); C. E. Lucas Phillips, *Cromwell's Captains* (London, 1938), p. 3.

89 *Letters of Theodore Roosevelt*, ed. Elting E. Morison (8 vols., Cambridge, Mass., 1951–54), 4: 1135; "John Hampden," *Leisure Hour* 20 (1871): 762. Cf. Donald Southgate, *The Passing of the Whigs* (London, 1962), p. 324 (on Lord John Russell's frequent identification with Hampden's defense of rights.)

Just the same, Charles Horne, a Nonconformist pastor and early-twentieth-century M.P. from Ipswich, compared Hampden's ship-money struggle to the effort of Horne and his colleagues in Commons to halt the ability of the House of Lords to vote on financial questions (W. B. Silbie, *The Life of Charles Horne* [London, 1920], p. 207). Cf. Norman Angell, *North American Review* 195 (1912): 759.

90 [Isaac D'Israeli], *Eliot, Hampden, and Pym, or a Reply of "The Author of A Book" entitled "Commentaries on the Life of Charles the First," to "The*

Author of a Book" entitled *"Some Memorials of John Hampden, His Party and his Times"* (London, 1832), pp. 25, 28, 34, 35; Robert Southey, *Quarterly Review*, Aug. 1832; *Whigs and Whiggism: Political Writings of Benjamin Disraeli*, ed. Wm. Hutcheon (London, 1913), pp. 52, 188, 335.

91 Walter Dodge, *King Charles I* (London, 1912), pp. 54–55, 94; Esmé Wingfield-Stratford, *The History of English Patriotism* (2 vols., London, 1913), 1: 317; Wingfield-Stratford, *Charles, King of England, 1600–1637* (London, 1949), pp. vi, 314–17, 318, 323.

92 Nugent, *Some Memorials of . . . Hampden*, p. 57; Sir John Skelton, *Charles I* (London, 1898), p. 112; G. M. Trevelyan, *History of England* (3rd ed., London, 1952), p. 392.

93 Elizabeth Charles, *On Both Sides of the Sea* (London, 1868), p. 382.

94 Nugent, *Some Memorials of . . . Hampden*, pp. lxiii–lxv; Lee, *Church of Thame*, p. 538; Swinstead, *Chalgrove Field and John Hampden*, p. 14. In 1863 Sir William Erle raised a monument to Hampden at Stoke Mandeville, celebrating his ship-money case, and in 1906 Swinstead raised funds for a John Hampden Hall at Chalgrove.

95 E. M. Whitby, *History of the Session, 1852–53* (London, 1854), p. 174.

96 *Notes and Queries* 1st ser., 5 (May 29, 1852): 517.

97 A. C. Ewald, *The Life and Times of the Honorable Algernon Sydney* (2 vols., London, 1873), 1: 17, 30, 34, 256; 2: 329, 331, 336, 338–39; Ewald, *The Right Honorable Benjamin Disraeli, Earl of Beaconsfield and His Times* (2 vols., London, 1881), 2: 588.

98 Mary Rowsell, *Traitor or Patriot?* (London, 1885); "Edna Lyall" [Ada Bayly], *In the Golden Days* (London, 1885), pp. 63, 68, 101, 312; *DNB*, Ada Ellen Bayly; J. M. Escreet, *The Life of Edna Lyall (Ada Bayly)* (London, 1904), pp. 3, 57, 111.

99 W. J. Escott, *Fortune's Castaway* (Edinburgh and London, 1909), p. 37; J. C. Ady, *Sacharissa* (London, 1925), p. 26.

100 *Roxburghe Ballads* 5 (1885): 424, 425, 431; G. M. I. Blackburne, *Algernon Sydney: A Review* (London, 1885), pp. 13, 119. Cf. "Algernon Sydney: Beheaded Dec. 7, 1683," *Saturday Review* (London) 58 (1884): 16.

101 Thomas I. Forster, *Letters of Locke, Sidney, and Shaftesbury* (London, 1830), pp. viii–xi, cxxi.

102 Landseer, *Sidney's Letter to Thomas Wyse*, p. 2.

103 William Cobbett, *History of the Protestant Reformation . . .* (London, 1824), letter XIII, para. 382; *The Diary of . . . Henry Sidney*, ed. R. W. Blencowe (London, 1843), p. xxxvi; Robert Plumer Ward, *An Historical Essay on the Real Character and Amount of the Precedent of the Revolution of 1688, in which the merits of Sidney are critically considered* (2 vols., London, 1838), 1: vi; 2: 200–322, esp. 286–87, 294–95, 312. Cf. "A Tory of the Old School," *The Reviewer Reviewed, being an Examination of a Crucial Notice in "The Edinburgh Review" of Plumer Ward's "Historical Essay"* (London, 1839), p. 20. Lord John Russell felt that the French-Canadian assembly's demand for reform in 1837 used "the weapons of Hampden, in support of the principles of Wentworth [Earl of Strafford, Hampden's

royalist contemporary]," in order to oppress British-Canadians (John Prest, *Lord John Russell* [Columbia, S.C., 1972], p. 129).

104 Wingfield-Stratford, *History of English Patriotism*, 1: xvii; Sir John A. R. Marriott, *The Crisis of English Liberty* (Oxford, 1930), p. 378; J. H. M. Salmon, "Algernon Sidney and the Rye-House Plot," *History Today* (Oct. 1954): 702, 705; H. M. Imbert-Terry, *A Misjudged Monarch* (London, 1917), p. 248.

105 T. B. Macaulay, "John Hampden," *Edinburgh Review* (1831), reprinted in *Historical Essays of Macaulay*, ed. George A. Watrous (New York, 1901), p. 108; Macaulay, *History of England* (5 vols., London, 1849–61), 1: 172.

106 Imbert-Terry, *A Misjudged Monarch*, preface, and p. 248.

107 *Notes and Queries* 1st ser., 5 (Apr. 3, 1852): 318; (May 22, 1852): 497; (May 29, 1852): 517; (July 3, 1952): 21; Ewald, *Life of Sydney*, 2: 325; William D. Christie, *A Life of Anthony Ashley Cooper* (2 vols., London, 1871), 2: 462; *Notes and Queries* 1st ser., 5 (May 1, 1852): 426; (May 8, 1852): 447; Reverend John S. Watson, *Biographies of John Wilkes and William Cobbett* (Edinburgh, 1870), p. 392. Mary Beny, editor of the Religious Tract Society's *Life of Lady Russell* (Phila. & London, 185?), quoted from Dorothy Sydney's letter to George Savile about "my Lord Shaftesbury's and Mr. Algernon's quarrel" over Shaftesbury's charge that Sydney was a "French pensioner." This might have served as some confirmation of Dalrymple's Barillon evidence, but instead Beny chose to dismiss both Dalrymple and Shaftesbury (p. 354).

108 Sir Leslie Stephen, *History of English Thought in the 18th Century* (London, 1876), 2: 115; Armand Carrel, *History of the Counter-Revolution in England* (London, 1857), p. 177; James MacKinnon, *A History of Modern Liberty* (London, 1941), p. 492; *Times Literary Supplement*, Nov. 15 and 22, Dec. 13 and 20, 1977, and Jan. 3 and 10, 1918, pp. 556, 598, 620, 637, 10, 22. Cf. Lord Brougham, *Old England's Worthies*, p. 170; and J. H. Plumb, *The Death of the Past*, p. 53.

109 Samuel R. Gardiner, *Cromwell's Place in History* (London, 1897), pp. 113–16.

110 Thus, upon their release from gaol in 1840, Peter McDouall and John Collins complained of the "shameful treatment" they had "received from the merciless Whigs," praised Chartists John Frost and William Lovett, "noble and patriotic friends" to "the cause of liberty," and were themselves advised by Manchester Chartists that McDouall's name would be "enrolled amongst those of the great and good men who in all ages have pleaded the cause of the oppressed against the oppressor." No mention was made of either Hampden or Sydney (Dorothy Thompson, ed., *The Early Chartists* [London, 1971], pp. 146–47). Similarly, in 1842 G. J. Harney's funeral oration for young Sheffield Chartist Samuel Holberry, seized for conspiracy in 1840, celebrated Holberry as "a martyr to the cause of Democracy": "With the Tells and Tylers of the earth, the name of Holberry will be associated, venerated, and adored" (Richard Gamage, *History of the Chartist Movement, 1837–*

1854 [Newcastle-on-Tyne, 1894], p. 215). See also Thomas Cooper's lines in "A Chartist Song": "For [Wat] Tyler of old, a hearty chorus bold, Let Labour's children sing!" (*Poetical Works*, p. 285); and "Wat Tyler," complaining of taxation without representation (*Hampden's* cause) in *Gauntlet*, Feb. 16, 1834, p. 857; Donald Read and Eric Glasgow, *Feargus O'Connor* (London, 1961), p. 96; *Gauntlet*, April 14, 1833, p. 159; Dec. 15, 1833, pp. 715, 716; Gamage, *Chartist Movement*, p. 74; *Reasoner* 4 (1848): 264; Ernest Jones, *Notes to the People* 1 (1851): esp. 499; J. Thelwall's *Tribune* 3 (1795): 226–30, 274; A. R. Schoyen, *The Chartist Challenge* (London, 1958), pp. 8, 42, 116, 123, 160, 161, 236; George Holyoake, *Sixty Years of an Agitator's Life* (2 vols., London, 1892), 1: 115, 189; C. Edmund Maurice, *Lives of English Popular Leaders* (2 vols., London, 1874–75), 2: 278–79.

111 See, for example, Edw. Knatchbull-Hugessen, *The Life . . . of Cromwell* (London, 1877), p. 2; Alex. Chalmers, *The General Biographical Dictionary* (rev. ed., 32 vols., London, 1812–17), 11: 71–76; W. D. Fellowes, *Historical Sketches of Charles the First, Cromwell . . .* (London, 1828), p. 258; Michael Russell, Bishop of Glasgow, *Life of Oliver Cromwell* (2 vols., Edinburgh, 1829), 1: ix; 2: 230–308, esp. 293, 295, 307; Robert Southey, *Life of Oliver Cromwell* (London, 1815); anon., *Oliver Cromwell; or, Cavaliers and Roundheads* (London, 1841); anon., *The Protector's Secret* (London, 1849), p. 2.

112 See for example, Daniel O'Connell (and his audience's reaction), cited in *Lancaster Gazette*, Nov. 1, 1845; anon., *Cromwell in Ireland* (3 vols., London, 1847), 2: 292.

113 Ernest Barker, *Oliver Cromwell and the English People* (Cambridge, 1937), p. 65 (on Walter Savage Landor's view of Cromwell); John Forster, *Oliver Cromwell* (2 vols., London, 1838–39), 2: 52, 64, 90n, 100–25, 299; Sir Edward Lytton Bulwer-Lytton, *Cromwell's Dream: A Poem* (London, 1839); Haydon, *Memoirs*, 2: 320 (for Lord Nugent's critique of Cromwell); Emery Neff, *Carlyle* (London, 1932), p. 24 (for John Stuart Mill's disapproval of the dissolution of the Rump). Cf. Oliver Cromwell [a descendant], *Memoirs of the Protector . . .* (London, 1820); Thomas Cromwell [another descendant], *Oliver Cromwell and his Times* (London, 1821), p. 67.

114 *Correspondence Infernale, ou Lettre d'Oliver Cromwell . . . à Henri Vandernoot, Ministre Plenipotentiare des Etâts Belgique-Unis* (n.p., 1790).

115 George, *English Political Caricatures*, 1: 207–8, 213.

116 John Thelwall, *Tribune* 3 (1795): 95, 226–27; John Baxter, *A New and Impartial History of England* (London, 1796), pp. 470, 476; R. Carlile, *Gorgon*, June 13, 1818, p. 28; Henry Hunt, *To the Radical Reformers, Male and Female, of England, Scotland, and Ireland* (London, 1822). Carlile considered Cromwell a "despot" as well for his abuse of Parliament, despite Carlile's own dislike of the Parliamentary system in 1822 (*The Republican* 5 [May 17, 1822]: 611).

117 *Political Papers . . . of Rev. Ch. Wyvill* (6 vols., York, 1794–1805), 2: 430; "A Member of No Party," *A Letter to Earl Fitzwilliam* (London, 1819), p. 82; George, *English Political Caricatures*, 1: 179, 187, 2: 102; Paula Preston,

"The Severed Head of Charles I of England: Its Use as a Political Stimulus," *Winterthur Portfolio* 6 (1970): 1–13.

118 I am indebted to William Thomas of Christ Church, Oxford, and 19C Cromwell for the information about W. T. Sherwin and the 1819 edition of the Titus-Sexby pamphlet.

119 Wm. Godwin, *History of the Commonwealth* . . . (4 vols., London, 1824–28), 1: 100, 319; 2: 6, 201; 3: 578–92; 4: 597; Wm. Cobbett, *Legacy to Labourers* (London, 1834), pp. 53, 56.

120 Ch. Westerton, cited in Bronterre O'Brien's *The Operative*, Dec. 16, 1838; O'Brien, "A Word to the Upper and Middle Classes," ibid., Jan. 27, 1839; "Vindicator," in *Northern Star*, July 11, 1840; Th. Cooper, *The Commonwealthman, or Chartist Advocate*, April 12, 1842; *Sketch of the Life and Character of Hampden*, pp. 5, 32; Hampden Club, *John Hampden*, p. 6. I am indebted to Raphael Samuel for the Cooper citation, to David Goodway for the information about Westerton, O'Brien, and Watkins, and to Robert Storch for the *Northern Star* citation.

121 Edm. Lodge, *Portraits*, 5: 75–92.

122 George Crabbe, "The Frank Courtship" (1812), cited in Christopher Hill, *God's Englishman* (London, 1970), p. 271; Wm. Jones, *Ecclesiastical History* (3 vols., London, 1831–38), 3: 646–59, cited in K. M. R. Short, "The Dissenter's 19th Century Dream of Republicans, Rome and Regicides," unpub. essay, ca. 1969, 19C Cromwell project; John Vincent, *The Formation of the British Liberal Party* (New York, 1966), pp. xxix, xxx; *Nonconformist*, Oct. 15, 1845, p. 709; George Dawson, "The Foreign Policies of Oliver Cromwell," in *Biographical Lectures* (London, 1886), pp. 48–50, 56–57 (I am indebted to Raphael Samuel for this citation).

123 Anon., *Oliver Cromwell: A Poem* (Edinburgh, 1829), pp. ii, xx, xxxii; Brougham, *Old England's Worthies* (London, 1847), p. 134.

124 Edmund Clarke, *Lectures on the Public Life and Character of Oliver Cromwell, Delivered to . . . the Manchester Mechanics' Institution, Spring, 1846* (London, 1847), pp. vii, 117, 159–63; Valerie Chancellor, *History for Their Masters* (New York, 1970), pp. 52–54.

125 I am indebted to Raphael Samuel for the "second Oliver" reference, which may be found in the Public Records Office, H.O. 42/123. See also *Bamford's "Passages in the Life of a Radical,"* ed. Henry Dunckley (2 vols., London, 1893), 2: 27–28.

126 *Poor Man's Guardian*, April 15, 1831; William Carpenter, *The People's Book: Comprising their Chartered Rights and Practical Wrongs* (London, 1831), pp. xxvi–xxvii; F. O'Connor to Lord Russell, *Northern Star*, July 13, 1839 (I am indebted to Stanley Shipley and Robert D. Storch for the last three references); *Westminster Review*, Oct. 1833, p. 225; Wm. Howitt, *The Man of the People* (3 vols., London, 1860), 1: 286–87; Engels, in *Neue Rheinische Zeitung*, Sept. 20, 1848, cited in Martin Berger, "War, Armies, and Revolution: Friedrich Engels's Military Thought," Ph.D. diss., University of Pittsburgh, 1969, p. 147.

127 *Gauntlet*, Aug. 4, 1833, p. 416; Elliot, *Poems*, 1: 114 ff.

128 Br. O'Brien, *The Operative*, Feb. 24, 1839; anon., *The Very Interesting Life of the Famous Oliver Cromwell* . . . (3rd ed., Manchester, 1840). Cf. John Robertson's very favorable essay on Cromwell in *London and Westminster Review*, Oct. 1839, pp. 181–256.

129 Articles on Cromwell appearing in British journals rose from an average of about five per decade in the early nineteenth century to an average of about twenty per decade for the period 1845–1925, while articles on Hampden or Sydney, popular in the early nineteenth century, dropped off to an average of three or four per decade after mid-century.

130 Emma Robinson, *Whitehall* (3 vols., London, 1845), 1: 180; 3: 21, 146; Henry Herbert, *Cromwell: an Historical Novel* (Aberdeen, 1848), pp. 27, 203, 290, 291.

131 A. R. Schoyen, *The Chartist Challenge*, p. 236; George W. M. Reynolds, *Political Instructor* 1 (April 20, 1850): 189; W. J. Linton, *The Republican* (1848), passim; Clarke, *Lectures on Cromwell*, p. 3. Henry Vincent, whose early lectures were critical of Cromwell's usurpation of Parliament, later changed his tune and, with Linton and Dawson, was one of the more Cromwellian lecturers. J. B. Leno recalled that "under [Vincent's] spell you could hear the sound of the great man's jack boots" (*Leeds Times*, Mar. 30, 1844; Leno, *The Aftermath* [London, 1892], p. 79. I am indebted to Brian Harrison and Raphael Samuel for some of this information on Vincent).

132 The citation is from the *Bradford Observer*, Dec. 26, 1849, and I am indebted to D. C. Wright of the City of Leeds College of Education for it. I am indebted to Tim Mason of St. Peters, Oxford, and 19C Cromwell investigators for the information about journalists' views of Cromwell's statue in 1845.

   One wonders what a Freudian psychologist would make of the fact that Sigmund Freud named his son Cromwell.

133 Linton, "Cromwell's Sword," *Northern Tribune* (Newcastle) 1 (1854): 147, 409–14; *The Red Republican* 1 (1850): no. 1, i; no. 6, 48; *The Times* (London), Sept. 16, 1856; Wm. Howitt, *The Man of the People* (3 vols., London, 1860) 3: 38, 95.

134 I am indebted to Raphael Samuel of Ruskin College, J. F. C. Harrison of the University of Wisconsin, and E. Royle of Selwyn College, Cambridge, for information about the impact of Dawson's Newcastle lecture, the Working Man's Friend series, and the debates of the Watlington Mutual Improvement Society. See p. 8 for more on Thompson and his Cromwellian listener.

135 *Historical Essays of Macaulay*, ed. Geo. Watrous (New York, 1901), p. 108; Hill, *God's Englishman*, pp. 267, 273; J. H. Merle D'Aubigne, *The Protector* (Edinburgh, 1847), pp. 202, 234–35, 256, 308–9.

136 E. Clarke, *Lectures on Cromwell*, p. vi; Howard Evans, *Radical Fights over 40 years* (London, 1913), passim.

137 W. J. Linton, *Memoirs* (London, 1895), p. 114; John Tullock, *English Puritanism and its Leaders* (Edinburgh, 1861), pp. 54, 156n; *Christian Commonwealth*, Dec. 21, 1882; *Liverpool Albion*, Dec. 13, 1860, p. 6; Reverend J.

Cranbrook, "Oliver Cromwell," in Liverpool Sunday School Inst., *Lectures on Protestant Nonconformists* (London, 1853), passim; Reverend John Clifford, *Oliver Cromwell and the Free Churches* (London, ca. 1899), p. 4; Adam Rushton, *My Life as a Farmer's Boy, Factory Lad, Teacher and Preacher* (Manchester, 1909), pp. 108–10; Joseph Barker, *The People* (Wortley, Leeds) 2 (1849–50): 28 (I am indebted to J. F. C. Harrison for this citation).

138 Carlyle, *Chartism* (London, 1840), p. 79; Carlyle to his brother, July 23, 1840, *The Letters of Thomas Carlyle to brother Alexander*, ed. Edwin Marrs (Cambridge, Mass., 1968), p. 499; David A. Wilson, *Carlyle on Cromwell and Others (1837–1848)* (London, 1925), pp. 184, 238; Emery Neff, *Carlyle and Mill* (London, 1932), pp. 24, 196.

139 Th. Carlyle, *Past and Present* (London, 1897), pp. 28, 388–93, 346, 335.

140 Walter Houghton, *The Victorian Frame of Mind, 1830–1870* (New Haven, 1957), p. 201; B. H. Lehman, *Carlyle's Theory of the Hero* (Durham, N.C., 1928), p. 49; Wilson, *Carlyle on Cromwell*, p. 330.

141 Sir W. Scott, *Woodstock* (3 vols., London, 1826), 1: 126.

142 Thomas Carlyle was to Cromwell what Thomas Hollis was to Sydney. For example, in 1873 he sent Harvard President Charles Eliot Norton a cast of Cromwell's death-mask, which Norton presented to Harvard in 1881 (Wm. C. Lane, *The Carlyle Collection* [Cambridge, Mass., 1888], p. 6).

143 *The Works of Thomas Carlyle* (15 vols., London, 1905–7), 5: 208–9; 9: 60; 10: 120.

144 Goldwin Smith, *Lectures and Essays* (Toronto, 1881), pp. 230, 233, 287; Smith, *The United Kingdom* (2 vols., New York, 1899), 1: 493, 598–601; 2: 48; Edm. Clarke, *Lectures on Cromwell*, pp. 45, 83. Similarly, E. Paxton Hood would later slight Sydney as a mere "theorizer" and praise Cromwell as one who "instinctively apprehended the wants of men," who "alone was able to govern without a theory, and therefore justly" (*Oliver Cromwell* [London, 1882], pp. 270, 273).

145 William Spurstowe [Nugent], *A True and Faithful Relation of a Worthy Discourse between Colonel John Hampden and Colonel Oliver Cromwell* (London, 1847), pp. 2–3.

146 Reverend Denis Murphy, *Cromwell in Ireland* (Dublin, 1883), p. ix; Crake, *Fairleigh Hall*, p. 183; T. Lathbury, *Oliver Cromwell, or The Old and New Dissenters* (Bristol, 1862), esp. pp. 3, 9; Lee, *Church of Thame*, p. 537; J. B. Mozley, *Essays Historical and Theological* (New York and London, 1878), 1: 294 (I am grateful to Eric Robinson for bringing this review to my attention). One Cromwellian devotee recalled being told by several "sentimental young ladies" who had " 'finished' their education" in 1882: "But Mr. Williams, I don't like Cromwell" (Houghton Festival, *Cromwellian Celebration* [St. Ives, 1883], p. 4).

147 Walter P. Dodge [a Middle Temple barrister], *King Charles I* (London, 1912), p. 54. Cf. Alan Smith, "The Image of Cromwell in Folklore and Tradition," *Folklore* 79 (1968): 17n.

148 John Robertson, *Patriotism and Empire* (London, 1899), p. 161; Reg. Palgrave, *Oliver Cromwell, the Protector: An Appreciation* (London, 1890),

esp. pp. xx, 2, 131; Tom Mann, *Memoirs*, pp. 154–56; J. M. Davidson, *The Annals of Toil* (London, 1899), pp. 199–228; *Clarion*, Oct. 15, 1898, p. 324 (I am indebted to Royden Harrison of Sheffield and Peter Cominos of Tulane University, 19C Cromwell contributors, for the last two citations). Cf. Karl Marx's similar views in *The 18th Brumaire of Louis Napoleon* (ed. C. P. Dutt [New York, 1935], p. 2) where he describes Cromwell as the leader of a "bourgeois" and "religious" revolution.

149 Many tradesmen and mechanics, and many Chartist Cromwellians were Dissenters as well, of course. And these dissenting, lower-middle-class radicals appear to have been the fiercest partisans of Cromwell.

150 Anon., *Oliver Cromwell: a Poem* (Edinburgh, 1829), p. xxvii; K. M. R. Short, "The Dissenter's Nineteenth Century Dream of Republic, Rome and Regicides," mimeo, 1969, 19C Cromwell, p. 23.

151 Clarke, *Lectures on Cromwell*, pp. 85–95; A. J. Bray, *Oliver Cromwell, A Lecture* (Watchet, 1869), p. 18; *Congregationalist* 2 (Jan., 1873): 50–51; Henry Bell, *Sermon on the Approaching Cromwellian Celebration* (St. Ives, 1883), pp. 5, 9–10; W. S. Fowler, *A Study of Radicalism and Dissent: The Life and Times of Henry J. Wilson, 1833–1914* (London, 1961), p. 24 (on Cromwell's being "the hero of Radicals"); John Bowle, *Politics and Opinion in the Nineteenth Century* (New York, 1964), p. 280 (on Thomas Green's love of Cromwell); Thomas H. Green, *Works* (3 vols., London, 1885–88), 3: 354; Robert Horton, *Oliver Cromwell: A Study in Personal Religion* (London, 1897), frontispiece, preface. Cf. G. H. Pike, *Oliver Cromwell and His Times* (London, 1899); Sir Richard Tangye, *The Two Protectors* (London, 1899). (I am indebted to Barrie Trinder, Brian Harrison, and J. F. Glaser of 19C Cromwell for the information about Henderson and the *Congregationalist*.)

152 F. W. Aveling, *Cromwell and Puritans, Ancient and Modern* (London, 1899), pp. 27, 30, 60–70, 72 ff.; *Daily News*, Sept. 15, 1900, p. 8, cited in H. C. G. Matthew, "Oliver Cromwell's Statue, Lord Rosebery and Imperialism," mimeo, 1969, 19C Cromwell. Cf. the views of R. W. Perks, M.P., who felt that Cromwell would have raised his voice in 1899 "against the overwhelming power of brute force in home and foreign affairs"; Leonard Courtney, a Liberal Unionist, who compared Cromwell to Paul Kruger, the Boer leader; and Lloyd George, who contrasted "the Protector's virtues and principles" to those of the hawkish Colonial Secretary Joseph Chamberlain (*The Times*, Apr. 26, 1899, p. 12; and Matthew, "Cromwell's Statue").

153 Aveling, *Cromwell*, passim; H. Price Hughes in *The Times*, Apr. 26, 1899, p. 12, and Apr. 27, 1899, p. 7.

154 Wm. Jones, *Ecclesiastical History* (3 vols., London, 1831–38), 3: 646–59, first cited in K. M. R. Short, "Dissenter's Nineteenth Century Dream."

155 *Congregationalist* 2 (Jan., 1873): 51; Reverend Joseph Smith, *Oliver Cromwell, or England in the Past viewed in Relation to England in the Present* (Dublin, 1851), p. 87.

156 R. T. Shannon, *Gladstone and the Bulgarian Agitation, 1876* (London, 1963), pp. 69, 73, 116, 138; *Northern Echo*, Nov. 14, 1876 (for which cita-

tion I am indebted to Hugh Cunningham of Sussex, a 19C Cromwell participant); E. P. Hood, *The Instincts of Liberalism* (Manchester, 1879), pp. 21–22.

157 *The Times*, Apr. 28, 1899, p. 8. Cf. J. Kirk Maconachie, *Oliver Cromwell, Christian Patriot* [a sermon delivered in a Congregationalist Church] (London, 1899), p. 22; and Rushton, *My Life*, pp. 108–10.

158 Cranbrook, "Oliver Cromwell," pp. 63, 87; *Eclectic Review* (1861): 84–104; A. J. Bray, *Oliver Cromwell, A Lecture*, pp. 4, 6; *The Times*, Apr. 26, 1899, p. 12; Apr. 27, 1899, p. 7.

159 Smith, *Cromwell*, pp. 5, 73; Maconachie, *Oliver Cromwell*, pp. 6, 23; Rushton, *My Life*, pp. 108–10 (I am indebted to Raphael Samuel for bringing my attention to this); Hood, *Cromwell*, pp. 19, 22, 278, 397–400.

160 E. Knatchbull-Hugessen, *The Life, Times and Character of Oliver Cromwell* (London, 1877), pp. 50, 54; Knatchbull-Hugessen, writing in *The Baptist*, May 4, 1877 (I am indebted to Hugh Cunningham, a 19C Cromwell participant, for this last reference).

161 From the *Penny Magazine*, 1839, a reference reported by Barrie Trinder to 19C Cromwell participants. Cf. *The Very Interesting Life of . . . Cromwell*; Haydon, *Memoirs*, 2: 310.

162 James W. Wellington, *Oliver Cromwell the Protector* (London, 1864), p. xvi.

163 Frederic Harrison, *Oliver Cromwell* (London, 1888), p. 102; Arthur Paterson, *Oliver Cromwell* (London, 1899), pp. 40, 192–93. Cf. François Guizot, *Histoire de la République d'Angleterre et de Cromwell* (Paris, 1853).

164 W. J. Linton, *The Republican* (1848), quoted by Dorothy Thompson in the 19C Cromwell correspondence; Linton, "Cromwell's Sword," *Northern Tribune* 1 (1854): 147; Smith, *Radical Artisan*, pp. 89, 179, 190, 214.

165 J. B. Leno, *The Aftermath* (London, 1892), p. 79; Ch. Reade & Th. Taylor, *The King's Rival* (London, 1854), p. 46; Charles, *On Both Sides of the Sea*, p. 395; Samuel Church, *Penruddock of the White Lambs* (New York, 1902), pp. 104–5; Gardiner, *Cromwell's Place in History*, pp. 28, 40–41, 113; Smith, *Lectures and Essays*, pp. 230, 233, 287, and *The United Kingdom*, 1: 493, 598–601; 2: 48; Smith, "The Great Puritan," *Atlantic* 94 (1904): 308 ff.

166 Henry Clinton, "An Oliver Cromwell Wanted," *Reasoner* 25 (Dec. 2, 1860): 10; Lt. Col. T. S. Baldock, *Cromwell as a Soldier* (London, 1899), pp. 523–24; Wm. O'Connor Morris, "Oliver Cromwell as a Soldier," *The United Service* (Philadelphia) 2nd ser., 9 (1893): 424; Leo Maxe, "Notes and Comments," *National Review*, March, 1900; Fredrick Payn, *Cromwell on Foreign Affairs* (London, 1901), p. 11n. (I am indebted to R. D. Storch and J. F. C. Harrison of the University of Wisconsin, E. Royle of Selwyn College, Cambridge, and H. C. G. Matthew of Christ Church, Oxford, all 19C Cromwell collaborators, for the information about Langford, Clinton, Maxe, White, and Churchill.)

167 John Tullock, *English Puritanism and its Leaders* (Edinburgh, 1861), p. 164; Dr. M. Macaulay, *Cromwell Anecdotes* (London, 1891), pp. 107, 114, 156.

168 Frederic Harrison, *Oliver Cromwell* (London, 1888), p. 185; Harrison, *George Washington and Other American Addresses* (New York and London, 1901), pp. 151, 154, 157, 161; Macaulay, *Cromwell Anecdotes*, pp. 107, 114, 156. Cf. C. V. Wedgwood, *Oliver Cromwell* (London, 1939), p. 92. (Harrison organized pilgrimages to Huntingdon and led a campaign to have Cromwell reburied in Westminster. Matthew, "Oliver Cromwell's Statue," p. 2.)

169 J. A. Picton, *Oliver Cromwell, The Man and His Mission* (London, 1882), pp. vii, 503; Charles Bradlaugh, *Cromwell and Washington* (London, 1883), pp. 15, 16, 19–20, 41; *The Harney Papers*, ed. Frank and Renee Black (Assen, Netherlands, 1969), 307–8. Similarly, Goldwin Smith linked Cromwell to the Union cause in the American Civil War (Hill, *God's Englishman*, p. 274). Cf. Loveland, *Emblem of Liberty*, pp. 140–42.

170 *Harney Papers*, p. 330. Perhaps Harney, the son of a sailor, resembled Sir Charles Dilke's grandfather who was "a conservative republican in old age, a radical republican in youth" (Roy Jenkins, *Sir Charles Dilke* [London, 1958], p. 67). But it is just as likely that Harney (and Dilke) always favored a strong, Cromwellian kind of government.

171 Payn, *Cromwell on Foreign Affairs*, p. 2; Lord Rosebery, quoted by Matthew, "Cromwell's Statue"; Rosebery, *Miscellanies Literary and Historical* (2 vols., London, 1921), 1: 98–99.

172 H. Johnson, in M. E. Sadler, ed., *Moral Instruction and Training in Schools: Volume I; The United Kingdom* (London, 1909), pp. 330–31.

173 Lord Nelson, of course, was not a *political* patriot but a naval figure. Inasmuch as this study concerns the use of political patriot-heroes as symbols, we will not concern ourselves here at any length with the Nelson symbol, except to note that the importance of this purely war-related patriot in Britain may be compared to the widespread use of war heroes in the naming of children in both Britain and America (see pages 207 and 208).

Nelson (and, to a lesser extent, Wellington) had many celebrators. In addition to the influential *Life of Nelson* by Robert Southey (1813) we can count at least fifty plays, biographies, novels, and poems dealing with the hero of Trafalgar and the Nile. Alfred the Great was, of course much admired throughout the middle ages and early modern era, but scholars agree that it was not until the nineteenth-century heyday of the British empire "that his praise rose to panegyric." Eleanor S. Duckett, *Alfred the Great* (Chicago, 1956), p. 201; J. Loring Arnold, "King Alfred in English Poetry," Ph.D. dissertation, Univ. of Leipzig, 1898; Viscount Stratford de Redcliffe, *Alfred the Great in Athelnay* (London, 1876); Alfred Austin, *England's Darling* (London, 1896), pp. viii, x, xiii; Beatrice A. Lees, *Alfred the Great* (New York and London, 1915), pp. 458–65. Cf. Reinhold Pauli, *König Alfred* (Berlin, 1851).

174 J. Willington, *Oliver Cromwell, the Protector* (London, 1864), pp. xi, 108. Caesar had been less attractive than Brutus to many antistatist, eighteenth-century Britons and Americans, and Brutus had been identified with Hamp-

den and Sydney. In the past century the roles have been reversed, just as they have for Cromwell, Hampden, and Sydney. Thus in September, 1971, a television commercial in the United States juxtaposed a paunchy, conniving Brutus to a handsome, heroically noble Caesar.

175 Horace Groser, *The Kingdom of Manhood* (London, 1897), esp. p. 26; Groser, *Popular Literature, Its Influence on the Young* (London, 1894), p. 8; Groser, *Oliver Cromwell, The Hero of Puritan England* (London, 1899), pp. 135–39. Cf. Chambers's Papers for the People, *Historical Celebrities: Oliver Cromwell, George Washington, the Emperor Napoleon, the Duke of Wellington* (London, 1887).

176 *Nonconformist*, Oct. 15, 1845, p. 709; W. J. Linton, *The Republican* (1848), quoted by Dorothy Thompson in 19C Cromwell exchanges; Smith, *Cromwell*, p. 3; Wm. Howitt, *The Man of the People* (3 vols., London, 1860), 1: 191n; Hood, *Cromwell*, p. 287n; Horton, *Cromwell*, p. 207. (I am in Brian Harrison's debt for the *Nonconformist* reference.)

177 It is possible, for example, that Lord Rosebery's invocation of Cromwell was politically motivated, responsive to perceived public sentiments. But I do not mean to imply that all such leaders are necessarily unprincipled weathervanes. The more successful ones are often successful precisely because their own sets of values *do* reflect those of a large enough public sector to insure their election.

178 *Daily Telegraph*, Apr. 23, 1878, p. 2; Houghton Festival, *Cromwellian Celebration*, esp. p. 2; *Catalogue of the Cromwell Museum* (London, 1889). (I am indebted to John Dunbabin, Peter Wyncoll, D. C. Wright, and Hugh Cunningham, 19C Cromwell collaborators, for much of the information in this paragraph.) It bears mentioning here, however, that many late-nineteenth-century Britons still regarded Cromwell as a destructive force. I am not arguing that *all* Britons became Cromwell admirers in these years (see p. 157, on the opposition to the Cromwell statue, for example).

179 Cecil Lang, ed., *The Swinburne Letters* (6 vols., New Haven, 1959—) 4: 152; A. C. Swinburne, "Cromwell's Statue," in *Algernon Charles Swinburne's Poems and Prose* (6 vols., London, 1904), 6: 340–41.

180 Matthew, "Cromwell's Statue," p. 3.

181 See the remarks of Sir Robert Perks, M.P., to Lord Rosebery, cited in my Introduction.

182 Lady Helen Clifford-Nellor, *Petition Against the Proposed Statue to Oliver Cromwell at the Houses of Parliament* (London, ca. 1899), pp. 1–4; *Saturday Review* 83 (Oct. 21, 1899): 510; *The Times*, Sept. 19, 1899, p. 6; Nov. 1, 1899, p. 8; Nov. 10, 1899, p. 8; Nov. 14, 1899, p. 7; 4 *Hansard* 34, c. 1189 (June 14, 1895). (I am indebted to Brian Harrison for this last citation of Balfour's and to H. C. G. Matthew for his stimulating analysis of the statue controversy.) Later, when Cromwell's likeness was omitted from a portrait-poster of Britain's "builders of Empire" by the 1927 Empire Marketing

Board, Cromwellians displayed similar outrage. F. L. Hayward, *The Unknown Cromwell* (London, 1934), pp. 40–41.

183 But in the 1950's a proposal to name a new college at Durham University after the Protector, who had first sought to establish a university in that town, was rebuffed, and in 1960 the Wallingford Borough Council rejected a suggestion that a road be named after Cromwell, "a malefactor of his class" (Hill, *God's Englishman*, pp. 178, 274). See also Joshua Brookes, *Vindication of Charles the First* (London, 1934), p. 252; and Noel Brailsford, *The Levellers and the English Revolution* (London, 1961), pp. 15–16, 649: "The nineteenth century, at the apex of its imperial glory, revelled in the tale of Cromwell's . . . megalomanic dream of . . . empire. For our generation this story has lost its glamour; our values have changed. The stature of the man still impresses us, . . . but . . . not a single social reform stands to his credit." Cf. Eduard Bernstein, *Cromwell and Communism* (London, 1895).

184 Henrietta Marshall, *The Story of Oliver Cromwell* (London, 1907), pp. vi, 109, 115; A. P. Ryan, *Mutiny at the Curragh* (London, 1956), p. 93; J. Drinkwater, *Patriotism in Literature* (1924), p. 182. Concurrently, Charles Ricketts praised Cromwell, but reconsidered the praise during World War I when he decided that Cromwell was "so dreadfully like the Kaiser" (G. M. Young, *Charles I and Cromwell* [London, 1935], p. 143).

185 Andrew Dakers, *Oliver Cromwell* (London, 1925), pp. 7, 9, 85, 154, 158, 190–91. Here Dakers resembled other pragmatists in admiring the ability of "strong men" to "balance" liberty and power. See also John Morley, *Oliver Cromwell* (London, 1900); John Buchan, *Oliver Cromwell* (London, 1934), p. 20; and John P. Diggins, *Mussolini and Fascism* (Princeton, 1972).

186 Ernest Barker, *Oliver Cromwell and the English People* (Cambridge, 1937), pp. 7, 16, 68–96. Cf. Maurice Ashley, *The Conservative Dictator* (London, 1937); Buchan, *Cromwell*, p. 20; Oliver Cromwell Ironside, *Ironside Politics* (London, 1909); Mary T. Blauvelt, *A Dictator's Tragedy* (London and New York, 1937); Ross, *Oliver Cromwell* (London, 1919) (a children's biography in the "Heroes of all Times" series), esp. p. 150; Walter Rye, *Two Cromwellian Myths* (Norwich, 1925); Frederick Varley, *Oliver Cromwell's Latter End* (London, 1939); Wilson, *Carlyle on Cromwell*, p. 295: "Cromwell's likeness should be in every school."

187 For late-nineteenth- and twentieth-century German views of Cromwell see B. M. B. Straeter, *Oliver Cromwell* (Leipzig, 1871); Fritz Hoenig, *Oliver Cromwell* (3 vols., Berlin, 1887–89); Wolfgang Michael, *Cromwell* (2 vols., Berlin, 1907); Helmuth Kittel, *Oliver Cromwell, Seine Religion und Seine Sendung* (Berlin, 1928); Heinrich Bauer, *Oliver Cromwell, ein Kampf um Freiheit und Diktatur* (Munchen, 1932); Herman Oncken, *Cromwell: Vier Essays über die Führung einer Nation* (2 vols., Berlin, 1935); Barker, *Cromwell*, p. 7; Maurice Ashley, *The Greatness of Oliver Cromwell* (London, 1957), pp. 15, 18.

188 Wedgwood, *Oliver Cromwell*, p. 241; The Cromwell Association, *Cromwell Speaks!* (London, 1941), pp. 3–4.

189 Randolph Churchill, *Winston S. Churchill, The Young Statesman* (Boston, 1967), p. 274. Cf. Edmund A. Lamborn, *The Arms of Cromwell* (London, 1941); Dorothy Muir, *Oliver Cromwell* (London, 1945).

190 Eventually, the admirers of Cromwell displayed the same fascination with the physical remains of their hero as had those of Hampden, Sydney, and Charles I. In April, 1911, on the same page of the *Times* (Apr. 19, p. 11) that announced the last of the statues built to honor Hampden, there appeared a letter from Karl Pearson of the Bimetric Lab at University College, London, concerning a head believed by some to be that of Cromwell. "No doubt we shall all like it to be Cromwell's head," Pearson remarked, but only time would tell. Twenty-four years later Pearson and G. M. Morant (*The Portraiture of Oliver Cromwell with Special Reference to the Wilkinson Head* [Cambridge, 1935]) reported the respectful analysis of the "Wilkinson Head" and concluded that it was indeed the venerable Lord Protector's!

191 S. R. Brett, *Oliver Cromwell* (London, 1958), jacket ad., and p. 94; Laurence Peach, *Oliver Cromwell* (London, 1963); Bernard Martin, *Our Chief of Men* (London, 1960), pp. 94, 141; *The Memoirs of General Grivas*, ed. Ch. Foley (New York, 1965), p. 153; Cromwell Association, *Oliver Cromwell: Order of Service for Cromwell's Day* (London, 1955).

192 County of Huntingdon, *The Cromwell Museum, Huntingdon* (Oxford, 1965). See Lady Antonia Fraser, *Cromwell: Our Chief of Men* (London, 1973); C. V. Wedgwood, *Oliver Cromwell* (new ed., London, 1973), p. 120 ("the atmosphere [toward Cromwell over the past generation] has changed"); and Isaac Levine, *Oliver Cromwell* (London, 1966), pp. 129, 145 (for praise of Cromwell's policy of religious toleration).

193 See, for example, John Baxter, *Resistance to Oppression* (London, 1795), p. 3; Pauli, *Cromwell* (London, 1888), p. 9.

194 Sir Henry Halford, *An Account of What Appeared on opening the Coffin of King Charles I* (London, 1813); Isaac D'Israeli, *Hampden and Pym* (London, 1832); Benjamin D'Israeli, *Sybil* (London, 1845), p. 292.

195 *Eclectic Review* (1861): 85; J. G. Gilchrist, "Charles I: A Martyr," [American] *Church Review* 47 (1886): 1; *Diary of George T. Strong*, ed. Allan Nevins and M. H. Thomas (New York, 1952), 2: 448–49; W. H. Davenport Adams, *The White King* (2 vols., London, 1889), esp. 1: 5, 140; Sir John Skelton, *Charles I* (London, 1898). Cf. Allan Fea, *Memoirs of the Martyr King* (London, 1904), p. vii.

196 H. S. Wheatley Crowe, *In Defence of a King* (Liverpool, 1904), introduction; Walter P. Dodge, *King Charles I* (London, 1912), p. 95; Anthony Ludovici, *A Defence of Aristocracy* (London, 1915); Mark Meredith, *Charles I, King and Martyr* (Liverpool, 1922), p. 7. Cf. G. M. Young, *Charles I and Cromwell* (London, 1935).

197 Thus V. S. Pritchett recalled that when his parents shifted him in 1914 from a "Cromwellian" school to one that displayed portraits of Charles and his

queen in its hall, he considered the move to have constituted "a rise in the world" (Pritchett, *A Cab at the Door* [London, 1968], p. 143). See also Wheatley-Crowe, *In Defence of a King*, pp. 33, 80.

198 Lady M. ("Pansy") Pakenham, *King Charles I* (London, 1936), p. 142; Thomas Kelly, *The Adventures of Prince Charles* (London, 1936); Sunderland Ross, *The Vagabond Treasure* (London, 1956); "Jane Lane" [Elaine Dakers], *The Trial of the King* (London, 1963), pp. 111, 159 (where Charles is compared to Christ); "Jane Lane," *The Young and Lonely King* (London, 1969); Evelyn Anthony, *Charles the King* (London, 1961); Freda Long, *The People's Martyr* (London, 1969). Cf. Esmé Wingfield-Stratford, *Charles, King of England, King Charles and King Pym* (London, 1949), and *King Charles the Martyr* (London, 1950); Margaret Toynbee, *King Charles I* (London, 1968); Christopher Hibbert, *Charles I* (London, 1968).

199 Indeed, the name appears to have been intended as a friendly gesture to the Scots, some of whom recall with fondness the Stuart pretenders.

200 John Skelton, *Charles I* (London, 1898), p. iv; A. M. Ludovici, *A Defence of Aristocracy: A Text Book for Tories* (London, 1915), pp. 105, 134, 165, 182; Charles Coit, *The Royal Martyr* (London, 1924), p. vii; Joshua Brookes, *Vindication of Charles the First* (London, 1934), p. 53; Evan John, *King Charles I* (London, 1933), p. vii.

201 Adams, *The White King*, p. 54; J. S. Fletcher, *When Charles the First was King* (3 vols., London, 1892), 2: esp. 40–41; Evelyn Everett-Green, *Ruth Ravelstan* (London, 1905); Wingfield-Stratford, *English Patriotism*, 1: 139, 363–75, and *King Charles the Martyr*, p. 200; Anthony, *Charles the King*, p. 109; Williamson, *Charles and Cromwell*, pp. 14–15.

7: Some Thoughts on Patriot-Heroes

1 This is also why many patriot-heroes begin as men (or women) of force—as military leaders, like De Gaulle, Washington, Sydney, Cromwell, Jeanne d'Arc, Nasser, or Andrew Jackson—before they become political leaders. Similarly, most are tragic figures, suffering in the fashion of the mythical, dying kings of Sir James Frazer's *The Golden Bough*. Hampden, Sydney, Cromwell, Charles I, Nelson, Jeanne d'Arc, Lincoln, FDR, JFK all expired in exalted or tragic fashion. Indeed, even Washington, dying on the eve of the nineteenth century, and Jefferson, dying on the fiftieth anniversary of the signing of his Declaration of Independence, acquired in death the mystical force provided one whose departure from the world of the living had been remarkable. Inasmuch as these militant and tragic features are found so uniformly among patriot-heroes, I have not given them much attention, for they do not help us to identify those different *types* of patriot-symbols that reveal for us the many changing facets of a political culture.

2 Indeed, many elites have, over the past century, become too cosmopolitan, too internationalist in orientation, to favor the sanctification of a purely national symbol of political virtue, in the very same time-span that the majority of the public were increasingly looking beyond local frames of reference

and were coming to identify vicariously with the nation-state (see my argument in J. Lovell and P. Kronenberg, eds., *New Civil-Military Relations* [New Brunswick, 1974], pp. 119–23).

3 For an insightful analysis of the localistic, anti-Establishment character of Senator Joseph McCarthy's popularity see Martin Trow, "Small Businessmen . . . and Support for McCarthy," *American Journal of Sociology* 44 (1959): 270.

4 Clinton Rossiter, *The American Presidency* (2nd ed., New York, 1959); Michael Novak, *Choosing Our King: Powerful Symbols in Presidential Politics* (New York, 1974), pp. 5, 233; *Time*, July 15, 1974, pp. 22–23; P. Abrahamson and R. Inglehart, "The Development of Systemic Support in 4 Western Democracies," *Comparative Political Studies* 2 (1970): 419–42.

5 Indeed, I would be surprised were FDR not to emerge as a key patriot-symbol. Compare, for example, Allan Nevins's description of FDR to any descriptions of Lincoln or Cromwell quoted herein: "Effective greatness—that is Roosevelt's title to a high place in the world's history. Intellect and character are not enough; to them must be added personality, energy, and an accurate sense for the proper timing of action. . . . He lacked the iron traits of Cromwell—but how incomparably more successful he was!" (Nevins, "The Place of FDR in History," *American Heritage* 17 [June, 1966]: 101, 104). I am reluctant to make the same prediction regarding Churchill.

6 In the process, some became a bit confused about what to do with the Republican Lincoln. In 1965 *Time* offered an antistatist critique of "Big Daddy, Alias Uncle Sam," and opined that "in the remote past, America's prevailing political philosophy held with Lincoln that government should do for the people only those necessary things that the people could not do for themselves." Actually, the observation was not an entirely inaccurate description of Lincoln's political philosophy, but it was the sort of philosophy that had in the past been linked to *Jefferson*, not Lincoln (*Time*, Nov. 5, 1965). Cf. Roy Basler, "Lincoln in Politics, 1948," *Abraham Lincoln Quarterly* (Dec., 1948).

7 Merle Curti, *The Roots of American Loyalty* (New York, 1946), pp. viii, 3. Cf. Joseph Morray, *Pride of State* (Boston, 1959).

8 For a good discussion of the matter see the *New Oxford Dictionary on Historical Principles*, ed. James A. H. Murray (Oxford, 1905), under the entries, "Patriot," "Patriotism," and "Hero." Cf. William Livingston, Jr., in the *Independent Reflector* 22 (1753): 208–9.

9 The author of the discussion of "Heroes" in the *New Oxford Dictionary* quoted from Ada Bayly's *In the Golden Days*: "For already Sydney had become his hero of heroes."

10 *Collection of the Maine Historical Society* 3rd ser., 1 (1904): 8–10, 21–25, 64.

11 Mary Follett, *The New State* (New York, 1926), p. viii; John Drinkwater, *The World's Lincoln* (New York, 1928), p. 25; John Drinkwater, *Patriotism in Literature* (London and New York, 1924), p. 13.

12 Godfrey Benson, Lord Charnwood, *Abraham Lincoln* (New York, 1917), p. 454; F. Harrison, *George Washington and Other Addresses* (New York and London, 1901), pp. 36, 183.

13 F. L. Bullard, *Lincoln in Marble and Bronze* (New Brunswick, 1952), pp. 85–86.

14 Harrison also compared Washington to Cromwell. Harrison regarded Washington as responsible for "the indissoluble union of an organic, industrial law-abiding nation with a boundless power of expansion and a paradise of prosperity before it" (Harrison, *Washington*, p. 12).

15 *Journal of Illinois Historical Society* (Oct., 1926): 110.

16 In this sense Britons and Americans resemble the behavior of Russians. As Michael Cherniavsky has shown, "Holy Russia" was an antistatist symbol to seventeenth-century aristocratic boyars, but nineteenth-century Tsarists adopted the symbol and sought to alter its antistatist quality by identifying "Holy Russia" with the Tsar (Cherniavsky, *Tsar and People* [2nd ed., New York, 1969]).

17 Goldwin Smith, *Three English Statesmen* (London, 1867), p. 1.

18 W. P. Webb, *The Great Frontier* (Boston, 1952); Sam Hays, "Political Parties and the Community-Society Continuum," in *The American Party Systems*, ed. W. M. Chambers and W. D. Burnham (New York, 1967), pp. 152–81; and Hays, "Introduction," in *Building the Organizational Society*, ed. Jerry Israel (New York, 1972).

19 It is worth noting, however, that the Lincoln of Daniel Chester French in the Lincoln Memorial (completed in 1922) (pl. 64) and Lot Flannery's statue of Lincoln in Judiciary Square (completed in 1868, removed in 1878, but replaced in 1922) both grasp columns of Roman fasces. The fasces undoubtedly represented the union of the states, but the coincidence of dates with the advent of Italian fascism is worth noting. Fasces also appeared on the 1917 quarter-dollar, and later on the dime, for the fasces were "symbolical of unity," as Treasury Secretary McAdoo put it. See F. L. Bullard, *Lincoln in Marble and Bronze* (New Brunswick, 1952), pp. 19–24; John Finnegan, "Military Preparedness in the Progressive Era," Ph.D. diss., University of Wisconsin, 1969, p. 203.

20 Roy Basler, *A Touchstone for Greatness* (Westport, 1973), pp. 204, 231, 241–42.

21 Theo. Greene, *America's Heroes* (New York, 1970), pp. 81, 117, 311.

22 A 1962 poll of French youth (ages 16–24) conducted by the Institut Français d'Opinion Publique found very little interest in "old style patriotism" or purely historical figures. John Ardgh, "French Youth . . . ," in *Everyman in Europe*, ed. A. Mitchell and I. Deak (2 vols., New York, 1974), 2: 361. See also Will Chambers, *Pedagogical Seminary* (1903): 110; Fred Greenstein, *Children and Politics* (New Haven, 1961); Daniel Boorstin, *The Image* (New York, 1971); Richard Hoggart, *The Uses of Literacy* (London, 1957), pp. 62–85; J. H. Plumb, *The Death of the Past* (Boston, 1970), p. 53; Stradling,

"Socialization of Support for Political Authority in Britain: A Long-Term View," *British Journal of Political Science* 1 (1971): 121–22.

23 The phrase, of course, is that of Erich Fromm (*Escape from Freedom* [New York, 1941]).

24 This by no means implies that either antistatism or localism has vanished. On the contrary, they continue as significant impulses in British and American life (see, for example, L. Free and H. Cantril, *The Political Beliefs of Americans* [New Brunswick, 1967]). There is some reason to believe that in 1970 antistatism was somewhat stronger in Britain than in the U.S. (see Jack Dennis et al., "Support for Nation and Government among English Children," *British Journal of Political Science* 1 [1971]: 40–41). But this is only a matter of degree. The decline in importance of Jefferson, Hampden, and Sydney as patriot-symbols is occurring in both the United States and Great Britain and is surely symptomatic of a general movement over the past three centuries toward executive consolidation and use of power and the public's general acceptance of that movement.

A Note on Sources
and Acknowledgments

I offer no formal bibliography since evidence of the use of patriot-symbols has no single character. Autobiographies, newspapers, paintings, poems, ballads, census returns, placenames, pamphlets, novels, and the like all served as evidence. The notes consequently are the only source citations; they are the ones I found most useful.

In searching for materials I made use of the resources of several repositories: in America, the Library of Congress; the New York Public Library; the Yale University Library, Beineke Rare Book Room, and Yale School of Music Library; the Newberry Library; the University of Wisconsin Library; the Milwaukee Public Library; the Carnegie Library of Pittsburgh; and the University of Pittsburgh's Hillman Library; in Britain, the Cambridge University Library; the British Museum; the Bodelian Library; the National Portrait Gallery; the Victoria and Albert Museum; the Dr. Williams Library; the National Trust; and the Mansell Collection.

I am particularly indebted to Roger Trieneus of the Library of Congress Rare Book Room, Doris Yokelson of the Hudson Institute (for her expert advice on public opinion polls), Andrew Matthews of the Prints and Drawings Room of the British Museum, E. J. Davis of the Buckinghamshire County Record Office, Herbert Collins of the Smithsonian Institution's Division of Political History, Maureen Hill of the National Portrait Gallery, Tim Mason of St. Peters College, Oxford, and several of the contributors to the "Nineteenth-Century Cromwell" seminar in 1969. (I have indicated specific indebtedness in my notes.) A number of mentors and friends offered help or advice: among them, Caroline Robbins, J. F. C. Harrison, H. Trevor Colbourn, James Morton Smith, Merle Curti, David Lovejoy, William Sachse, Stanley Katz, Jerry Frost, Eric Robinson, E. P. Thompson, Avery Craven, Sam Hays, Tim Mason, Alfred Young, David Montgomery, Seymour Drescher, Barry Bruce-Briggs, and Stuart Brandes. Once more I am indebted to the careful efforts of Margaret Jefferson of Pittsburgh, whose preparation of the typescript copy of this essay surely entitles her to call herself an "editor" henceforth.

The American Philosophical Society and the Faculty of Arts and Sciences of the University of Pittsburgh made a good deal of the research for this essay possible. Neither of these institutions nor any of my generous colleagues are responsible for errors either of commission or omission in this essay.

241

Index

DESIGNED BY TED SMITH/GRAPHICS
COMPOSED BY FOCUS/TYPOGRAPHERS, ST. LOUIS, MISSOURI
MANUFACTURED BY CUSHING-MALLOY, INC., ANN ARBOR, MICHIGAN
TEXT IS SET IN TIMES ROMAN, DISPLAY LINES IN PALADIUM

Library of Congress Cataloging in Publication Data
Karsten, Peter.
Patriot-heroes in England and America.
Includes bibliographical references and index.
1. Great Britain—Politics and government—
1603-1714. 2. United States—Politics and govern-
ment—Revolution, 1775-1783. 3. United States—
Politics and government—1783-1865. 4. Statesmen—
Great Britain. 5.Great Britain—Kings and rulers.
6. Presidents—United States. 7. Patriotism—
Great Britain. 8. Patriotism—United States.
I. Title.
DA375.K3   301.2′1′0941   78-53286
ISBN 0-299-07500-1